Coming to America

Why Vietnamese Immigrants Came to America

Lewis K. Parker

Why Vietnamese Immigrants Came to America

On Deck™ Reading Libraries
Published by Rigby
a division of Reed Elsevier Inc.
1000 Hart Road
Barrington, IL 60010-2627
www.rigby.com

Book Design: Mindy Liu and Erica Clendening
Text: Lewis K. Parker
Photo Credits: Cover © AFP/Corbis; p. 4 Lee Lockwood/TimePix; pp. 5, 20 © MapArt; pp. 6–7, 10, 11, 12, 13, 21 (top) © AP/Wide World Photos; pp. 6 (inset), 8–9, Still Picture Branch, National Archives and Record Administration; p. 15 © Alan Levenson/TimePix; p. 16 © Ted Thai/TimePix; pp. 17, 21 (bottom) © Catherine Karnow/Corbis; p. 19 © Oak Ridge National Laboratory, photo by Curtis Boles

09 08 07 06
10 9 8 7 6 5 4 3

Printed in China

ISBN 0-7578-2464-1

Contents

The Vietnam War

In 1954, Vietnam was separated into two parts—North Vietnam and South Vietnam. North Vietnam had a communist government. South Vietnam had a government that was against communism.

The Fact Box

A communist government owns all property and controls the way things are made.

These women are working in a rice paddy. Many rice paddies were destroyed during the Vietnam War.

North Vietnam wanted to take over South Vietnam. In 1955, a war started between North Vietnam and South Vietnam.

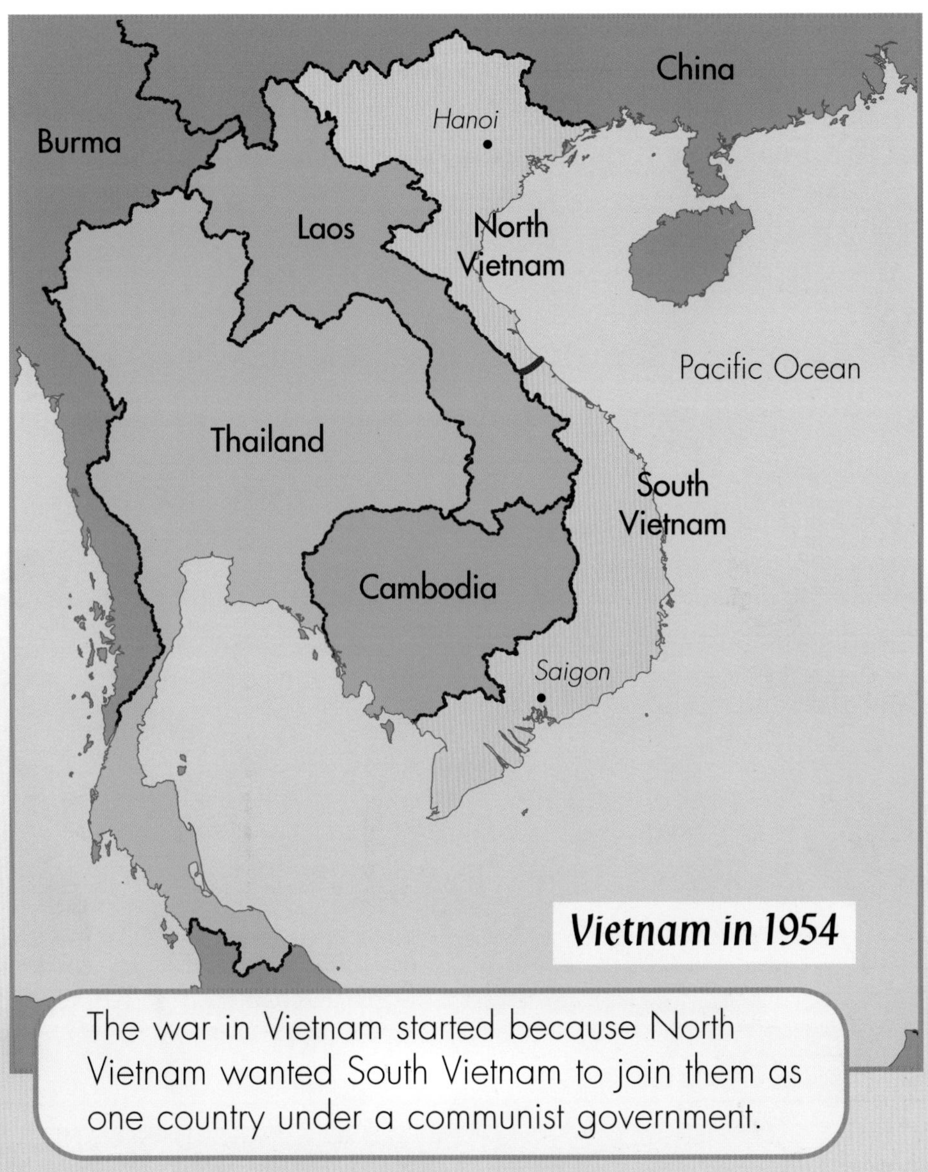

The war in Vietnam started because North Vietnam wanted South Vietnam to join them as one country under a communist government.

The Vietnam War made life hard for the people of North and South Vietnam. Villages and cities were destroyed. Over three million people living in Vietnam were killed.

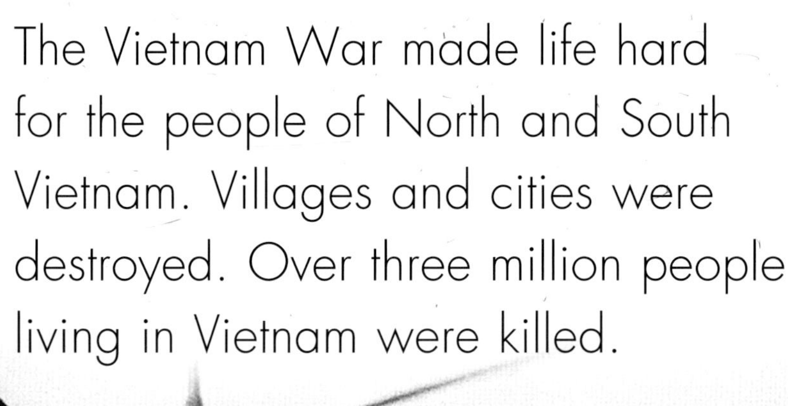

During the Vietnam War, about 58,000 American soldiers were killed in Vietnam.

By 1962, the United States had sent about 11,000 soldiers to South Vietnam. Their job was to help stop North Vietnam from taking over South Vietnam.

The Vietnam War ended in 1975. North Vietnam won the war. North and South Vietnam became one country with a communist government. Vietnam was a poor country. Millions of people had lost their homes, jobs, and businesses.

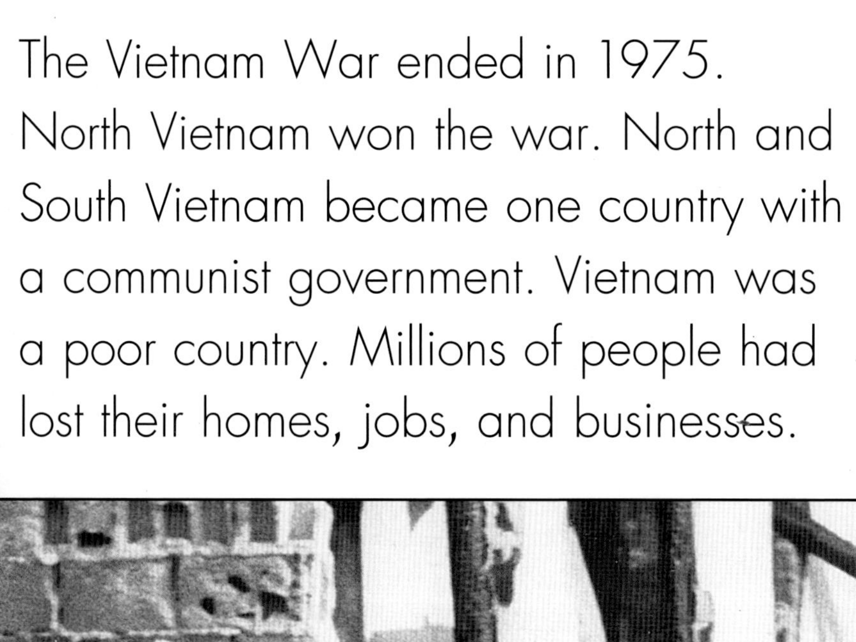

Many buildings and homes in Vietnam were destroyed during the war.

The Fact Box

When the Vietnam War ended, more than ten million people were homeless.

Leaving Home

After the war, over 200,000 people left Vietnam to find a better life. Many of these people escaped from Vietnam in small boats and sailed to nearby countries. From those countries, most of the Vietnamese people traveled to America on boats or planes. The trip out of Vietnam was dangerous and many people died.

Many people who left Vietnam were called "boat people" because they had to travel on crowded boats.

"My mother was hesitant to get on board [the boat] because she had to choose between leaving us or staying to see her mother for the first time since 1954. As the boat pulled away, I can still remember my mother standing on the dock, crying and waving to us."

— Darlene Nguyen Ely, who immigrated in 1975

Life in America

When the Vietnamese immigrants came to America, they sometimes stayed in army camps where they learned how to speak and read English. They also learned about life in America.

U.S. soliders helped Vietnamese people leave their war-torn country.

After arriving in America, many Vietnamese immigrants went to U.S. army bases.

The new life in the United States was not easy for Vietnamese immigrants. Many Americans helped the immigrants by giving them housing, food, and clothing.

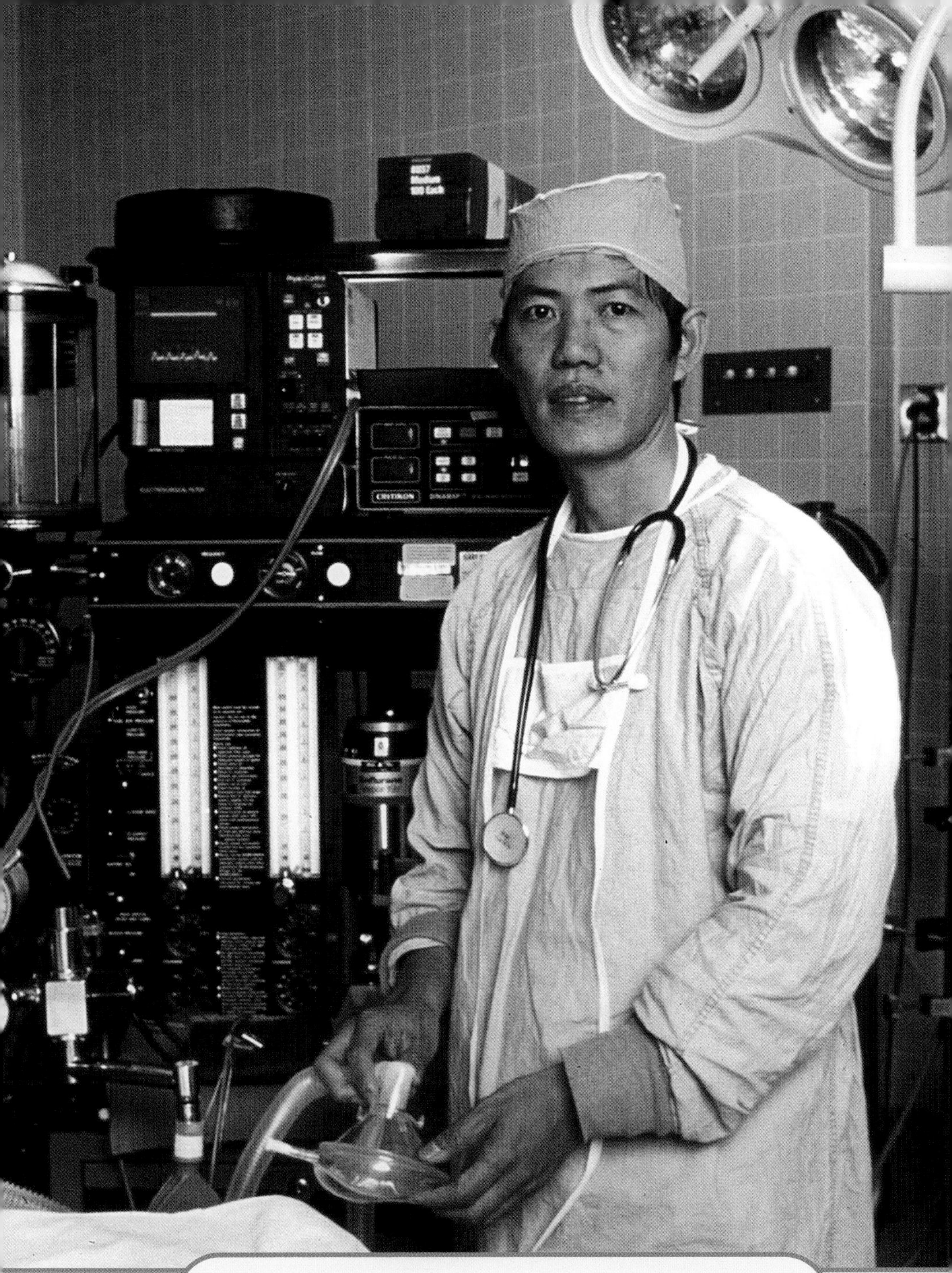

Many Vietnamese immigrants worked hard at low-paying jobs. They saved their money and sent their children to college.

Many Vietnamese immigrants moved to large cities where they could find work. Others moved to coastal areas and worked as fishermen. Like other immigrant groups, Vietnamese people often lived near one another in small communities.

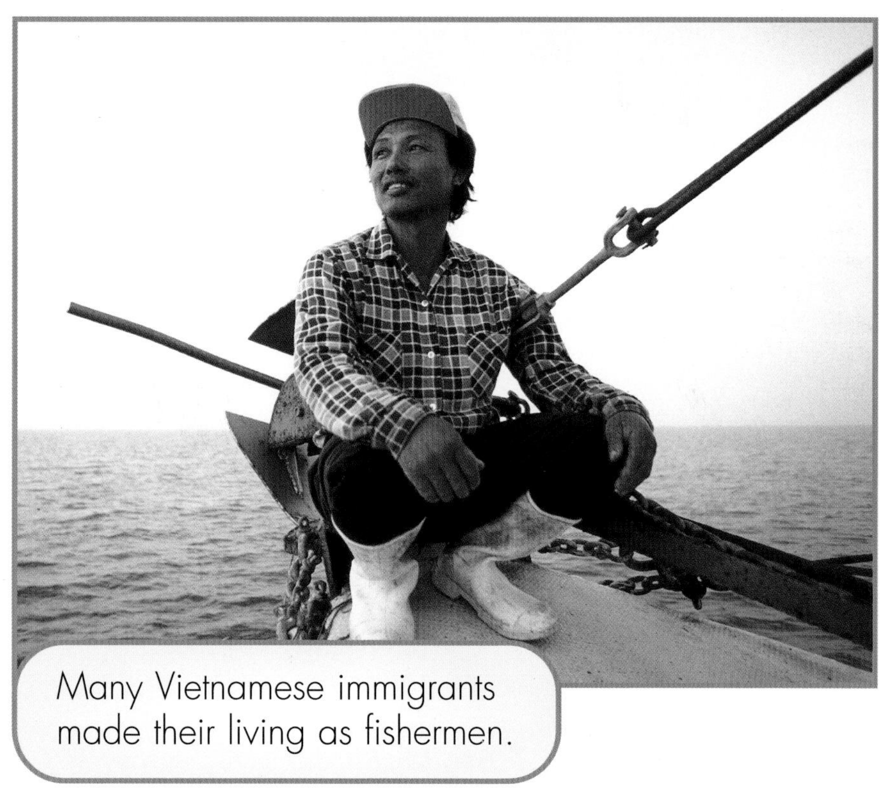

Many Vietnamese immigrants made their living as fishermen.

Vietnamese immigrants set up Little Saigon, a community near Los Angeles. More than 200,000 Vietnamese Americans now live in Little Saigon.

Vietnamese Immigrants Today

Most Vietnamese immigrants have only been in the United States for about 25 years. Many have started their own businesses, such as restaurants and jewelry shops. Others have become lawyers, doctors, teachers, and scientists. Each year, thousands of Vietnamese immigrants still come to America for a better way of life.

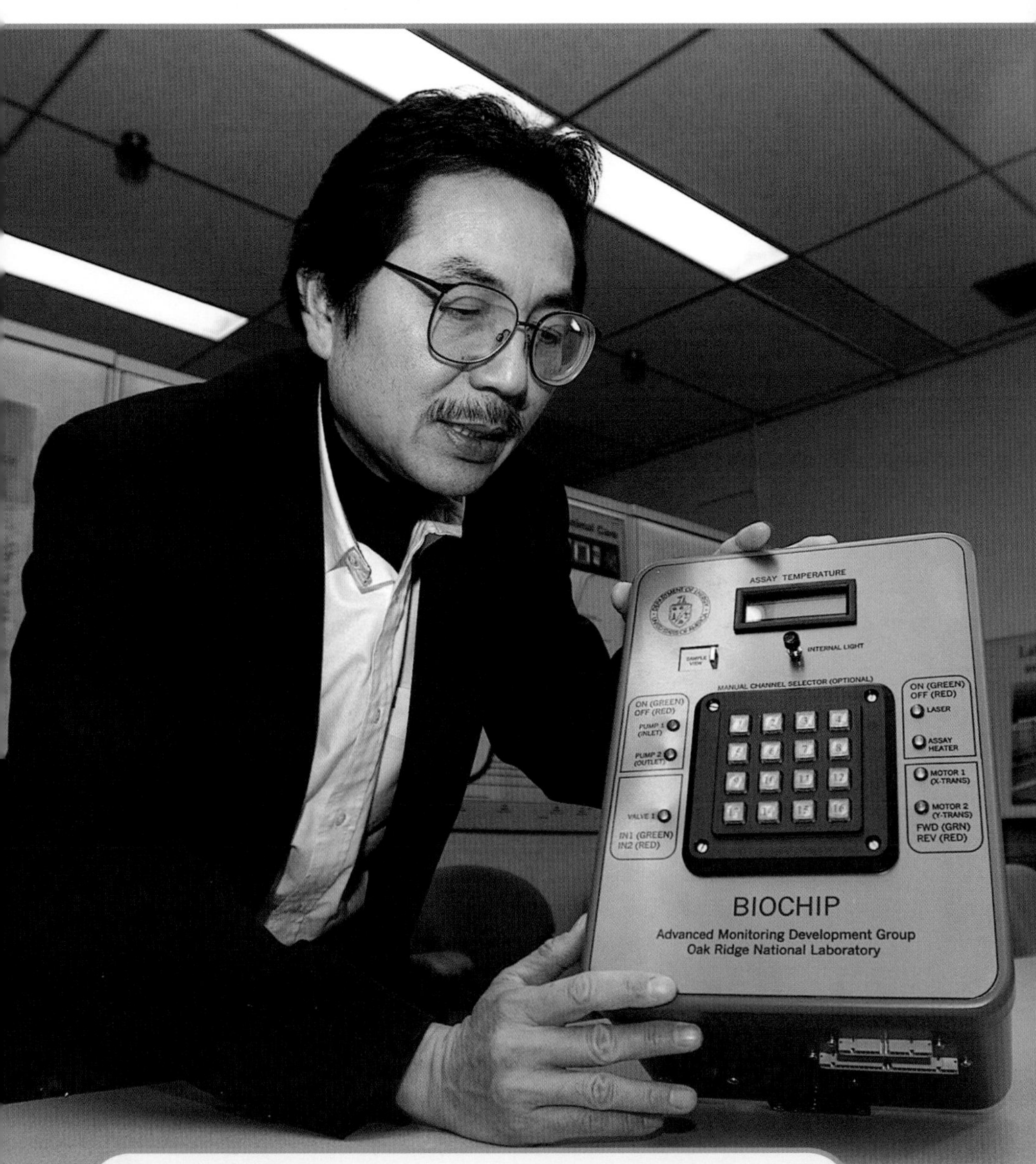

Tuan Vo-Dinh is a Vietnamese immigrant who has become a successful scientist. He invented an important machine for testing blood.

Between 1990 and 2000, the number of Vietnamese people in the United States almost doubled. Today, about 1.2 million Vietnamese people live in the United States. The Vietnamese, many of whom escaped their small, war-torn country, are helping to make America successful.

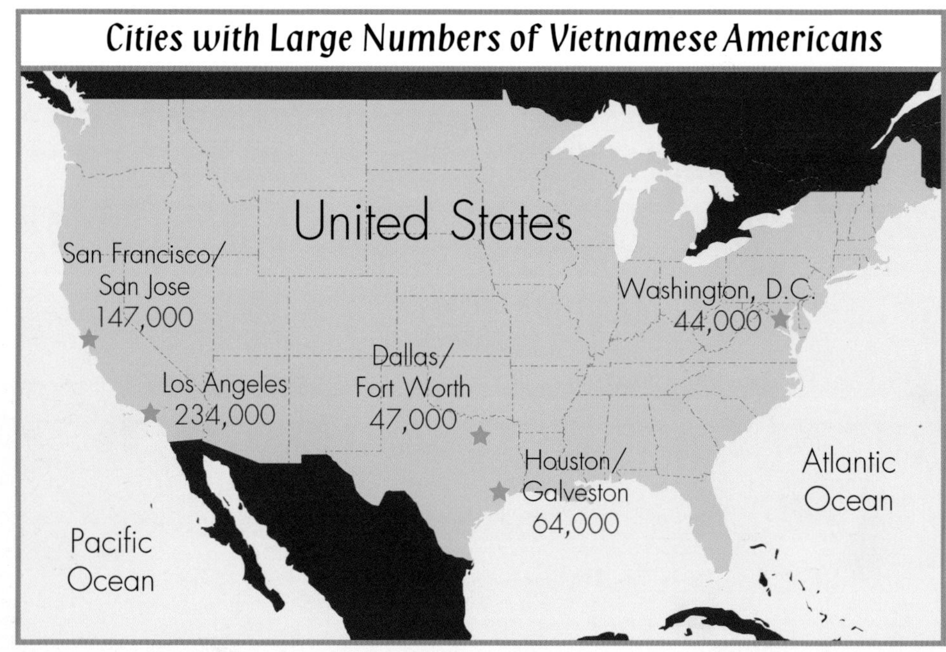

Vietnamese people celebrate Tet, the Vietnamese New Year, at the end of January or early February.

Many Vietnamese immigrants have made a new life for themselves in America.

Glossary

coastal (**koh**-stuhl) having to do with land that is next to the sea or ocean

college (**kahl**-ihj) a school where people can study after high school

communism (**kahm**-yuh-nihz-uhm) a type of government that controls people's jobs and everything they own

communist (**kahm**-yuh-nihzt) supporter of the idea of communism

community (kuh-**myoo**-nuh-tee) a group of people living in the same place; the place where they live

immigrant (**ihm**-ih-grunt) someone who comes into a country to live there

paddy (**pad**-ee) a wet field where rice is grown

restaurants (**rehs**-tuh-rahnts) places to buy and eat a meal

separated (**sehp**-uh-ray-tuhd) keeping two things apart; divided

Vietnam War (vee-eht-**nahm wor**) battles from 1955–1975 in which the South Vietnamese people, with help from American soldiers starting in 1962, fought communists from North Vietnam

Resources

Books

Vietnam: The Boat People Search for a Home
by John Isaac and Keith Elliot Greenberg
Blackbirch Marketing (1996)

Two Lands, One Heart: An American Boy's Journey to His Mother's Vietnam
by Jeremy Schmidt
Walker and Company (1995)

Web Site

Meet 5 Young Immigrants
http://teacher.scholastic.com/immigrat/bio/van.htm

Care was taken in selecting Internet sites. However, Internet addresses can change, or sites can be under construction or no longer exist.

Rigby is not responsible for the content of any Web site listed in this book except its own. All material contained on these sites is the responsibility of its hosts and creators.

Index

ALSO BY AATISH TASEER

FICTION

The Temple-Goers

Noon

NONFICTION

Stranger to History: A Son's Journey Through Islamic Lands

TRANSLATION

Manto: Selected Stories

THE WAY THINGS WERE

THE WAY THINGS WERE

AATISH TASEER

FARRAR, STRAUS AND GIROUX
NEW YORK

Farrar, Straus and Giroux
18 West 18th Street, New York 10011

Printed in the United States of America
Originally published in 2015 by Picador, Great Britain
Published in the United States by Farrar, Straus and Giroux
First American edition, 2015

Library of Congress Cataloging-in-Publication Data
Taseer, Aatish, 1980–
The way things were : a novel / Aatish Taseer. — First American edition.
pages cm
ISBN 978-0-86547-824-4 (hardcover) — ISBN 978-0-374-71277-8 (ebook)
1. Families—India—Fiction. 2. India—History—20th century—Fiction. 3. India—Social conditions—20th century—Fiction. 4. India—Social life and customs—20th century—Fiction. 5. Domestic fiction. I. Title.
PR6120.A74 W39 2015
823'.92—dc23
2014049064

Farrar, Straus and Giroux books may be purchased for educational, business, or promotional use. For information on bulk purchases, please contact the Macmillan Corporate and Premium Sales Department at 1-800-221-7945, extension 5442, or write to specialmarkets@macmillan.com.

www.fsgbooks.com
www.twitter.com/fsgbooks • www.facebook.com/fsgbooks

1 3 5 7 9 10 8 6 4 2

To what shall I compare my literary pursuits in India? Suppose Greek literature to be known in modern Greece only, and there to be in the hands of priests and philosophers; and suppose them to be still worshippers of Jupiter and Apollo; suppose Greece to have been conquered successively by Goths, Huns, Vandals, Tartars, and lastly by the English; then suppose a court of judicature to be established by the British parliament, at Athens, and an inquisitive Englishman to be one of the judges; suppose him to learn Greek there, which none of his countrymen knew, and to read Homer, Pindar, Plato, which no other Europeans had even heard of. Such am I in this country: substituting Sanscrit for Greek, the *Brahmans*, for the priests of *Jupiter*, and *Vālmic*, *Vyāsa*, *Cālīdāsa*, for Homer, Plato, Pindar.

William Jones

The god of love invented the strangest arrow in the world, one that can kill you if it strikes – and kill you if it doesn't.

A Prakrit verse from the Śṛṅgāraprakāśa of Bhoja

To what shall I compare my literary pursuits in India? Suppose [illegible] literature [illegible] in [illegible] obscurity, and them to be in the hands of [illegible] and philosophers, and suppose them to be still worshippers of Jupiter and Apollo: suppose [illegible] successively by [illegible] and lastly by [illegible] then suppose [illegible] to be established by the British parliament [illegible] Athens [illegible] an inquisitive [illegible] to [illegible] of the [illegible] suppose him to [illegible] there, what [illegible] of the [illegible] and Homer, Pindar, Plato [illegible] no other Europeans had [illegible] such [illegible] Phaedo [illegible] the [illegible] *Eleusinian* [illegible] *Odyssey* [illegible] Homer [illegible]

—William Jones

The Indian [illegible] among the [illegible] and all your [illegible]

—A Hindu [illegible] from the [illegible] of [illegible]

I

Skanda is deep into his translation of *The Birth of Kumara* when his mother calls to say his father is on his deathbed.

Uma has many flaws, but falsity is not one of them. She does not even pretend to be sad. In that special way of hers, part convent school, part cafe society, she says, as if Toby were dead already, 'Well, darling, it was bound to happen one day. I hope you're not too sad. You must be. He is your father after all. Skandu? Jaani? Say something. Are you in shock?'

'A little, Ma. It's only 6 a.m. . . . How do you know?'

'Sylvia called me.'

'Sylvia?' he asks, wondering why his stepmother would have called his mother before him or his sister.

'Yes. One has to be gracious in times like these. And she's very good in these respects. Very correct. "*I vaunted to geev the cheeldren som tayme, Uma.*" Must have been such a relief after me.'

And here she gives the first of many little laughs.

'Have you spoken to Rudrani?' he says, thinking of his sister in Connecticut.

'She won't go. She's on one of her trips. India doesn't exist for her. She's Mrs Glowitz and that's the end of it. That girl, I tell you, she will wake up one day unable to remember the life she escaped to find herself in the one she's in now. So unlike me! I always took things head on, even when I was just an air hostess without a clue about the world.'

His mother does not mention that time in her life very often. It makes him wonder what the prospect of his father's death is making her feel.

'Should I go?'

'Of course, you must. To Geneva first, and then India—'

'Ma!'

'I just want you to be prepared. He'll have to be taken to Kalasuryaketu. And I'm certainly not . . . Women, besides, have no role in these things.'

'What condition is Baba in?'

'Sylvia says hardly conscious, unable to recognize anyone. But it may just be, now that he's passing on,' – and, here, she gives her little laugh – 'that he's in no mood to recognize her.'

'Will you come to Geneva?'

'No, not to Geneva. It's no place for me. And your father . . . Who knows! Might be a nasty shock after all these years, might hasten him on his way! I'll see you in Delhi, should that be the way things go.'

'But how do you know he wants to be taken back?'

'He does want it.'

'Really, Ma? He left for good in 1992. Never went back. Why take him now?'

'Apparently he gave Sylvia some indication before he . . . well, before he couldn't.'

'That he wanted to be taken to Kalasuryaketu?' Skanda says cautiously.

'Yes.'

'Will you come?'

'I won't, darling. It's been too long. It feels like a buried life.

But you must go. There'll be a lot to handle, mind you,' she says, changing the subject. 'Indian customs. The drive down there. The cremation. Bureaucrats, collectors, local bigwigs. I'll make sure someone from Mani's office is there . . .'

'Ma.'

Mani is Maniraja, Skanda's stepfather of many years. They try usually to avoid him in conversation.

'Oh, come on. What does it matter? Just to get you through.'

He doesn't say anything.

'And at the other end, there'll be plenty of people to help. Tripathi and gang. The people there have great regard for Toby. Listen: get your act together; go to Geneva. You must, it's your duty . . .'

'I will.'

Once he is resolved to leave, he leaves Manhattan quickly, in the modern way: hurried calls to friends to say goodbye, a chat with Rudrani, emails to professors. The parting glimpse of a long glittering city, islanded and on the verge of summer, supremely indifferent to his departure.

The night his father dies, a late spring storm plays mutely in the windows of the Geneva clinic. Electric spiders appear in the darkened glass, which, like a doubly exposed photograph or a matting effect in film, already bears the motionless reflection of foam ceilings and tubelight. He and Sylvia keep vigil. His father, tubed-up and hardly breathing, eyes dim, is visible past the door's long pane of wire mesh glass. The fear, even more than of death, is of an extended period of unconsciousness, the pacemaker heart continuing to beat even as the body fails. Who will bear responsibility? Sylvia, nurse to the long illness, already looks in need of release.

But at 2 a.m., just as he's stepped out for a cigarette, and is trying to protect its papery tube from the rain, he receives a text from Sylvia. His father's blood pressure has crashed. 80–40. By 4 a.m. it's over.

A kebab and a beer at dawn. The wet tarmac of the street brightens with the first light, a petrol rainbow eddies and opens out gently in a puddle.

Inside – eager to get the dead weight off their hands – the hospital management assail him with forms, and the names of funeral homes. Sylvia's soft but insistent crying mingles with the clipped but urgent tone of a Swiss German nurse. By morning, with the broadening of day in the city outside, a set of interlocking agencies and institutions have taken over. It may seem daunting to move a body from Geneva to Delhi, but it has been done before, a process need only be initiated. Sylvia won't come; she took him away from India alive three decades before, she does not want to take him back dead. This is where her responsibility ends.

Night, his father in tow. The embers of unvisited cities burn below him while his ears ring with the screams of the deportee. She boarded in Brussels, escorted by two men in grey uniforms. She was short and plump and dark, with lifeless shoulder-length hair. And she was sick with hysteria. 'India,' she yelled, the 'd' hard and bludgeoning. 'No want to go to India. Hate India. My life in India is bitch. Hate India. No want to go to India.' Again and again, her screaming, wild and full of ill omen, rang through the nervous silence of the plane. When at last Skanda stopped one of the stewards, he said, 'It's only for now, sir. It'll stop as soon as we're in the air. You see, sir, the only way she can get off is if the captain refuses to fly her.'

When they are cruising – and the plane is quiet again – he asks the men in grey, her escorts, what her life in Belgium had been. They explain, with her in earshot, that most of it was spent in a detention centre outside Brussels. So: no boyfriend? No job? No nice little apartment? No, they say, and smile. She listens, then with a sidelong glance, she says, in Hindi, 'But it was better than India. They gave me a cappuccino every morning. I felt free.'

In the morning, the light of India presses red against the shuttered ovals. He lifts it a crack and a fierce blaze sweeps searchingly over the cabin walls. Grīṣma, Skanda says almost aloud, as they descend. From *gras*: to swallow, to devour, to consume. Summer, in a word. Indian summer, real Indian summer. Not some mere extension of good weather, but a season of glare and hot winds, of bleached land, its beige-brown parcels visible from the air: a season of white skies, of wheeling kites; a season of death.

A game of cognates – a game his father had taught him – begins on the plane with the flight map. Distance to destination. Destination: *gantavya*. The place to be gone to. Gerundive of *gam*, an old Indo-European thread which takes little leaps of meaning as it travels west: turning go to come. In Gothic, *qvam*; in English, *come*; in Latin *venio* for *gvemio*. He makes an effort to stop. Theo Mackinson, his professor at Columbia, mocks him as a collector of cognates. But it is oddly comforting; it gives an illusion of continuity, helps thread past and present together.

And there is a lot to thread together, a lot that is erased with this new arrival. The airport of his childhood is gone. In its place, a many-armed sprawl of green glass and moving walkways. Gone, too, are the red-painted buckets labelled 'Fire' whose sand was hard and paan-stained, littered with cigarette butts; gone, the heavily tinted windows, from whose corners the peeling laminate left long sticky triangles of undarkened glass. Instead, there are springy carpets in a red and beige Kandinsky-esque pattern, and swift-moving carts, driven by men in attractive uniforms.

He spends six hours at Indian customs, though here the men his mother has arranged from Maniraja's office take charge. And they, in a deep sense, deeper than he will ever know, speak the same language as Mr Sitamani, the customs officer, a caste-marked Tamilian, who wetly stamps his documents red. His office, with its red ink pad and its yellow desk sponge, still suggests the old country. The game resumes: maṇi, like Maniraja – cognate with the Latin *monile*, necklace; the English mane – is jewel.

Once his late father is loaded in – reappeared magically now like a piece of lost luggage, his air-conditioned coffin bearing a wide range of stamps – they leave the wastes of Delhi in convoy, he in one car, his father in another. A pale iodine sky darkens and brightens in cycle after futile cycle. Occasionally there is a gulmohar in bloom, the tendrils of its flowers a scorched red, dark as sunspots. It's years since he has felt the breath of summer against his skin. The wet cotton of his shirt scorches his back. And he's happy for it all, happy for its intensity; he feels a swell of relief.

Tea and snacks in Dholpur. By evening, the landscape has changed. The old eggshell hills, bare and worn down to their core, are covered in a burnt yellow grass; in places they appear charred, as though someone has extinguished a giant cigarette on their furrowed faces. This is the landscape he has always associated with the approach of the Tamasā. The river. He can see it now in his mind's eye: broad and green, the surrounding land white. And little Kalasuryaketu on its banks. The landscape brings on a feeling of anticipation, as certain Mediterranean landscapes bring on an anticipation for the sea.

His phone vibrates. An email from his mother:

> Janum, forgive me: still in Bombay. Can't make it to Delhi after all, but will try to be there on your return. Good luck with everything. Tripathi will be there to help. I don't think you have to stay the full thirteen days, since there isn't going to be a Raj Tilak as such. (Although, for me, you are now the little Raja of

Kalasuryaketu.) I don't know what condition the Shiv Niwas is in, but I'm sure a room or two should be habitable. Also, send something along these lines to people in India and abroad:

I am sorry to inform you that His Highness the Maharaja of Kalasuryaketu my revered father passed away on Sunday 31 May. The family was in attendance and he passed on very peacefully. The spontaneous farewell from the town was unprecedented in our history and we are all humbled.

He BBMs her back: 'His Highness?'

'To many, he was,' she replies.

'And no "spontaneous farewell" so far.'

'Don't worry; there will be. ☺'

And she's right. As the car begins the climb up to Shiv Niwas, people start appearing along the sloping streets. Out of barbers' shops, pharmacies, little road-side shrines. Out of their houses, and businesses, from auto-repair shops, where inner tubes are being checked for punctures in shallow dishes of water. The old men raise knotty folded hands over their heads; the women, on cue, begin to cry; adolescents take pictures on their phones and project a kind of sulky curiosity, while children run alongside the car, trailing their fingers along its flank. Everyone acts instinctively, everyone knows what to do, and as they come nearer Shiv Niwas, the streets clog, as though word has been travelling with them. Just before the gate, one young man, running purposefully alongside the car, pushes the children away and jumps in at the front. The driver, who he addresses directly, clearly knows him. The car slows outside the vast whitewashed gate, where the road rises sharply up to Shiv Niwas, and magically, it seems, an older man, long-toothed and smiling, appears with folded hands, in a grey safari suit. In a wordless exchange, the young man gets out, the older man gets in, and the young man now waves the car on, as though it has been awaiting his permission.

After a moment's silence, the older gentleman turns around and extends his hand, and, with eyes dancing behind their bifocal lenses, he says, smiling knowingly, 'So, Yuvraj saab, you've forgotten me?'

Silence.

'Tripathi!'

'No! . . . Oh, my God, of course not, Tripathi saab! How can you say that? I just got—'

'Been travelling a long while?'

'Too long, Tripathi saab. Can't tell day from night.'

Tripathi gives a long rasping laugh.

'I loved your father. Maharaj saab and I . . . we grew up like brothers. He was a very great man. Very learned. We shared a passion for Sanskrit, you know?'

'I know, I know, Tripathi saab. He would tell me what a great teacher you were.'

'What great teacher, saab? I was nothing before him. But, yes, this much is true: my memory was better than his. When he was compiling his great textbook in the summer of 1975 – the year Mrs Gandhi declared the Emergency, I still remember – he would often say, Tripathi, give me an example of a saptamī tatpuruṣa from Kāvya – what I think in English you call the dependent locative – and, phat, I would produce something out of God knows where, and he would be speechless. Tripathi, he used to say, you may in some respects be a useless bunch, you pundits, but you have something. No doubt, no doubt!'

Tripathi is still laughing when the car swings round a corner. And Skanda sees, for the first time, from a great height now, the river, a meandering vein of green on the pale dry earth. The Tamasā!

THE EMERGENCY (1975)

The Creation of Poetry lecture was, half out of principle, half out of habit, always the first Toby gave on landing in India. He delivered it that June afternoon in Delhi at the India International Centre.

'In his rage,' Toby said, 'Valmiki curses the hunter from Nishada. "Adharmo 'yam iti," the twice-born sage says. "This is unjust. Since, Nishada, you have, at the height of your passion, killed one of this pair of kraunchas" – curlews! – "you shall not now live for very long."

'The curse of an angry sage,' Toby continued, 'is nothing we have not seen before in Epic. But what happens next is unprecedented: it is what makes this among the grandest openings to any work of literature. Because, within moments of uttering his curse, Valmiki regrets his terrible words. The question,' Toby breathed, 'is *why*? Why does the author of the Ramayana regret cursing the man from Nishada who, in killing the male of this pair of birds, has shattered his reverie and caused him such grief?'

The lecture came usually to Toby without mental effort; with such ease, in fact, that he feared he sounded mechanical. But that afternoon, despite the familiar subject and audience of friends, he was unable to concentrate. His gaze kept finding its way back to her.

And she seemed to notice. Her large liquid eyes seemed to return his look; there was a trace of movement in her lips.

'We are not told,' Toby said, trying hard to focus his thoughts, 'Not told why he regrets his curse. But in what follows we are given an important clue. For, in the next instance, Valmiki utters what we consider to be the first verse of Indian poetry. "Fixed in metrical quarters," the sage says, "each with a like number of syllables, and fit for the accompaniment of stringed and percussion instruments, the utterance that I produced in this access of śoka, grief, shall be called śloka, poetry, and nothing besides."'

Toby looked long at the audience, and, coming now to the end of his lecture, said, 'He regrets his curse, I feel, because he knows that his grief at the killing of the bird – grief, he feels interestingly, not for the dying bird, but for its mate, the hen, whose song turns to a piteous lament – has set free his inspiration. It is the dirty secret of his art. Known among poets as the ādi-kavi – the first poet, a Sanskritic Cædmon, if you will – he is the first to recognize, twenty centuries ago, that, however much poets wish not to cause pain, there is no poetry without pain, no poetry without pity. And from here on, in the Indian imagination, śoka – sorrow or grief – comes to be fused, both conceptually and phonemically, with śloka, poetry! It is this, and nothing besides, that we consider to be the birth of poetry.'

In India, the use of English could, at times, come to feel like a performance in itself. People came to listen to it as people might come to listen to music in other places. In a country so accustomed to high languages, to benedictions and mantras, whose sound itself was beneficial, it was no great matter that not all of what Toby said was understood. It was a ritual. And once completed, the IIC intellectuals, with their yellowing beards and bad teeth, were keen, after a bit of late-afternoon English, to get on with the other elements of the ritual: the vote of thanks, the bouquet of gladioli, the tea and the samosas.

A few stayed behind to ask Toby questions. 'But, Raja saab,' one old man in a Himachali cap said, 'you have said nothing about 1857?'

'Should I have?' Toby asked.

The man gave him a wink and a smile. An elderly lady, breathless from her walk up to the stage, said pointedly, 'So, Mr Ketu, you have learnt Sanskrit then.' This was not a question. And she seemed not at all uncomfortable by the silence it produced. An old bureaucrat, in beige and brown, cut in, with a burst of raucous laughter, 'Well, Raja saab, the return of the native, eh?'

From out of this fusty crowd, Toby felt a hand, soft, dark and jewelled, clutch his. He knew immediately whose hand it was. But he caught only a glimpse of her. She was beautiful. Her eyes bigger, mistier and yet more melancholy than they had seemed from the stage. She had long black hair and was dressed in a green chiffon sari, with a single emerald edged with diamonds around her neck.

She said, 'I hope I'll see you later tonight at Bapa's.' Then – adding, 'That was amazing, by the way' – she pressed his hand and withdrew quickly.

He was so overcome he had not been able to reply, and, when finally he was able to get away and go out to look for her, he was detained by an unusual man, a man who stood out at first glance.

Toby was in a hurry, but there was something arresting and assertive in how he had stopped him in his tracks and introduced himself in the corporate way, energetically shaking his hand while at the same time presenting his card. Toby at the time recalled thinking, *This is someone completely new*. The ring of Hessonite on his fingers, the little moustache, the slightly unhealthy pallor of skin, had all suggested one kind of person. But his careful, accented way of speaking, his beautiful clothes and shoes, and . . . and, well, his intensity, the fire in his eyes, singled him out, as someone who, in Toby's considerable experience of India, was utterly unfamiliar.

And he seemed ready to assault Toby with his question: 'The Ramayana, Professor Ketu, or should I say, Raja saab: what is it to you? Myth or history?'

Had Toby, in a hurry to find the woman in the green chiffon sari, answered this man's sincere question with a fudge, an intellectual swipe? Perhaps. He had said, with a smile, 'Why not stick with the Indic definition? Of Itihāsa! Which is a compound, as you know, iti-ha-āsa, and when broken down, means, literally, The Way indeed that Things Were. That covers everything: talk, legend, tradition, history . . .'

'That's very glib, Raja saab,' the man said. 'But that doesn't answer my question, does it? Do you regard it as history, in the sense of it having all really happened, of Ram having really existed, or would you say it was myth?'

'These things, especially in an Indian context, are not so easy to classify. And I'm not sure it's so important . . .'

'Oh, it is important! If tomorrow you told a Muslim Muhammad did not exist, he would consider it important.'

'What I was going to say was I'm not sure if it's important for these things to meet a Western standard of what is historical or not. Which is maybe too limited for the Indian context. People, after all, have all kinds of ways of thinking about their past, and the important thing is to discover how they saw themselves, rather than how we see them today.'

It was an academic's answer, and Toby's interrogator sensed its safety.

'Let me ask it more simply, Raja saab: do you, as a professor, believe that such a man as Ram ever existed, the way Jesus—'

'Jesus is not a historical—'

'OK, fine. Muhammad, Queen Elizabeth, Shakespeare . . . I don't care. Do you believe that there was ever a king in India called Ram?'

'There may well have been one. But no – by the standards *you* are applying, he is not historical. But neither, as you mentioned, is Jesus nor the Buddha—'

And here there was a crack in his interrogator's composure. His eyes swelled round and white in his head; his lips trembled.

'Buddha, Ram not historical? Shit Muhammad historical?'

Anger came now to Toby too.

'What do you want me to say? Mr . . . Mr . . .' He glanced at the card in his palm. 'Why don't you just come out with it?'

'You people, you have a full agenda. In league with those Islamic shits—'

'You stop that. Don't you dare use that kind of language—'

'I suppose you'll be saying next that there was no destruction of temples. Vijayanagara not destroyed. Vedic culture not Indian culture; the Aryans came from elsewhere. That's what you want to say, no? India zero, a big fat anda? No?'

'Vijayanagara,' Toby said, interrupting firmly, '*where*, incidentally, I'm headed myself in a few days, was destroyed. And we know that because the Muslim historians, who you despise so much, have recorded it. As for the Aryan migration, which, if it occurred, occurred thirty-five centuries ago, you should ask yourself why it bothers you so much? What is this obsession in India with origins? This need to have people spring from the ground. Thirty-five centuries is a long time. Longer than the histories of Greece and Rome. Why is it in India alone that the mere suggestion that the Aryans might have come from elsewhere causes such discomfort? Can you tell me that, Mr—?'

Before he could look at the card, the man replied, 'Yes, I can, Raja saab. I'm not . . .' He hesitated; his lips were dry, a fragment of spittle clung to them, 'I'm not afraid to take things head on. I can tell you just why. It's because *you* . . .' Here, again, he paused and – as if wanting, now at this bitter end of the conversation to make amends

– took the trouble to correct himself. '*They*, the white man and the Muslim,' he said, taking Toby by the hand with his two hands – not now the corporate shake – 'made us believe we have nothing of our own!' Then, making to go, he added, 'Raja saab, please: if I have said anything untoward, forgive me. And if I can be of any assistance to you at all, during your stay in India – these are delicate times! – do not hesitate to be in touch.'

With this, he swung round and vanished ahead of the small crowd of people leaving the IIC. Toby, seeing his card face down in his palm, turned it over. Mahesh Maniraja, CMD Mani Group. It was a name he would have cause to remember.

Evening fell. A queue – people clad in beige, cream and white, with the occasional green and red of a sari – formed before a table draped in satin; the clatter of crockery merged with the clamour of human voices, and the drone of insects. Toby knew a sudden feeling of confusion and melancholy.

The auditorium had been full of his friends but they were gone now. Only Tripathi, who had been with him since the airport that morning, when he landed from London, remained. He now approached.

'Raja saab,' he said, 'your friends Mr Mohapatra and Gayatri madam told me to tell you to come this evening to Bapa saab's in Sundar Nagar. They're all having dinner there. They said they were sorry for having to run off in a hurry, but their father was among the politicians arrested last night, and there are a million things to be tended to.'

'I know, I know. I was meant to be staying at Nixu Mohapatra's house on Aurangzeb Road. He was going to give it to me for the summer, in return for my flat in London. But he's not going to London now. It seems like everybody is here all summer.'

'Have you made alternative arrangements?'

'Yes. My friend Viski Singh Aujla is going to give me a discounted room at the Raj for as long as I like. Well, until, I finish my textbook, at least.'

Tripathi smiled, and, seeing some disappointment in Toby's face, but unaware of its cause, he said, 'I think everyone's been a bit thrown off with this Emergency business. It's all been very sudden.'

Toby feigned interest, but the antics of the modern Indian state left him cold. It was such an anxious and clumsy entity, now invading alpine kingdoms, now abolishing the princes, now spoiling the skylines of temple towns with concrete water tanks. Emergency, immujency, immjunsi. He had heard the word, fresh both in sound and meaning, ricochet around the city all day, acquiring new significance as it moved.

Driving in from the airport, he had seen sandbags in the shade of trees still festive from their May blossoming. In the dead white light of that June day, he saw men, Jats invariably, in olive-coloured uniforms, their handsome faces beaded with sweat, take their positions behind barricades. He had observed the blue metal barrels of guns cast their blank and cyclopean gaze over the still and scorching streets. It had been a day of stealth, and heat, and the crackle of radios, whispered conversations in darkened shops and houses. A day without newspapers, save for a few – where the government had forgotten to turn the power off.

'Will it last long, Tripathi? This Emergency?'

'Who can say, Raja saab? At the moment the elites are most affected, the newspapermen, the politicians. The public, the truth be told, are quite relieved. They feel there'll be some proper governance for once.'

'It'll be bad in the long run, Tripathi, you watch. This kind of thing always is.'

They stood like that for a while, the occasional IIC member, tea and samosa in hand, giving a little bow or a smile as they went past.

Observing the descent of evening over the IIC, and the park at its rear, ornamented with tombs, Tripathi muttered, 'Go-dhūli.'

'Yes!' Toby said, feeling his spirits lift a little at this reference to the earth-dust hour, so resonant in poetry.

He had intended to say something about it in his lecture. But he had forgotten. Rifling through his reference cards, he handed Tripathi one dated 26 June 1975. Tripathi put on his spectacles and read aloud in a low murmur, 'The majestic sun is setting bringing on gracious night . . . here, carrying their water pots, are the sages returning in a group . . . their bark-cloth garments soaked with water . . . the smoke, pearly as a dove's neck, carried by the wind . . . the trees all about . . . seem to have grown dense; the horizons are all lost to view . . .'

'That is my India, Tripathi,' Toby said, when Tripathi looked up. 'A place of sages returning home in the evening, of smoke visible from their sacrifices; of trees filling, as they do here, with the sudden violet density of dusk. This, for me, is the real India, the India that lives on. Not this shabby Sovietic state the witch and her son want to shove down our throats.'

'Careful, Raja saab,' Tripathi said, and laughed. 'You've only just arrived.'

'The hell I care. By what I gather, I have more friends in jail than out. But, listen, Tripathi, we'll have some good times together now that I'm here.'

'Will you stay for a while this time?'

'Maybe,' Toby said with a grin. 'Maybe for a long while.' Then, recalling the secret cause of the elation he felt, he said, 'Tripathi, tell me: did you see that lady sitting next to Isha Singh Aujla? The one in the green sari?'

'Viski saab's wife?'

'Yes. No, I mean. Not her, but the one next to her.'

'Her sister? Mishi madam, I think.'

'Mishi? Is that her name?'

'No. Uma, I believe. Odd choice of name for a Sikh girl. Punjabis, I tell you! They give a girl a name like Uma, then call her Mishi. Ishi and Mishi!' Tripathi said and laughed. 'Why? Some problem?'

'No, no, nothing.'

Skanda is alone after what feels like days. And back in Delhi.

He had feared dislocation, feared things not ringing true. But it had not been like that. From the moment he set eyes on the Tamasā he had known a great sense of familiarity. And later, when they had all come down to the banks of the river – to the uninhabited left bank, at the shmashana ghat – and the Tamasā was visible behind the veil of sooty smoke and orange oblation-fed fire, he had known a sense of purpose too. When in the hour before the cremation the sky darkened, robbing the river of its glitter and threatening rain, he had, despite the entreaties of the Collector to wait for the arrival of an important MLA, given the priest permission to begin. Just as well. For the MLA did not arrive for another hour. And by then it was dark.

He had feared passivity, withdrawal, his tendency to retreat behind the walls of some inviolate system or structure; what his sister, Rudrani, angry that he was angry (for her not coming) had called his 'little fortresses'. 'That's right. I'm really to learn how to take things head on from you, Mr Let-me-find-the-most-complicated-language-in-the-world-to-lose-myself-in – a dead one at that! – and-if-I'm-lucky-it-might-just-get-me-through-my-entire-life. Give me another one, Skandu. At least I have a relationship with a human being, someone I love; I have children. It could be said that I'm living my life. That I don't want to come to India is my business. Everyone deals with these things in their own way. And Baba, more than anyone, would have understood.'

But grief was not purely a private matter. There was Kalasuryaketu to think of. His father had made it clear what he wanted; and someone had had to execute his wishes. He, Skanda, had done that. He had cremated his father. He had watched as the fire rose and darkness fell; watched as the flames, overcoming their initial reluctance, coaxed the flesh off his father's body. He had watched them make a cathedral of his ribcage and give to his mild face a fierce and aboriginal aspect. Then, when the priest instructed him, he, Skanda, had smashed open the back of his father's charred skull, so that there would be an aperture for the spirit to escape its earthly prison.

Had that not all been real life? What could be more real than death? And had he not lived through it? Had he not done all that was asked of him? He had taken his father's body from Geneva to Kalasuryaketu, returned with his ashes in a terracotta urn so that they could be immersed at the Confluence.

A message on Skype informs him, 'Theo Mackinson is online'. He has been fighting to keep awake. Drinking black coffee, eating peanuts. Narindar has left him a Coke on the desk, his father's old desk. And, in a moment, he brings up his class in New York on his computer. He can see them all ranged around a large brightly polished table: Liese, the yoga teacher; Diksha, the exchange student; Kris(hna), a Californian Brahmin; and Alexis Dudney, a thin pale-faced scholar of Indo-Persian, who adds Sanskrit to his repertoire of languages the way a sexual adventurer might add a redhead to a catalogue of other conquests.

'Skanda Mahodaya!' Theo Mackinson says, his image lagging. He is from the west coast, Oregon perhaps. He is in his early thirties, with short brown hair and brilliant blue eyes; his handsome face has hard edges, and a glow: a real tranquillity, Siddhartha-like, a mixture of Indic and west-coast serenity.

'Skanda Mahodaya,' he repeats in a more solemn tone now, then looks about the classroom and thinks better of it. Hurriedly he types a message: 'Everyone is here at the moment. But I'm very sorry for your loss. If you'd like, we can arrange a chat next week.'

Skanda: 'I'd like that very much.'

Theo: 'Great!'

Then aloud, Mackinson says, picking up the thread of an earlier discussion, 'What we have here, in *The Birth of Kumara*, is a dual narrative. There is the realm of the gods and the realm of men. The two narratives breathe easily next to each other; rarely is it made explicit that one is aware of the other, but we, the readers, on some implicit level, will always sense the presence of the other. Here, in the second canto, the gods, harassed by a demon called Taraka, have been told by Brahma that only a son born of the seed of the great god Shiva can kill Taraka. For this to happen Shiva must fall in love with Uma, the beautiful daughter of Himalaya. Uma, who, like an embodiment of the female principle, is central to this poem. Uma, "whose waist is altar-shaped, with three beautiful folds, which are like a ladder for Love to climb." The only trouble is that Shiva is deep in meditation and cannot be disturbed. Which is why, at the end of this canto, the gods will recruit Kama – Love – to go into the forest and disturb Shiva's austerities. And, for this,' Theo says, with mock solemnity, 'Love will die. Skanda Mahodaya, 2.10, if you will: ātmānam ātmanā vetsi . . . You know the self by the self.' Then, teasing him for his love of cognates, he prods: '*Vetsi*? From *vid*, like *veda*, cognate with . . . ?'

In the world of Indology, these are the cheapest of cheap thrills. But his father had understood. *After the material from which we're made*, he would say, *this shared history of sound and meaning is our deepest affinity.*

'The Latin *videre*, to see,' Skanda answers. An old beautiful root, which fuses words of seeing with words of knowing. 'Related also to the Dutch *weten*, the German *wissen*; in Old English *witan*. And wot: singular present of wit.'

'Right, Skanda Mahodaya!'

Now, Dudney, the most Indo-European of them all, cannot contain himself either. He says, 'It's the source of such words as video and vision. And I read somewhere – in Calasso, I think – that the reason veda has the same derivation is because the seers did not, as is commonly believed, hear the Vedas. They saw them!'

When it is over, he is drained. Over-caffeinated and sleepless. It is only 10.20 p.m. or so. Not yet 1 p.m. in New York. On his iPad, the Leonard Lopate show is still playing. They are predicting clear skies over Central Park, and temperatures for the first time in the high 70s. He is not homesick, but a feeling of dislocation is setting in. And the flat is eerily unchanged, a monument to his parents' relationship. When, at length, his mother calls, she says, reading to the bottom of his mood, 'And so, then? Are you going to just stay on there? Indefinitely? You can, you know. I have no objection. In fact, it's nice for me to have you there, nice for the flat to be used. But what about your college? Your degree?'

'Well, we've broken for the summer. I just had a make-up class via Skype.'

'Great! Well, then, stay. Stay as long as you like. Skype, did you say? I love it: a man sitting in India learning Sanskrit via Skype from New York. Your father would have loved that: no greater comment,' she says in a heavy voice, 'on the state of Indian learning in India. Good. Well, you have everything you need?'

'Yes.'

And now, as he rings off, in earnest, he wonders, *Why not?! Why not stay awhile? I do have everything I need, why not stay and let the heat build and the rains come? Why not translate – for this is due quite soon –* The Birth of Kumara *here, in this place where my father has lived, and was for a while at least very happy, and where the city beyond is full of acquaintances, if not friends? Why not?!*

He drags his status from Do-Not-Disturb to Invisible, and watches for a while as his Skype contacts, their day in New York under way, check in and out.

Turning over thoughts of leaving and staying, he remembers the ashes. His father's ashes, and their immersion at Prayaga. With this in mind, he calls his mother back.

'Darling, how should I know? Your father would have known. But he's not here to ask. Why don't you ask Tripathi?'

'OK. I will. Just tell me this: is there any particular time before which I must immerse them?'

'I suppose,' Uma said. 'You can't just leave your father's ashes in a biscuit tin on top of the fridge.'

'They're in an urn.'

'Ah, good. Then relax. Ashes don't go off.'

It was 1972 when Uma Fatehkotia decided to become an air hostess. It happened after a conversation with her friend, Priti Purie, the daughter of a navy admiral. Uma sat in a chair by the telephone table, in the great gloom of Fatehkot House, as Priti's brassy voice came down the line.

'Mishi, darling, I just went to him, my father, and I told him I'm doing it. He said, in his best Admiral's voice, "Prits, are you asking me or are you telling me?" I said, "Daddy, I'm telling you." And then . . . he let loose. "Air hostesses, little better than whores. Sailors of the modern age. The kind of women who become stewardesses . . . Admiral's daughter this, Admiral's daughter that . . . Did I send you to the best schools in the country so that you could mince up and down aisles serving white men their coffee?" I let him have his fill, Mishi. But my mind was made up: I was doing it, regardless of what he thought. I wanted to get out and it was the only way. And, let me tell you, Mish, it's been what . . . three years now? . . . and I've loved every minute of it. Nairobi five days . . . Singapore, the Raffles Hotel . . . Mauritius, Dubai, Hong Kong; I've lived in London. Gloucester Road . . . King's Road . . . free tickets, phalana, phalana. And when I began, haw, nothing could have been more shocking; and, now look, the doors are wide open: girls of the best families are doing it. Meeting their husbands on planes, if you please. The eternal promise of trolley to lolly.'

Priti Purie was a beautiful green-eyed girl; tiny, fair-skinned, articulate. She spoke in that accent known as 'educated subcontinental' and Mishi drank in her words, making all her reasons and experiences her own. No one had spoken more directly to her. For she also longed to get out, longed to slip the leash of an evil bureaucracy with its P-1 forms, host letters and currency restrictions; most of all, she longed to escape her mother and the stifling gloom of Fatehkot House. Within days of this conversation she went off to the British Airways office in Connaught Place, with its darkened windows and potted plants. It was as busy and social as the Oberoi Hotel, and Priti was right: everyone from the daughters of army chiefs and bureaucrats to those of businessmen, old feudals and even a few princes wanted to be air hostesses.

Six months later she was in the air. She was twenty-two.

Mishi's decision gave her already strained relationship with her mother, Deep, a new line of tension. The announcement came only weeks after the wedding of her younger sister, Isha, to the heir of a rich Sikh family and it seemed to Deep like some final act of self-destruction. True, many good families, in those lean days, had become acquainted with air-hostessing. But that was not to say it did not shock. The idea of girls from good families, who had never so much as made a cup of tea for themselves, scurrying up and down the aisles of aeroplanes, serving strange men their meals, was abhorrent even to Mishi's father, the Brigadier, who generally had a more philosophical outlook on life. For Deep, bourgeois to her entrails, it was worse than being an actress. A dance girl. 'You've done it now,' she said bitterly, 'you've signed away all hope of your ever marrying. So, bas, my work is done. What is left? I wash my hands of the situation. We'll put something aside. And you, you make do the best you can. What else is there to say?'

Mishi had not meant to laugh, but her mother's hysteria always produced in her a nervy feeling of lightness and hilarity. She gave a clear crisp little laugh, which seemed to come from a place of total contempt for her mother and her values. But, though she seemed uncaring on the surface, inside she was wretched. She was desperate to get out and to be, in some way, her own woman. As long as she remained under her mother's roof, she felt her life was shaped by her displeasure. She felt it become nothing more than an act of rebellion.

She flew for three years, and, though it gradually lost its charm, she clung to it, as her only escape from the oppressiveness of life in Fatehkot House. Then, one day, on the flight back to Delhi from London, an incident occurred that in a roundabout way brought her time in the air to an end.

It was that hour after dinner when the cabin acquires the air of a late-night bar. Dinner had been served; the lights were dim; some passengers were drinking brandies and coffee. The smokers congregated at the back of the cabin. One man, particularly, had made several trips there. He wore jeans, a blazer, soft red leather shoes with tassels. He was balding, attractive; there was an air of good living and reading about him. Mishi, on her barrelling journeys up and down the aisle, had on more than one occasion caught his eye. Peering up at her over his glasses, a book, a cigarette, a glass of red wine, all hanging off his hands with a kind of studied ease. This was a man, she felt instinctively, who could make love to her as easily as he could solve the crossword puzzle.

Mishi, at twenty-five, was sexually inexperienced. Not out of prudery, but because the few men she had been with had seemed to her more fumbling and inexperienced than she was herself, and, finding herself in unsafe hands, she had decided to hold out for better things. She was at that age when the mind is ready, but the body, untested, craves a guiding hand.

Glances turned to smiles; there was the odd banal exchange: 'How tiring it must be to serve dinner to a plane-load of people'; there was a furtive and generous refilling of his glass. Then the darkness deepened and Mishi, casting her eye up and down the aisle, saw nothing but a dim expanse of sleeping bodies, and the man she had admired still drinking and reading in the light from a single spot overhead. He seemed to be waiting for her.

She was right. He was self-assured; he spoke and moved fast; within minutes of her approaching, she felt his fingertips graze and trail the woollen expanse of her skirt, pinch the flesh at her waist. But, though deft, he was not gentle; there was, in fact, something brutal, something urgent and hurried about him. And quickly she saw that his main interest lay in seducing an air hostess – a local one at that – and, while still in the air, fucking her on the aircraft.

'It will be something new,' he said in an accent that as far as she was concerned could have been French or Spanish or Italian.

New? she thought. *For who?* It was all new for her.

'I go,' he said, jumping his eyebrows in the direction of the toilet, 'and you come.'

'No,' she said firmly, 'I will lose my job.'

He became impatient, and the hand that had been trailing the inside of her stocking, made a sudden leap up her skirt, and a thumb, poised and prodding, forcefully massaged her clitoris, as though seeking to flip a switch that would change her mind.

'No!' she said, and pushed him away. Then, straightening her skirt and blouse, she added – such was her uncertainty! – 'We can have coffee in Delhi, if you like. But, for now, let's just talk. Tell me: what are you reading?'

His plans spoiled, he smiled at her, and now frank and naked in his face, she saw his contempt for her.

'We talk?' he said. 'What we talk of?'

'What are you reading?' she repeated.

'What'm I reading? I'm reading a history of Vijayanagara. You know Vijayanagara?'

She didn't.

'Hampi? You never heard of Hampi?'

She shook her head.

'You see, you rich Indian girls! All the same. What is there to talk to you about? No history, no culture. Just good for one kind of humpy,' he said, and laughed, taking a foreigner's pleasure in the pun, 'then marriage, children and game over. If it was not for us, you people, you wouldn't know nothing.'

Mishi reddened. She would have liked to slap him or spit in his face. But she felt ashamed by what he said, and did not want to react in a way that would seem too scripted. That would have drawn a smile from him, as if this, too, like her ignorance, he had anticipated. 'Swine,' was all she managed, hissing it under her breath. And, walking away, she heard the sound of his laughter behind her.

Safe in the knowledge that she would never see that man again, Mishi was able to consider what had occurred with an open mind. And what stood out for her was not what he had done, but rather her own meekness. The way she had fallen in line. His easy power over her. He had spoken, she knew, with his own ends in mind, but what he had said was true. How effortlessly he had been able to take her measure, to know the kind of girl she was, whereas she had nothing comparable to say about him. She had no world view in which she could locate him as he had located her. And there was something else: when he was at his most insulting, when his face was a sneering mask of contempt, she had found him sickeningly attractive.

Skanda is invited to a party. The price one pays for venturing out in a city such as this!

The morning begins in frustration. He is working on a compound at his father's old desk. A special kind of compound called a bahuvrīhi, which is exocentric, referring to something outside itself. So, what might mean strong horse would – if a bahuvrīhi – mean he whose horse or horses are strong. The compound is:

lalāṭikā | candana | dhūsar' | âlakā

Literally: tilaka | sandalwoodpaste | grey | lock (as in hair).

The difficulty lies in identifying – from left to right – the relationship between each two elements. So, lalāṭikā | candana. A genitive relationship, it would seem, as the sandalwood (paste) *belongs* to the tilaka on her forehead. The next step is to figure out what relationship this fragment of meaning – the sandalwood-paste-of-the-tilaka – bears to the colour grey. Dhūsara. Is it *because of* or *by way of* the sandalwood (paste) that the lock of hair is grey. Which would suggest an instrumental relationship. *Or* . . . and here Skanda feels himself making mistakes.

His eyes begin to wander. To the cracked and almost petrified surface of the old desk. An inkwell, its thick glass chipped in places.

A wrought iron paperweight of George V. A cream-coloured wall from which the paint cracks and peels. One kind of frustration excites another, and soon he is watching a video he has been following for days: *Dora Venter Dog World.*

Dora in an arid plain. She stumbles along, her flesh-coloured dress torn, her slender and small-breasted body visible. Her blue eyes are blackened with kohl, her fair hair wind blown: *a wild angel has appeared to him, the angel of mortal youth and beauty, an envoy from the fair courts of life, to throw open before him in an instant of ecstasy the gates of all the ways of error.* She has a clear bottle of amber-coloured spirit in her hand. She spills it on herself and on her shaved pussy. Men in boots and fatigues, wife-beaters – four, in a menacing circle – assemble, their uncut cocks in their fists. And soon little Dora is on her knees, then in their hands, her little aureate body arced and passed about. DP'd, TP'd almost, and Dora laughing through it all. She is trying to make it all seem as if it were part of the plan. Her plan. She is fighting to suppress the pools of kindness and innocence that rise to her eyes and spoil it all. Dora laughs it all away. There are drums in the background. And Navajo flags. Dora is showered in semen in the sunlight on the dry earth, the shadows of denuded branches long across her back. Dora is asleep, alone – poor Dora! – with nothing but Enya for comfort.

He squeezes out a last drop, puts the tissues in the ashtray and heads out.

Khan Market. On the surface it is exactly as Skanda remembers it, but the shell of the old market is full of new shops and cafes; there are patisseries selling ten-dollar éclairs; and even the back streets teem. All along an arterial section, darkened flights of stairs lead up to air-conditioned restaurants. Gunmen sit outside on wooden stools, and at their feet, nourished by a drain, are sprigs of fresh peepal.

He is stepping out of a bookshop when, from a crowd of people picking their way over the uneven flagstones, a graceful and raspish voice says, 'Skanda?'

He looks up and sees . . . he is not sure! But he knows this face. A youthful face, with long greying hair. The eyes bright and warm and dancing. Who is this woman? So familiar and yet . . . he can no longer conceal the questions in his face, and she says, a little accusingly, 'Kitten Singh!'

Kitten Singh! He now knows exactly who she is. A strong aversion for her rises up in him like an instinct. He finds himself staring emptily at her face. She's had a lot of work done and it has left the texture of her face uneven: in places, lined and expressive, in others, taut and immobile. It gives her facial gestures an unpredictable quality; there is almost a kind of delay, as with an actor whose lips are out of synch with his song.

'Please accept my condolences. I used to know Toby very well in the old days. Both of them.'

'Thank you,' he says, though he is never sure if that is what one says.

'Bete, this must be a difficult time,' she says hurriedly, 'but, if you'd like . . . *if* – no pressure at all – if you'd like to get out and see some people, I'm having a Sunday lunch; there'll be many people from the old days there, and many young people too; I'd love for you to come.'

'Thank you for asking, but—'

'Leave it open. Think about it. Maybe in a few days you'll want to.'

'OK.'

'Chalo, I'm off. Please give my best to Mishi, sorry, Uma.' Then she pauses and says, half in earnest, half, it seems, out of malice, 'Does she still go by Uma? Or is it Mrs Maniraja . . . ?'

'Still Uma.'

She gives a frosty smile and pats his cheek. 'Such a handsome boy! Just like your father.'

The approach to the flat is through a great whitewashed arch, as cool and dark as the entrance to a mosque; the arch, in turn, is framed by a red brick doorway and festooned with creepers whose leaves have withered in the heat. Beyond is a garden, a bald patch of pale earth. And, though nothing else seems to move through the day, and even the shadows can barely bring themselves to inch forward, there is a continuous circulation of cars around the little square garden, for on its one flank stands the Raj Hotel, whose doorman, red-turbaned and dressed all in white, a Sikh, as doormen so often are, casts a solemn unweary eye over the slow progress of the afternoon.

Inside, Narindar, an old and seasoned practitioner of daytime darkness, schooled in the rituals of a north Indian afternoon, does not allow the day to enter. The flat is a place of old rasais, of reddish-brown rugs, of orange-spined paperbacks, termite-eaten with yellowing pages, of low dusty lamplight, and the occasional looming shadow of a Kurkihar bronze.

He turns his attention back to the compound from the canto entitled 'The Goddess Reborn' and cracks it immediately:

Lalāṭikāyāḥ candanam tena dhūsarāḥ alakāḥ yasyāḥ sā.

It was the instrumental after all: she whose locks were grey because of/by way of the sandalwood (paste) of her tilaka.

Uma, from then on, passionately in love, found no respite in her father's house, even on thick slabs of ice, Uma whose locks were grey from the sandalwood (paste) of/from her tilaka.

There was nothing accidental about the gloom of Fatehkot House. It had its origin in the story of Deep Fatehkotia, who, at an age when she was too young to see in her own experience the experience of others, returned home one humid afternoon in September 1947 from a picnic at the Qutab to discover that the young soldier she was engaged to marry in December that year had been bankrupted by the Partition of India. Beggared down to those little things that hurt most: the only existing photographs of his late father; the Purdey shotguns; a Samurai sword, with a red lacquer sheath, that he had taken off the body of a slain Japanese soldier in Burma, some years before.

Deep had assumed her father, Rai Bahadur B– Singh, a peasant contractor from Punjab who had amassed a vast fortune from work given him during the building of British Delhi, a man whose name was etched in stone on one of the Secretariats, would call off the marriage. Which until that moment had tilted in Deep's favour: for while she was but the daughter of a contractor, albeit a rich one, from a lowly Jat clan, the man she was marrying was the sardar of a grand Sikh family; a missal family; a man whose ancestors had been among the handful of chieftains who had propped up the throne of Ranjit

Singh, when his kingdom had stretched from Kabul to Delhi. Her fiancé's wealth before the Partition included a dozen or so villages with tenants; a well-sized fort; houses in the hills and some 6,000 acres in the gold heart of Punjab.

But, though all this was now lost, Deep's father refused to call it off. He had, in fact, made it his business to lend support, moral and material, to his Sikh co-religionists, so many of whom the Partition had displaced overnight. Had Deep been older, she might have seen the nobility of her father's actions. She might have seen that she was but a small casualty in a great human disaster, touching the lives of millions around her, and that her father was one of its heroes. A Schindler to those Sikhs who had lost their homes and properties, and who the upheaval had impoverished overnight. But Deep's world view, either as a consequence of her youth or temperament, was not generous enough to take in the larger implications of the tragedy, in which her own misfortune played so small a part. In her mind, the great event of the Partition was reduced to the manageable proportions of her own private loss.

She was nineteen; in the bloom of her youth, she had believed; and now, in one stroke, her father had snuffed the bloom out, robbing her of illusions.

Another kind of person, more daring, more of a risk-taker, might have sought a different revenge on the world. She might have run away; had an affair and eloped; slit her wrists, who can say? But Deep, influenced perhaps by the spirit of passive resistance, so prevalent at that time, chose for herself a unique form of revenge. She decided to make her life a monument to the early injustice she had experienced and to forgo all the things that made life worth living.

Her father, trying to make up to her for what she had lost in marriage, gave her a lavish trousseau of suitcases full of Wedgwood, Mappin and Webb silver, fine crockery, enough for two dozen people to eat off, beautiful Banarsi saris, boxes upon boxes of jewellery,

Toosh shawls in every colour and stripe. But she refused to have them unpacked, let alone used. She had a car and driver at her disposal, which she kept idle, choosing instead to send out for a rickshaw every time she wanted to go out. Her father had given her two sprawling bungalows in Lutyens' Delhi with lawns on all sides. But nothing that could be described as cheer was ever allowed to enter them. They remained in a permanent state of semi-darkness. The carpets, the heavy furniture, the objets, all were of a piece: each achieving the amazing distinction of appearing both ancient and valueless. The tablecloths were frayed and stained; the napkins never of a set; meals were a disorderly affair; and the kitchen was so dirty that the smells would carry into – and fill – the house every time its white swing door, finger-marked and begrimed, swung open. Nothing life had denied Deep could compare with what she was willing to deny life. And it was a very studied kind of gloom, indeed, that pervaded Fatehkot House.

If Deep lived with hope at all, it was that one of her daughters, either Isha or Mishi, would, through marriage, restore to her the glory that she had never believed truly to be gone, but merely occulted, like the Mahdi. In her two girls, she had, with the precision of the creator herself, planted two perfectly symmetrical complexes: in the older, Mishi, she had instilled the belief that she was intelligent, but ugly, talkative and unmarriagebly dark. Meanwhile, she had convinced the younger, Isha, that for all her classical Punjabi beauty, she was an abject fool. Till marriage appeared on the horizon, the girls had been roughly equal in the affections of their mother, with the balance, in fact – for Deep fancied herself as a bit of an intellectual – tilting in Mishi's favour. But when, at the age of twenty-one, with her older sister still unmarried, Isha became engaged to Viski Singh Aujla, the heir to an immense Delhi fortune, the advantage, with the sudden frostiness of the sun gone behind a cloud, shifted away from Mishi.

In fairness to Deep, something must be said about the Aujla fortune, for it was, and still is, legendary in Delhi. And any mother, especially one nursing an ancient grievance, might be forgiven for discovering a special store of affection for a child who had allied herself with it.

There was the Raj, of course, that art deco marvel in the heart of Delhi, the brightest jewel in the crown of the Aujla fortune, which, though less grand than it is today, was nonetheless one of the city's great hotels; there were whole quadrants of Connaught Place that belonged to them; there were several properties in Lutyens' Delhi, so many that it was only on roundabouts, with the radial spokes of the city's streets coming at them, that they could even remember the ones on which they owned houses; there was sugar and jute in the east; and, in the west, in Punjab, there was rice and wheat, carefully apportioned into land-ceiling-proof parcels. There were old-fashioned houses in the hills with wooden floors and carved eaves and falling-to-pieces bungalows in various small towns across U.P. and Punjab. There were peripheral plots of land, each several acres large, on what was quickly ceasing to be the periphery of Delhi, and a farm the size of an Argentinian ranch on the border of Pakistan . . . Or had that been acquired by the government? A lot had been acquired. In fact, such was the extent of the Aujla wealth that, if just what had been acquired by the government was given to a single individual, he would, on the crumbs that had fallen from the Aujla table alone, have been one of the richest men in the city. Such – mashallah! – was their wealth. And once Isha put herself in proximity to it – at the very same time that her sister decided to become an air hostess – the game, as far as maternal love went, was up.

Transfigured by this new reality, Mishi's life, in the eyes of both her mother and herself, came to seem like one long act of defiance. A series of unconnected incidents – her referring, as a little girl, on her father's prompting, to her mother as 'the contractor's daughter';

her cutting her hair in open disobedience of the Sikh injunction not to do so; her smoking as a teenager; a disastrous episode involving a driving lesson in an army town that had ended in recrimination, and a girl with a broken arm – all came to seem like example after bitter example of Mishi's defiance of her mother.

The Fatehkotia sisters did not allow their mother to affect their relationship. They remained close, full of love and friendship for each other. And, when Mishi returned to Delhi, after the incident on the flight with the European, Isha was the first person she told. She did not mention the inexplicable attraction she had felt for the man who insulted her and Isha could not understand why it bothered her so much.

'What does it matter, Mishi? Hampi? Some old ruin in Karnataka. Means nothing to nobody. Why should you care? The man was obviously a low-grade cheapo, trying to take advantage of you. Brush it aside. Come instead this afternoon to meet a guest of Viski's. He's giving a talk today at the IIC called "The Creation of Poetry"; then you'll see the other side of Europe. The good side. Cheapos exist everywhere.'

'OK, Ish, but listen: I have to get waxed first. I have a forest on my arms,' she said, running her hand over her bare arms, and causing the little bristly hairs to stand on end.

Isha laughed and mashed out her cigarette in a bronze ashtray. They sat in the smoky cool of the one air-conditioned room in Fatehkot House. A fierce June blaze pressed against the curtained window.

Later that morning Mishi heard in detail about the Emergency from Kuku-Waxing.

Kuku, who went about her tasks, heating wax in a stainless steel katori and preparing the long strips of cloth, while, at the same time, watering a money plant by the window and wiping away sweat from her brow, said, 'She's done a very good thing, Mishi. You don't know, dear, you've been gone a lot, it was terrible. Protests, rallies, court judgements: they tied her hands. How patiently she bore it all. But after a while, you know, everyone has a breaking point. Arms and legs?'

'Arms, legs, back and anything else you can find, Kuku.'

Kuku, a fat woman, with an awful leech-like mole on her cheek, from which some truly evil hairs sprouted, gave a loud bronchitic laugh. She moved swiftly around her cramped parlour, and soon Mishi felt the first strips come long and hot upon her legs. Except in the more delicate areas, where the skin was not firm, she enjoyed the pain. Enjoyed breathing into it, and thinking of its smooth and satisfying result.

'Tell me, Kuku, this Emergency, will it mean everything will be closed?'

'Like what?' Kuku said abstractedly, as she fastened her fingers around the first little strip and tore it from Mishi's body.

'Shops, museums, businesses?' she said, thinking of the lecture later that day as a way to take her mind off the pain.

'Oh no, everything will work better than ever before. I'm sure of it. Rani saab Chamunda was in here earlier. They're trying to arrest her mother. Naturally! Jan Sangh types. There were a lot of arrests last night apparently.'

'Really? They're trying to arrest her mother, and she came to be waxed?'

Kuku laughed. 'We all have our priorities.'

'Who else?'

'This morning? Just you and her.'

'No, no, Kuku! Who else have they arrested?'

'Oh, opposition leaders, journalists, trouble makers, you know.'

Kuku moved fast, applying and tearing away the strips. Mishi's body felt scorched and raw; her head seemed in the darkness to swoon a little; a cooler whirred, projecting a pale choppy light over the room.

'Ms Isha, you know . . .' Kuku said.

'Yes, my sister, Kuku,' Mishi answered, trying to ward off an indiscretion.

'She came in some days ago.'

'And?'

'Well, she wanted, apart from the usual – pits, arms, legs, back – some waxing in her down-there parts,' Kuku said proudly. 'You want heart, ma'am?'

'Maybe, Kuku,' Mishi said tentatively, 'let me think about it.'

The Emergency. Chamunda. The dreary south Delhi afternoon, the little parlour in the over-furnished flat. All of it conspired to remind her of the stifling smallness of this world. Was it normal to feel such urges, for flight, for escape, for a world elsewhere? Did the others feel them too? Did they also have a hard hungry knot lodged in their stomach that craved experience? The flying had got some of it out, but it had, in exciting her imagination, and putting her half within reach of a different kind of life, also made things worse, made her more aware of how much she wanted something to happen to her.

'Kuku?'

'Yes, ma'am?'

'Heart hi de do.'

'Good choice, ma'am. It's the fashion now.'

When it was over, she picked her clothes off a chair in the dark. They slipped and slithered against the soapy smoothness of her skin, and she could not help but reach to touch, with her unpainted fingertips, the newly depilated skin around her vagina. It felt as arousing and new and unfamiliar, as if it were somebody else's, the dark folds tense and prominent. *Oh God – Fucking Delhi – I'm so horny!* She felt around for her sunglasses; Kuku saw and flipped the switch, and, with the light, they came suddenly into her hands. She drove their ends into her thick hair and stood for a moment in her heels, purple tinted lenses on her head, an expression of puzzlement on her face, as if trying to remember something. Kuku still charged around the room in her grubby white frock, tidying up.

'Kuku?'

'Yes, ma'am?' she said, stopping to look up.

'Do you know what . . . *where*, I mean, Hampi is?'

'No, ma'am. Restaurant?'

'No, no. Nothing.'

Mishi returned to Fatehkot House to find her mother morose. The Brigadier's wife adored Nehru; she had, in solidarity with his freedom movement, and despite the disapproval of her father, worn khadi blouses under her silk saris; she had, in support of that movement, given her own pocket money to the future prime minister for his autograph. That the daughter of that beautiful man, who to her mind represented all that was good and hopeful in her youth, should now suspend the freedoms he had fought so hard for was as disillusioning a thing as she had ever known. She was, for once, speechless. She sat with her elbows on the dining table, in the late-morning gloom of Fatehkot House.

Mishi, sailing in for lunch, before heading out for the IIC with Isha, could not help but taunt her. 'So, Mama! Have you heard the news? Oh Boy! Heard what the great paean of democracy has been up to? Dear Pundit ji's daughter! Looking forward, Mama, to a patch of benign despotism?'

The old woman did not reply; she was too close to tears.

*

Ordinarily, Deep would have prepared something for her daughter's return from the IIC. Something snide and biting about her life and prospects, something slow-acting, that a few hours later would return to nag Mishi, and would – though she would tell herself it did not matter – spoil her evening. Yes: ordinarily the Brigadier's wife would have struck back. But she did not have the chance.

The reason was that, as evening fell, and the girls returned from the lecture, they were in a wonderful mood. They filled the house with their talk and laughter. And they did not exclude their mother, but tried to bring her in. They told her all kinds of fascinating things about what the lecturer had said about Sanskrit and the Ramayana and the Birth of Poetry: of how śloka, poetry, was connected etymologically to śoka, grief. In all this, the Brigadier's wife forgot her own grief about the Emergency. The girls said how they would be meeting the professor who gave the lecture later that evening at their friend Bapa's house, and how he was a prince, but not a prince; Indian, but, at the same time, a bit of a foreigner. And it was not just Isha who was in this light and happy mood, but Mishi too. Mishi especially. She seemed to exude something so positive and benevolent. Mother and daughter exchanged a look which, though edged with suspicion, was tender. Something cautiously affectionate passed between them, something that seemed to be part of a spirit of new beginnings. A mother's heart being what it is, the ill feeling Deep had nurtured from the morning evaporated in contact with this new warmth.

The lights came on in Fatehkot House, though dimly; the Brigadier had his first whisky; upstairs there was the happy commotion of women dressing for dinner. And just a little while later, on the back of a furious clatter of heels, the permanent gloom of Deep's house was momentarily interrupted by the Fatehkotia sisters sweeping out into the night, leaving in their wake a trail of perfume.

*

'Down or up?' Isha said, turning the car window's handle.

'Down, Ishi. Please. In any case, we're going to arrive with big dark patches . . .' She raised her arms.

Isha, trying to make out her sister in the cavernous interior of the car, said, 'No, no, you're fine,' and touched her kurta at the armpits, just to be sure. Then, in the yellow light that entered from outside, she thought she saw something else.

'Eeeeeks! What is it? A creepy crawly?'

'No, no, calm down . . . Ek minute, Hira, ek minute. Sundar Nagar. Bapa saab ke kar.'

The car, its air petrol infused, began to move. Isha handed her sister on her fingertip the burnt red petal – gulmohar – that she had removed from her hair. Mishi took it and tossed her hair back in relief.

'Haan, tell me, what were you saying?'

'I was saying: you and Mama seem to be getting along.'

'I wouldn't say that. Just a ceasefire.'

'And are you pleased you came today?'

'I couldn't be happier, Ish. It was wonderful. *He* was wonderful.'

Isha gave a little laugh; the car trundled through the empty streets; shafts of yellow light waved them along on their way.

'Well, have a little scene, if you like. But don't get too serious.'

'Why?' she asked, though she had a good sense of what her sister might say.

'It never works, you know. Even though he's probably more knowledgeable about India than we are.'

'Not probably; definitely.'

'Definitely. But still: the mentality is very different. You'll forever be looking over your shoulder to see if he's OK. And you don't want that: you want the man to lead.'

'I don't know, Ish . . . Maybe I don't want to live here at all. Maybe I want to get out for good.'

'You think that now. But trust me: our kind of person can't manage abroad. Doing everything for yourself. The poky little flats. All those khit-pitty Angrezes, with their precious little manners: it's death. You'll go mad.'

'I don't know . . . I really felt something today.'

'Like what?'

'Like a sign.'

'What kind of sign?'

'Well, do you remember the episode I had on the plane with that rude man?'

'The humpy story?'

'Exactly.'

At that moment, just as they were crossing the intersection, an expression of amazement came into Isha's face.

'Mishi, wait, one minute, look at that. Hira, araam naal.'

The car slowed, and down the long deserted street, lining it on both sides, the women saw armed men in the shadows of trees.

'My God!'

'It's all real. We're in for it, Mishi. Till this moment . . .'

'Me bhi soch reya si . . .'

'Chup kar, Hira! Jaldi agge chal.'

The car sped on.

'A police state!'

'I know. Just like that. One day to the next.'

The sisters, in the hope of recovering their composure before the party, tried to pick up the thread of their earlier conversation. But the car had already entered Sundar Nagar and they drove along a street that had houses on one side, and a high stone wall with iron spikes – the wall of the Delhi zoo – on the other.

'You were saying, a sign . . .'

'He didn't even know I was listening. But I heard him mention it . . . Hampi this . . . Vijayanagara that . . . and I thought it was so strange because it was the only other time in my life—'

'We're here. Tell me inside.'

Soon the two women were crossing the small front garden of Bapa's house, where, past open doors and muslin curtains catching in the hot wind, there was the comforting sight of a lamp-lit drawing room, from which they could already hear voices and laughter.

'Systole and diastole . . .' Theo Mackinson says, slipping past the camera. 'Skanda Mahodaya, wait: I see that you have a coffee. Let me get one too.'

He is dressed in olive-green khakis and a red-checked shirt. Past the polished surface of his desk, once the camera's eye has adjusted to the change in light, Skanda sees, in the long rectangular window, a glimpse of the city he has left behind. A newly green branch, tense and sprung, sways lightly in the breeze. Beyond, a facade of blackish-brown-yellow brick. The faint screech of a siren carries up from the street. Seen from the thick night of a Delhi summer, it seems so mild and clement an impression of spring. Spring! Which, at this very moment in his translation of the Birth has, in league with Love, stolen unseasonably into the ascetic's grove, where Shiva is performing his austerities.

'Skanda Mahodaya? You there?'

He swipes the pad; the screen brightens.

'Much better.' Noticing his reddish eyes, Theo says, 'How late is it for you there?'

He searches the screen.

'About 1.30.'

'That late! You should have told me. We could have found another time.'

'It's fine. I prefer working at night these days.'

'The heat?'

'Yes. And the glare.'

'I remember. I once spent a whole summer like that in Varanasi. Speaking of which, have you been down that way yet?'

'To Varanasi? No. Why?'

'To Prayaga. I thought you might have—'

The Confluence, the ashes. He has not thought about them in days.

'No. Not yet.'

Silence. Give Mackinson a difficult compound and he'll flush out the derivatives and internal bahuvrīhis, but people, emotions . . . Well, it is one of the reasons why one becomes a Sanskritist.

'All well, though?'

'Yes, yes. All fine.'

'And do you have friends and family in Delhi?'

'Some. Cousins and things. Grandparents I was very close to. Maternal. But both dead now. Not too many friends. But I'm going to a party in a few days,' he says, with uncertainty. 'So I might make some.'

Theo laughs. 'Where were we?'

'Systole and diastole.'

'Ah, the two narratives, and the relationship between the two. So, yes: I like to think of it in terms of the basic motion of the heart. Of course there is a relationship. A vital relationship. But the two actions, like the two narratives, are also discrete. Every now and then we will be slipped a little clue – such as when Kama is in conference with the gods – that one is aware of the other. It is an intelligent breathing relationship, a porous relationship, but also subliminal. The larger machinery for the most part remains concealed. Which I think is nice. But, you, Skanda Mahodaya, should not, beyond a point, concern yourself with these things. They are too *meta* for your purposes. They are there for your interest and amusement. But your main focus must remain the text. And try to read from within the tradition. Let the commentators guide you. Let the great Mallinatha guide you; you couldn't hope for a better teacher than him. My job is just to hand you over to him.'

Skanda loves the commentators. They answer in him a deep need for teachers. And, even more than the main text of the poem, it is that paragraph of gloss, which unpacks the verse and seems to contain the ghost of the tutorial, that really excites him. His father used to say that that was the true link to the past: that was where you could actually hear a voice from ancient India.

'Out of interest,' Mackinson says, 'where have you got to?'

'The third sarga.' Glancing at the open book – M.R. Kale – next to the computer, he reads:

> Kāmas tu bāṇ' | âvasara | pratīkṣaḥ
> pataṅgavad vahni | mukhaṃ vivikṣuḥ
> Umā | samakṣaṃ Hara | baddha | lakṣyaḥ
> śar' | āsana | jyāṃ muhur āmamarśa

'Oh! A wonderful moment, Skanda Mahodaya. Love and Spring, in league with each other, have entered the forest, forcing the hot-rayed sun north. There is now suddenly a fragrant breeze in the woodlands. In which, the red palasha flowers, curved and crescent, appear like nail scratches. The female elephants – always a sign in Sanskrit poetics of rut in the air – are offering trunkfuls of water, scented with the pollen of lotuses, to their mates. Shiva is deep in meditation. And look at the descriptions of him here. Do you have the David Smith with you?'

'No.'

Mackinson hurriedly searches a shelf of turquoise-coloured volumes. He finds the one he wants and flips fast through its rustling pages.

'"The fierce pupils motionless,"' he reads, and looks up with a smile. 'Then, look at this, the classic description of meditation: "By restraint of his internal currents he was like a cloud without the vehemence of rain, like an expanse of water without a ripple, like a lamp in a windless place absolutely still!" One trembles at the thought that this is the man Kama is to disturb. Kama who comes into the forest, "avoiding the lamp of his eyes". And now at the verse you are at we find him poised. "Kāmas tu bāṇ' | âvasara | pratīkṣaḥ . . ." What do you have for that, Skanda Mahodaya?'

A little embarrassed now of his own translation, he says, 'It's still very rough, Theo.'

'Never mind.'

He reads, '"Having espied the opportunity for his arrow, Kama . . ."'

'Fine. And for "Hara | baddha | lakṣyaḥ"?'

'"His gaze fastened on Shiva."'

'Yes! Then?'

'"With Uma near . . . in proximity".'

'Lovely: "vivikṣuḥ"? Do you see the desiderative here, reduplicating the verbal stem *viś*? Which related to the Latin vīcus gives us such words as vicinal and vicinity, and means here: to enter, enter in, go into. In the desiderative, it is the wish to enter.'

'Yes. Kama is described as a moth wishing to enter the mouth of the flame.'

'Very nice. Fine. And, at last, coming at the end, the actual predication.'

'I had trouble here.'

'The verb is *ā-mṛś*. To touch, to stroke, to handle, to finger. Here it is reduplicated, and in the perfect. So: "He, Kama, fingered . . ."'

'"His bowstring"!'

'Exactly. Again and again, Kama fingers the bowstring of his bow made of flowers, ready to shoot the arrow that is Fascination. The arrow that kills if it strikes, and kills if it doesn't.' Mackinson pauses and says with a smile of pure and childish excitement: 'Skanda Mahodaya . . .'

'Yes, Theo?'

'Love is poised to strike!'

Toby looked a foreigner in India. It was not just the light eyes, nor the fair skin and floppy blondish-brown hair; it was that, above and beyond these things, there was an innocence, a naivety in his face that gave him away as someone who could not have grown up in India. Not, at least, in north India, where even the stray dogs had a knowing and watchful look. It was strange: there was never a man who knew more about India and, yet, knew India less, than Toby. He was like one of those men who fall in love with the idea of a woman, while all the time insulating themselves from her reality. At Oxford, a student of his, a girl from Bengal, had said, 'Professor Ketu, it's as if you rather wish modern India didn't exist.'

And, laughing, he had replied, 'Don't we all?!'

Toby's deep knowledge of classical India made the real India remote, made it more concept than reality. For there are few places where the past continues as seamlessly into the present as India and, yet, where the people are so unaware of it. All around him Toby saw the remnants of the Sanskritic past: there in the names that were compounds, the analysis of which he would do silently in his head; there, in the low-lying colonies that had dressed themselves up in grand names from the Epics, to which his mind could not help but go; there in the nursery down the road that had named itself after Indra's capital; or in the chemists that had taken for themselves the names of the twins who were physicians to the gods; and there in the people's language, which even in English adopted words like 'only' and 'just' to compensate for lost particles of stress and emphasis – words such as 'hi' and 'eva' and 'khalu' – that had come down to them from Sanskrit.

Everywhere he looked, Toby could see, under layer upon haphazard layer of borrowed and vernacular language, the glorious and systematic bedrock of Sanskrit. It held for him all the frustration and excitement of seeing beneath a thick encroachment of slum and shanty the preserved remains of a far grander city, of gridded streets, sophisticated sewage systems, of magnificent civic architecture. But, thrilling as it was – to find extant around him the language he had dedicated his life to – it was a private thrill. For as much as the language limped on, as much as it was still visible under the vulgate, all awareness of it had gone. It was not apparent to those living among it; it was there in the form of ruins, and nothing more. The people, moreover, had no means to assess its beauty and this could produce either embarrassment or false pride.

The knowledge of decay made Toby seem passive when it came to India. The country already, to so large an extent, existed for him privately, in his mind and imagination, that he let all of it become illusory, all shadows on the wall of a cave, all a pale emanation of some far grander and irrecoverable reality. He was like a man who, having known the forum in the days of Trajan, returns to see it as spolia on people's houses.

That attitude – his aloofness – made him for all the wrong reasons attractive to people of a certain class in India. They confused his distance, which came from an uncompromising love for what had been lost, with their own deracination. For them, he seemed to answer a need: to both be in India and to stand at a distance from it. The members of this class, who were already set apart from the rest of the country by the loss of language, by privilege, of course, and by what had come to seem almost like racial differences, had no desire to shed their distinctiveness. They clung to it, in fact, wanting nothing so much as to remain inviolable and distinct: foreigners in their own country.

And yet – strange as it must seem – they had a corresponding desire to make a great show of their Indianness, to talk of classical dance recitals, of concerts, of textiles, and spirituality. To throw in the odd precious word or phrase of Hindustani, to upstage their social rivals with a little bit of exotica so obscure that no one could be expected to know it. India was their supreme affectation! They wore it to dinner, as it were; and, of course, the ways in which they were truly Indian – their blindness to dirt and poverty, their easy acceptance of cruelty – they concealed very well.

They spoke rapturously of India, but dreamed of the West. Of European cities, of shops and duty-free goods. They spoke of eternal India, but, in their hearts, they were hungry materialists, who wanted nothing so much from life as a Japanese washing machine or a German toaster. Their contradictions were glaring and, in trying to hide them, they fell into cynicism and hypocrisy.

For this class of person, Toby was irresistible.

'Come here, this minute, you, Lawrence of Belgravia!' Vandana bellowed, on seeing him enter the room. 'Giving lectures on Ram, little swine. I'll tell you about Ram. He was a bloody weakling. A wimp! Come here!'

She was a great fat woman, loud and boisterous, with a fierce red bindi and the expressive eyes of a dancer, a Bharatnatyam dancer; she had, though it was hard to believe now, been trained as one. Like many bullies, she was painfully shy and unsure of herself, easily wounded.

The daughter of Marxist intellectuals, and a graduate of the National School of Drama down the road, she would perhaps have wanted a career in the political theatre of the time, which was so vibrant; or the new-age cinema, of the Shabana Azmi ilk, who, incidentally, was a classmate. But nothing had materialized and her talents had been squandered on very successful impressions of politicians in general, and Mrs Gandhi in particular. This had given her a modicum of drawing room celebrity. Taking leave of Toby's old friend, Mahijit, the Raja of Marukshetra, whom she had been flattering quietly in a corner, she rollicked across the room, swaying her great backside as she moved, flailing dimpled arms, spilling Scotch and ash.

She was getting ready to do one of her famous performances, in which she mocked the epic hero, Ram, for forcing his wife, Sita, under public pressure, to prove her chastity through a trial by fire.

'Sita, my dear, forgive me,' she said, in a simpering voice, 'you see Mummy says that your reputation is now tainted. And, because I'm a typical ball-less Indian wimp – the first, I might add, but not the last! The ādi-wimp! – I will please be requiring you to self-immolate your own good self.'

Cries of laughter and amusement went up in the room. 'O Vandana!' 'You're too much!' 'Such a little performer.'

Mahijit, spitting into his brass spittoon, jumped his eyebrows at his friend, who, all too familiar with Vandana's antics, smiled at the others in the room, but was inwardly fatigued at her approach. Bapa, their host, the second son of a second son, and a great social figure in Delhi in those days, famous for organizing music recitals in his garden, came up quickly. He was dressed, as he invariably was, in white from head to toe. 'Don't listen to a word of it,' he said to Toby. 'You were brilliant. This lot are too colonized to know a thing.'

'"Yes, yes, Sita,"' Vandana pressed on, her eyes flashing wildly, '"Go on, jump in, burn yourself alive. So that Mummy and the rest of us can be assured of your purity. And then we'll probably burn you alive anyway because your dowry was not large enough. Come on. Jump!"'

She swung her bottom into the air, and made a little pushing gesture with her hands, as though really prodding someone to enter a pyre. Then she threw her head back and laughed raucously. 'If it was me, I would have been on the first flying chariot back to Lanka. Give me dark sexy demons – dripping coconut oil – over wimpy Ram any old day. Or perhaps I would have stayed, and had a naughty little affair with Lakshman, who seems so much sexier . . .'

Vandana, still performing, now firing invisible arrows into the air, now prancing around the room in imitation of the epic hero, was intercepted by those who could see – Gayatri Mann, namely – that Toby was in need of rescuing.

'Namo Namaḥ, Raja saab,' Mann said smokily into his ear.

He gave her a relieved smile.

Gayatri Mann was the consummate professional Indian. She lived abroad with her husband, the publisher Zubin Mann, and, at a time when her country felt closed and remote, when the news was all famine and insurgency, she wore saris and high heels in Belgravia. She made documentary films on Bangladesh, on secret India, on the timelessness of Hinduism. She wrote books on pseudo-spirituality and the Princes, many of whom were her friends. She appeared on television shows to chasten those who threatened to spoil the magic by overplaying the wretchedness of India. 'Poverty?' she once told Louis Malle, 'I don't know why people keep going on about poverty. Everyone I know in India has a car.' And everyone she knew did.

In the West, she traded on India; and, in India, starved for news of the West, she carried back stories of the latest fashions, of books and movies, of Polanski and Kapuscinski, of how London was changing. She had sole monopoly on the exchange of pop culture and exotica, and she could only have thrived in a world where the exchange of goods and ideas was restricted, where news and information were scarce, where distances were real. Anyone might have told her that she would not survive the Internet. And, truly, much later, in that other time, when change came at last, it singled her out for extinction with a fury that till then had only been reserved for such inanimate things as the post and the landline.

Her father, the politician Sarat Mohapatra, was among those arrested the night before. And it was one of the many pretensions of this political family to refer to him – Mohapatra, *their* father – in the English way as simply Father, as though he were everybody's father.

'Wow-zee, Toby saab,' she now began, 'what times we live in! Father, you know, he was so stoic. He was ready for them when they arrived. And he, of course, was great friends with Pundit Nehru. So what a blow, so personal, you know. The daughter of your old friend sending around the police to arrest you. Horrific, and so bad for India, for her image. Forgive us for not being able to host you. Nixu's been in a flap about it all morning. *Because*,' and here, looking over at her brother who was in earshot, she gurgled with pleasure – nothing pleased her more than to run someone down, even her own brother – 'apparently when they came around to take Father away, he told the servants not to bother to wake Nixu. So it was only this morning, when the servants brought him his orange juice and paper, that my darling brother discovered Father was gone.'

'Shut up, Gayatri,' Nixu said. 'He'd have done just the same if it was you.'

'Nonsense! Father and I, you know, Toby, were very close.'

'*Are* very close, Gayatri. He's in jail, not dead.'

Ignoring her brother, she said, 'If he was not so staunchly opposed to all this dynasty business, which frankly he considers the height of vulgarity, he would have quite liked me to follow him into politics. I was the only child of his that he would discuss these things with,' she said, glancing at Nixu. Then seeing Toby's attention drift, she added quickly, 'But enough, enough political gup-shup, Toby ji.'

Toby, even in that quick survey of the room, had seen the person who'd been on his mind since that afternoon.

'Who—?' he began.

'Who?! Who, what! Tell me about yourself. You were marvellous today. I tell you, if only we'd grown up knowing these things. All they ever taught us, in bloody Tara Hall, was Billy the Bard, the Brontë-Shrontes, "I wandered lonely as a cloud" . . . It's such a handicap, you know. They were so systematic, Les Angrez, in stamping out our culture.'

'And a very good thing too,' Nixu said. 'Where would we be without them? Chanting-shanting. Burning women. Drowning girl children. The Horror that is India, I tell you . . .'

'Gayatri, who—?' Toby tried again.

By this point, Mahijit had approached. Nixu, on seeing him, sang, 'There was a rich Maharaja of Magador . . .'

Bapa heard and came over. Making a little napkin dance by its corners, he sang in a strong tenor, 'Who had ten thousand camels and maybe more.'

Nixu snatched the napkin, and flourishing it over his head, went on with abandon, 'He had rubies and pearls and the loveliest girls.'

Then they slipped their arms into Mahijit's.

'But he didn't know how to do . . . ?'

Mahijit, who'd clearly been through this many times before, looked straight at Toby, and muttered deadpan into his moustache, 'The rumba.'

At which, Bapa and Nixu laughed and laughed, till they had tears in their eyes.

Mishi had seen Toby come in. They had stopped just short of meeting each other's gaze. Or had they? It was hard to tell. There were such treacherous currents swirling around them that evening. Gayatri, for one, she could see, would sooner die than let him come over to her. She was, at that very moment, probably saying: 'Oh, some little air hostess, I don't know. Vapid as hell. I don't know why Bapa invites this lot . . . The B-team, if you ask me.'

And how could she, Mishi, just go over? Her boldness from earlier that day had deserted her.

She sat with Isha and Chamunda, whose large solemn eyes grew wider and wider, as her boyfriend, the green-eyed Ismail, gave a long praising account of the Emergency, interspersed with the filthiest language:

'This madarchodh country, you think it can be ruled by anyone not willing to, bhenchodh, give it to them in the gandh? For centuries they've, bhenchodh, been getting it up the you-know-what, had people rogering the hell out of them. Country with her damn legs open. Lying back, and enjoying herself. You think they understand any other language here? Let me tell you: they don't. And, let me tell you also, it was not her idea; it was his. It was her son, my friend, who finally decided that, bhenchodh, enough is goddam enough. Have to take this place into hand. Give this swine JP any more rope, and he'll, bhenchodh, hang the lot of us with it. Democracy-shamocracy, it's a damn good thing this has happened. The guy's a visionary. He'll whip this namby-pamby country into shape, you watch. Give him five years. Bloody place will be looking like Singapore.'

Chamunda had her bare feet on a stool, and though she remained perfectly still through this torrent, her dark toes, with their rings of faded gold, occasionally twitched, as if out of nervousness. She was beautiful, but her self-confidence had been damaged in a bad marriage. It had left her the kind of woman who either sought out men like Ismail, who were rough and abusive and treated her a little badly, or settled for men so tame and domesticated that she soon tired of them and was forced to have affairs on top of her affairs, forced to find new lovers to compensate for the inadequacies of her existing lovers.

Mishi, until now, had shown an exaggerated interest in the conversation. She laughed at key moments, energetically asked questions: the kind of thing we do, when our night has a secret purpose and we don't want to be found out. But, as the evening wore on, and dinner was served, and the lights guttered with a fluctuation, and an even layer of noise and laughter began to settle over the room, a mild depression took hold of her. She began to doubt anything would happen. She began to feel she had misjudged the situation. To be sure, she had felt his eyes on her through the lecture; and, later, when she had come up to him, she was certain she had seen something dazzled and grateful in his expression. He was speechless, and she was the cause, she knew. But had it been only temporary? Had he arrived at Bapa's, seen his friends, and changed his mind? Perhaps he was already committed, attached, and his reaction had been that of a helpless man. There had been no time to speak to Viski about it. But, surely, if this man was interested, he would have found some way, by now, to approach, to send her word of some kind . . . ?

She felt her earlier energy leave her; it, too, had been part of her secret hope for the evening. And, now that that was thrown into doubt, she was suddenly hot and bothered, bored of the conversation. The room felt congested, the air thick under the wheeling monotony of ceiling fans.

'Where are you going?'

'To have a fag.'

'Have one here!'

'No. I want to sit in the cool for a while.'

'Should I come?'

'No, no, stay. I'll just be back.'

In those days, most houses had a single air-conditioned bedroom. During parties, it became a smoking room, with people lying louchely on the bed, the sheets in a squalid swirl, the bedside tables cluttered with glass ashtrays. Mishi, receding into the back of the house, prayed it would not be like that today. She needed a moment alone. And, opening a door at right angles to a tube-lit kitchen, from which there came the steady exchange of food and dirty plates, she was relieved to find an empty room. The bed undisturbed; the air smoke-free and cool. She was tempted to lie down, put her feet up, and, with her head against the board, close her eyes for a moment. Her body felt so heavy, every joint hard and strained. It was so good to rest it, to feel its new waxy smoothness. To feel the ribbed contours of the Fabindia bedcover under her body. To gaze with a dreamy eye at a bookshelf lined with P.G. Wodehouse. She now stood up, went into the bathroom, and, leaving the door open a crack, began to pee in the dark.

Who has not done something similar? Not answered the urge to have something happen to you by creating the glimmer of a situation in which it might. Oh, and the peace of the bathroom, away from the harsh sounds of the party, with nothing but a laser-slim strip of light breaking in! The torrential rush of at least one kind of release and beyond, the small risk that she might be discovered, that there might suddenly be voices in the bedroom. But of course there weren't. It was quiet. And she had only just eased into it, let a light and defenceless swoon come over her, when the quiet was broken into by a thievish flash. The bathroom door gaped, a figure entered, and, with the firm click of a bolt, the darkness returned, pitchier and more closeting than before.

'Who's there?' she said, feigning panic. 'Who's there?'

Silence. This new and securer darkness did not respond. A tap came on. And, over the chortling sound of water, the consumptive wheeze of a drain, she heard a voice say, heard *him* say, quite softly, 'It's me.'

She smiled. A smile into the darkness is like a smile on the telephone: one of those rare moments, when we make an expression of joy purely for ourselves.

'But what if it had not been me?' the voice probed, making her laugh out loud.

'Then I would have raised a hue and cry.'

'Oh, would you have?' he said, and she could sense he was smiling too, but she could not gauge the distance at which he stood.

'You know, I really do need to finish peeing.'

'Go ahead. Please.'

And it was so odd: the way he said it, she felt she could.

Later, she never forgot the feeling of safety he had given her, the steadiness of his hand; the sense, very early on, that she could be naked before him. Later, she found other things, but never again that security. It was the closest thing she had known to the protections of childhood, and it stayed with her forever: the running tap, the entombing darkness, her allowing herself to pee in the presence of a stranger, who stood waiting, as if he had been waiting forever, and would go on waiting, until she was ready.

But, of course, she was ready. For she had been waiting too.

‘But what is this waiting?’ the girl Skanda has just been introduced to asks.

She is tiny, scrawny as a bird – her wrists scarcely two inches round – but her eyes are vast and liquid, full of the alarm and wonder of a child. Kitten Singh brought her over with a triumphant, ‘Meet Gauri! She was married to a Sanskritist.’ But it is not Sanskrit that draws them to each other; it is their need for a quiet corner away from this brunch of politicians, TV anchors, writers and journalists. The moment he is with her the room recedes. The guests, so threatening till a moment ago, become like a carousel of half-familiar faces, gliding by them as they speak.

He notices his father’s old friend, the Raja of Marukshetra: a heavy-set, elegant man, with a stern moustache and large eyes. He’s dressed that afternoon in a tight white churidar and a pale blue kurta; he has a spittoon in one hand, a Bloody Mary in the other. Skanda can also make out a dark-skinned woman, a little fat, magnificently unmade-up, with no jewellery save for a gold star anise in her nose. Chamunda! Beside her, a much larger woman, full of laughter and boisterous conversation. Vandana, he suspects. It is still the city of his childhood, but there are changes: Gayatri Mann is in a wheel-chair.

Her head drops to one side and she speaks with difficulty out of the corner of her mouth.

'It happened,' Kitten Singh had said earlier, trying to catch him up on everyone's news at once, 'when she was in New York. Bapa is not with us anymore either. He passed on last year. But, you know who's flourishing? Nixu Mohapatra. He's Chief Minister of Odra, for the umpteenth time! He still doesn't speak a word of the local language. Can you believe it? But the people, they love him for it. They say it protects him from corrupting voices. This must be what your father used to describe as "that innate Indian distrust of oneself".'

Soon after this survey of the room, Kitten Singh had brought Gauri over. And it was a relief.

'This waiting?' Skanda says now. 'It is a description of those periods in our lives when we suffer . . . for love – or for our art . . . You said, you were a writer, yes?'

'Hardly a writer. I write copy for websites.'

'Well, anyway, the canto I'm referring to is called "Asceticism Bears Fruit". And it is Uma who has taken up the ascetic's robes.'

'But what is the fruit?'

'The love of Shiva.'

'Oh, romantic. Is this what the English call sentimental poetry?'

He feels his gorge rise.

'More sentimental than the sonnets?' he says.

'Ah, but there the language is very specific. Very concrete. It brings something real to mind. Here it is all red lotuses and thunder clouds. Moons, creepers, rivers, submarine fires. It's so stylized. What was that funny word you just used? You know, for the colour of Uma's robes?'

'Babhru?'

'Yes, that's the one! Babhru to you too! Sorry! I'm being a little supercilious, aren't I?'

'It's a word for brown,' Skanda says calmly. 'Reddish-brown.

Tawny. It is described as the colour of a young or infant sun. It has the same origin as brown in English or *braun* in German.'

And now, for the first time, into those elongated eyes some respect seems to creep. She says something he likes; she says, 'We, in India, prefer to take the long road back to India, don't we? Via the West, preferably. Like this house – look at it: all this beaten brass and floral ceramics, the block print cloth . . . it feels like India . . .'

'. . . Returned to India via the Kings Road?'

'Yes!'

Emboldened, he says, 'And, Gauri, this colour she wears, it is very specific. It is the most Indian of Indian colours. It is that smoky-saffron-brown colour. Which is the colour of the rising and setting sun here, and practically nowhere else. I've seen it a thousand times myself from the window of a train or car, leaving the city at dawn.'

'I haven't left the city much recently; and never at dawn, at any rate. *I* have a young son myself . . .'

Something about the way she says this makes him feel that there is more to her antipathy for Sanskrit than he first thought.

Kitten Singh returns.

'I wanted to ask you,' she says, with sudden urgency. 'Did you tell your mother you were coming here?'

'No, we haven't spoken . . .'

'Good move. I'm fine with her, of course; and I'm in touch with your Isha Massi—'

'Will she be coming?' he interrupts.

'Here? No, no. But I see her occasionally. Your mother, however, I think she still bears a grudge from the old days, from Gulmarg, you know.'

He feels a stab of guilt – he should not have come, he knows – but before he can say anything more, she says, 'But the reason I came to find you is to tell you – I can't believe I just thought of it! – you know what day it is today?'

'No?' he says.

'It's 26 June! The day I first met your father, some thirty-five years ago. Would you believe it? And what a night we had that night. We were at Bapa's house, I remember – it was just after the Emergency was declared. And we went from there to the Cellar after Bapa's . . . you're too young to remember: it was a famous nightclub of that time. And then, finally, we ended up, all of us, at the Oberoi coffee shop. We must have been out till dawn that night. Drinking, smoking joints, phalana-dhimkana . . . What times those were, mad times! There was such a . . . I don't know. I see you children today and you've seen it all. We were such innocents. But willing to try anything. Once, you know! And, your father – tobah! – was *he* a wild thing! So bold.

'We had to get him out of town that night, you know. Because – this is so funny! – while we were in the Oberoi, the lights suddenly went out – you know, the usual power cut/shower cut. And, with everyone several sheets to the wind, he leaps up onto a table, your father, and makes an announcement in the dark, if you please. He says he will give any man willing to assassinate Mrs Gandhi £1,000. Now, my God, Skanda, all hell broke loose. Can you imagine: a man, just after Mrs Gandhi has declared a state of Emergency, offering money to an assassin to kill her. Meri to uddhar hi nikal gayi. When the lights came on, pin-drop silence. Not a squeak. I said, "Toby, tu iddron nikal. There are intelligence men everywhere; the management is up in arms; you'd best get out of here." He said, "Kitten, I was meant to leave for Hampi in a few days." I said, "Leave now. This minute. Phoran. Just go."'

Gauri says, 'But how would they have known it was his voice if the lights were out?'

He likes her for asking this; nothing passes her by.

'Gauri, my dear, don't be so silly. They have their ways. And the accent, no? Unmistakable. How many people would have spoken like that? And a prince, to boot; they would have flayed him alive. Old Mrs G, you know how she despised the princes!'

'And did he leave, my father?'

'Oh, that very night. Or morning, rather. At sunrise.'

'With my mother?'

'I don't think she was in the picture yet.'

'I'd always heard they met that night?'

'Well, maybe she was there. I don't remember. But romantic, no? Foolhardy! An outlawed prince leaving town at dawn . . .'

'When the sun was but an orange-brown infant?!' Gauri offers.

'Screw you,' Skanda says, laughing.

'It's straight out of . . .' Kitten begins, 'I don't know.'

'Mills and Boon?'

'No, no, silly girl, Shakespeare, Cervantes. Not Mills and Boon. Chalo, I must tend to my guests. You two are fine?'

'Fine.'

'Good. I'm sure you'll get along famously.'

He thinks not, but then he wonders . . . It feels like one of those remarks one remembers later. And even this meeting, it has an odd feeling of significance to it. There's something about Gauri.

Once Kitten Singh has gone, she says abruptly, 'It has a bad reputation, you know, your great language. Here, at least, it has been co-opted by all the worst people. Every Hindu nut from here to Kanyakumari.'

'I know.' He wants to say, *More than you could ever know*, but he stops himself. 'What can I say? People will have the past speak in ways that have more to do with the present than the past.'

'You're smart,' she says prissily, spoiling the intimacy that has grown between them. 'I hope to see more of you. There are not too many people in this town who – to steal a phrase from Proust – are part of "the aristocracy of the mind".'

He wants to get away again, but she unexpectedly says, 'Skanda, if you're in Delhi for a while, I'd like you to meet my son, Kartik.'

'Your son? Why?'

'Oh, because,' she says, coolly, 'I think it will be nice for him to meet a likeable Sanskritist for once. It'll be a change after that swine, his father.'

'I knew it!' Skanda says and begins to laugh.

'Knew what?' She says defensively.

'That you had married a rotter, and that it had coloured your view of Sanskrit . . .'

'My view of Sanskrit is not coloured.'

'Come on!'

She laughs now too. 'Well, a little perhaps. Yours would be too, if you lived with an abusive little shit who thought he was Shiva, and found all the validation he needed in Sanskrit texts.'

As they're leaving, she says, 'I mean it, Babhru. I really do want you to meet Kartik. I'll call you soon.'

A fat orange sun, sulphurous as a bomb, rose over the land outside Delhi. It burnt away every trace of the night, under whose cover so much had been possible. The two people asleep in the back of the Ambassador were in that state before wakefulness, when the mind tries frantically to reconstitute the fragments of the night. Which, having known no unity save the now dispersed darkness, resist being threaded together.

The car barrelled south; they came in and out of sleep. But, every now and then, an eye, red and sticky, glued together, would open and gaze furtively at the semiconscious form of the other. The lolling head; the drawn lines; the faces soggy with sleep and drink; the muscles around the mouth tightening and flexing – the hint of stale breath – the sudden flicking back of the head in the eternal (and futile) search for a better resting place. It was such intimate company for two strangers to find themselves in. And it was with a mixture of wonder and awkwardness, the night's memories returning as a flood, that they became aware of their flight from the capital.

*

The night before, there was this exchange outside the coffee shop of the Oberoi.

'In Sanskrit, Mishi . . .' Toby said, and stopped. 'Mishi? What kind of name is that?'

'It's short for Michelle!'

'Michelle? Is that your real name?'

'It's actually Uma, but—'

'Uma! You can't have as grand a name as Uma and call yourself Mishi! No, no, no. You must go back to Uma. And, as I was saying, Uma – yes, Uma! Much better . . . So, as I was saying, in Sanskrit we have a dual number. A whole declension for things that come in twos, such as Toby and Uma . . .'

'If I'm no longer Mishi, surely you can't be Toby.'

'All right then. What shall I be?'

'Whatever you really are!'

'But I'm really Toby.'

'I mean whatever you are, if you're not Toby, the way I'm Uma, if I'm not really Mishi.'

'Oh, you mean what I really-really am!'

'Yes. What you really-really are, if you're not really Toby.'

'No.'

'No? Why no?'

'It's too long.'

'What do you mean too long?'

'It won't work. What I really-really am is too long.'

'Try me.'

'Ghanashyama Mayurdhvaja Pashupati Rao . . .'

'OK, OK. Toby.'

'But you are definitely still Uma.'

'I've never been called Uma.'

'But now you will be. And as I was saying, Uma, in Sanskrit we have a dual number, devoted solely to those things that come in twos. So, for instance, if I were to say, we go, as in we all, you, me and this rather annoying woman called Kitten Singh – and we thought we had problems! – who has attached herself to me and won't let go, and who wants me to leave town for what I just said, a moment ago, when the lights were out, but who I suspect is one of those women who creates false intimacies just so that she can get into one's trousers . . .'

'One's trousers?'

'My trousers. Now, if I were to say, we all go, and I meant to include her, I would say, gacchāmaḥ.'

'Gacchāmaḥ?'

'Correct. The first person plural. But, if for instance, Uma, I wanted to say, let's you and I—'

'When the evening is spread out against the sky?'

'Yes! If I wanted to say, let's just you and I, having successfully ditched this old bore Kitten Singh, go, then I would say – wait for it – gacchāvaḥ. The first person dual.'

At this Uma, for that was who she was now, drove her index finger into the front of his trousers and drew him close. 'OK, Ghanashyama Mayurdhvaja Pashupati Rao of Kalasuryaketu, aka Toby. Gacchāvaḥ!'

Moments later, as the sky brightened, they stood outside the Oberoi Hotel before a sleeping encampment of Sikh taxi drivers.

'Where are we going?'

'To Hampi.'

'What? In a car? I thought it was hundreds of miles away.'

'It is.'

'Satzriakal, ji. Sanu taxi di lodh si gi.'

'You speak Punjabi?!'

'Just a little.'

'Kithe jaana e ji?'

'Gwalior.'

'Gwalior?'

'Gwalior?'

'We can't tell him Hampi; he's never heard of it. Let's just take him out of his comfort area gradually. Lunch in Gwalior; then, with a little incentive, cocktails in Kalasuryaketu; and once we've picked up my writer friend, old Vijaipal, we'll head south. Then, on the banks of the Tungabhadra, I will ask you to marry me.'

'Bloody fool!'

But, even as she said it, she could see it was not a joke. Not, at least, in the sense of the very idea of it being a joke. And if she'd been having lunch that afternoon with a friend, instead of going south with him, and the friend had said, so, what is he like?, she might have said, 'He is the kind of man who, having only just met a girl, can tell if he means to marry her.' 'Wow, ya, really? Sounds great. Romantic, yaar.' 'Yes. In the sense of him knowing who he is. But don't get me wrong: I'm not saying he has drive or ambition or any of the other things we associate with this kind of confidence. In fact, I wonder if his certainties are not just a way to keep the world out.'

Would she have known so much so early? Hard to say. But – as much as she would later tell her children, 'Oh, you kids, you're so cautious these days! With me, I just jumped into a taxi with your father one morning and that was it' – when she saw the tall sleepy sardar driver emerge from the canvas tent outside the Oberoi Hotel, she was not acting as spontaneously as she liked later to make out. She was, in fact, thinking, *If getting into this taxi now means, goodbye to air-hostessing, goodbye to respectability, goodbye to my relationship with Mama, even if it means goodbye to Delhi, for a long, long time, then so be it, and good riddance – for, as far as I'm concerned, someone has shown me an out, thrown me a line, and I would be a fool not to take it.*

The car barrelled south; the sun rose; the heat was exquisite. It was worse with every hour; it was as if they were making a journey to the source of the parching breath that blew in through the open windows. The enemy of moisture. It did not even make them sweat; to sweat would have been better; but it seemed by just blowing over them to rob their body of its liquids. They soaked her shaneel dupatta in water and draped it over the Rexene seat. They took turns lying in each other's laps. By 3 p.m., the arid hills had begun to appear, and the land grew scorched and ravined.

The driver, alone, was serene. He had a wet handkerchief rolled up behind his neck. And, save for a brief query at Gwalior as to whether they wished to go further – receiving, in reply, new and more generous terms – he said nothing. By late afternoon the bare and eroded kernels of hills that must once have been mountains began to appear. Hills covered in burnt yellow grass.

'You can see why we have so many words for brown,' Toby said. He was sitting up; the sight of the hills had revived him, the hills that anticipated the Tamasā.

'I can't think of even one.'

'Oh, there are many. It's like ice and the Eskimos: aruṇa, piṅgala, kadru . . .'

'Go on!'

'It's true.'

'I mean: go on.'

'Oh, what, just off the top of my head? Babhru. Like *brun* and brown.'

'Wait. Are you making this stuff up?'

'What stuff? The cognate stuff?'

'Yes. What does that mean anyway, cognate?'

'It means born together with, *co* + *natus*. And *natus* from *(g)nascor* is cognate with the Sanskrit root *jan* from where we have janma and the Ancient Greek gennáō, to beget. Genesis, too. Or, here is another one: *lubh*, to be perplexed or disturbed, become disordered, go astray; to desire greatly or eagerly; to entice, allure . . .'

'Oooh, how exciting. What *cognates* does that have?'

He smiled. The car had begun to climb for Kalasuryaketu. The heat was gone. Soon the Tamasā would be visible. Soon they would be having drinks on his terrace. Soon she would be bathed and dressed. And beautiful again. But, for now, she was sprawled out on the car seat, her head in his lap. Her face was covered in a film of sweat and dust; her hair was rough and dishevelled; even her dark breasts, pressing against the black cloth of her kurta, had a moist and begrimed look about them.

'With the Latin *lubet*, *libet*, *libido*; the German *liob*, *lieb*, *lieben*; the Anglo-Saxon *leof*.'

'Toby!'

'In English?'

'Yes, in English.'

'Love only.'

The Shiv Niwas was less a palace than it was a fort, a line of rooms and terraces on a high rampart overlooking the river. Which, at that hour, was dark and scarcely visible. There was no moonlight on its broad expanse, no riverfront as such. The only sign of the river at all was the weak reflection of electric light, lapping black and yellow on its margin.

Most of the year, the place was closed up. And there was great excitement that Raja saab had arrived from Delhi. In one day, and with a lady friend!

'Why didn't you tell me? I would have driven up to fetch you.'

'Oh, there's no need, Labu, it was painless.'

'No, but really: it's the limit. And madam, can you imagine making her drive up in heat like that?'

'She's a tough old thing, Sharada.'

'Haw! The way you talk. Now, tell me quickly, should I set drinks on the terrace? Or will you eat something first? I've put two buckets of hot water, for you and madam.'

'Drinks, then dinner. Has my guest arrived?'

'Yes, yes. He's been here for days. Reading, writing, visiting temples and whatnot. Such a strange man. Looks just like an Indian, but speaks like a pukka Angrez.'

'He's never lived here, Sharada; he is a pukka Angrez. And show some respect: he's a famous, famous writer in the West.'

'But, on the face of it, he could be from here. Not like you, Raja saab. So fair and European-seeming, but, in your heart, a pukka desi.'

On the terrace, some moments later, Vijaipal said, 'And your friend, Toby? Will she be joining us?'

'Any moment, Vijay. She's still recovering from the drive up, I imagine. I'm dying for a drink. What are you having?'

'I'll have whatever you're having. I bought some whisky for you from the duty-free in London. Do you want that?'

'No, let's save that for the trip. Here, I have . . .' He tried in the faint tube-light from a battery-powered torch to make out the labels. 'There's some Scotch, some Indian whisky, which you don't want . . .'

'Yes, let's give that a miss.'

'Beefeater—'

'Lovely, Toby. I'll have the gin with what? . . . Soda, I suppose.'

'Soda.'

Once Toby's back was turned, his mind raced. In the early hours of a romance, when you think you have it in you to be holed up for days, there is nothing more tantalizing than not being able to do so, to have to come down for drinks or dinner, to behave normally in front of a guest, to conceal your desire, to speak of the Emergency and of the decay of Hinduism, when all you want to be doing . . .

And it had been so much stronger than anything he could have imagined. Seeing her unbathed in her kurta, searching for clothes in his cupboard, for soap, for shampoo, her legs exposed, the most evil reek wafting past him. Of armpits, of unwashed hair, of sweat turning to vinegar in the crevasses, pits and folds of her body. It had produced in him the unquenchable arousal of the morning, when it seems like nothing will release you from it. And when he blindsided her on the way to the bathroom, and she stood on her tiptoes clenching her fists against the wooden cupboard and muttering, 'But your friend, Toby, your friend,' he had, inhaling her, feared something would not give, and would leave him aching with desire. Right to the end, when she was a flood under him and he could still smell her on his mouth, he had feared that. And nothing had helped: not the nails she dug into his back, not the fist she fastened around his testicles as if meaning to tear them off, not her arcing her body up and driving his face into her armpits, nothing, till, at last, she had, with a surgeon's precision, dug her one red-nailed digit an inch into what was like the source of his resistance, conquering, in a sharp stab of joy and surprise and release, the little redoubt of sphincteral tension.

Then, for many minutes, with the gratitude and fatigue of a child, he had watched himself make his way out of her: a cautious, nacreous stream picking a course through the inflamed folds of dark skin.

'Extraordinary, Toby, to have done it all in a day, the drive. I think the staff here are quite amazed!'

'Well! I had a supportive team. And, besides, it's such a relief not to be spending the night on the way, Vijay. What about yourself? Did you get here easily enough? I suppose this Emergency business has thrown your writing plans into a swivet?'

'Not at all, you know, not at all. India has this way of distracting one, of luring one into her little problems, so that you forget the big ones, the ones you could see easily when you first arrived . . .'

'A pageant / to keep us in false gaze!'

'Yes! Very nice. Nice to hear it used like that.'

He handed him his drink. The weak but constant white light, edged now with a better though less reliable light from the fanooses, sank deep into the patchwork of Vijaipal's face, which was drawn and pulpy by turns. There was something serious, and a little embittered, in that face. Toby had never minded it before. But his mild impatience now told him how much Uma already possessed him, how much he wished her there, with her femininity and laughter, to cut the gaunt seriousness of this man.

'No, I think all it will do, this Emergency, Toby, is allow Indians to see themselves a little more clearly.'

'How do you mean?'

'Well, by shattering the illusion of liberal democracy. It's very bad, you know, Toby, when you're such a third-rate place, to parade around high notions of liberalism and democracy, which, as you know, developed at the height of another civilization's achievement; and which, in a place like India, only mask the reality. Hide the decay. Much better the end come fast.'

At this Vijaipal laughed and Toby was surprised to find that, though he said nothing he did not agree with, he was unable to share in his pessimism. He found himself distracted, looking back at the dimly lit rooms behind him. Without even being asked, he said, 'I'm sure she'll be here any minute. We had a very late night, then the drive . . .'

'But, Toby, you must tell me of your own interest in Indian things, in Sanskrit. Because in my experience with Indians, the privileged ones, at least, they either have open contempt for their culture or they revere it away with foolish pieties. *Sanskrit is the mother of all languages*, that kind of thing, you know? Which is another way of not dealing with it.'

Toby nodded his head vigorously, then, unable to control himself, cried into the back of the house, 'Sharada, take a look to see if the Dilli-wali-madam is all right, see if she needs anything. Tell her we're sitting out here.'

When he turned back he saw Vijaipal was smiling, a smile at once generous and accusing.

'Is it all very new?'

'Yes!' Toby said sheepishly, and felt a great sense of relief, felt he could now talk to Vijaipal properly, now that he knew.

'You look very much *in* . . .' Vijaipal paused, searching for the right word.

'In something! Yes. I fear so.'

'You'll tell me about it later, Toby, you'll tell me all about it later, yes?'

'I will.'

Now they stopped talking, for there were padding sounds of footsteps behind them, and, a moment later, out of the darkness, with the rustle of a bush or some potted plant, Uma appeared. In grey Adidas track pants, her hair wet and twined, pulled over one shoulder, where it soaked the thin muslin of an oversized kurta, making visible, even in the darkness, her bra strap and skin.

'I'm so sorry. You won't believe it . . .'

'You fell asleep?!' he said without thinking, in his enthusiasm at seeing her, in his wish to suppress with words, any words, the power of the impression she had made on him. But it had the opposite effect, for the look that passed between them contained all the secrets of the bedroom. And she was twice – no, three times – embarrassed: for her lateness, for the way she was dressed, for the intimacy that had become evident, and that excluded Vijaipal. Vijaipal, in whose easy admiration of Uma, in the frank pleasure of his gaze – his evident delight that she had joined them – Toby was able to relive his own pleasure at seeing her.

He left them to get her a drink and to recover his equanimity, to revel in the passive pleasure of listening to someone, for whom your feelings are new and strong, make conversation with someone who is a stranger to them, but not to you. He poured the drink slowly, as conversation began behind him, with the shy discomfort of musicians warming up, every note seeming at first to sound false.

By the time he'd returned with Uma's drink, he had almost to fear for his own inclusion.

'Toby, Mishi was just . . .'

'*Uma*,' he said, handing her her drink.

'Uma?'

'It's true. It's my real name.'

'Is it really? And they called you Mishi? I'm afraid Toby is right . . .' He stopped himself. 'These names! Where do they come from? From an embarrassment with Indian things, no doubt, an embarrassment even at the sound of Sanskrit?'

'It's funny you ask,' Toby said, suddenly at his ease. 'People have a strange relationship with these things. No one would seriously give their child a name like Mishi or Toby, never as their real name – they would only ever give them a Sanskrit name – but as—'

'I know what you mean. In the place where I grew up, a terrible place, not worth mentioning, I used to know some people, so culturally denuded, that their names had become Neel and Diamantine. You, Toby must know—'

'Nala and Damayanti?' he said, laughing, and glanced at Uma, who had drawn up her feet and was leaning back against a bolster.

'Exactly! People would have you believe that none of it was important; they would have you believe these are trifles: but, of course, it is important: important how India is thought of in India, no? How, for instance, Toby, is your interest in classical India regarded among your class of person?'

'With dismissal, at best. Or suspicion.'

Toby felt her gaze on him, a questioning gaze. He felt her form her earliest impressions of him.

'Right! Suspicion that you might have some right-wing political agenda, that your interest is but a cover for a hatred of Muslims or some such.'

'Yes. But for so many it is. And I've always regarded the men in saffron as the true enemies of the Indian past . . .'

'Because . . . ?'

'Because,' and now he looked at Uma, to make sure she was interested in their conversation. 'Because . . .' he repeated abstractedly, then the words came: 'they would see it reduced – all the glory of ancient India – to *slogan*.'

'To slogan, yes! Slogans and pamphlets. Very nice, very nice thing to say. And then, of course, in that form it has no meaning. It is no longer an intellectual thing, no longer interesting.'

'No,' he said, trying not to look, but afraid they were boring her, 'in that form it is worthless.'

Silence.

He interpreted it as brought on by them having lost her, but it was broken – to his great joy! – by a question of some intensity from her. A question that made him feel that the thing he loved most in life might one day get along with the thing he was beginning to like more and more.

'How did it begin for you?' she said. And, though Vijaipal had asked him something similar a moment before, it felt so fresh and heartfelt coming from her that he was almost flattered by it.

'You know,' he began, addressing her, then thinking better of it, turned to Vijaipal, whose drink he could see was empty, 'I think it was Latin and Greek in school.'

'In England?'

'In England.'

'Oh, I see, I see. The regard one place has for its things producing in you a similar regard – a need, even – for your own things. I understand that very well. I've known such a need myself.'

'It's true. Because, you know, here, the Sanskrit teacher is invariably a figure of fun.'

'A kind of holy fool, no doubt! Caste-marked and full of outdated ideas. Probably everyone in the school had a kind of contempt for a man like that. Not attractive and interesting-seeming, not like the English teacher, say?'

'That's it. But once I was able to connect the Sanskritic world with the classical world at large, it came to seem like the greatest discovery of my life.'

'How so?' Uma asked.

Again he felt a flush. 'Well, I think more than anything, in a country where so little was planned, everything haphazard and shoddy, here, at least, was an example of the most exquisite planning. Proof that things had not always been as shitty as they are today. Because, Vijay,' he said, turning to the writer, 'if we were to associate the genius of a place with one particular thing – the Russians with literature, say, or the Germans with music, the Dutch and Spanish with painting – we would have to say that the true genius of Ancient India was language. Not so much the use of it as the study of it: their grammars were peerless, easily the most profound meditation on language in pre-modern times. And once I discovered them I could never again think of India as merely the shabby place I saw around me. It changed my entire relationship with what remained of old India in India . . .'

'To the past?' Vijaipal said.

'To the past, yes. But also my idea of East and West.'

'Those distinctions would have broken down. Of course! It would have come to seem like a shared past.'

'It *is* a shared past,' Toby said. 'Where these languages are concerned – the Indo-European ones, at least – it is most definitely a shared past. And while, in Europe, this is only a point of curiosity – a confirmation of the Biblical idea of the Tower of Babel, say – in India, it was like permission to respect oneself anew.'

Suddenly he became aware of her presence. Uma, who had been sitting across from him, got up, as if drawn to him by his intensity, and came to sit next to him.

Vijaipal glanced at her, then laughed. 'Like discovering, while mired in deep poverty, that you are, in fact, the first cousin of the King.'

'It's true, Mr Vijaipal!' Uma said.

'Vijay, surely!'

'Vijay. Because we grew up with so little. We had nothing. And the worst part was that we made the people below us, who did have something, believe that what they had was worthless. We forced them, if they were to enter our ranks, to surrender their culture.'

'Such a bad business, isn't it? Confusion heaped upon confusion. The more I travel in the colonial world, the more it feels like a general condition.'

For some time now Laban had been waiting. Seeing an opening, he said softly, 'Khana.'

Dinner had been laid out for them in a partially enclosed veranda overlooking the river on three sides. They discussed the trip ahead, how long they would wait in Kalasuryaketu, how long the drive would be, where they would stop, where they would stay.

At one point Uma said, 'What makes it so important, Hampi? Why do you people keep going back?'

Her question produced an awkwardness among the two men, as

though they both acknowledged their reasons as being very different and wanted, out of courtesy, to give the other way.

'My reason is simple, Uma,' Toby said. 'I find it beautiful. But hear Vijaipal out.'

'I'll tell you, Uma, I'll tell you. In my work it is not so important to have historical information as it is to have a historical sense. To be able in some way to give the past shape. And you will see how a place like Vijayanagara, with its unique history, will do that for you automatically.'

He said this and looked out at the Tamasā, where through the gaps in the muslin curtains it was possible now to see the lit shapes of long boats on its dark surface.

Midnight in the flat. No sounds from the city, the air still and dry. Skanda lies on a faded sofa, the nap of its floral upholstery coarse under his back, staring up into the musty darkness. A single light, a halogen light – rare piece of refurbishment! – shines on the flat's most beautiful object, bought years ago in the south, somewhere near Hampi, in anticipation of Skanda.

It is a picchvai of peacocks. At the centre of this ostentation of white birds there is a single blue peacock. The peacock is Skanda's mount. A foolish and haughty bird. Orgulous. In the picchvai, the peacocks dance under a bruised monsoon sky. A sky due any moment in Delhi. Of heavy wandering clouds. Nabhas in Sanskrit, *nebulosus* in Latin, like *nebula*, 'mist'. *Nifol*, in Anglo-Saxon: dark. Daytime darkness, he likes to think. When *by th'clock 'tis day, / And yet dark night strangles the travelling lamp.* The trees acquire that special density and their white flowers seem to prick the canvas, as though it were a canopy, with nothing but starlight behind. The miniature painters devoted such attention to the trees, distinguishing the lighter and big-leafed banana from the darker entanglement of mango. And, fountaining up over every copse, was always the prickly canopy of a palm.

It is a scene that awaits rain. Who knows why these vain birds need the rainy season to come alive? Or why they are so dejected when the rains are done? But it has always been so. In the Ramayana – when the monsoon is over – the peacocks glimpse the sky free of clouds and their tails droop. They are described as gat'ôtsava – robbed of festivity – and, in this mood, they fall to contemplation.

In the picchvai, they are in disguise. As with Shakespearean comedy, it is the great theme of Sanskrit literature. In The Birth, Shiva comes in disguise to Uma, who has taken on asceticism to win his love. It is a test of sorts. 'He wants,' Skanda recalls Toby saying, 'to see if his world is suited to hers.' And so, disguised as a student, with matted locks, an antelope skin round his waist, a staff of palasha wood in his hand – the mark of the student – he enters the ascetics' grove and, on seeing Uma, questions her as to the cause of her asceticism.

The David Smith, which Skanda feels is more beautiful than his, has Shiva saying: 'Why in your youth have you discarded your ornaments and put on the birch bark . . . is [night] ready for the red morning when it's evening and the moon and the stars are out?! / If you're seeking heaven, your effort is in vain – your father's dominion is the land of the gods . . . if you're seeking a husband, have done with meditation! A jewel does not seek. It is sought.'

Uma does not reply. But a girlfriend informs the ascetic that the man she seeks is none other than Shiva. 'Shiva!' the ascetic cries: 'that beast, that wild man, that dweller in the places of the dead. Shiva, whose body is covered in the ash of funeral pyres, whose elephant hide garments drip blood, Shiva, the skull-bearer, this jewel of a creature seeks him?! Surely this is some kind of joke?'

'While the Brahmin was saying these unpleasant things, she, [Uma] looked at him sideways' – this is the Smith.

Skanda's is: 'She looked at him askance, with eyes whose corners were bloody, her brows contracted into creepers, her lower lip trembling with rage.'

And then, after tearing into him, she pulls away, her breasts break against their bark garment, stana | bhinna | valkalā: that is the compound; bhinna, related to the Latin *findo*, the German *beissen*, meaning to break, shatter or pierce; in English, it gives us bite. Breasts biting in anger against their bark garments until Shiva reveals his true form. Then she is neither stayed nor gone. With one foot raised to go, her body moist with sweat, Uma is, the poet tells us, like a river whose course is obstructed by a rock.

'O you of stooping limbs' – Shiva says – 'I am from this moment on your slave.' When the moon-crested Shiva said this, she cast off the weariness of her exertions, for with the fruit exhaustion turns into freshness. But since this is a dual narrative – its two arms working in tandem, one energizing the other – the fruit varies from narrative to narrative: for Uma, it is the love of Shiva; for the gods, it is the birth of Skanda, their general.

Skanda asleep on the sofa, under the dim lights and high ceilings of the flat in Delhi.

Uma never forgot that first morning in Kalasuryaketu, of sitting out on the terrace of Shiv Niwas, the sluggish green expanse of the river sprawled out over the bleached land beneath her, the sound of bells carrying up from the scorching ghats. It was a glimpse of an India that the thin but culturally impervious layer of post-colonial life in Delhi – the world of clubs and convent schools – had never before allowed her to see.

And soon after, there would be the sight of Vijayanagara at dawn, the veil of morning mist hanging over the ruined city, giving it the aspect of a place still smoking from siege. The surrounding land was covered in gigantic boulders and paddy fields, in whose glassy surfaces shoots of rice burst through the repeating tableaux of blue sky and clouds. The Tungabhadra – reflecting pool of a river! – negotiated a placid course through this plateaued country, its path obstructed with dancing rocks. Kishkindha! Where in the vast ruins of a great capital, amid wide avenues and shattered aqueducts, there were still palaces where musical columns could be played.

Before leaving Kalasuryaketu, she had called her sister, Isha, from Tripathi's house in the bazaar. Toby stood outside, in the light of a kerosene lantern, now smoking, now negotiating with a man selling fruit.

'Does Mama know?'

'No, you fool. I've been covering for you, of course. From the moment she called, I said you were with me . . . But Mishi, there's a limit . . . I'm all for breaking the rules . . . but I hope, you know . . . thodi reputation di bhi fikr kar . . .'

'Ish, I think it's fine.'

'Fine? Are you mad? The whole town's talking, Mishi. Kitten Singh saw you two taking off . . .'

'No, I mean. I think it could be serious.'

'Are you completely off your bloody rocker? You've been gone less than two days. How—?'

'Is it that little? Really? It feels so much longer already.'

'Mishi!'

'Chal, well, let's see. Now I'm gone, I'm gone. Anyways, I was away a lot. Say I'm off flying or something, no?'

'Arre, at least, show your face at home?'

'I can't.'

'Why?'

'I'm not in Delhi. I'm somewhere in the wilds of M.P., about to head further south.'

'South? Where?'

'I'm not sure. Hampi.'

'No! With him only?'

'Yes, obviously. And some writer chap. Vijaipal . . .'

'Sooprasaat?'

'Yes. How did you know?'

'Oh, he's famous, yaar. I've read about his books in the papers. *Man of Hidden Shallows*. *India and Oblivion*. Get something signed, no?'

'I'll try.'

'And, Mishi . . .'

Already she felt she did not answer to that name.

'Yes?'

'Don't say anything stupid.'

She laughed. 'I'm not the stupid one. Remember?'

She stood there a little while longer, observing Toby. It surprised her that, in such a short time, she was hardly able to separate his smell from her own. His pale nakedness, at first so strange to her – the pinkish nipples, edged with thick brown hair, the ridged crevasse of his chest – no longer held any secrets. His erudition ceased to intimidate her. The love affair of thirty-six hours had already blurred these lines. She felt in possession of him. And the thing that surprised her most was how little any of it surprised her. She must always have expected something like this would happen to her. Now that it had, she felt entitled to it, felt it her due. She had spent a long time in the wilderness, waiting for it, among people who had tried to diminish her. She would almost have liked to retain some bitterness for them, but it was impossible. Her happiness was too great.

They made a journey south over several days, stopping at Dak bungalows on the way, skirmishing with the approaching rains. Toby and Vijaipal, perhaps because Uma was seeing with fresh eyes what they had seen before, made a great fuss over her.

At first it had seemed like an odd grouping, the two lovers and Vijaipal. But, in fact, it worked very well. In the day they would go out separately – Uma and Toby together, Vijaipal alone. They had an arrangement to meet at a given time at the giant statue of the Nandi if they were interested in having lunch together. Otherwise, they would spend the day apart and meet for drinks in the evening, at the cottages where they were staying. A place in the paddy fields owned by a friend of Toby's, where the coffee was very good and strong, and where a bottle of whisky was kept for them in a locked cupboard. After a day on their own, some of it spent swimming in the Tungabhadra, some climbing to a high summit with views of the surrounding land, some spent sleeping and making love in the shadows of giant rocks, Vijaipal's company in the evening was a welcome thing.

His learning, when it came to Indian things, was not as extensive as Toby's. But he was, in a sense, the shrewder observer, less romantic, less invested in pleading the cause of one culture over another. And the men would frequently argue. Over whether India had a history-writing tradition or not; or whether there was anything resembling the realism of Virgil's *Georgics* in Sanskrit literature; any writing, that could be compared, in its specificity, to Varro's description of his Aviary. Uma listened with interest, but could not make out the contours of their conversation. She did feel though that beneath everything they said, so dispassionate and cerebral, there was a great underlying tension.

One morning Toby felt unwell, and said he would not go out. Uma thought she would stay in with him, but Vijaipal offered to take her, and Toby insisted she go. 'His view is not mine,' he said to her quietly, 'but he's thought very hard about these things. And you should go out with him. It'll be a real learning.'

Soon after, she sat pillion on Vijaipal's Enfield, as they made their way along dirt roads, past the glassy fields, to the main site. It felt strange, so much was she full of Toby, to be so near another man. She tried holding on with her knees alone – this felt less intimate – but she didn't trust herself and had eventually to rest her hands on his waist; with the rush of air, his smell – something oil-based and discreet –

would occasionally reach her; turning a corner or accelerating, their bodies would collide lightly against each other.

It was a still hot day, the impression of the sun keen and hard in the reflecting fields. Gone now, now appearing as a dancing ball some distance away, now on their left, now on their right. Sometimes the fields would darken and a breeze would blow over them, rippling their surfaces and obstructing their powers of reflection. Then, in a blaze, as if in revenge, sun and sky would return at once, bringing a greater and more ominous stillness, ionizing the air with uncertainty.

Vijaipal was dressed that morning in jeans, hard brown shoes and a pale blue (almost white) oversized shirt, which was tucked in and gave a sense of the smallness of his frame, the clothes seeming to balloon off it. His mood was very different – more sombre and serious – from when they would meet for drinks in the evening. He seemed to be working, adding what was useful to a narrative already forming in his head, discarding what he did not need. And, though he seemed closed-off, private, absorbed in what he saw, he was full of a kind of generosity for Uma, as though wanting her, with her gaze unsullied by politics, to be able to see what he saw.

'I find it helpful,' he said, even before they had approached the site, while he was still looking for his notebooks and pens, 'when considering the history of a place like Vijayanagara, to think of what was happening in other places. To think of history laterally, as it were. And Vijayanagara, which was founded in 1336, and only lasted two hundred years before it was destroyed – and destroyed completely – by a confederacy of Muslim princes, has a very interesting history in that respect. For we have literally – and, I think, 1336 is the date it began – the Hundred Years War between France and England, on one end, and the birth of Shakespeare, with all that that signifies, on the other: 1564 he was born, 1565 Vijayanagara was destroyed. Don't do anything with this information; just keep it in mind. It will help lay out the field.'

She had no idea what the Hundred Years War was; Shakespeare, she knew, but not what his birth signified. Still, she liked the intensity with which Vijaipal spoke, and didn't want to interrupt him. He seemed to sense the dull impact of this information on her, for just as they were entering the monuments, he said, with fresh urgency, 'And please don't believe these things don't matter; or that they are trivial. I know, despite Toby's protestations, that Indians have no time for history, no way even to assess the passage of time. A hundred years, two hundred, a thousand, five thousand: it's all the same to them, isn't it? They have no markers, no points of reference, and, so, no way to value the past. I know, too, that for most Indians history begins for them with the birth of their grandfather; everything else is prehistory. But please, do not, for one moment, believe it was always that way. When Toby says that, in his commentaries, a man writing in fourteenth-century Andhra Pradesh might effortlessly reference another writer, writing eight centuries before him, in an altogether different part of the country, with a casual "iti-daṇḍin" – as Dandin says – he has a point. I don't know if it establishes what he thinks it establishes, that Indians had a history-writing tradition, but, yes, they certainly seemed to have been able to go back further into their past than they can go today. So that inability now, to be able to go no further than fifty or seventy years, is not to be seen as a feature of your culture. It is new, this ignorance; it is part of the shattering of a wholeness, part of *your* ruin. But we will not get into the cause of it or Toby will accuse me of poisoning your mind.'

Toby, Toby, Toby! She'd never seen such vehemence about things that seemed, well, hardly to inspire it; things that to her, at least, were so insignificant. But as fast as it had come over him, this mood – and it was a rage – it was gone. Once they entered the enclosure of the monuments, either in response to the soothing effect of their beauty or to her own quiet and puzzlement, Vijaipal was calm.

'You don't take pictures?' she said, hoping to restart conversation.

'No, I don't. I find they erase the impressions my mind makes. Which, though less detailed, are often stronger.'

'Such as?'

'Well, take this day, for instance, Uma. A day of sun and clouds, of brief breezes and strong sunshine, of sudden stillness . . . And I would remember it in this impressionistic way: I would remember your company: my uneven mood, seeming to correspond to the changes in weather . . . I would remember the enduring splendour of the monuments; there, even after multiple viewings . . . Well, if suddenly I was handed a photograph from this day, this broad range of impressions would not survive the exactness of the photograph; they would be subsumed by it. Do you know what I mean?'

'When you put it like that . . .'

'Intuitively, you do.'

'Intuitively, yes. I do.'

'Good. Come with me. I don't want you to make too much of my earlier outburst. I am not a man of prejudice, but I feel strongly about these things. They can upset me. But, please: don't, for a moment, believe I romanticize the past of this unfortunate city.'

He had a way, Vijaipal – it was an aspect of the intensity with which he spoke – of making you feel you understood what he was saying, even when you didn't, of making you take seriously the things he took seriously.

They stood now on the central axis of the city. The great avenue, still partly facaded, and occupied by people Vijaipal referred to as 'matchstick folk', stretched up before them. Behind them was a temple, still in use, where pilgrims came, their bright clothes visible even at a distance.

'They still come, you see,' Vijaipal said, 'but none of your lot ever will. Unless, of course, some foreigner makes it fashionable.'

She laughed, and then he, looking at her, laughed too. In a lot of what he said there seemed to be either the possibility of further rage, bordering on violence, or great comedy, big, dangerous laughter. And, for the first time now, she was able to see that though he was, in fact, an ugly man, short, dark, built like a sparrow, he was a very attractive man. The kind of man, who, as you grow to know him, seems a man apart from the one you first met.

It was a long day. They had lunch; they rested; at one point there was a mild drizzle, large warm drops of rain landing in dusty splashes on the stones and dry earth; then the sky cleared and they carried on with their 'looking'. They saw palaces, and stables, and royal baths, before returning more or less to where they began. At about 4 p.m., they found themselves in a room enclosed on four sides by high stone walls; its roof was gone and it was open to sky; at the centre was a statue of Narasimha. The sky had clouded again, and the return of afternoon darkness gave the lion-headed statue, fanged and fierce, a special menace.

Vijaipal tired at last, rested on the statue's pedestal, washing his face and neck with water from a flask.

'In the end, you see,' he said wearily, 'a place like this does not speak of a vital culture. It is almost inevitable that it was destroyed.'

'I thought you found it painful, its destruction.'

'I do. But I can also see that what they were doing was not an expression of genuine renewal.'

'What were they doing?'

'Repeating the past. Shoring up what had already been done before. And though anyone, from anywhere, visiting Vijayanagara in the early sixteenth century would certainly have been impressed by it, by the scale of it, they might perhaps have also found it decadent. Oppressive, heavy, too filled with ghosts, if you know what I mean. And so, I suppose, the question arises: how does genuine renewal occur? How does a modernizing spirit enter a moribund culture and transform it completely? Release it, either from a state of perpetual decay or from imitation, either of itself, in the form of parody, or of others, as mimicry?'

She had walked over to the statue and was inspecting it, when suddenly she felt him behind her. Not threateningly, not advancingly, but there. Breathing. Still. Observing her observe the statue. And she knew – and what frightened her was her own fragility, her own lack of resolve – that he was very near to making a pass at her. Very near to acting on a tension, as distinct as the possibility of rain, that had arisen between them over the course of the day. What would she do if he did? What would she do if, at that moment, his body had so much as grazed against hers, or his hand come to rest on her waist? And she, supposedly, in love with someone else . . . Was she mad even to consider it, mad to half-want this small, ugly, brilliant man to fuck her on the stone floor of this room, exposed to the vagaries of louring monsoon clouds?

The force of her desire made her start; and, with that sudden movement, the gaping tension of that second when anything could have happened was shattered; she had pulled away. She had swung around, and smiling, a smile almost of aggressive placidity, cold water over what had passed between them, she said, 'How does it happen? How does genuine renewal occur?'

He smiled; there was a trace of bitterness in his face. Not the full bitterness of a man thwarted in his advance, but something residual and lingering.

'I don't know, Uma. It is one of the great mysteries of the world: how an old culture, moribund and decayed, regenerates. I suspect it comes at a time when men acknowledge the past as dead. But what kind of men are these . . . who see what no one else has seen till then, who have the courage to admit that the past is dead, and that they must begin again . . . I don't know. It's impossible to conceive of such men till they exist; and then, once they do, it is impossible to imagine the world without them.'

'Men like Toby, perhaps?'

For a moment Vijaipal had the stunned expression of a man who'd been hit in the face, then it melted fast into a livid mask of scorn and contempt. He could see what she was doing – making up for what had almost occurred between them earlier – and he was determined not to spare her.

'Toby, Uma? Toby? Toby! Are you . . . ? Toby, with all his weakness and dilettantism, the little Sanskritist, a man so drunk on his safety and security that he would have a renaissance unto himself, a drawing room renaissance! . . . You think a man like that could be the agent of genuine renewal? Oh no, no, no, Uma. Either you've misunderstood me or you're lying!'

'Vijaipal!'

'Don't you see what Toby is? Don't you see that his little rebellion against the Anglicized ways of his friends is a society stunt, an affectation? Like that foolish business of him offering a reward to someone willing to kill Mrs Gandhi. Don't you see how they love him for it, his society friends? He's a performer . . . these are the actors and the actresses of society, Uma! These are not serious people. And now that you've brought it up . . . I've been meaning to ask you: I hope you won't be so foolish as to marry a man like him? Like Toby. All very well to have a little fling with an Indian prince, something for the diary, but Uma—'

'Vijaipal, stop. You know I—'

'You'll need someone more dynamic than that, more real, Uma. You're a passionate intelligent woman. Toby fiddling about, now deriving cognates, now writing little textbooks that no one is going to read . . . that won't satisfy you. You'll be bored to tears in five minutes flat.'

'Vijaipal!' She made for the doorway of the little sanctum, open to sky.

'Well, since I have gone this far,' he said, blocking her way for an instant, 'let me go a little further: let me answer your question: that other kind of man, the anti-Toby, rougher, less polished, less precious than him – the kind of man you, Uma, might really be happy with, might really love – he might also be the one to usher in an era of change into this deadest of dead countries.'

Skanda is in front of his laptop, waiting for his sister to stop being Mrs Glowitz. But he can see she's revelling in it, making a show of her busyness. She has appeared twice before the camera to say she'll just be back. Once with his nephew, on his way to school. 'Say goodbye to Skandu Mamu . . . in India! . . . Because, darling, when it's morning here, in Connecticut, it's night in India. And your Skandu Mamu is an owl who sleeps in the day and wakes at night.'

While he waits for Rudrani to return, his fingers, guided as if by a cognition of their own, explore his stepfather's company's website, which is designed in the shape of a 3D diamond. At its core are images of coal manufacture, of heavy machinery, of furnaces. The group's mission statement reads:

> Like the many-faceted jewel, we at the Mani Group have, from our beginnings in pure carbon, including interests such as coal services and logistics, power trading, mining equipment manufacture and civil works construction, branched out into areas as diverse as tulips, wine and the Maniraja Classical

> Library: a project which aims to publish, with all the style and commitment we can muster, the great works of Indian literature . . .

On the clickable facets of the diamond-shaped site are: fields of tulips; Maniraja, himself, in gardening gloves, sipping red wine (they've even managed a mist!) in front of a trellis of grapes. One rhomboid facet shows customers in a high-ceilinged bookshop with wood panelling and a single malt corner; and, in gold leaf along the cornice of the shop, Skanda can make out his own contribution. Valmiki's 'Creation of Poetry' verse.

Rudrani returns; Skanda can see immediately that she is in one of her taunting moods.

'You should go,' she says, picking up the thread of their earlier conversation.

'Why?'

'Because it's good for you to face these things, your demons. Did you say that he had his secretary invite you? I love it. When it comes to newer and more innovative ways of being a pure dick, Maniraja really raises the bar. What is it? Some new foray into the arts, no doubt? A chair in some college? A library? A seminar on the ancient art of oenology in India?'

'An event for the MCL,' he says, glancing at the web page open before him.

'Ah, your employers!'

'Not my employers,' he says, closing the page. 'They commissioned a translation, that's all.'

'That man, I tell you! He'll do anything to retain his control over us. Probably it was our dear mother who suggested it: *Why not give Skanda a translation to do? That way we can keep his scrotal sack in our fist a little longer.* And Maniraja must have jumped at the idea. Baba's death, I suppose, has done nothing to pacify him. He still doesn't feel he can sit back and relax. Who knows? He might return from the grave and steal our mother away. Is she going to be in attendance, by the way, Her Ecstasy, The Ballbreaker of Kalasuryaketu?'

'No. She's travelling.'

'She still hasn't been down to see you, has she? How long have you been there? Six weeks?'

'About that long.'

'Incredible. You can't make them up, this lot. If they were parents in a novel, no one would believe it. I'm afraid, brother dearest, on this front, we've been dealt a pretty shabby hand. All the more reason to ditch the fuckers and get on with our own lives, no? Which brings me to something I've been meaning to ask you: why aren't you back yet?'

'No reason, really,' he says, after a pause. 'It's just nice to be here after so long.'

'Nice to be there? Skanda, it's 120 in the shade. Nobody thinks it's nice to be there. I hope you're not crawling into one of your dead moods: "Let me just find a little cave somewhere, where I can do Sanskrit for the rest of my life. And hopefully, when I next look up, my life will be over. Yay!"'

'The rains should be here soon.'

'So? Then it'll be humid, and there'll be mosquitoes and Dengue. Hell! What are you talking about? And Sanskrit? Columbia? What about all that?'

'It's the summer, Rudrani.'

'Still! You have a life here. Friends, family, me! I don't like the idea of your staying on there indefinitely one bit. *Unless* . . .'

'Unless?'

'Unless you've met someone.'

'No, but—'

'No but what?'

'But something.'

'You know you've got to stop living in this way.'

'Which way?'

'Of refusing to try anything for fear that it might not be perfect. There's more to life than being unassailable, Skanda. "No but" what? What were you going to say?'

'That I did meet someone I quite liked the other day . . . and she's meant to be coming over in a day or two.'

'Who? Where?'

'She's called Gauri. I met her at the house of this woman called Kitten Singh . . .'

'This woman called Kitten Singh? Skanda, are you out of your mind? You know perfectly well who Kitten Singh is. You remember what she did that summer in Gulmarg?'

'I do.'

'I do? But you went to her house anyway. Skanda, you frighten me. Does Ma know you went to Kitten Singh's house? I mean, I'm no fan of mommy dearest, but even *I* wouldn't go to Kitten Singh's house . . .'

'I don't know why I went, Rudrani. I realized too late . . . And, what can I say? I was curious, I suppose.'

'Curious? About what?'

'About seeing who'd be there from the old days.'

'That's a very odd thing to do, Skanda. You have a very strange relationship with that time, you know.'

'How so?'

'Well, on the one hand, you're so aloof from it – hardly even aware of it – but, on the other – in that passive way of yours – you seem to want to slide back into it.'

'I was hoping Isha Massi would be there. That's all!'

'Another of our mother's favourite people! What is this? Some kind of revenge?'

'Why are you being like this?'

'Like what?'

'So unpleasant.'

The meanness drains from her face.

'Because I love you, and miss you, and I see what you're doing.'

'What am I doing?'

'Not living in the now, raking up what's dead and gone.'

'I am living in the "now", Rudrani. I even have a date in a few days.'

He doesn't tell her more about Gauri, though. He doesn't tell her she was once married to a Sanskritist, or that she has a young son . . . She is bound to read into it.

'When did this happen?' Rudrani says abruptly.

'When did what happen?'

'When did I end up your older sister?'

'You're not my older sister. You just saw less than I did.'

'Saw less of what?'

'The rot. Now listen, tell me: I was trying to remember the other day. The picchvai with the white peacocks . . .'

'The one they bought in the south? On honeymoon, or whatever they were on.'

'Yes. What is the story about it?'

'You're really the master, Skandu. A master in the arts of evasion and passivity. When did you first start to believe that if you didn't see something, it wasn't there?'

'In Gulmarg. Now fuck off. No more lectures.'

'You know something, Skandu?'

'What?'

'It wasn't all bad. I remember.'

'I know. I do too.'

*

That night, a dream. Not recurrent now for years. A dinner party. Everyone from the old days is there. Chamunda. Isha Massi and Viski. The abusive Ismail. Nikhil, and the black-gummed Gayatri Mann, with her evil mole. His whole childhood world. Everyone, including his mother, but, notably, not his father. He comes in, in his night suit to say goodnight. Everyone is drinking and smoking and laughing. And just as he approaches his mother someone from behind yells – 'Ohhoho, Yuvraj saab, the little prince of Kalasuryaketu.' The next minute someone has pulled down his pajama. 'Look, look, the crown jewels.'

And everyone's laughing, and he's looking at his mother, his cheeks scorched with shame. And she? . . . Is she laughing too?

Once Vijaipal left them – and he left the day after the episode at the monuments – they gradually made their way back north. The rains encircled them en route and made driving hard. But Toby seemed not to mind. He told Uma how old and romantic an Indian impediment this was. To be delayed by the monsoon. The time when kings have ceased their campaigns, and their armies retreat. When roads and hostilities, by equal measure, are blocked with water. When clouds as big as mountains cover the sky. The sky – 'nabhas, Uma' – *seems to have wounds bound up with the dressing of soft clouds, red with the colour of sunset but very pale at the edges.* At night . . . *lashed by lightning as if by golden whips*, the sky – 'ambara, Uma' – *makes thundering sounds within, as if in pain.* And the sky – 'kha, Uma, cognate with the Latin *halo*' – *is darkened in all directions, favouring lovers.*

'All the time, Valmiki compares the seasons to the abducted Sita. The flashing of dark clouds to the anguished Vaidehi twisting in the arms of Ravana. I'm not boring you, I hope?' Toby would suddenly say on those rain-drenched afternoons, when, in the front room of some rest house or Dak bungalow, they would watch, through grilled windows, the water stream onto the veranda.

'No. I love it.'

'All right. But stop me if I'm getting carried away. I have that tendency. I will say though, Uma, that if there is anyone to whom this season truly belongs, it is the peacocks.'

'Of course it does, Toby. Everyone knows that.'

'But not just because they're happy when it rains – *anyone*, as Bob Dylan will tell you, *can be happy!* – but because of how sad they are when it stops raining.'

Uma did not forget his words, and, a few days later, at an antiques shop in the south, belonging to a woman called Dhanalakshmi, the peacocks returned.

Toby had for many years been a serious collector of Indian art. He had bronzes, Kurkihar and Chola, a seated Paravati and the Saint Mannikkavachaka; a Ganesh from Vijayanagara; stone heads from Gandhara and miniatures from various schools. But, of all these things, the collection that was the oldest – he had bought his first when he was still at university – and today the largest, was his collection of picchvais. These depictions of Krishna, almost always with his gopis, almost always during the rains, almost always playful, held a special appeal for him related to those forms – like the Annunciation, say – in which the fame of the scene places certain restrictions on the artist, but can, by virtue of those very constraints, draw out the best in the best artists.

'Like the sonnet of painting,' he told Dhanalakshmi, 'in nine out of ten poets it brings out what has already been done. But in that one poet it will reveal an imagination that leaves the form forever changed.'

Dhanalakshmi was a large dark woman, with a handsome, cratered face, horsy teeth and short white hair. Toby knew many dealers around the country – fey Parsi gentlemen in Bombay; stylish operators like Reggie Kumar in Delhi, with his velvet suits and ivory cane; greasy smugglers like Popli, the cut-serd of The Singing Bell – but none with the drama and easy erudition of Dhanalakshmi. She was of a grand Sri Lankan family – her father had been Governor General. But she had run away from them as a young girl to marry a toothpick of an Australian jockey whom she kept in great style. She smoked sixty cigarettes a day; drank large whiskies neat; and there was not a person alive who knew more about artistic traditions, south of the Narmada, than Dhanalakshmi.

It was from her that Toby first heard the princes were being raided. 'Every last broken-down royal, Tobs, from Bapa to Marukshetra to the Kusumapurs, of course. Gun salute or not, they're all bloody having their trousers pulled down and their willies inspected. It's terrible. She's always hated them, the dragon on Safdarjung road, and now she's having her revenge on the lot of them. And, naturally, if you raid princes, you're going to find something or the other. Not always buried gold, like they found in Kusumapur—'

'They found gold in Kusumapur?'

'Kilos of it. Some bloody little government inspector tripped on a tile – and voilà! – there were stairs leading down to an underground chamber full of gold. Probably there from Mughal times. Now, Tobs, think about it, you think anyone who knew would have left it there?'

'Probably RM Kusumapur herself didn't know.'

'Of course not. Old HH whatshisname died in a polo accident. He might have known. But he didn't have time to tell anyone, did he? So now everyone's in for it. And naturally it's very popular. Raid the rich bastards who've oppressed you all these years. Obviously they're finding things – nothing special, mind you – but a Lalique dining table here, a few silver chairs there. You better watch out. The little firang Raja of Kalasuryaketu. They might even connect you to the "foreign hand". And then I heard about your little antics at the

Oberoi on the night after the Emergency was declared. Damn fool thing to do, if you ask me.'

'You heard about that? From who?'

'Oh, you know, the usual Delhi gossips.'

She flared her eyes and gave a loud snorting laugh.

'You don't think it'll get back . . . ?'

'Of course it will. They probably already know. Nothing will happen though. They've got bigger fish to fry. But you'll be raided, for sure . . . Are you joking? You have only so much as to own a bloody air conditioner these days to be raided. The only reason I've been spared . . .'

And now she paused and glanced at Uma, who, while they were speaking, had been walking about the room looking at its many treasures. In part she was doing this because of the beauty of what the room contained, but also because, from the moment they had entered, she had felt a distinct frostiness from Dhanalakshmi.

It was not obvious. Dhanalakshmi had greeted her perfectly cordially; she had shown interest in her impressions of the trip; she had displayed a curiosity, which was really malicious amusement, on discovering that she was an air hostess. But, once they had sat down and the formalities were over, she addressed not a single word to Uma. More than that, she had steered the conversation away from anything Uma might be able to participate in, either with an involved discussion over the workings of some gallery or museum, an auction of bronzes in London, or else intimate conversations about friends she and Toby had in common. Uma tried to join in, asking how Dhanalakshmi had begun as a dealer, but Dhanalakshmi fell silent, and smiled knowingly at Toby, as if to say, 'You tell her.' When Uma rose to look at the art in the room, Dhanalakshmi ignored her, and redoubled her effort to keep Toby engaged in conversation.

At last, when Dhanalakshmi said, 'The only reason I'm not . . .'

– and paused, Toby said, 'Oh, don't be silly! You can talk freely in front of Uma.'

At hearing her name Uma swung around. And, now looking at Dhanalakshmi, she said, 'Would you like me to leave the room? I can.'

'Oh, no, no! Don't be silly, darling,' Dhanalakshmi began. 'A friend of Toby's is a friend of mine.'

'I'm not his friend.'

'Uma?'

'Yes, yes, of course,' Dhanalakshmi said, 'foolish of me to have said that. I was just being extra cautious, you know. So, it's nothing. It's just that the PM's daughter-in-law frequently buys antiques from me, which is why I have been spared *la terreur*. That's all; nothing, really, you see. Shall we go outside and take a look at the new things, Toby? I've had some fabulous stuff come in. What with everyone trying to get rid of it as quickly as possible! Come, come. Uma, I hope you'll join us.'

'I'd love to, Dhanalakshmi.'

And so, with everything a little on edge between them, they went out to the warehouse and showroom Dhanalakshmi had behind her house. Evening was falling. Not the long melancholy evening of the north, but something swifter and spongier, an expansive humid darkness of big leaves and naked bulbs.

'I wish I could have done more bandobast,' Dhanalakshmi said, gesturing to a trolley on which there was ice and soda and a bottle of Black Dog. It stood at a pebbled intersection between the warehouse – a corrugated roof with canvas curtains for walls – and the showroom, a well-lit place, beyond whose glass doors the bright colours of paintings and the long shadows of bronzes were visible.

'You don't have anything softer, do you, Dhanalakshmi?'

'No! Uma, dear! I only wish,' Dhanalakshmi said, with an incredulity that had the effect of making her apology seem both exaggerated and insincere. 'We're all Scotch drinkers in this house.'

'That's fine. I'm happy with Scotch.'

They made their drinks and were heading towards the warehouse that housed stone sculpture, when Uma said, 'You know, I think I'll see the showroom first, then join you outside.'

'But it'll get dark,' Toby said, 'You won't be able to see a thing.'

Dhanalakshmi's large lawyerly eyes swelled in anticipation, as if to say, 'See, Toby, what a fool of a woman you've found.'

'Never mind,' Uma said. 'I'll see what I can.' And with a long meaning smile, as if to say goodbye, she peeled away from them.

'OK. We'll see you outside then,' Toby said airily.

As she walked away, sipping her strong and unfamiliar drink, Uma had the first taste of a feeling that she would come to know well. It was not, as Vijaipal, had anticipated, a feeling of contempt for Toby's weakness; Toby was not weak, it was something else. Without trying too hard to analyse its cause, it was a feeling of being alone around Toby, even when – *especially* when – Toby was present. It was a kind of metaphysical solitude, confined to the unit of two. And this feeling, at least, of being alone when he was there, of which she had the first taste that evening, would prove to be a corrosive influence on their relationship, especially when blacker times approached.

Apart from the force of her emotion, making her receptive in ways she might not have been, deepening her sense of solitude in the showroom, a place of gleam and shadow, where the antiquities seemed still to possess something of the violation of being torn from their natural nooks, she was aware of the earliest beginnings of a sensibility she had never possessed before. These objects of devotion, the gods alone, or with their consorts, sometimes seated, sometimes standing, now in bronze, now in stone, had never made any kind of impression on her. She had never even thought to consider them as objects of beauty. She would not have known what to look for. They had no context for her; they were simply of the past. A vast and amorphous past, without feature or point of reference. She might more easily have been able to give shape to the history of England: she might have been able to locate the Battle of Hastings, Shakespeare, Elizabeth I, the Industrial Revolution on a timeline. India's history – British presence excepted, events such as Plassey and the Mutiny of 1857 – was all fog.

But, now, fresh from the past few weeks with Toby and Vijaipal, she had, for the first time, the vaguest impression of the terrain, its contours and its fault lines. The coming or not coming of the Aryans; the role of Sanskrit, purely liturgical for a period, a language of literature and statecraft thereafter; the contest between Buddhism and Hinduism; the emergence of vernaculars at the same time as in Europe; the arrival, violent or non-violent, of Islam. She now also had a scatty knowledge of the gods and their lives. And these things had changed her way of looking. They made her look with feeling at what had been closed to her before. She did not have knowledge as yet, but she had the whisper of a way in.

Walking by a Kushan Bodhisattva, ashen-faced and long-moustached, Uma saw that the label read Gandhara, second to third century AD. Gandhara! Such an evocative name, seeming to contain resonance even to the untrained ear. And had she not heard Toby just the other day say, 'I can never look at the art of Gandhara without seeing in it the faces of the Frontier.' Or the fat Khmer Ganesh she passed . . . Had Toby or Vijaipal not said, 'It was one of the most amazing transmissions of culture the world has known. No army, not a drop of blood spilt, no colonization, as such, and yet, by the end of a few hundred years, south-east Asia, all the way to Java, was dripping with Sanskritic culture . . .' Or, most wonderful of all, after their conversation about peacocks, a twelfth-century Ganga period Skanda, astride his peacock.

It was, by far, the most beautiful thing in the room. From the hard realism of its clawed feet, to the graded and stony play of light on its tail, to the Skanda himself, god of war. His many arms casting wild shadows over the room. His one exposed leg, blacker and shinier than the rest of his body, gave an indication both of the height he would have sat at in the temple from which he had been wrenched, and the regard people had had for him over the centuries: touching what was beautiful, bringing it to shine.

It was like this, her anger slaked, that she, in a reverie of sorts, found herself in a distant room at the back of the showroom. A storage area of a kind. Damp and musty, illuminated by the light of a bulb hanging from a long wire.

It housed what the showroom could not hold. Uma went through a pile of miniatures stacked neatly on a table; *nothing so special*, she thought to herself. She sat on her haunches and fanned through a dozen or so Tanjore paintings that had been left leaning against the cemented wall of the backroom. She was about to go out when she heard voices in the showroom, and, from a childish desire to be found, rather than to find and risk appearing aimless and lost, she decided to stay on in the dingy backroom. She spotted several large picchvais – she recognized them from Toby's descriptions – leaning one against the other. She went over and began to go through them, when she stopped at the picchvai of the peacocks.

Even from the limited view she had of it, she could see it was something very special. Even in that dim light it stood out from the rest. Its near-total whiteness made it seem like a blank or unfinished canvas. She had just about managed to get it out when Toby entered. The sight that greeted him was of Uma standing in front of the most beautiful picchvai he had ever seen.

The painting adhered to every convention of the form while subverting them all. The dark hills; the monsoon sky; the play of thunder on the crests of the hills; a river meandering down: virtual clichés of the form had been compressed into a six-inch band at the top of the painting: a panoramic miniature. The rest of the canvas was devoted to great pluming explosions of white, feathers ostrich-like in their size and flamboyance. White on white: a joyful homage to this – what does one even call it? – shade, pigment, colour, this notoriously difficult thing to bring texture and distinction to. There was something euphoric about the way the paint, almost like plaster or lime, had been smeared on to the canvas. And, from this formless pallor, the artist made the smallest concessions to form, to the reality of what was, in fact, being represented. White dancing peacocks. Here, barely distinguishable, was the outline of a plumy eye, there a pair of real and beady eyes, small and black and hard; now a beak, now a vicious clawed foot. At the centre of this formless eulogy to white was a single perfectly realized blue peacock.

'The Krishna,' Toby breathed.

He was behind her now. She could almost feel him against her. And for a moment she did not understand what he meant.

'You see what he's doing? Instead of taking the Krishna, the god, as his subject, he's playing on the very meaning of that word Kṛṣṇa, which before it is applied to the god, simply means black, like Černyi, in Russian. He's taking this essentially devotional form of art and making colour – he's a painter, after all! – the object of devotion And, look: at the centre of his tribute to white, there is – in disguise, mind you – the god whose name means black. It's exquisite, Uma. A mor kuti picchvai. And we were only just talking about peacocks.'

'I thought of you the moment I saw it.'

'It should be ours. I'll speak to Dhanalakshmi. It must be ours.'

'Ours?'

‘Yes, *ours*. And then his whose inheritance it will be one day.’

‘Who’s that, Toby?’ she said, though she knew perfectly well. She wanted to hear it from him.

‘Skanda, of course.’

‘Toby?’

‘Yes . . .’

‘Are you asking me to marry you?’

Gauri is in the flat, standing before the picchvai of the peacocks.

'They're in disguise!' she says casually. 'Krishna and his gopis. Krishna is the blue peacock, the white peacocks his gopis. Yes?'

'Yes.'

He knows that he will sleep with her. Not because he is attracted to her, but because it is not frightening to sleep with her. Her frail, small-boned body, seeming to speak of pain and damage, comforts him. He knows, if his mother or sister met her, they would say, 'Skanda is drawn to birds with broken wings.' But they do not think of him – and here an exocentric compound would have been useful – as one whose wings are broken too.

He is at the ṣaṣṭha sarga, the sixth canto: the betrothal.

'Who is being betrothed?' she asks, on the first afternoon they sleep together. It is raining at last. And even in that dark flat, into which Narindar has never allowed white light to enter, there is now an imperceptible softness. Like the passing of a threat, like a fear proved false.

'Shiva and Uma, of course. And it is she who proposes: "dātā me bhū | bhṛtāṃ nāthaḥ pramāṇī | kriyatām iti . . ."'

'Easy, Tiger. Slow down.'

She is lying on her stomach. Her hips are wide, her bones visible, her breasts sallow and low-slung. It is a miracle she's forty-three; she seems like a child, a knowing child, but a child nonetheless.

'Dātā me?'

'"The giver of me – my father: the Lord of Mountains gives me in marriage," she says, "you must recognize his authority."'

'Bold,' Gauri says.

'Yes. The women in this poem have nothing to do with what the men in saffron say the ideal Hindu woman should be like.'

'In the sense . . . ?'

'In the sense that they are far from demure; they are sexually liberated and experienced; they drink wine. Even if you take the moment when Shiva's wedding procession passes through the streets of Himalaya's capital, Oṣadhiprastha . . . The windows of the town are filled with the faces of women who reek of rum or spirit. And whose eyes are vilola . . .'

'Vilola?'

'Moving to and fro. Agitated. Tremulous. Like swarming bees. And their girdles are only half-done up. They're dropping jewels as they run to the window. One woman's waistband comes undone as she goes to see Shiva go by, and she doesn't even bother to do it up. She just stands there holding it. And Kalidasa describes the rings of her hand as illuminating her navel. Another has only a single eye kohled – such is her urgency. Still another has lost the ribbon in her hair and the mass of it has come undone.'

'Are these prostitutes?'

'No, no! These are the beautiful women of the town. My father would always say, "These goons in saffron, they say they want a Hindu renaissance, they have no idea what a Hindu renaissance would entail. Their shitty little values about sex and food would be the first thing to go out of the window". But try telling them that!'

'Did he try, your father?'

'In his way, he did, yes. But he was very passive.'

'And your mother?'

Ah! That moment when a girl first asks you about your mother.

'Not passive,' he says and laughs.

'Not passive? What kind of answer is that?'

'An evasive one. I'm joking. She was a dragon and she ate him up.'

'A dragon!?'

'Well, maybe, not a dragon. But tough. And she couldn't stand what she thought of as his weakness, his aloofness, his fatalism. Call it what you want.'

'How did it manifest itself?'

'In many ways. But the first time was soon after they were married. There was a raid on our palaces in Kalasuryaketu.'

'On our palaces in Kalasuryaketu! . . . Oh, look at you, the little lord Fauntleroy . . .'

'Trust me, if you saw them, you wouldn't be saying that.'

'Why! In bad shape?'

'Holes in the ceiling. Returning to dust, virtually.'

'Oh. I'm sorry. Go on.'

'Well, it was the time of the Emergency so the raid in itself was nothing out of the ordinary. Everyone was being raided in those days. It was more the way my father reacted to it. His equanimity in the face of it, his resignation. A foretaste of things to come. And my mother, I think, was alarmed. It was also incidentally the first time she met my stepfather.'

'At the raid? How?'

'Ironically, my father, who had met him some months before in Delhi, called him in to help.'

'Isn't it always that way? With certain people.'

'What way?'

'They put in place the mechanism for their own undoing.'

'You've been reading too much Marx. I think he just thought of him as someone who might be able to help. He felt he spoke the same language as the taxmen.'

'Yes. But these things are never as random as they seem; they always represent something important, a shift, you know. And women are better able to discern these things.'

'What things?'

'Shifts of power. The irrelevance of one class, the rise of another. Over-refinement in one place, vitality in another.'

'Why?'

'Why, what?'

'Why are women better able to see these things?'

'I'm not sure. And not all women, you know. Only some.'

'What kind of women?'

'The ones who are made uneasy by weakness, by what is obsolete and therefore dangerous.'

'I thought women liked men who were dangerous.'

She laughs. 'That's another kind of dangerous, bozo.' Then, after a pause, 'Where is he?'

'Who?'

'Your Dad,' she says somewhat coyly.

'Dead.'

'I'm sorry. I didn't realize.'

'That's fine.'

'How long?'

'How long what?'

'How long ago did he die?'

'Eight weeks ago.'

'What?! Holy shit.'

She sits bolt upright in bed.

'What?'

'No, no, no!'

'No, no, no . . . what?'

'Skanda, you do *not* look and behave like someone whose father died eight weeks ago. There's something wrong.'

'Wrong? Why? How does someone whose father died eight weeks ago look and behave?'

'Like he might still be dealing with it. Skanda, you don't seem to be dealing with anything. If this is not easy for you, it should be impossibly hard. You're either some kind of sociopath or you're suppressing something . . . Your mother said your father was passive?'

'Pathologically passive.'

'Skanda, you have some strain of the disease too.'

Toby and Uma were married in August. A small irregular procession consisting of both men and women – whoever could be found of the drawing room set in August – snaked its way through the streets of Lutyens' Delhi. Many who ordinarily would have been in London were in attendance, due to the Emergency. Marukshetra; Chamunda and Ismail; Nikhil Mohapatra, even though Gayatri Mann, having bitterly prophesied – 'I give it six months' – had returned to New York; Viski, but not Isha, obviously: she waited with her sister at Fatehkot House. Bapa, who, though still in white, had draped a beautiful old jamavar over his shoulders. There was almost no one from Toby's side, except for his half-sister, Usha Raje, who was, in fact, the true Rani of Kalasuryaketu – Toby being of a morganatic marriage – but was not thought of as such. And she, in turn, by marrying a Mr Malhotra from Bombay, had ruled out all chance of her children inheriting.

At Fatehkot House, the Brigadier awaited the procession with his brother, cousins and eighteen-year-old son, Inder Pratap, known as I.P., Isha and Uma's beloved brother and the apple of Deep Fatehkotia's ever dimmer eye. Fresh out of the Doon School, and on his way to Stephens to read English literature, I.P. was full of a natural intellectual curiosity and loved Toby within hours of meeting him.

His father, the Brigadier, liked Toby too.

The Brigadier's nature was very different from his wife's. He did not share her pessimistic view of the world. Nor did he have any time for her feeling of historical grievance. His own family had known such gains and setbacks – had seen honours turn to shame – that history was nothing to him, if it was not irony. And he delighted in its reversals and bitter symmetries.

The Fatehkotias were among those families whose fortunes had been made during the Mutiny of 1857. An ancestor had collaborated with the British in defeating the Mughal in Delhi, for which – awful phrase: 'services rendered' – he had been generously remunerated with land and honours. In a cantonment somewhere in, say, Hoshiarpur, where Hodson's or Skinner's or Somebody's Horse was headquartered, there hung in the officers' mess a portrait of this ancestor. He was dressed in a dark-blue tunic with scarlet facings, the cuffs heavily laced with gold, and, round his waist, he wore the embroidered red cummerbund of the 9th Bengal Cavalry. He carried a sword; his beard was long, white and a little straggly; medals and decorations hung from his breast. The caption – galling to the Brigadier! – read, Risaldar Major M– Singh, C.I.E. Sardar Bahadur, Order of Merit.

But, though honoured and decorated in his lifetime, history, as it does so often on the subcontinent, had trifled with him. Once the pride of his tribe and community, he had finished by being a source of embarrassment to his descendants. The Brigadier and I.P. regarded him as a collaborator, a soldier of fortune: the archetypal man the British made easy use of to gain mastery over India. When, in the 1947 Partition, the Fatehkotias lost all that had been gained in 1857 and more, the Brigadier saw the tragedy as a kind of retribution. He felt almost relieved of a historical burden, felt he had paid his dues. There was something fitting, he thought, something neatly symmetrical, in arriving penniless in 1947 to the same city his ancestor, in cahoots with the British, had helped subdue only one hundred years before.

Unlike his wife, the Brigadier, when he cast his mind back on the past, did not see a dhobi list of wrongs done him, but rather a sweetly painful record of equal and opposite ironies. In fact, his special sensitivity lay – and what a dangerous sensitivity in a soldier! – in being able to see the mirror image of the troubles he (and his community) had endured, in the lives (and communities) of his enemies. His eyes could still well with tears at the thought of the Japanese soldier he had killed in Burma. 'He was no older than me, you know. And, when I collected his effects, I found letters from his family to him in English. In English! So, you can imagine . . .' Here, he would pause, and prodding his listener to the natural conclusion with a smile, add softly, 'must have been of good family.'

Then there was the story from his childhood in that part of Punjab that was today Pakistan: of the car, carrying him and his grandfather to Fatehkot, breaking down at the side of the road. Evening is falling; two Muslim truck drivers offer them a lift. They arrive in Fatehkot late at night and his grandfather tries to offer the men some money for their troubles, but they refuse. 'Sanu sharminda na kar na.' Once they leave, his grandfather discovers a little briefcase containing his pistol and quite a lot of money has been left in the glove box of the truck. The next day the drivers, who would already have been hundreds of kilometres away, return with the money and the pistol. Again they refuse payment. Again they say, 'Sanu sharminda na kar na.' 'Who would do it today?' the Brigadier would say at the end of his story. 'Who would do it? You tell me.'

Deep, listening, would become irritated. She knew that behind this ostensibly benign story, a tale of graciousness from another time, a clean chit was being handed the Muslims of Pakistan. The very same Muslims who had brought about the Partition that had snuffed out the hopes and dreams of her young days. And, every time the story was told – and it was told many times – Deep would let out an angry 'Pfffffff', and then rise to attend to some errand, till now forgotten about. The Brigadier, if ever he noticed her annoyance, batted it away, with a fanning of the hand. He seemed to say that his stories, with their special nuance, were not for people of his wife's sensibility. Not for the daughters of contractors.

In Toby, the Brigadier immediately recognized a kindred spirit.

'You know,' he said, on their first meeting, 'it was me who gave her this name, Uma. *Not*, I think you'll agree, a very common name amongst us Sikhs. But I thought it beautiful. It is, of course, you being a student of Sanskrit will know . . .'

'A name for Parvati.'

'Yes, but do you know how it actually comes about?'

'It means,' Toby said, catching Uma's eye, 'oh no! It is what her mother says when she decides to undergo austerities to win the love of Shiva.'

The Brigadier's wife gave a contented laugh, as if all her own trouble with her daughter was contained in this story. The Brigadier saw, did not like what he saw, and gave Toby a secret look, as if to say, *Don't mind her, she's a fool*. As far as he was concerned, Toby was passing all his tests. But he had one more little one up his sleeve, to really separate the gandham from the chaff.

'"Tāṃ Pārvat" îty ābhijanena nāmnā",' he began by rote, though his Sanskrit pronunciation was hardly good, and he was forced quickly to switch to English. '"Dear to her kinsfolk, they gave her the name of Paravati, derived from her father's . . ."'

'". . . u m" êti",' Toby completed in Sanskrit, for by happy chance the Brigadier was quoting the Birth. '"It was only later when her mother tried to stop her asceticism by saying 'U ma, Oh no!' that the fair-faced girl went by the name of Uma."'

'Yes, yes,' the Brigadier said, throwing up his hands, 'that's it. Excellent. I'm so pleased,' he said, looking at his eldest with love, 'that your real name has been restored to you, not that foolish name my wife's family' – by which, he meant, his wife – 'used to call her by. Uma. Lovely!'

And, with this, Toby had all the Brigadier's approval. Which, though not easy to come by, once given was irrevocable. Later, when Uma herself tried to persuade him that he had been wrong about Toby, he would listen, as fathers must, but once she had finished speaking, he would pretend he had heard something altogether different: 'Yes, yes. Quite right, quite right. A very fine man. Do you remember that day when I quoted something to him from Sanskrit literature? The only bloody verse I knew. And he completed the verse for me. You won't find two in this town who can do that. Very fine man.' Then he would look mistily away, as if the rest of the conversation was for the women to have.

Toby had the Brigadier's approval, yes, but Deep, who put her name to unhappy prophecies as easily as some people signed petitions, was less sure. 'Pffffff! Raja-types. Khamagani-this, khamagani-that. Their back never straightens only. Can't imagine my headstrong daughter kowing and towing like that.'

'Kow-towing, Mama,' Isha said.

'Pfffff. Can't see it working, but chalo! We say thank you for little mercies: at least the air-hostessing days are over!'

On account of the weather – it was August, virtually the first auspicious day after the summer – the wedding was short. A small sangeet at Fatehkotia House, which Toby and his friends crashed; a 10 a.m. wedding and reception lunch.

It was from this lunch that the majority of the wedding pictures came. They were black and white photographs of a clouded late-monsoon day. They showed the groom in a linen suit, with flared trousers, a pair of aviators propped into his longish hair. The bride was in heavy clothes and, with her face virtually concealed in jewellery and fabric, she had something of the expression of livestock being led to the shambles.

The raid began on a hot night in September, a few weeks after they were married. The rains were late that year, and the air, weeks away from Dussehra, was still moist and gassy. The power had failed many times through the night. At last, Uma, in frustration, had thrown open the windows of their room in the Raj, which let in nothing like a breeze, but only a soft tepid damp, suffused with the singing of crickets.

'Try to go back to sleep,' Toby said.

Just then, seeming to shake the suite to its foundations, the phone rang.

Toby returned from answering it, his body drenched in sweat. And, though it was a warm night, Uma would always recall that sweat as cold. It seemed to flow from all the wrong places; it gave to his attractive body a sad and drooped aspect. The hair about the nipples pasted down; the rich axle line, wet and shining, sunk into its crevasse; the outline of his shrunken penis visible through the soaked muslin, showing fear and alarm.

'That was Laban calling from the bazaar.'

'At this time? What's the matter, Janum?'

'They've raided the city palace.'

'In Kalasuryaketu?'

'Yes.'

'What do you want to do?'

'We should go.'

'Let's go. Now?'

'Now.'

'Do you want to call anyone?'

'Like who?'

'Viski? Ismail? Someone close to government? Someone who might be able to help should it get ugly.'

'No. Let's wait. Usha Raje is already down there. We might yet get off lightly. And if it comes to that,' he said – thinking no doubt of Maniraja's offer of assistance during these 'delicate times' some months before – 'I know someone who might be able to help.'

The trip south was not what it had been a few months before. They fought all the way down. About big and small things. About whether to take a private car or a hotel car. Whether to pack lightly or to be prepared to stay awhile. 'Toby, you took me down there once already with nothing. I'm not doing it again. I'm your wife now.'

They fought about what to say, and when. About what would happen if the government men questioned Toby in connection with what he had said on the night of the Emergency. They fought about whether they should take their passports or not. They fought about where they would stay. At the Shiv Niwas or the City Palace? The City Palace belonged to Toby's sister. 'Over my dead body am I staying there. I can see that woman's contempt for me a mile off.'

'That woman, Uma? That woman? My sister!'

'Sister-shister, she thinks I'm trying to usurp her place as the Rani of Kalasuryaketu. Kalasuryaketu! Bloody joke of a tin-pot kingdom. Not worth one air-gun salute. Like I would want to take it from her.'

When she said this, Toby fell silent, as if a line had been crossed. He could see that in the attack on the sister was a more serious assault on him, on who he was. And Uma, to her credit, the moment she saw his expression, clutched his hand and said she was sorry. It was that first frightening moment when a fight brings to the surface things no one knew were there. Toby, in turn, did something that would become part of the grammar of their marriage: he withdrew.

They swept through Delhi's empty streets and reached the U.P. border in less than an hour. A sandstone arch, and a frail yellow-armed barricade, policed by two sleeping men. Beyond, dark open fields and faintly lit villages. The occasional thunder of a truck. The heat and stillness of night; the permanent unhealthy rattle of the car. In the morning a damp and steaming light that broke over fields to which the rains had brought the first signs of life.

They stopped for tea. In a thatched hut, where a sleepy boy in a frayed vest cleared away steel plates, still smeared with the hard remains of rice and dal, blue flames crept cautiously out of a mud stove and licked at the base of a heavily dented aluminium kettle. The earth, wet with dew, turned to a gritty paste at their feet. An expression of remorse and forgiveness passed between them. But there was also a kind of surprise. The overwhelming return of love, coming, as if to a room where a party has been held, and finding, in the unforgiving morning light, a scene of devastation: the remains of half-drunk drinks, cigarette butts unpeeling in them, stains and spilled peanuts, broken glass.

Suddenly Toby rose and went to the back of the hut, where their driver, a thin-faced and moustached man from U.P., after a night of driving, rested on one of the wooden benches. After a brief exchange with him, she saw the driver get up and escort Toby out of the hut.

'Where are you going?'

'To make a phone call. I'll be back in a second.'

They reached the City Palace just before 8 a.m. Outside its black wrought iron gates a small army of policemen had assembled. At first, they prevented the car from entering, but then one of the men – a boy, whose education had been paid for by Toby's family – recognized Toby, greeted him apologetically and waved the car through. They drove along the red earth drive lined with gulmohar, in whose ferny canopy there was still the occasional scorched blossom. The lawns had begun to revive after the monsoon and there were islands of thick clumpy grass spread across them. The palace, a pale pistachio jewel box, had never looked more beautiful. Some mixture of rain and decay, and perhaps the violation of the government cars, with their carbuncular red lights, parked in its porch, gave it a pitiable and fragile aspect, as if something old and refined and graceful was on the verge of destruction.

Its entrance hall had been turned into a government office. The interior, a cool block of churchy shade, was rent, as if from the ground up, by the violent and rhythmic clacking of typewriters. The wicker furniture had been swept aside and in its place had come four workmen's tables, at which Usha Raje's staff were lining up to give testimonies, recorded with assiduous care by the typists. When they saw Toby, they broke ranks and came in floods of enthusiasm and hopefulness to greet him. They clasped his ankles, they reached up to touch his hands; some of their faces were wet with tears. It was a scene at once moving and repulsive; it could tolerate no witness. And, though the raid was an official affair, when the interrogator emerged out of this commotion to break it up it was clear from the distaste in his face that, for the power he represented, nothing was more threatening than the mixture of servility, affection, attachment and reverence that had brought these men and women to their knees at the first sight of Toby.

The interrogator was a short bald man in his forties, thin-lipped with large protruding eyes. At seeing what had occurred he was forced to remove his thick bifocal glasses and wipe them clean, as if they had deceived him. He was in plain clothes, sandals; there was a red-bodied Parker in his hand – a gift, of course! – whose springy button he thumbed furiously, as if extending a tic from his person to the pen. Finally, having taken Toby in, passing a cool uninterested eye over Uma and the staff gathered at Toby's feet, he cried with something like anguish, into the vault of the room, 'Who is this?!' Then, a hushed shriek, 'Who is this?'

Someone from the crowd at Toby's feet said, in a tone that seemed to urge him to kneel too, 'This is our Raja saab.'

'Did I ask you?' the interrogator spat out. 'Did I ask you? There are no rajas in this country. Understand? Our leader got rid of them, so that you . . . But what could she do, if slavery courses through your veins. Give the whole damn country a blood transfusion?'

At this, his joke, he gave a shrill little laugh. His assistant, a darker man, with wavy strands of white in his thick oily hair, joined in. And, for a moment, the drama, which had seemed to be building up to a boiling rage, was suspended in comic relief. The interrogator, it seemed, was a man of many colours. In what was now a very calm voice, he said, 'You can't be here. I don't know who you are; I don't know why you were let in; who told you there was a raid going on. I don't know. But you can't be here. You must leave. Please, immediately, this minute—'

'Usha Raje is my sister—'

'But you haven't answered the question.'

'What question?'

'Who told you there was a raid going on?'

'Someone called—'

'Find out who it is,' the interrogator shrieked, 'find out who it is.' Anger and urgency returned at once. Speaking rapidly to his assistant, 'I don't care if you have to round up the whole jingbang lot of them, I want to know who is calling out. Find out, Reddy. This is not a joke.'

Reddy went half about his task, as if expecting any moment for another mood to come, and for the order to be rescinded. And he was right. Suddenly the interrogator was prying and curious; he seemed even to smile.

'Are you foreigner?' he said to Toby.

'No.'

'Looks like foreigner.'

'My mother was Scottish.'

'And your father?'

'Indian. He was the old Raja.'

'Oh, Raja saab had foreign wife.'

'Yes. Like Rajiv Gandhi have foreign wife.'

'Who said that? Who said that?'

It was Uma.

'Who are you?'

'My wife,' Toby said, throwing a scolding look back at her.

'Madam, please let me inform you. Not to be speaking in this way of Madam PM's family.'

'In what way?'

'In this . . . in this . . . Why are you people here?' He cried again, as if in pain. 'I have already told you there is a raid going on. You cannot be here. Please go.'

Then Reddy whispered something in his ear and a bright wheedling smile rose to his lips.

'But maybe,' he said, 'you know about the tunnels.'

'They're full of snakes,' Toby said, bringing an expression of astonishment to his wife's face. 'No one's been down there in centuries.'

'Yes, we know about the snakes. Snakes guarding treasure, no doubt. We know what you people have been up to. We know how you have looted us common people. We found gold in Kusumapur, you know. Hundreds of kilos of it. It is this that our leader wants to get back, to distribute among the common man.'

'I can't help you into the tunnels. I've never been there myself.'

'Can't? Won't. I think you will, I think you will.'

In the face of this new menacing tone of inquiry, Toby fell silent. But the interrogator had now decided that they should stay. He gestured to two women inspectors in khaki saris, with thick oily plaits and discreet red ribbons in their hair.

'Take them upstairs to where Usha Raje is. We'll deal with this lot later.'

On the wide marble staircase, leading up to the bedrooms, Uma said, 'What is the matter with you?'

'What do you mean what is the matter with me?'

'Why are you being so meek, such a coward? These people are dirt, and they ought to be treated that way.'

'It won't help our case . . .'

'Ay, ay,' one of the women inspectors said, annoyed to hear this whispered conversation in English. 'No talking. There's a raid going on.'

As they passed the rooms whose doors had been sealed with an untidy splatter of red stamped wax, the inspector said, 'You will only be allowed to use one room for the duration of the raid. You cannot leave it unaccompanied, even if you want to go to the bathroom. Understand?'

They did not reply.

Murky sunlight poured in past a glazed veranda at the end of the corridor, where painted wicker furniture stood in front of a console on whose green marble surface there were crested silver frames of the old rajas of Kalasuryaketu. They showed them standing next to animals they had hunted and killed; they showed them jewelled and in fine clothes photographed by Man Ray. Faintly visible beyond the high garden walls of the palace was Kalasuryaketu, still enveloped in a morning mist: a town of low whitewashed houses, arranged as a petticoat, over the steep escarpment of the Shiv Niwas, past whose ramparts lay the Tamasā.

They came around a corner and found themselves, for a few moments, in near pitch-darkness. Then the door of Usha Raje's room swung open and they saw, in the light breaking into the corridor, that they had been standing under the vacant, glittering eyes of mounted animal heads.

A stale stench of socks carried out of Usha Raje's room. And immediately its source was clear: a woman police officer, with her hair in greasy pigtails, had removed her shoes and sat on the bed, dangling her feet like a child. Small dark feet with badly chipped red nail polish. Next to her was a stack of old fashion magazines; she flipped through the pages with a studied mixture of boredom and intense curiosity, as if she needed one as a cover for the other. Her face was small and cherubic, her skin gleaming with oily good health, the lips tense with garish red lipstick and mischief. On seeing Toby, a shy and demure look entered her eyes, as if a suitor was being presented to her, but, at the sight of Uma, her malice returned.

'Why is the maid being allowed in?' she said to her fellow police officer.

The woman blushed, then giggled; Usha Raje, sitting by the dressing table in a peach chiffon sari, choked with laughter. She had, beneath the pinched respectability of chiffon and pearls, that distinct bitterness – Mrs Gandhi-like – of a woman who has married a man many times her father's inferior. Mr Malhotra, standing by her, gave a happy snort. Uma was about to answer the police officer when Toby stopped her.

'She's my lawful wedded wife,' he said rigidly in formal Hindi.

'Dharmapatni!' the officer shrieked. 'How chweetly the white man speaks Hindi. Hay!'

'His father was Indian only,' her colleague chimed in.

And for a while the two women were beside themselves at the rare and wonderful sight of the white man who spoke heavily Sanskritized Hindi. The rules about silence were abandoned, and they did everything in their power to make him speak, asking their questions in English and howling with laughter when he answered in Hindi. How long you driving? Stopping on way? Having breakfast? Here, she did a little imitation of a man eating. You show us gold in gupha? Big, big snake! Very scaredy!

At his every answer, which he gave with reserve and patience, the women laughed till they cried.

'Did you hear he said "sarpa" for snake! "Swarna" for gold! Cho chweet. Hay, I've never seen something like this. He could put the pundit in my village to shame!'

Uma watched all this with creeping horror. She had never seen him out of his element, never seen him as anything but the most stylish man she had ever met; and now, before her eyes, he became a kind of clown. She felt almost frightened for him. She sensed his vulnerability. She wanted to get away from the room, away from the smell of socks, away from her husband as an object of ridicule. She made for the door.

'Ay ay, where you going, madam?' the officer said.

'To the bathroom.'

'Not going unaccompanied,' the other officer said, and reached to touch her arm.

At this she swung around and growled under her breath: 'Khabardar. Don't you dare touch me!'

Usha Raje and Malhotra gasped. 'Uma . . .' Toby began.

But the officers seemed, in fact, to fall in line.

'I'll take her,' one said quietly.

As they left the room, the devilish poopie yelled after them, 'No bathing. Just bathroom.'

When the door shut behind her, she put her face in her hands. No tears, just a dry and wrenching feeling of helplessness. A strange glut of emotion rose in her like an ache but died in her throat, leaving a raw and unswallowed lump. Was she overreacting? Were they right to behave as they did? Was it naive of her to believe that if they showed some gumption these jumped-up creatures of officialdom would back down? In front of her, through the gaps in her hands, a Lalique dressing table caught the morning light. On its white glass surface were two sets of Mason Pearson hairbrushes, Oil of Olay, a bottle of Miss Dior, a silver tray filled with Revlon lipsticks. Artefacts that spoke both of luxury and isolation. The little things they lived by! In the room beyond she could hear Usha Raje and Toby, with the odd insertion from Malhotra, arguing in hushed tones about how her behaviour would make things worse for them. Then Usha, in P-language, began to tell Toby that she had smuggled out an emerald Ganesh from the Puja room before the raid began. It was concealed in her blouse; they needed to get the women officers out of the room for a moment so that it could be saved. And that was when, from the depths of a feeling of irrelevance, she heard Toby say:

'Apāi hapāve capālled apa mapān whupū apāi thapink capān hapelp.'

'Whupū?'

'Apān apāwfapul lapitaple mapān capālled Mapanapīrapājapā. Hapī wapill knapow hapauw tupū tapālk tupū papīppul lapīke thapis.'

'Hay, hay,' she heard the evil nymphet say, 'enough you two. There's a raid going on. No talking.'

A few moments later Uma, washing up in the sink, a solid silver tub flashing in the mirror before her, felt her stomach churn. She was violently sick.

And then, thirty-six hours after it began, the raid was over. Not too much material damage: just two carved silver mirrors and a cigarette box, made for Toby's father in England, mysteriously missing.

But there was immaterial damage, such as the tone Toby took with Maniraja after the raid.

He had come down to Kalasuryaketu on Toby's request. He drove a Toyota, which, in those days of deprivation, was as good as a Bentley, and he wore a beautiful suit. But under those fine clothes, he was a tough-talking, brass-balled business type. He spoke to the inspector as he ought to have been spoken to.

'Oh, Mr Chawla, did you always want to work for the tax department?'

'No, actually, sir,' wheedle wheedle, 'I was a vet at first.'

'Oh, a vet! How interesting. And why did you stop being a vet and come to work here? Was it the money . . .'

'No, no, sir, how you talking. I'm only a poor man trying to do my job under great pressure.'

'Oh ho, well, I must tell my friend, Dikshit who is the head of the

Tax Department, to take some of the pressure off. Perhaps to take it off completely.'

'Oh, Mr Dikshit, your friend?'

'Very close friend. Like a brother. And such an honourable man. Hates corruption, in all its forms. Especially, harassment . . .'

'Yes, yes. We, of course, know your family. Big factories. Cars, sweets, coal.'

'Yes, we've had the privilege of having your boys over.'

'How come you here, Mr Maniraja?'

'Bas, passing through the area. On my way to Delhi. My friend Ismail Mujib, great friend, you know . . .'

'Who does not know Ismail Mujib?'

And so, it continued, the dialectic of the influential and the influenced, flowing easily to a place of rest and mutual understanding.

It did not end the raid, but a new tone was set. Samosas and tea would arrive frequently from the bazaar. Oil-daubed newspapers over Wedgwood plates bearing the Kalasuryaketu crest. An inky blue Skanda astride his peacock. In the background was the Kāla | sūrya, which, in myth, was the sun at the end of Time.

'Very grateful to you, old boy,' Uma heard Toby say to Maniraja once the taxmen had left. 'I mean, you know . . . people of your world . . . I would never have known how to speak to them.'

Ah, the errors of judgement we make! And, tragically, in those early days of a relationship, there is no distinction between behaviour that is out of character and that which seems to reveal true character. Unluckily for Toby, with his sister there by his side – a cruder, more thankless reflection of himself – Uma felt she saw her new husband for what he really was: a foolish ineffectual snob.

'It was after the raid,' Skanda says, 'that my mother felt sure she was in trouble with my father.'

'She would tell *you* these things?' Gauri asks in disbelief.

'She always told me everything. And it was my misfortune that I never forgot a word.'

'What did you say?'

'I said, "Why didn't you do anything then?"'

'And what did she say?'

'She said, "How could I? I was married barely a few months. I had just escaped the clutches of your evil nani. I was newly pregnant with you. I had to wait it out."'

They are in the flat, where the time is no longer stopped at his arrival from Geneva. It has made one of those sudden leaps that makes you sit up. 'A change in the weather', Proust tells us, 'is sufficient to create the world and oneself anew.' Never is this more true than with the rains, which arrive like a person arriving, and, one hour to the next, everything is altered: the character of the heat; the quality of the light; the colour and smell of the earth. And there are things that lie on one side of the rainy breach: Theo, Skype, his father's ashes, the white light, the dry heat; on the other: Gauri, and

Gauri alone: and there are things that knit the time together: Sanskrit and The Birth.

'But it should not have affected you,' Gauri says, picking up the thread of their earlier conversation. 'Kartik, you know, asked me the other day if I loved his *deddy*. "Tum mere papa se pyaar karte ho." "Absolutely not," I told him. "Bilkul nahin." But then I tempered it quickly by saying, "It's because I love you so much, Kartik; I have no space in my heart for anyone else but you." He liked that. And, your mother, did she mitigate what she said? To make you know that even if she no longer loved *deddy* dearest, she still loved you?'

'All the time. But because there was so much of him in me, it was impossible for me not to see the connection, between myself and the man she came to loathe.'

'Loathe is too strong a word, surely.'

'It *was* loathing, Gauri. I'll tell you why: because *she* left, and he never recovered. When you cause pain to those weaker than you, the guilt turns to loathing. Into a most secret and profound loathing, for we can never name it as such. We explain it away in other terms, but we, and we alone, know it to be the most animal of all hatreds: our hatred of weakness.'

'So what then?' Gauri asks, after a pause. 'Was it all just downhill after that?'

'No, no, not at all. Quite the opposite. The raid was put down to a bad patch at a bad time, and halcyon days followed. *The years*, my father would say, *when the days went by like leaves falling from a tree.* The years of babies and brunches and long summer holidays. My father, with his textbook to write, had endless amounts of time for us. There were zoos, and birthday parties, and a great sleep in Delhi. I can't tell if it was because I was a child or whether those were, in fact, sleepy days . . .'

'They were sleepy days. But not politically, mind you. You were too young to remember . . .'

'What year were you born in?'

'Will you still love me if I tell you?'

'I'll love you more.'

'1970. And you? Two thousand and . . . ?'

'Shut up. 1976.'

'A baby! And your sister?'

'1978, 13 April. The day the trouble in Punjab began.'

'Early for that, no? Punjab didn't get going till much later. I remember. Not till 1982, at least.'

'No, no. 1978, 13 April. It may have been a speck on the horizon, but that was the day Bhindranwale, then still an unknown village priest propped up by the Congress, clashed with the Nirankaris. That strife between the priest and the heterodoxy: that was the true beginning of the Punjab problem. That was when the ball was set rolling. Trust me, I know: Punjab was another slow fuse in our lives.'

'And when was it over?'

'Punjab?'

'No. The relationship. Your parents.'

'Hard to say exactly when.'

'How did it happen?'

'Slowly. There was an incident concerning my uncle I.P. in 1984; a long separation; my father leaving for Kalasuryaketu . . .'

'Then Europe?'

'No, that was later, and Gauri . . .' he says, and stops.

The rain is too loud for him to continue.

In 1978, the trouble in Punjab was still remote. After the boredom of the Emergency – and yes: that is what it became: interminable: like a monsoon or war without end . . . And Tripathi had been wrong: after the initial disruption to their lives, the rich – though some of their relations remained in jail – were hardly affected. It was the poor who felt the sharp edge of the family planning programmes, of the forcible sterilization, of the midnight vans, of the tyrannical beautification programmes (read: slum clearance). When, in the election of 1977, they had the chance to express their anger, they threw Mrs Gandhi and her horn-rimmed son out.

Toby was at the Kumbh, with Tripathi and Baba ji, a roguish ascetic, full of yoga and politics, when elections were announced. It was the famous Kumbh of 1977; the entire press corps, forbidden under censorship from writing political stories, was in Allahabad. And, unbeknownst to them, Mrs Gandhi had come too. It was there over the loudspeaker that she, in her thin voice, announced the elections that would put an end to her Emergency.

A few months later, on the night of the results, Uma and Toby, newly moved into their flat, newly parents, took Skanda in their arms and drove down to Bahadur Shah Zafar Marg in an old black Fiat.

It was a beautiful March night and thousands had gathered outside the *Times of India* building, where, on black billboards, the results were posted liked cricket scores. There, they found friends, and so many other people besides that traffic on the arterial street had stopped. And when, close to dawn, it became clear Mrs Gandhi and her son were going to lose their own seats, a roar went up from the street. Just before the first light, dancers began to appear, with drums about their necks, and people had tears in their eyes. Never before, or indeed again, had an election been so much about the freedoms on which the modern nation was founded, and never before had the people spoken so completely in one voice. They – Isha, Viski, Uma and Toby – returned at 5 a.m. to Fatehkot House to find the Brigadier and his wife listening to the BBC on a shortwave radio. Even Deep Fatehkotia, not usually one to be swept up in a public festivity, could not contain herself. She looked her son-in-law in the eye and said, 'Toby saab, you must know my general contempt for the Indian public. But today, I hand it to them: we must salute the Indian voter.'

And, on hearing this, the younger generation found themselves full of emotion, for there was such innocence that night, innocence as there had not been since Mrs Gandhi's father first roused a sleeping nation to light and freedom. Their generation had never known anything like it. They were people stranded between the spoilt hope of Independence and the still distant promise of Liberalization. And, though more isolated than their parents, they were also ironically the most colonized: the first to lose language and faith and culture, the first to feel the certainties of tribe and community crumble about them. But that night – the night Mrs Gandhi and her son lost the election – was their night and they exulted, even if briefly, in the hope it had restored in them.

A few weeks later, Uma discovered she was pregnant again.

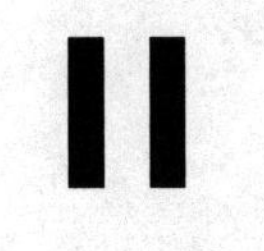

The general fog that lies over Delhi brings to this most fragmented of cities a surprising unity.

The cities within the city, each endowed with an island mentality, merge magically into an urban whole, achieving what no number of flyovers and metro lines have been able to. In this new harmony, temporary and unclean, the glittering glass offices of Gurgaon, their aircraft warning lights flashing red in the haze, are united with low-lying gated colonies to the south, east and west. These, with their bright markets and bald communal gardens, and the occasional tomb of a forgotten medieval official, are, in turn, stitched together with the radial sprawl of Lutyens' city.

Here the murk has sunk deepest. Tonight, the British city, with its low domes and bungalows, is like a submerged necropolis. The rickshaws glide along its streets, with that stealthy sense of purpose with which single-beam submersibles in documentary films explore the ocean floor; the yellow streetlights, buried in the canopies of trees, have the nested glow, at once inviting and dangerous, of marine wonders behind screens of sharp coral; and, everywhere, the dense cold air, sulphurous and full of particles, closes over old wounds. Even where the scar tissue runs deepest, the line between the British city and the Muslim town to its north, where the escapees of one upheaval came to populate the abandoned places of another, the fog, easy and billowing, brings a feeling of continuity, at once even-handed and insensitive, like the blanketing hush of a first snow, like curfew in Srinagar.

The house on Curzon Road, down a long tree-darkened avenue at the heart of the British city, shows its wounds too.

A cement scar has appeared across the full length of its pale yellow facade. It is visible from the street. Long, saw-toothed and smiling.

'Hai, Jaanu!' Gauri says, 'Where have you brought me? And on such a night . . .'

At the gate, men, with an exaggerated concern for the cold, stand around a cement dish, from which a good fire climbs high into the murk. On seeing the car one pries himself away from the orange warmth. A face, small and ravaged, eyes clouded. They appear bluish-white behind their bifocal lenses till the driver of the car, always quicker to take offense than the owner, strikes fear into them. Grovelling apologies; anger ricocheting among the men huddled by the fire; and, at last, the house's green gates fly open. Shelves of fog rise in sudden alarm, stumble along the red sandstone of the drive and cascade down to some further place of rest. The car's beams chase off the remaining wisps of fog to reveal a scene of devastation.

'What were you saying?'

'Tch, tch, tch! Now look at this!'

The white headlights sweep over an arcade of palms. They are ranged around the red sandstone rim of a central oval whose wet earth is bare and upturned, like a freshly ploughed field. Etched blackly onto the pale trunks of the colonnading palms are terms of abuse and the promises of lovers. The capitals of the palms, frayed and burnt brown in the acid winter air, overlook a fountain whose basins are dusty and dry, its Egyptian needle a shattered stump. An unplastered brick wall, perpendicular and precise, comes from one edge of the property to cleave the central basin of the fountain unevenly in two. The wall climbs the house's shallow steps, spoiling the symmetry of its pillared entrance, and plunges deep into the hulking shell of the Lutyens mansion.

Standing outside, Gauri says, 'This is your real massi's house?'

'Real massi. Isha massi. Mother's sister.'

'They had some family feud or what?'

'Brothers. Property.'

'Typical, no? Wherever money's involved. When did you last come here?'

'I virtually grew up here, Gauri; I was here for countless Holis and Diwalis and birthday parties, but I haven't been back in – what?! – twenty years.'

'Twenty years! So long. How come?'

'Just . . . I don't know. We drifted apart, I guess.'

'And, out of the blue, she called you, this Isha massi of yours?'

'Out of the blue. She heard I was in town from Kitten Singh and called. She said they were having a party.'

'Not much of a party, Janoo,' she says, wrapping her shawl more tightly around herself.

'Maybe we're in the wrong place.'

Breathing in the thick night air, and letting her teeth chatter for effect, she says, 'What a night!' She draws him close to her, and, seeming now to want his attention, says, 'How do you say night in Sanskrit, baby?'

'Rātri, of course,' he says easily.

'Ah, yes, of course.' Then, half teasing, half humouring him, she says, 'And does it have any cognates?'

She turns away, missing the smile her question brings to his face. The cognate game, introduced to him by his father – and something of a joke between him and Mackinson – has, in the six months Skanda and Gauri have been together, been appropriated by them.

'Making fun of me or what?'

'No, truly! I want to know.'

'Well, the answer is, no. No cognates.'

'How boring!'

'Baby.'

'What?'

'Baby!' he says, now wrapping his arms around her.

'What?!' she says, embarrassed.

'*Any cognates*?! I love you!'

'Shut up, fool.'

'No cognates for rātri, but I might be able to rustle some up for nakta.'

'Nakta?' she repeats carefully. 'Is that night too?'

'Yes, a long dark nocturnal thread.'

'Go on.'

'On one condition?'

'What?'

'A kiss for every one.'

'Silly fool.'

'Agreed?'

'Agreed.'

'*Nox*.'

'Ooof, I knew that.'

A grudging peck.

'*Núx*.'

'Again?!'

'No! *Nox* Latin, *núx* Greek.'

'Oh, fishy, but OK.'

A taut and withheld one; a have-a-good-day-at-the-office kind of thing.

'Then?'

'*Nakht-uru.*'

'Eeeks! What is that? German?'

'Zend-Avestan.'

'Oh, baby. Come here. You're so sexy.'

A real kiss, something long, and ponderous.

'Go on.'

'*Nacht.*'

'What?! Bloody cheat. Making a fool of me?'

No kiss; a shove instead.

'No. I promise. This is the German,' he says, extracting his due.

'The next one better be wildly different.'

'*Naktis*,' he says sibilantly into the night, seeming now not even to want a kiss.

'Oh, what's that?'

'Lithuanian, my love,' he says airily.

'Come here, little bugger.' And she gives him a kiss that's like a spanking.

'And?'

'We may already be at the end of the thread.'

'Oh! That's not so impressive.'

'*Nahts*!'

'What's that?'

'Gothic.'

And now she takes his face in her two hands and gives him the best kiss of the night.

Still being kissed, he murmurs, '*Neaht, niht.*'

'What . . . ?' she mumbles with her mouth full.

'Anglo-Saxon,' he mumbles back, and the kiss deepens.

'Any more?'

'*Nošti*, Slavic.'

'Not cheating, I hope.'

'No, Gauri. Deep all-enveloping night, Finnegan's Night – the dark night of the soul – where under the cover of fog and darkness, we enter this shell of a house together. Look,' he says, and points to the light in the portico of the house. A few naked bulbs extend from long wires. They reveal a construction site of sorts, and, hanging from a line, the frayed vests and paint-spattered trousers of labourers.

'Inside?'

'Inside, yes. We have to find this party.'

Only once they enter is it possible to see the extent to which the wall has shattered the wholeness of the house. Undetected, it has followed them down a handsomely proportioned central corridor. A floor of marble diamonds, coated in a fine white dust and strewn with nails, rushes to meet the pale glow entering at the end. Now inside the baggy husk of the house, the wall separates bedrooms from adjoining bedrooms, blinds corridors and casts sunny terraces into gloom. It appears framed in a teak doorway, lit by the light of a single naked bulb. And, though the strangeness of seeing it in the house distracts from the impression of destruction, this is an illusion: all beautiful and complex things when they are crudely destroyed – or partitioned – produce at first a kind of wonder before the horror of their destruction sinks in.

Gauri draws her head back from peering up into a cavity, out of whose damp darkness a black and yellow braided wire descends magically.

'Oooof! So sad. Such a beautiful old house.'

'But always gloomy, for as long as I can remember. It was the first thing that hit you as you came in: the gloom!'

'Bad history or what?'

'Very bad. My uncle Viski's mother – Teji – was a famous beauty. "And she vuz," as my grandmother used to say, examining her nails, "a pross."'

'Tch, Skandu. What a word.'

'She slept with half the Punjab.'

'In those days?'

'Yes. And when her husband, old man Aujla, got to know about it, he threw her out from this house on Curzon Road. Not that she cared much, mind you. By that point, she had moved on from small-town doctors and the staff of his hotel to a rich industrialist called Reggie Hotelier. A pincushion of a man, with his own chain of hotels and a magenta Mercedes.'

'Embellishing or what?'

'No, no. God swear. And the worst part was – awful irony: I tell you, these things only ever happen in real life! – he had a twenty-year lease on the Raj. Which meant that when old man Aujla threw his wife out, he had to suffer the ignominy of her, newly disgraced, leaving his house in her lover's Mercedes, only to move into the presidential suite of *his* own hotel.'

'No!'

'I'm telling you. And, to really drive the knife in, she was forever decorating and redecorating it, according to her whim and fancy, as if it were her own drawing room.'

'Then?'

'Then, what! The old man did a terrible thing. The thing that is responsible for the unhappiness of this house, and for this wall.'

'What?'

'He threw out his youngest two children – a boy and girl – with his wife, bag and baggage, refusing to acknowledge them as his own.'

'And your uncle, Viski?'

'Viski, he kept. But, with the other two, he was a veritable Leontes: *Hence with it, and together with the dam / Commit them to the fire.* Viski spent his whole life trying to make up for what his father had done. He tried to give his siblings their fair share of the properties, gave them half the Raj. He was eaten up with guilt and managed, in the bargain, to spoil his own marriage – which became pretty violent

– all in the most desperate attempt to regain the love of his mother and siblings.'

'And?'

'And what? They took everything, while all the time hating him for being the one who could give, and, when the time was right, they turned on him. It destroyed Viski. Not that they had conspired to do him out of his property – he cared nothing for money; but that even after all his efforts his brother and sister, who he adored, still despised him. Gauri?' he says into the dark.

'Yes. I'm here. Come and look at this, Skandu.'

She is in the dining room where there is now a bladeless fan and a long table, its white cloth flecked with dried cement. The wall, though only partially built here, rises up between the hub of the fan and the table, then smashes past the gaping jaws of a smallish fireplace, dislodging and cracking its pretty lintel of mustard stone. There are still photographs on the walls, still modest works of art, still a jib cabinet, which, on being prodded with one knee – as Skanda does now – springs open to reveal breakfast things. Marmite. Jam. Churan. A Japanese toaster. A funny little green-handled cutter which can be pressed down on a piece of fruit to cut it into eight pieces.

'You know it so well, this house.'

'I told you: I virtually grew up here.'

'How so?'

'We were here for many of the difficult periods in our life.'

'In '84?'

'No, not then; not during the riots, at least. But others.'

'Such strange things on the walls!'

There are photographs and posters, the height marks of growing children engraved on the long flank of a crockery cupboard.

'Fareed, Iqbal,' he mouths the names after an age.

'Who are they?'

'Cousins. Isha's children.'

He points to black and white pictures of them on plastic potties, looking up at the camera, the top-knot of Fareed's long hair coming loose and falling to the side.

'I'm sure they don't look like that now,' she giggles. And, as she says this, he realizes he has no adult picture of them in his mind.

There are photographs from Gulmarg and Pahalgam too. Of Viski playing golf; of tattu rides; of the frothy Leedar river; of their cottage, CM1, and him in his mother's room.

'You?' she says, pointing to one of the photographs.

'Me.'

'Baba! In your little Kashmiri dressing gown. How sweet you were.'

The picture brings up a painful memory, which his mind shies away from unpacking.

'Do you know *Rama's Last Act*?' he asks Gauri.

'No. What is it?'

'It's a famous Sanskrit play that my father translated. It was part of a compilation of his called *Three Sanskrit Plays*. It's by the eighth-century playwright Bhavabhuti.'

'Bhava-who?!'

'Bhavabhuti.'

'Why did you think of it?'

'Because this – us, here – reminded me of it. It opens just like this: Ram and Sita in a picture gallery. And they're looking at a painting exhibition of events from their lives. The whole epic is there in pictures on the wall for them to see. The breaking of the bow, the abduction of Sita . . . And they're laughing, and crying, and at times fearful. *Lacrimae rerum*, you know.'

'*Lacrimae* . . . ?'

'Tears of Things. *Lacrimae*: tears, like aśru in Sanskrit and *dákru* in Greek.'

'Tears of what things?'

'All things, and no things, Gauri. Things past and present.'

'Strange.'

'It is. It's there as a framing device. The play begins in the picture gallery, where they, Valmiki's epic characters, are looking back on the events from the epic. And it ends with a play within a play, a new offering by Valmiki.'

'What is that? Meta-fiction?'

'Meta-fiction, yes. Bhavabhuti, Sheldon Pollock says, was the most *meta* of all the pre-modern writers. Which is really saying something because they were all deep into this stuff, the Sanskrit writers. Valmiki, Vyasa, you name it. Meta-fiction was like the biggest game in town. Inductions. Plays within plays . . . Are you cold, by the way?'

'No, not at all. I have my shawl. Here, give me your hands.'

'We should really find this party, you know.'

'We will. But slowly. I'm enjoying being here with you in this house. It reminds me of my childhood, of exploring – I don't know! – some ruin or something. But, go on: why the meta-elements?'

'In drama, it's obvious: I mean the reason why someone would want to do it. Because it's right there, the line, you know, between the audience and the stage: the line between the real and representational, art and reality. It's so tantalizing and physical. How can one not play with it? How can one not consider its implications, its tension? Shakespeare loved it too. His plays are full of reflexivity. In Bhavabhuti . . .'

'Bhava-who?' she says and grins.

The teasing is her way of keeping his pedantry in check. And he likes her for it, likes her for protecting him from his genetic fate.

'Am I boring you?'

'No. But look: this amazing picture. All the different generations together. Who is that?' She points at a boy in shorts and a blue and red striped T-shirt.

'My cousin Iqbal.'

'Will I meet him tonight?'

'I hope so. The toddler, in case you were wondering, is me.'

'Oh, look, baba. All sad-eyed and staring up.'

'The young man in the white turban and jeans, standing by the bar . . . that is my uncle I.P. as a young man. This picture would have been taken in the early eighties.'

'Real uncle?'

'Mother's brother.'

'Will I meet him tonight?'

'No. He had trouble with the police in 1984 and he now never comes to India.'

They are halfway around the room. In the semi-darkness, above a facing fireplace, there is a kitschy picture of the Golden Temple, its outline beaded with red and blue flashing lights.

'And this?' she says, pointing to a picture of children with black painted moustaches and wooden bows covered in chintzy satin.

'The Playhouse school, my nursery. My mother taught there for a while.'

'How old were you when your father started teaching you Sanskrit?'

'It was there right from the start. He taught me all the way through, from when I was a child. He just worked it into my upbringing, I suppose.'

'And your sister's too?'

'No.'

'No? Why?'

'I don't really know. Perhaps he saw some kind of native interest or ability in me. He could be very intuitive in these ways.'

'And he was a good teacher?'

'Oh, the best, Gauri. They still use his textbook, you know. The one he wrote in the seventies when he was with my mother. It's very special: it was my textbook at Oxford.'

'Really?'

'Yes. So, in a sense, even when he stopped teaching me, he continued to teach me.'

'What made him such a good teacher?'

'He had this way of always teaching from within the tradition, and of bringing alive the Sanskritic world. The play I mentioned earlier, *Rama's Last Act*, he taught it to me when I was still a child. Not all of it. Just the benediction. And, even though I didn't understand it, I fell in love with the sound of the words.'

'How does it go?'

'In Sanskrit or in English?'

'English, please.'

'It begins with an ode: "This we offer with an expression of homage to the poets of old. Let us also pay reverence to language, a deathless thing, a part of the soul."'

'The soul,' she says softly into the darkness. 'Ātman.'

Then, taking his hand, she leads him out of the dining room. And they go deeper into the house.

THE RIOT
(1984)

The hour of juncture – saṃdhyā – juncture between day and night, enveloped the flat. And it brought all variety of distractions to be found at such a junction. Uma, in blouse and petticoat, made-up but unperfumed, hair twisted into a knot, was in between dressing and giving Rudrani a bath. Narindar, flitting along the flat's freshly painted walls like a moth, turned on lights as he went by. They had been outside together a moment ago, Narindar and Skanda, outside where there was now the screech of birds, voices calling children in, bicycle bells, the slow rumbling tread of a dark blue truck pumping Malathion into the October air. His uncle I.P. was due soon, and the excitement of this made Skanda restless, as did the guttering of the lights: a fluctuation! A new and adored word. In the tentative air of this juncturing hour, in the general storm of a day winding down, his father alone was still and calm, unperturbed by the transfers taking place around them, as if there were no dinners or card parties to be gone to, no baths to be had, no drinks to be laid out, no night to fling its cloth over the sky.

'Ātmanaḥ,' Toby said. 'What case is that in, Skandu?'

Aḥ? The aspiration had thrown him off. A single index finger shot out of his closed fist, and wiggled tentatively before his father, who looked at it with mock horror, eyes wide, as if it were an insulting gesture – an expression sure to provoke uncontrollable laughter – before bringing a large hand, open and smothering, paper trumping rock, closed over the little fist.

'First? First?! First?!!!' Peals of laughter by the time the third First is said. 'Look again, Skandu. Is it an "a" final?'

'No!' He could tell it wasn't from his father's tone.

'Is it an "as" final, like manas?'

No. Because it would retain its 's' if it was in the singular, unless . . . vocative? O Soul? No, that can't be: the soul is not being addressed. So . . .

'I'll give you a clue,' his father said, and leaned back in his chair. 'It is in the same group as rājan. Now, come on, concentrate – rājā, rājānam, rājñā, rājñe . . .'

'Rājñaḥ!'

'Exactly!

'And so?'

'It's the sixth case, baba: ātmanaḥ is ātman in the sixth case!'

'Correct. *Of* the soul: ātmā, ātmānam, ātmanā, ātmane . . .'

And together in one voice they say, 'Ātmanaḥ!'

'Now, get your poor father a drink before he faints . . .'

'Baba, are you and mama going out for dinner?'

'You know we are. To Isha Massi's. For a card party . . .'

'And is I.P. Mamu going to come to be with us?'

'Why are you asking questions you know the answer to? Of course he is. And your father, in the meantime, will be emptying your mother's family's pockets.'

'Winning, or what?'

'Big time! Rich banne vale hain hum.'

'Richer than Viski Masardji?'

'Richer than him even.'

'*Toby*, come on! Let him have his bath. And get dressed yourself.'

He winked at his son, and, getting up, mouthed, 'Rich,' which made Skanda laugh hysterically. Then pouring himself a Campari soda – for some reason available when hardly anything else was – he swung around, and still standing at the bar, did a little jig: 'Money, money, money . . .'

He was in the middle of telling Skanda that rich, rājā and *rex*, like Rex Harrison – Skanda's favourite actor – all had the same root, when the doorbell rang.

Narindar opened it. It was I.P. with his luggage.

'Ohohoho, sardar saab . . . !'

'Mamu!'

'*Toby!* He's here, and you're not even dressed.'

'I will, darling. Not to worry. Sardar saab, what are you drinking?'

'Greetings, Highness . . .' I.P. said, half in irony. Then, in between setting down his bags, he removed his kara from his wrist so that Skanda, ever fascinated by its size and the fact that he could open bottles with it, might play with it.

'Highness! You mustn't call me that, I.P. I am but a mere princeling, and more ling than prince, if you ask me. Skandu, you better go for your bath. Or your mother will . . .' he smacks his fist into his palm '. . . us all. Go on.'

'But afterwards can I sit with I.P. Mamu?'

'Of course you can. He is here to sit with you *only*.'

With a question in his face, Toby made a flicking action with his wrist. 'Scotch, if you have it,' I.P. said, in reply to the gesture.

'I certainly do. Come, sit down, tell me of your travails. Is your mother still trying to get you to give up teaching for a life of boredom and dissipation on a hundred barren acres in Haryana?'

'Oh, Toby saab,' I.P. said, laughing with the relief, and pre-first-drink excitement, at the raising of a subject so near to his heart.

'Don't ask. She may well succeed.'

'Don't do it, brother-in-law. Don't do it. Believe me. Soda?'

'Pani. Flat's looking lovely.'

'All thanks to your sister. She's chosen all of it, the upholstery, this shade of cream, which I like so much more than white.'

'Don't believe a word he says, I.P. I've married a bloody cushion scatterer. Toby, are you getting dressed? Or are you going in your jeans?'

'Coming!' he said, and winked at I.P.

Toby loved I.P. He always had, ever since their first meeting in 1975, when I.P. was an eighteen-year-old student on his way to Stephens. He was one of the joys of Toby and Uma's marriage. In those early years of marriage, when children are still very young, and the world feels so near, too near to give a sense of the shape of one's life together, I.P. gave them a foretaste of later life, of what it would be like to have grown-up children. He allowed them a glimpse into the satisfactions and quiet contentment of having made it, of having got through.

I.P. had an effortlessly close relationship with his sister; and, as an extension of that closeness, he adored Toby.

It helped too that he had an intellectual frame of mind, a love of history and literature. And there were not many people to share this with in his own circle. The conversation among people of his class, school and tribe – Feudals, Doscos and Jat Sikhs – was limited invariably to talk of fishing, shooting, School, with a capital S – which is to say the Doon School – and the purchase of land and machines, the latter two an extension, no doubt, of an ancient and tribal instinct, at once martial and agrarian. Only when they got drunk did they touch upon two additional subjects: their lost homeland beyond the Hindu Kush and the sacrifices and valour of the gurus who gave them their religion. But even this slightly wider interest was spoiled by the chauvinism and pieties it inspired.

For I.P., newly discovering intellectual life in India, Toby was a rare thing: a man without an agenda, without a tribe. A man willing to let history be what it was, without wanting to ram it into a frame which answered the needs of a particular group or caste or faith. I.P. was at that age when our sense of who we are, or of who we have been told we are, chafes against what we discover in our reading. And immediately a choice seems to appear: to let the reading show us the way forward, like water picking its course over unfamiliar ground; or to direct the reading, to channel the stream, so that it confirms what we already think we know. I.P. was among those few people who could do the former. He had a mind that welcomed doubt and uncertainty; he revelled in it, in fact; he was not one to ever make the perilous decision of deciding to know. His mind was happy to grope its way to its own conclusions, happy to breathe easy in a state of unknowing.

It gave Toby immense pleasure to see him encounter the great mysteries of Indian history, to see him absorbed in questions that had obsessed Toby as a young man. Questions of whether the Aryans had come from elsewhere or sprung from the soil. Did they invade or migrate? What did that awkward gap of a few centuries between our last date with the Indus Valley and our first date with the Aryans signify? And was their culture – the Vedic culture – absorbed by the Indus Valley civilization or did the one supersede the other? How was it that there was such a dearth of material from that early Vedic period? A highly complex language, a whole system of thought and belief, but hardly a copper bowl, a seal, a stone, a dwelling, so little to say they really existed. And, this, when their texts spoke of jewels and gold ornaments and great palaces. Was that all but a paean to the glory of their gods and not a realistic description of their environs? What of Sanskrit? Who spoke it? When? Where? For how long? How did it break its liturgical function to become a language of literature? What was the nature of its transmission east into south-east Asia?

And was it the coming of Islam that caused it to retreat? Or had the decay already begun? These questions did not need answers. They could be left as questions; the raising of them was all. They were part of the natural complexity of living on soil that was old and alluvial to its depths. But too often, I.P. found, people either fled from these questions or rushed to fashion a version of events that would suit the requirements of some particular group.

And one of the things I.P. and Toby had in common was their mutual frustration with intellectual life in India. On many occasions, I.P., much to the annoyance of Deep Fatehkotia, would take the bus down from Dehradun and stay a few days with Toby and Uma, complaining to them about his job at the school. Then, grudgingly, once he had got out some of his angst, he would move to Fatehkot House, where his mother would, with renewed energy, apply pressure on him to leave teaching and farm the Fatehkot land in Harayana.

I.P. was among the most natural teachers Toby had ever met. He was gifted, generous, patient as a lama, and it made Toby sad to see him full of self-doubt that October evening.

'I had an interesting run-in with Sarkar,' I.P. said, following Narindar with his eyes who, placing a wooden coaster on the peg table next to him, laid his drink down.

'Is he new?'

'Narindar? No, of course not. He's Labu and Sharada's son. From Kalasuryaketu. Saab pooch rahe the ke aap naye aaye ho, kya?'

Narindar blushed. 'Kahaan naya hun? Main toh kab se aap ke saath kam kar raha hun.'

'Perhaps he's just grown up.'

'Perhaps. But what were you saying about Sarkar?'

'Oh, nothing. I was teaching the boys something from the end of the Birth, something that, in fact, you had put me on to. I was giving it to them as an example of eroticism in our literature, of how the classical world thought of sex and love . . .'

'Do you remember what it was?'

'Not entirely. It's from the Consummation, I know that much. There is, following an extended period of love-making, this great moment of realism. Uma is fastening her garment, which has come loose, and Shiva . . .'

'Is – yes! – hṛta | vilocana. One whose eyes are seized.'

'You remember by what?'

'Of course. By the scratches at the top of Uma's inner thighs.'

'Exactly! So you can imagine that the boys had quite a giggle at this. And invariably old Sarkar came to find out.'

'His Bengali sensibilities must have been terribly affronted.'

'Oh, they were! He called me in to give me a little lecture about the canon, if you please. "I.P., my boy, we want our young students, embarking upon the noble discovery of literature, to be acquainted with the canon. There will be time later for other things. But first, they must know the canon. The canon, I.P."

'I said, "Sir, what is uncanonical about Kalidasa?" And, Toby, he gets this tortured expression on his face. Literally I thought he was going to burst a blood vessel. Nothing coherent comes out of his mouth. He just grips the table and says, as if the words were being wrung from him, "Sentimental poetry . . . English . . . The greats: Chaucer, Shakespeare, Milton, the Romantics. The boys are giggling, I.P. The boys are giggling. I will have complaints from the parents soon."'

'What did you say to that?'

'I said, "Sir, if giggling is what you're concerned about, there's plenty to giggle about in Shakespeare."'

'"But I.P.," he says, "they won't mind if it is Shakespeare; they will if it is Kalidasa. They don't spend good money to send their boys to Doon School only to learn Kalidasa."'

'Conversation over?'

'Pretty much. Can you imagine, Toby, in a country like ours, talking of canons? Where history has played such tricks with us: to talk of canons! The thousand years of Persian writing in India. Is that canon? The Sanskrit dramas and poems, the epics . . . Not canon? The Brontës canon? I wanted to say to him, Sarkar, the Yanks are on their way up now. So, what? In fifty years, is our canon going to consist of Twain and Emerson and Melville . . . Out with the Angrez, in with the Yanks?'

'Yes. Apparently, every time there is an ascendant power in the world, India will remake herself in its image! It's ludicrous.'

'That's it, that's it. I tell you, Toby, there is slavery in this country's blood. You can't get it out, no matter how hard you try.'

'You mustn't say that, I.P. Men like you will change it. The spread of new ideas will change it.'

'I don't think so, Toby. We have no memory in this country. Just amnesia. I was reading this novel on the bus down from Dehradun.'

He took a big sip of his drink, then went over to his canvas bag and removed a dog-eared copy of the novel from somewhere near the top of the bag.

Seeing it, Toby said, 'Oh, I know Rushdie, I.P. I may not follow contemporary literature, but who doesn't know Rushdie? He won a big prize for it.'

'Yes, he did. But listen to this . . .' He took another big sip of his drink, drenching his moustache and the little triangle of beard below his lip.

'Listen! Have you read it?'

'No, not yet. But I hear it's very good, so is the new one apparently. *Shame.*'

'Listen, listen,' he repeated, reading and pacing. '"Today, the papers are talking about the supposed political rebirth of Mrs Indira Gandhi; but when" . . .' he paused to smirk at Toby, '"*but when* I returned to India, concealed in a wicker basket, 'The Madam' was basking in the fullness of her glory. Today, perhaps, we are already forgetting, sinking willingly into *the insidious clouds of amnesia*; but I remember, and will set down". . . so on and so forth. But look at that phrase, Toby: "*the insidious clouds of amnesia*". That is what gets this place time and again. It never learns from the past; it just keeps forgetting. Look at the Emergency, that's what Rushdie is referring to . . . Nine years ago. The year you were married. I remember. And less than a decade later . . . ?'

'Forgotten. It is true.'

'A lifetime away. The witch is back in power, turning her evil eye to Punjab this time, which is already in flames, and no one says a thing. No one even remembers. It's maddening. It's enough to make you want to retire early, as my mother will have me do, and farm some land somewhere, live a quiet life, you know, of reading and contemplation.'

There was a rustle of cloth behind them; the noise of heels, sounding out like shot; the wafting herald of perfume. I.P. saw his sister and a smile of pure pleasure broke over his face. But it soon darkened again. Toby sensed Uma behind him, and reached his hand back, which she took, standing there quietly, allowing her brother to finish.

'And I'll tell you something, Toby. There's nothing benign about this amnesia. It conceals some pretty awful things. I don't want to make some Santayana-like pronouncement about the price people who refuse to remember the past eventually pay. But, let me say this much to you: there is nothing benign about this amnesiac fog, nothing benign at all.'

There was now the slapping sound of wet rubber slippers. And soon I.P. was enveloped in the affection of his sister and nephew.

The mention of Punjab made Toby aware that I.P. was not wearing his turban. Just a baseball cap over his juda. And, recalling the new hostility against Sikhs, he wondered for a moment if I.P. was trying to conceal the signifiers of his faith.

He said, 'I.P., you're not wearing your turban?'

I.P., with Skanda in his arms, gave him a sidelong look that seemed to say, *And so?*

'I hope it's not because—'

'Toby! Are you insulting me? You think I'm afraid of these coward cops. I'm a Sikh, for Christ's sake. I'm not wearing my turban because I was wearing my helmet. That's all.'

'Toby, really?' Uma said. 'What a thought! We're not like your lot, you know, quaking at the knees every time a government inspector shows up. We're not religious people, but we would never hide the fact that we're Sikhs.'

'I just . . . Never mind. I'm happy to be wrong. I.P., we'll see you at the other end? Once we're back.'

'Of course. I have a party to go to afterwards. But I'll be here till you get back. Are they meant to be asleep?'

'Rudrani already is. And Skandu will fade soon.'

'I won't!'

Uma looked at I.P. and mouthed, 'Five minutes.'

They stand – Gauri and Skanda – in the shell of the drawing room. The fog comes in through the high transoms and seems, even on this moonless night, to be full of light. At the centre of a large balding carpet, a chandelier lies on its side. Crawling along the maroon margin of this vast room are white mosaic letters. Gauri, following them down, reads haltingly, 'Rai Bahadur Rajwant Singh, 1936.'

'Who was that?' she asks.

'Viski's grandfather,' Skanda replies. 'He was one of the earliest occupants of this city. A real frontiersman. A peasant-contractor from Sargodha who, under Lutyens' supervision, helped build this necropolis from the ground up.'

'Necropolis? Why do you keep calling it that?'

'It has the air of one, doesn't it? The air of something built and abandoned, the lifeless majesty of the mausoleum or tomb?'

She nods, but does not answer. Instead she follows the mosaic margin right to the end of the room. He watches her go, putting one foot after the other. His thoughts drift into silence, but Gauri remains their focus: And Rajwant Singh, he almost says aloud, knew this city from its inception, knew it when it was just brown scrubby land surrounded by the ruins of other Delhis. He had been witness to all the original arguments. Over site. Over style. Over significance. Over the choice of architect. He had seen the case being made for the northern site, which would have given the new city a closer relationship to the Muslim town it was meant to supersede, a closer relationship to the river. He had seen that case demolished on the grounds that the malarial swamps in the north were a hazard. He had seen the Ridge – where the British made their last stand in 1857 – dismissed on the basis of – what? Bad memories? Perhaps.

Rajwant Singh – Skanda imagines – had seen the planners' eye drift south, even from that spot where their monarch had laid a token foundation stone in the year of the durbar. He had seen that eye continue on its southbound journey till it rested on the wilderness that was Raisina. And the old contractor must have asked himself, Why? Why this arid plain, cut away from nature and history, with nothing to recommend it but ruins on all sides? Why this necropolis?

Then, one day *he must have seen*, Skanda thinks, his eyes still fastened on Gauri. Rajwant Singh must have seen the English, for the first time, as they saw themselves. They would have been laying down the roads of the city and fixing upon perspectives, and vistas. 'This avenue must run into the humped mass of the purana qila. And from here the Qutab must be visible, from there the Jama Masjid. And we must do something about the grouping of Lodhi tombs.' Hearing this talk – 'Tughlakabad this, Indraprastha that' – the contractor must have seen, for the first time, the extent of their ambition. And it would have been far grander, far more hubristic, than anything he had imagined until then.

The planners wanted this site, this blank page with history pressing against it on all sides, precisely because it answered their needs like no other. They did not just want to build an adjunct to an existing Delhi; they did not want simply to add on to what had come before; they wanted to build a final Delhi, an ultimate expression of their belief that they were the last stage of Indian history. It was as if they sought to knit together the different cities of Delhi, to make a whole of the disconnected past. And this imperial capital, this city on a hill, with the ruins of other Delhis on her petticoat, was to have been the capping stone of history. The end of history. That was their ambition, even as the next decade saw them wrapping up their empire and abandoning the newly built capital.

Gauri, having walked around the room, returns. Skanda, thinking still of the building of this imperial city, says, 'And don't forget: this was the age of Mussolini. The agency that built EUR was created in 1936. It was an age of utopias. Which,' he adds, ' – I mean, the idea of utopia itself – are always violent. Violence by another name.'

'By what name?' Gauri says, with interest.

'By the name of purity,' he answers, seeming half to be asking himself a question. 'Every man who ever dreamt up a utopia was animated far more by the wish to purge, Gauri, than to build.'

'Pakistan was a utopia,' she says, as if challenging him.

'It was. And we need go no further in making the case for their intrinsic violence than that.'

'But what was being purged?'

'India, of course! By which I mean Hindu India: the contamination of it, you know.'

'Khalistan . . .'

'A Utopia too.'

'What was being purged there?'

'The same thing.'

'The same thing? Surely not, Skanda. Sikhs are Hindus.'

'Try telling a Sikh that.'

'But, come on—'

'No, no, Gauri. A Sikh is not a Hindu, not merely a Hindu. He is more like a Hindu looking at himself through Muslim eyes. And he does not like what he sees. He wants to be rid of it, *purged* of it.'

'Of what?'

'Of cowardice, of weakness, the taint of defeat.'

'You go too far . . .'

'I grew up with a Sikh mother, Gauri. And nothing the Muslims have to say about Hindus can compare with what Sikhs have to say about Hindus.'

His answer silences her. She begins slowly, as if measuring the room, to walk down its short side.

'Believe me,' he says, somewhat imploringly, 'it was something that had begun to affect my parents' relationship. Just look at that remark: "We're not like your lot, you know: quaking at the knees every time a government inspector shows up." Many things had seeped into their lives by this point. Things they were dimly aware of, and things they knew too well. Some came from the environment – and what a toxic environment it had become! – some they generated themselves. A lot had changed, you see, and . . .' he trails off, as she walks out of earshot, driving his thoughts inward.

Two dates less than a decade apart, he thinks – 1975 and 1984 – and what a gulf lies between them! Mullahs in Tehran. Soviet tanks in Kabul. Bhutto's head in a hangman's noose. The return of religion, of conservatism. Of Reagan and Thatcher. How keenly my father must have felt it when an English friend of his in 1981, soon after John Lennon was killed, said – and truly, it could not have been said earlier – the Sixties are over.

When Gauri returns, Skanda, as if all this while she has been following his train of thought, says, 'And Baba, Gauri, was such a child of the Sixties.'

'In the Western sense?' she asks. 'In the sense of flower power and free love?'

'Yes, but not just in that sense: in the Indian sense too. In the sense of innocence. In the sense of that time of chiffon saris and sweetly melancholy film songs, of bougainvillea and cantonment towns. Of the sight, as evening fell in Delhi, of a cream-coloured car with a single red light, negotiating the city's broad streets. "And to anyone who knew," he would tell my uncle I.P., who himself was too young to know that time, "it meant that a gentleman prime minister was on his way to dinner." *That* innocence – one may blame the Emergency, though perhaps it could not have lasted anyway – was irrecoverably lost by 1984. Rage had entered the system, Gauri, rage and criminality.'

'But, Skanda,' she says, answering urgency with urgency, 'what has all this to do with a marriage? Especially when two people are weathering these things together?'

'That is the point: they were not weathering them together. To one, India was becoming every day more remote, every day beyond grasp. And to the other? Well, she was better able to cope, better able to take things head-on. And – I don't know! – people always say our literature is crammed full of big events. Of riots, and partitions, and emergencies. Some must ask: is this really the stuff of everyday life? Surely some people must just be living quiet lives with quiet problems, unaffected by these cataclysms? My answer is no. It is as Naipaul says, "The train has many coaches and different classes, but it passes through the same landscape. People are responding to the same political or religious and cultural pressures." And the difference, I feel, between places that work and those that are in turmoil is that, in the former, people don't have to think about politics; in the latter, they can't help but think about them.'

'Look at Punjab . . .' Gauri says with energy.

'Exactly,' he replies, 'just look at Punjab, look at how it had crept up on everybody. 1978,' – the history of those years, like a verse learnt by heart, is always ready on his lips – 'Bhindranwale, still an unknown village priest, clashes with the Nirankaris, whom he considers to be apostates. A classic move, by the way: purge the faith first, before you move on to the enemies of the faith. He was like an early bin Laden, Bhindranwale. 1980, the Nirankari guru is killed and Bhindranwale expresses his approval. The next year – 1981 – the cops arrest him for the assassination of a local newspaper editor, Lala Jagat Narain . . .'

'Then Blue Star?' Gauri inserts casually.

'No, no, not yet,' he says, with irritation, as if she has misquoted a line of the verse. 'First, there's Bhindranwale's bungled arrest at Mehta Chowk, which turns into a show of strength for him. Then, in 1982, the year of the Asian Games, Sikhs are pulled off buses on the borders of Delhi. The next year – 1983 – brings massacres and terror on night buses. Bhindranwale, taking Shabeg Singh with him, moves into the Golden Temple, into the precincts of the shrine itself. *And then*, in June, 1984 . . .'

'Blue Star?'

'Blue Star, yes: Mrs G sends tanks into the temple, signing, in effect, her own death warrant.'

Recalling this roll call of events, he wonders why the history of these years possesses such power for him. Some of it must come from the fact that it lies on the edge of his memory, on the edge of lived life. But some of it is surely real. The details! Done, as if by an artist's hand. First, the shrine – later, the scene of the siege – in whose frilled arches there is always the reflection of water, always dancing veins of gold; then the liturgy that never ceases, even once the firing begins; and then, the cool and magical impression the tank around the temple makes even on a hot day. And June would have been hot! What menace there is in thinking of this beguiling shrine as the backdrop for the battle. The water clouded purple; blue-turbaned men firing from the gaps in the marble stairs; the trapped pilgrims, the white sky, the dazzle of sunlight on water; and then, the village priest and renegade general caught in a Hitlerian trap, even as the army closes its clumsy circle around them.

'And when it was over,' Skanda says aloud, 'Blue Star, that is, people were left with a terrifying spectacle: the charred shell of the Akal Takht – the seat of the Timeless one.'

Gauri's face is turned away, but he can sense she's listening.

'It had been built a foot higher than the throne of the Mughal Emperor in Delhi, and it was the ultimate symbol of Sikh defiance, of their unwillingness ever to accept overlords. So, the sight of it destroyed like that was a signal to every Sikh, believing or unbelieving, that there would be retribution. Paid and repaid in double measure. That now the blood would begin to flow.'

'You're such a drama-baaz,' she says, laughing.

'But it's true, Gauri. That must have been what it felt like, for people going into that terrible winter of blood and gas.'

'Or not? Probably it just felt like any other year, with everyone caught up in the usual Diwali festivities, no?'

'I doubt it.'

'I mean, what did people feel in August '47? Or 1914? Or even 2001. I'm sure they sensed trouble was on the way, but probably you always just go around a corner before you realize that it was a turning point. And October in Delhi, as you know, is so hectic, with Diwali shopping and card parties and whatnot. Such a beautiful month, no? Not like tonight.'

'No, and especially evocative for my father.'

'Why, for religious reasons?'

'No. Because of the literature. It's a big trope in Sanskrit poetry, that season. It's the time when the skies are at last free of clouds, the autumn night washed with moonlight; a time of festival, of activities resumed after the heat and rains, a beneficent time, you know, when – what is it they say? – In the mansions of the sky, auspicious configurations become possible again; and "rivers, little by little, reveal their sandbanks as bashful women, in their first sexual encounter, reveal their loins . . ."'

'You naughty boy,' she says and laughs. 'Should we just do it here? Right now? In this dark abandoned house. On this rickety . . . what do you even call this thing?'

'An opium bed?' he offers, watching her raise herself on to its rotting mattress. 'Then? Should we go for it on this termite-infested opium bed, or will your massi find us and give us two tight ones . . . ?'

Observing his smile fade, she says: 'Skanda . . .'

'Gauri.'

'Tell me something.'

'What?'

'So, it all came together that October, or what?'

He nods.

Yes, he thinks, that October, with the air in the evenings, now chilly, now smoky, now cloyingly sweet with the scent of saptaparni, it did all come together.

It was in October that Uma, after nine years of marriage, first became aware of her restlessness. It came upon her almost as a memory of restlessness from another time. A time when it was not so much that her dissatisfactions were acute as that her wish for change was strong. The moment of discovery came as it had in 1975: in the form of signs. She looked feverishly for them in the world around her. Skanda might ask, 'Mama, does aberrant mean something repugnant, something hateful?' 'No, Skandu, that is abhorrent you're thinking of.' And, suddenly, not one paragraph down, in the book she was reading there it was: abhorrent. Why had the word appeared magically like that at the very moment when Skanda had asked its meaning? It was not a common word. What was it that attracted these coincidences? And, in those days, there seemed to be many. Numbers; dates; words. Odd, and seemingly pregnant, synchronicities showing up out of nowhere. Odder still was her wish for them to keep coming, and for them to mean something.

She was surprised to find herself reading horoscopes. She waited for hers every day in *The Hindustan Times*, reading it over Rudrani's shoulder as she brushed her hair, trying to make its brief and elastic message fit the contours of her life. She ignored the romantic bits, as one does temptation and infidelity. She concentrated instead on the career advice, which she adapted to her life as a housewife. She looked, all the while, for hints of change: for cataclysm, even; anything that would reconfigure her life. One day, well into her having become a hawkish addict of the future, her daughter asked her a question with that cruel simplicity that is a child's alone.

'Mama,' she said, as Uma, putting Rudrani's hair into pigtails, pulled apart thick black bands baubled with red plastic strawberries, 'why do you read the horoscope?'

There was no reason to have felt it as an accusation; no reason to have felt it as sharply as she did; it was an innocent question; it could easily have been deflected. But, for some reason, it tore off the protective screen behind which reflection and self-examination lay. And what was laid bare in that instant was her unhappiness. She felt come thick and choking into her heart, mind and throat, pulling at the lachrymals, an answer: *Because I desperately want something to happen to me.*

She did not say it aloud, but no sooner had it been admitted into her heart than it set to work, undoing her faith in what till then she had believed to be nine happy years of married life. She was perhaps especially sensitive that morning to such an anti-narrative. For only a few hours before she had received a call from Priti Purie – yes, the very same one! The Admiral's daughter who had first got her into flying. But not Purie now: Hirachand. She had made good on the eternal promise of the airlines: trolley to lolly. She had found a rich businessman husband – a biscuit tycoon! – while flying, 'and, Mishi darling, what can I say? He grounded me.'

To hear that clear crisp voice, still full of the shrill optimism of the convent, was disconcerting. After a gap of a decade, for it was at least that long since she had last heard it, it came through over the telephone that October morning like a broadcast from another country. Uma felt the light of appraisal fall over her own life. It made her contemplative; it was a sudden reminder of the passing of time. She found her own voice – not faltering, no . . . but unable to compete with the rich timbre of Priti's. There was something busy about that voice: it was full of news. Priti's life, which she had made in Bombay, seemed more vital than her own. It was a life of travel, of dinner parties and turnovers; it reeked of sex.

It made Uma aware of the placidity of the morning scene around her, in her own flat, a scene that was like a microcosm of her life: Skanda watching a film on the VCR; Toby, reading the newspaper – full of bad news from Punjab – about to sit down to a morning of work. Which, even after all these years, remained impenetrable to her, seemed to lack an arc or sense of purpose, but consumed him entirely. It was not that Uma was dissatisfied with what she saw around her; it was just that she was, for the first time, aware of it. So, it was not that she thought: *Oh, how awful my life is*, but, rather, *Oh, this is my life*. All of it, and there might never be anything more.

Had she thought there would be? Yes. Yes, she had. Not necessarily in material terms. True: Toby was not as rich now – or, at least, did not have as much money on hand – as when she married him. Court cases with his sister; land ceiling acts; a portion of the rent lost from the flat in London; translations and the publication of his textbook held up – these things had eaten away at his income. But Toby would never be poor. And there was very little she wanted that they could not afford. There had been foreign holidays; months in Gulmarg over the summer; the children' school, clothes, birthday parties . . . No, none of this had been a problem. In fact, she almost wished it had. For it might have given their life together a kind of urgency? A pulse? A charge? All the things that she sensed the presence of in Priti's voice – sex, money, travel – were there in her life too, but in smaller amounts with each passing day. Her life had widened out like the Tamasā at Kalasuryaketu and, though full of breadth and volume, it seemed hardly to flow.

She had done things to give it meaning. She had, when the children were very young, worked at the Playhouse school; that was fine so long as the children were there. But once they went on to real schools, it had not held her. Neither had the various interests she had tried to cultivate: the sitar, which she had played in school, and tried unsuccessfully to take up again; the painting, for which she had once believed she had a genuine talent, and which had fallen away from her; she had tried to read more seriously – the classics – the canon, a concept she would hear debunked later that evening; she had even, at the height of her love for Toby, tried to learn Sanskrit. But it hadn't worked. In fact, she had come to resent Toby's passion for the language, an all-consuming passion with no care for a result. She learned with something like horror that he could be immersed in the scholarship of this language all his life, and it mattered not a jot to him whether it yielded anything. She had nothing like that in her own life. And when she asked him – first gently, and later aggressively – what he wanted from life, even in the narrow sphere of Indology, he had replied, with a smile and a phrase from the Gita: 'Mā karmaphalahetur bhūr.'

'What does that mean, Toby?! Really, what does that mean?'

He tried to explain. 'It is an important verse . . .' he began.

'Important?!' She gave a sharp and mocking laugh. 'Why is it *important*? For what, Toby?'

'It's not *for* anything, Uma.'

'Well it must be for something. You've devoted your whole bloody life to this stuff, this language. It's the only thing that excites you, and now you're teaching it to our son, as if his life depended upon it. The other day he says to me, "Women neither like nor dislike anybody; they are like cows in the forest, always seeking fresh grass" . . .'

Toby began to laugh.

'It's not funny! This is the kind of crap that you're bringing him up on.'

'Uma, it's from the Hitopadeśa.'

'I don't give an F where it's from . . .'

'He's reading it because the Sanskrit is simple. It's over ten centuries old; it's bound to contain a few anachronisms. But there's more hita in it – more benefit – than harm.'

'What benefit? How will it help him to learn this dead language?'

'It'll give him a feeling for the country he lives in, for its past, for its other languages; it'll give him a sense of how things hang together; it will deepen his sensibility.'

'But what will be gained by this "deepened sensibility"?'

'Everything, Uma. Everything is sensibility. Not just in my work; in all work, in science, in mathematics . . . Men need an idea of human possibility, of who they are, and Sanskrit—'

'Sanskrit what?'

'Sanskrit will automatically give that to him. It will help him join the dots—'

'How, Toby? How will losing himself in a lifetime of futile study help him join any dots?'

Silence.

'I'm sorry.'

'It doesn't matter.'

'No, really, I'm sorry. I didn't mean that. Please tell me what you were going to say . . .'

He looked long into her face, as if to search it for any remaining rancour. Then he said, 'It will give him the ability to see through language. Not just in India, but across the Indo-European belt. It will give him an instinctive idea of the past. And, in a country like India, where people have so few means to possess such an idea, it will give him a kind of confidence. There is a world coming into being, Uma –

not just here, but everywhere – in which nobody from here to bloody Peking on one end, and Rabat, on the other, is going to be able to tell his arse from his elbow. What Skanda knows of language will protect him; it will put him on sounder footing; he'll have a higher idea of things.'

She gave a weary smile. 'What were you saying earlier? The verse from the Gita?'

'It's nothing. It just says, one should . . . *you* should not let the fruit be the aim.'

'Of what?'

'Of action.'

She rolled her eyes; he laughed.

Some part of her growing impatience with him came, no doubt, from the impatience she sensed among others.

It was a country with a very strange relationship with foreigners; and Toby, for all practical purposes, was a foreigner. In India – unlike, say, Russia, or China – the foreigner was welcomed as a king at first. People regarded him as something rarer and more precious than they were themselves, someone who stood neutral to their own violent differences and internal suspicions. The foreigner, flattered by the attention, was feted; invited everywhere; he was encouraged to believe he had made lasting friends. And, so far so good. If, at this point, he was to leave, if he was to refresh his foreignness, as it were, he was safe. But if he stayed on and became more implicated in Indian life, if he let his foreignness wear too thin, if he married an Indian woman, say, and had half-Indian children, he was doomed. He became something repugnant to the Indians; neither a man they could assimilate into their own familiar likes and dislikes, many of which had their origin in caste, nor one they could raise above themselves. Worse: he became a fallen reminder of the glamour and power they had once invested him with. They hated him for standing aloof, they hated him even more for trying to draw nearer; he became an annoyance; a faulty mirror, rusted and flaking, in which they could see their own self-loathing. A deposed Kurtz who, in another time, they might even have sought to destroy.

Had something along these lines begun to happen to Toby? In some respects, yes. So long as he had come and gone, he had been a novelty; he had brought cheer, and news of the West, to the boredom and malaise of drawing room life; he was someone the ladies could fight over, someone through whose favour hostesses could show up their rivals; they loved that he knew them all, and yet was not compromised by belonging to any particular camp; they giggled over his exaggerated reverence for the Indian past, and allowed themselves to feel a degree of feigned shame at their own ignorance and deracination. But all this was contingent on Toby being a man of hotel rooms, of linen and safari suits, in whose pockets there might be the stubs of boarding passes – Heathrow–Palam – and loose foreign change, a large dark blue British passport, say, with the mysterious name – G.M.P.R. Kalasuryaketu – written in blue ink on the white oval window at the front. A man, in short, who could at any time be asked when he was leaving, and, from whose date of departure and port of arrival, the imagination of a Delhi grand-dame, on a hot dusty day, might extract some pleasure – from the distant and clement dream of a day spent shopping in Knightsbridge.

When he no longer could be asked when he was leaving, when he appeared every other day at their parties alongside a woman they thought no better than themselves – and some thought considerably worse – when his children went to the same schools their children went to, smashed open the same piñatas, took the same riding lessons at the President's Estate Polo Club, he became, for every notch they had placed him above themselves, twice diminished. They sneered at his learning, they rolled their eyes at his mention of classical India; they told him they loathed the sound of Sanskrit.

'But for the Indian woman,' Naipaul writes, 'a foreign marriage is seldom a positive act; it is, more usually, an act of despair or confusion. It leads to castelessness, the loss of community, the loss of a place in the world; and few Indians are equipped to cope with that.'

Did Uma feel this loss? She did. Gradually, the phone rang less and less; people were out of town a lot; and, though it seemed they saw each other as much as ever before – and Delhi people will always let you know this – they saw Toby and Uma less and less. They became an unfashionable couple; they vanished from the premier drawing rooms of the city; they came to be seen as déclassé. And, unthinkable as it might have seemed in 1975, they became more and more dependent on Uma's family, I.P., Viski and Isha – who had invited them to dinner that night – for support and company. Did it affect them? Not easy to say. What cannot be denied is that the change in their status did away with what in 1975 had been taken for granted: that it was Toby who would bring the world to Uma.

'And him?' Gauri asks. 'Your father? Why does he seem so weak?'

Skanda does not reply.

In the musty darkness of the abandoned drawing room, shot through with the light-infused fog, billowy and tumbling in, as if coming off the slide of the transom overhead, they sit on the opium bed, smoking and staring blankly out at the large empty room.

'Tell, no?' Gauri presses him.

'Tell, what?'

She comes behind him; he feels her breasts on his back; she slips her feet inside his legs, so that his balls rest on the hard skin of her heels.

'Why was he so – I don't know – dead, yaar!'

Then, placing the burning cylinder of the cigarette on the edge of the opium bed, she reaches with both hands for his penis; and, with the ease of someone removing something distasteful from her own body, squeezes out a last bead of semen from the fast-shrivelling folds of his foreskin. She holds it up before him, with a child's mixture of revulsion and delight, as if it were an insect or a blackhead, then slides it deep into the wet tube of her mouth, seeming to say, *I, for one, am not afraid of life.*

If it is her intention to intimidate, she does. A little. If to arouse, that too: nothing sexier than a girl not squeamish about these things. But, if she means to make some larger philosophical point about passion and daring, about putting one's hand in the fire, well then she must be replied to. Because it is not enough to say the other side is simply afraid of life, too weak-stomached for its big impulses, too – what are you if you're not red-blooded . . . ?

'No, Gauri. It's not just people who are *dead* who don't want scenes and dramas, who want to avoid saying what they don't mean; who – yes! – want in some ways to be unassailable; whose definition of love is not a cycle of big fights and big make-ups; who don't want to get themselves dirty in the shit pool of uncontrolled emotions—'

'I lost you: too many negatives. Are you saying people should be like this or should not be like this?'

'I'm saying that this is not the only definition of being alive. There is such a thing as an internal life, a life of contemplation, a life of peace on the surface, and a long labour below; it need not be written off as "dead". Or, un-Indian . . .'

'Un-Indian?' she says with genuine surprise.

'You know perfectly well what I mean: land of spices, hot weather, melodrama, Bollywood . . . Anyone who wishes to be a little more low-key, written off as a wuss, a foreigner, someone who doesn't have what it takes . . .'

'What are you getting so worked up for?'

'I'm not getting worked up. And, if you want me to get worked up, all you have to say is, "What are you getting so worked up for?"'

Silence.

One cigarette is extinguished, another continues to burn, though its cycles are shorter and fiercer.

'Sorry.'

'I don't know what got you started.'

Gauri lights up again.

'Tell me what happened to your uncle, I.P.?'

After a prolonged silence, he says, 'We must go and find this party.'

'Skanda . . .'

'Nothing happened, Gauri. He was picked up the night before Diwali by the cops. He vanished into Tughlak Road Police Station. That's all. You know Tughlak Road Police Station? Where there is now a metro stop and a newly whitewashed police building, and where the cops – such is their new sensitivity! – have preserved an arch from the British days. That is where I.P. spent some of his last nights in India. And were it not for our servant Narindar, ending up there himself for some rowdy behaviour on Diwali night, we might never even have found him. It was what my grandmother, poor woman, could never get over. They kept looking for him all over the city – pulling every damn string in the business – and, all the time, he was just down the road, shouting distance, almost . . .'

'And what? This was Diwali time?'

'The night before the amāvasyā. Which does not, by the way, mean moonless; it means a dwelling together – amā, together; vas, to dwell. The night the sun and moon dwell together and, so, moonless because—'

'I get it, Skanda, I'm not an idiot: the moon, busy *dwelling* with the sun, fails to makes its appointment in the sky. The dwelling together, I get it. It's lovely.'

That night Toby, Uma and I.P. remained together a long time. Frosted light fell from the keystone of the sunken arch outside their flat, and made loom the shadows of creepers. The air was cold and dense and particled from watchmen's fires and crackers. There was a feeling of warmth from within the house, of children asleep or nearly asleep; their young uncle, in blue jeans and a white shirt, a Scotch in his hand, had come out to say goodbye to the departing adults. Uma, in a black and gold sari, leaned against their blue Willy's jeep, in which a single orange light burned, and Toby's fingers rested against the perforated face of an engine heater.

The familiarity of the scene concealed her unhappiness that night. Her dissatisfactions remained; they were, in fact, built into the shape of her life, but, seen from another angle, they seemed, as with a flight of Penrose stairs, to vanish, seemed almost to be a trick of the eye.

The familiarity that was secretly galling to Uma – that same force of habit – was reassuring to Toby. He felt none of her ambiguity. He had around him all that he wanted from life. He was not blind to his wife's restlessness – he had noticed the rolling eyes, noticed her impatience with him – but he could not imagine the world otherwise. Nor was he wrong to trust in this blind way to habit, for it is so often what keeps people together, just as a cataclysm, an event in the world beyond, can make real the possibility of a life apart.

An event such as this – the kind that shows us the cracks within – entered Toby and Uma's life one Wednesday and was gone the next. Wednesday – the 24th – was the amāvasyā, Diwali. On the 31st – a week later – Mrs Gandhi was killed. *All the interim is like phantasma.* It made the Tuesday – the night of the dinner at Curzon Road – stand out in both their minds. If for nothing else than the pretty banalities of that night. I.P. leaned against the arch, sipping his whisky, while Uma was brushing off the powdery whitewash from his jeans. The lights in the flat within. The odour of mothballs and old perfume in Uma's shawl, newly removed from steel trunks for the winter. The diesel-smell in the Willy's; the cold Rexene seats . . . later, they came all to feel, these banal details, like an achievement. They were proof, even when the world that made them possible crumbled, of their nine years together.

The sight of Uma freshly bathed and dressed and ready for the evening, especially if she was wearing a sari, the tips of her hair wet, her skin, soft and scrubbed, held great power for Toby. It was like a ritual re-enactment of their earliest attraction for one another. And, every time she came out like this, perfumed, her hair brushed, ready to go out, he assumed the grateful expression of a man who had been granted a fresh start. He liked nothing more, in these first moments, than to follow her with his eyes, even as she wore an air of distraction about her which seemed to conceal the coyest and most touching concern – the kind that never leaves a woman, no matter how much age or weight or illness ravage her beauty – for how she was looking. In the past, he might have done something, even while they were still in the flat, and she was pacing about in search of things to put in her evening bag, to break through the protective layer of her abstractedness and feast on the shyness he knew to lie beneath. But now, after children, that rite, for it invariably involved an intimacy, was confined to the moments before he turned the key in the jeep's ignition.

It might be a long meaning look; a hand on hers; the fixing of an earring that sat badly on her earlobe. A tiny tenderness. Nothing, really. Nothing, and, yet, all. And not so nothing that he did not now sense her impatience with it. The gesture rebuffed, the hand removed. She was like a woman afraid of betraying her own grievance, afraid to let habit encircle her again. But, because it was nothing she was brushing off, she could also say, when asked what the matter was, if everything was all right, that it was 'Nothing'. Then, masking her earlier irritation with a smile, she might add, 'It's just that we'll be late; that's all.' *Late? Late by five minutes for a dinner at her sister's?!* An inward thought, for, if he put it into words, he could be sure he would be accused of making something out of nothing.

Theirs was not the only house in which the week of Diwali that year – 1984 – came to feel like a ceasefire in a larger conflict, a spontaneous laying down of arms – 'Stille Nacht' carrying up into the night air of a field in Flanders.

In the house on Curzon Road, Viski had been raging for months. He had thundered abuse against the Brahmin's daughter on Safdarjung Road; he had, eyes bloodshot, beard hoary and fierce, slammed down closed fists on dinner tables; he had, in a state of anger verging on tears, been led away on more than one occasion by Isha. The features of that solemn Jat face, which, even when at rest, had something martial and bellicose in them, and in which there was in equal measure the potential for joviality and thunder, had since the trouble in Punjab darkened permanently. The drawing room set felt that he took it all too seriously. But they did not know what it was like for a proud and – it must be said – warlike people to suddenly, and with Dreyfusian insidiousness, find they had, in a city they thought they knew, in a city some felt they had built, become overnight the object of suspicion. And for the Sikhs, whose entire sense of self dwelt in notions of honour, of iron-spined courage, of holding one's head high, to have a distrustful and sceptical eye – and a Hindu one at that! – look askance at them . . . Oh, it was galling.

In his more drunken moments – it was true – Viski's anger at what he saw happening around him turned fast into chauvinistic rage. 'The little fuckers,' he would begin, when he was sure there was not a Hindu in sight, 'time and again, they've come running to us, with their balls in their mouth, black faces terrified, quaking in their bloody chappals. "Save us, Save us! Sword-arm of Hinduism. Our women are being raped, our children massacred." And time and again, we have risen to fight the invader, whether he be Muslim, British or Chinese. Time and again Sikh regiments have stood like a bloody wall behind the Hindu. In all the wars, it was us – us in 1947 against Pakistan, us in 1962 against China, us, again, in 1965 against Pakistan and *us* in 19 bloody 71 – who were out there fighting. Sikhs! General Shabeg, a bloody war hero. Why did he turn on the state? Why was he in there fighting alongside Bhindranwale in the Golden Temple? I'll tell you why, I'll tell you – I'm not afraid to say it – the treachery of the Hindu! As much as there is courage and honour in our blood, there is treachery and cowardice in his. Smiling badh-badh-ding-ding treachery. Under all that head-shaking – "yes sir, no sir, two bags full, sir" – treachery. Shabeg Singh, a bloody war hero, and you sack him in disgrace, two months before he is due to retire? Why? Because he uses a couple of army trucks to transport cement to a retirement home he's building?! Are those grounds on which to dismiss the hero of Bangladesh? The man without whom there would have been no Mukti Bahini?! I ask you!'

Viski's forefathers had been liberators of the Golden Temple. When Massa Rangarh turned the shrine into a den of vice, a place of louche parties and dancing girls, it was his mother's ancestor who had gone in there and separated Massa's head from his body. Both Viski's grandfathers had been in Punjab politics. His mother, after she was thrown out from the house on Curzon Road, had defeated her father-in-law, Viski's grandfather, in a famous election. And only the other day – before the siege – she had arrived in her Mercedes at the Golden Temple, when it was infested with militants, and made a speech warning those who dared to hang their undies in the house of the guru, that they would meet a sticky end. All around her there had been the crackle of AK-47s being fired into the air. But old Teji Kaur was unperturbed. After delivering this brave speech, she completed her circumambulation of the shrine and sailed away in her magenta Mercedes.

But Mrs Gandhi's siege of the temple had stopped her mouth, as it had Viski's. It had left them all part of a great collective silence. A silence that had prevailed since June that year. The strangest thing. It was as if an entire community, on seeing the spectacle of the Akal Takht, charred and ruined, had held their breath together. Not in a threatening or ominous way – though that was the effect – but almost in a half-curious way, for as Viski would later say, 'You see, we all knew, every Sikh worth his salt knew, that for what she had done the witch would die . . . it was just a question of how.'

On the night before Diwali, when everyone was due at the house on Curzon Road, Isha had made Viski promise: 'Please, I beg of you, no politics tonight. No Punjab, no Blue Star, no nothing.' And, in truth, he was not in the mood either. He was in a festive mood and dressed splendidly in a peach-coloured pug with an olive-green safa, his grandfather's buttons gleaming on his bandgala. The same grandfather whose name wound its way around the perimeter of the drawing room in curly mosaic letters, and where that evening there was a great feeling of pre-Diwali cheer and festivity. Of card tables; of bank notes; of clear beakers of soda in which bubbles fizzed and died on the surface. Men in white, the blue R of the Raj embroidered onto their pockets, threaded their way around the Formica tables – not baize, for even the rich were not rich in those days! – laying down bottles of whisky and unopened decks of cards.

It was the kind of room where the chandeliers were crystal but the light in them was dim, the drops a little dusty. Viski's grandfather – because he had worked on the Vice-Regal palace itself – had had special access to the best stone. And it was these aspects of the room – the floors, the Jaisalmer stone around the fireplaces, the art deco pelmets, of a rich honeyed wood – the things that endure, and that socialism cannot beggar, not, at least, immediately, that survived the ravages of that time and remained beautiful. Otherwise, the upholstery on the sofa, though with an attractive patina, had grown stiff and coarse over the years; the cutlery was fine silver, mixed in with stainless steel; there were some beautiful glasses, but others no better than what one would find in a cheap hotel. Everywhere, as with the fine old cars outside, Jaguars and Pontiacs whose engines had collapsed, and into which Viski's parasitical cousins threatened to install Suzuki engines, there was the evidence of decay. Of genteel poverty. Of great personal style whose decline was being painstakingly managed. It was a room that awaited either further destruction, final and swift; or else breath-taking renewal from the ground up.

Viski circled it, a cigarette in his hands – for that was the kind of Sikh he was: irreligious to his nicotine-stained fingertips – checking to see if there was enough Scotch in the bar, if the coals in the angithis on the veranda burned brightly enough, if the giant slab of ice he had ordered had arrived, if the caterers from the hotel, in their bulb-lit encampment of great iron vessels and red gas cylinders, were setting up. He was in a festive mood, but an unsettling thought – for once, unrelated to Punjab – played darkly at the back of his mind.

He had received a call that morning from his sister-in-law, Mishi – still Mishi to him. She had a friend in town, from her days in the airlines. A girl who'd made good. Married some businessman in Bombay. Priti Purie; he remembered her vaguely, Admiral Purie's daughter: pretty Priti. Mishi wanted to bring her and her husband – Shashikanta Hirachand, a biscuit tycoon – to their dinner that night. Such a small thing; she needn't even have asked. 'Of course,' he had said, 'this is your house.'

But it had sat badly with him, the idea of having a businessman, who no one knew, come to his house; which, it was true, would spoil the intimacy of the evening. But no; Mishi could bring whoever she wanted. It was not that; it was something else. Something in the decorousness of her tone which had made him suspicious; something clipped and over-polite, as though formality were being used to conceal some rougher emotion. And, as he went about his inspection of the house, Viski realized that he knew what that tone was: it was the unmistakable tone of a woman wanting to bring to the house of an unsuspecting friend or family member the man she is having an affair with. Had it been a man Mishi wanted to bring over, Viski would immediately have drawn those connections. But a woman? An old friend from the airlines? Why did her voice have that note of strangled excitement?

Whatever it was, it made him sorry for Toby. This city, this country, he had seen it wear down his old friend's confidence. He had seen it bring a note of apology to his face, seen it shame him for his sensibility and knowledge. There had been nothing more dazzling than the Toby of the seventies; the Toby of Oxford, of the flat on Cheyne Row. Toby, who used all his royal connections so as just to be able to sit for hours on end in some musty library in Bikaner, studying old manuscripts. The Toby who had told him of eighth-century literary theorists in India and who had patiently answered all his questions about history and migration; Toby, from whose lips he had first heard the words Proto-Indo-European; the same man, who, mildly and persuasively, had corrected each of his prejudices. Viski had watched Delhi, through the cold light of its neglect, make Toby's great erudition seem worthless.

'I say, Shashi-cunt, fellow . . .!'

'Kānta, Viski,' Isha said, trying hard to calm the tension that had arisen between the two men sitting at the card table. 'Kānta.'

'Hello, fellow! I thought it was cunt, like nīla-cunt, the blue-throated one . . .'

'Firstly, Viski,' Isha said, emphasizing the third of Sanskrit's five nasals, 'that's kaṇṭha.'

'Cunṭ?'

'No, aṇṭha, ṇ, ṇ,' Isha said, exposing her teeth, and drawing her tongue back into her mouth, in a retroflex motion, so that its ridged back and blue vein were visible.

'Ṇ, ṇ, ṇ,' Viski repeated, like a chastened child.

Everyone at the table smiled slyly into their cards. Except, of course, Shashikanta Hirachand.

'Kaṇṭha, kānta, can't you hear the difference?'

'I say, fellow,' he said, his eyes bright with mischief, 'she's like bloody Professor Higgins . . . kaṇṭha, kānta, can't. You tell us, O Sanskritist, which is it: Shashi kaṇṭha, kānta or Shashi-can't, can or won't. Or just plain cunt . . .'

'Viski!' And, flaring her eyes, Isha silenced him.

'Why don't you ask him, whose name it is?' Kitten Singh said, with that syntax that was every bit her own. In the pause that followed the arch musicality of her question, her thin red lips gleamed. She rearranged her three-card hand in her soft and veined fingers, which, large and blazing with rings, had the immobility and heavy ornamentation of a pair of cicada wings.

'*Because*, Kitty-kat,' Viski said, taking a deep sip of his Scotch, 'my dear brother-in-law, my dear, dear, brother-in-law, he knows more about these things than – please forgive me, Shashi-can or can't – the average native. Shall we do a test? What say you, fellow? First we ask Shashi-can or can't – I don't know! – what his name means? Then we ask brother-in-law, here, and see who gives us – how does one put it? – the fuller answer. Yes: the fuller answer. What say you, Hirachand? Eh? What does your name mean?'

The businessman smiled insolently into his moustache. He had for some time now become the target of a scarcely suppressed rage in Viski, but he was not without his share of blame. When they had first sat down at the table, Viski had been courteous enough. But one or two things had occurred in quick succession to set the evening on its unfortunate path. The first little irritation was Hirachand's request that they introduce variations into the game, ridiculous things with ridiculous names, like AK-47 and Tambu mein Bambu, which for that generation of purists was an inadmissible corruption of the game. When everyone on the table objected, Hirachand began churlishly to play his every hand blind. Then, when three rounds later, he had still not picked up his cards and Viski said, 'What, fellow? Blind again?', Hirachand gave a pedantic answer, which only further annoyed Viski. He detected in it that smiling Indian smugness which was just the thing he had in mind when he spoke pejoratively of the badh-badh-ding-ding Hindu.

'I know, you Delhi-wallas,' Hirachand said, 'are very fond of your teen patti. But speaking strictly on the level of probability, which must ultimately be the level upon which all games of chance are decided, this beloved game of yours is extremely flawed.'

'Oh,' Viski said.

'Yes. Because, speaking strictly on a probability basis, a Trio should not rank higher than a Pure Sequence. It is analogous to a pair being higher than a sequence. So, please, I will, in light of this logical flaw, play my every hand blind.'

Had he said nothing else all evening – into which Viski would have read many things: *chippy little Bombay businessman*; *greedy Gujarati bania can't bear to part with his money*; *coward Hindu*; *nerdy snitch*; *vegetarian!*; *just the kind of punk I used to thrash in school* – this remark alone would have been enough to damn him in Viski's eyes. But Hirachand, blithe and contented, seemed bent on a course of further self-destruction. And, as conversation turned, as it so often does in Delhi, to politics – to the toppling, in fact, of Tariq Mattoo's government in Kashmir earlier that year – Hirachand, in a tone of studied boredom, as if concealing the pain of exclusion, said, 'Ah yes, you Delhi people, you like so much to talk about politics.'

Isha saw Viski's face sour and said, 'He's a friend, you see, Tariq. That's all. We were up there when his government fell. He was giving the kids rides on his motorbike in Pahalgam, while Mrs Gandhi was toppling him in Srinagar!'

She had meant it as a joke, something to lighten the air. But it was lost in what Hirachand said next.

'Friend or no friend,' he said, his voice full of taunting righteousness, 'she had no choice but to dismiss his government. What else could she have done? Muslim CM conspiring with Khalistanis to break the country up again. She had to fight these fissiparous tendencies. Someone had to!'

Fissiparous tendencies! So quaint and obscure a phrase today, almost like irredentism. But, in those days, it was as much in vogue as Islamo-fascism today. And, on that table, the echo of this remark, more for its banality, its *Pravda*-ish adherence to the party line, than any offence it caused, reverberated in the long silences that are an invariable part of the rhythm of conversation on a card table. In the heavy interim, between the making of a move and the resumption of conversation, no one said anything, but everyone seemed to look longer and harder at their cards; the sipping of a drink, the lighting of a cigarette acquired a noirish significance.

It was Toby's turn.

And he might well not have said anything either. He had seen an ugliness creep into the public discourse over the past many years, an ugliness that seemed, as with so many other evils, to have been introduced into the system in those years after the Emergency. More and more, Toby had learned to hold his tongue. The remark which in 1975 would have produced a severe rebuke – akin to the one he had once given Maniraja – was in 1984 the kind of thing he might let slide. For one of the peculiarities about prejudice is that it seems always to speak from the heart; it seems, in some daring way, to be speaking the truth, to be saying what others secretly believe, but do not have the courage to say themselves. And the man who speaks against prejudice can often come to seem like the peddler of shop-worn banalities, while the voice of prejudice can seem bold and original; a lone voice with the power to drown out others, the power to subdue.

But that night, for a number of reasons, Toby did not feel subdued. He did not feel the crippling effect of a reserve that had become second nature to him. For one, he was drinking large drinks – Viski's trademark – Old Monk, nimbu and soda. Two, he had a brilliant hand – a seven trail – which is enough to make even the meek feel bold. And, three, Uma was provoking him.

From the time they had arrived at Curzon Road there was something exaggerated about her. In her excitement at seeing Priti Purie; in her embraces and girlish laughter; in the showy fun she seemed to be having. It was as if, compared with her earlier sullenness in the car, she was trying to tell him how relieved she was to be out of the house, away from him, away from their life together. These things can always seem – in fact, they're intended to seem – like figments of our imagination. But he knew he was not imagining it. Her excitement was contrived and stagey. It had an edge; it was as if she wanted to ward him off. Never had fun seemed so much like rage.

Rebuffed a few times, and gradually drunker, he seemed to absorb the rage too. He let the old enemy of their relationship, Kitten Singh, her hair now wilfully grey, bringing to her yet unlined face a severity and gravitas, flirt shamelessly with him. He allowed Viski to make him drink after stronger drink. He began also to make a show of having a good time. In this mood, angry and a little wretched, he sat down to cards on Viski's table. The room, by then, was full of people. In the din of noise and laughter the card tables felt, as with clearings in a forest, like pools of calm and quiet, with a life all their own. It was soothing to withdraw to them.

But there was that one discordant note on their table: Hirachand. Everyone noticed and slowly the table began collectively employing long silences and hidden allegiances to undermine him.

'Fissiparous tendencies!' Toby said, with a smile, laying down his chal in the cut-glass bowl at the centre of the table. 'I suppose we'll be hearing of the foreign hand next.'

Viski gave a snorting laugh. Kitten smiled; Isha, being the hostess, suppressed hers. Nikhil Mohapatra, who hadn't said a word thus far, and was precariously balancing a Dunhill in the same smooth dark fingers in which he held his cards, mumbled, 'Charges of treason? Blasphemy? The burning of a witch perhaps?'

'Fellow!' Viski cried. 'An auto-da-fé, I say!'

Everyone began to laugh. The noise of it drew Uma and Priti, who had been smoking at a distance, nearer. Hirachand, seeing his wife approach, felt emboldened. He said to Toby, his English suddenly in retreat, 'You, as foreigner, must best be knowing about the foreign hand.'

Toby, feeling Uma's eyes on him, sensing that she was observing the tension and thought him its cause, and would interpret it as an insult to her friend visiting from Bombay, wanted to put an end to it all. He muttered, 'Rather have a foreign hand than a blind one.'

This made Viski – and no one else – laugh out loud.

But now, for some mysterious reason – perhaps it was the delayed effect of Hirachand's earlier remarks – it was Viski who seemed in some drunken and half-mocking way to take real offence. 'Bilqul sayi keya, main kehnde hun bhaga do behnchodh firangiyun nu.'

Hirachand, presuming Toby had not understood, replied in curt Hindi, 'I'm not saying that. But the threat of the foreign hand is real.'

'Absolutely,' Viski thundered, still in Punjabi, 'that's why I say. Let this son-of-a-bitch foreigner not even play his bloody foreign hand. Now, this minute, let's send him packing.'

Hirachand, lured into the trap, gave a contented little laugh. He winked at his wife; a boyish wink that seemed to say, *Don't worry, I'm fine, darling. I'm having fun. Everyone here likes me.* Toby's face, three-card-poker straight, gave nothing away.

'What do you say, Uma?' Viski continued, 'what should we do with the little foreign spy. Chase him off?'

Uma smoked and made no reply. But Hirachand, now wildly amused, for nothing excites the provincial more than a bit of xenophobia, said, 'How are you talking, man? To his wife, you are saying such things?'

After a pause, Toby said, mixing Punjabi, Hindi and English, 'I know, Viski! Tu vi had karda. Wife de saamne meri beizzati.'

The joke unveiled, a little laughter rose from the table. Hirachand saw that it had been on him all along. But Viski was not satisfied and soon they were at the point where Viski, ever more aggressive, was saying, 'What say you, Hirachand? Eh? What does your name mean?'

Hirachand, who could see now that sympathy was coming over to his corner, played the victim. He said, in response to Viski's question, 'Shashi means moon. And Kānta,' he added carefully, 'means beloved, desired . . .'

'Oh, moon, does it?' Viski said, cutting him off, 'We'll see about that, my little desirable cunt.'

'Viski!' Isha said, seeing how upset Uma was becoming.

'No, now no "Viski!"' Viski said. 'I'm going to show this little punk who the foreigner is. Go on, tell me why does shashi mean moon?'

'Why does it mean moon? It means moon because it means moon. Why does moon mean moon?'

'Oh, getting clever, cunty-wunty? Brother-in-law, why don't you tell us, why does shashi mean moon?'

'Viski,' Toby said, glancing up at Uma, 'I'm not playing this game.'

'And why? Have I been discourteous? Can we not sometimes say something back too?'

'Very discourteous, Viski. Now stop it,' Isha said.

'I will not stop it. This little pilpilla toad thinks the whole bloody country belongs to him. Thinks, just because he's got a few CR in the bank, and a reedy little moustache, that he's the great defender of Indian culture. Defender, my foot. When the invader was coming, it was our lot, and Raja saab's lot, who were defending this country. While this little shopkeeper here was rolling over onto his back and dreaming of akhand Bharat! Ha! I'm not leaving this table,' Viski said and brought an open palm face down on the surface of the card table, causing it to shudder, the glasses to tinkle and the banknotes in the kitty to fly up, 'until Raja saab tells him what his damn name means.'

'Tell him, please,' Isha hissed, looking desperately up at Toby. Who could feel Uma's eyes on him. The table was rigid with tension. Only Hirachand, knowing that he now had everyone stitched up, was serene.

'If I tell him, Viski,' Toby said at last, 'will you stop all this?'

'I will,' Viski said with drunken solemnity, placing a palm on his heart. 'God swear.'

'Śaśa,' Toby said, with a sigh, 'like the German *Hase*, means hare. Śaśin, of which śasī is the nominative singular, means hare-possessed or having a hare. It is called that because the spot on the moon was thought to resemble a hare. For the same reason the moon is known as śaśāṅka – a bahuvrīhi – "whose mark is the hare."'

'I say!' Viski thundered. 'How lovely! Now was that so painful?' And suddenly he was playful again. He turned to Isha and said with a broad grin, as if Hirachand was their son, 'See, I just wanted the boy to learn.'

Hirachand, his wife behind him, her hand coming slowly to rest on his shoulder, rose without a word and left the table.

It all occurred on that practically moonless night. The next day – Diwali morning, the 24th – the sun was late coming up. Its pale wintery disc – sooty, orange, anaemic – rose over Deep Fatehkotia walking to Toby and Uma's flat in search of I.P. She wore her sneakers and salwar kameez, a harassed lock of silver hair falling over her forehead. Deep, who when she had had nothing to complain about, complained continually, but who now, when faced with a real crisis, and every right to throw her fists up at the sky, was eerily calm. So calm it was as if she feared the force of her emotion; or else, she was insulated by some deep martial instinct which, dormant within her, must have for centuries, like an opiate or paralysing enzyme, protected the women of her tribe from the pain of losing sons in battle; or perhaps it was the doctrine of her faith, which, founded in a time of persecution, was never so contemptuous of anything as it was of weakness, that allowed her to walk over to Toby and Uma's flat on that dismal Diwali morning in search of I.P., as if she had come looking for a lost pair of spectacles.

*

'But first,' Skanda says, 'there were a few more hours of darkness.'

'What is this looping,' Gauri says. 'Why must we keep going round and round . . . ?'

'Because that is how things really are. And all the old books, Gauri – the ones that were oral before they were written – were ring-shaped, concentric, more an echo than an arc. My professor at Columbia, Theo Mackinson, his whole study of the epics was this: ring-theory. The repeating and rippling shape of life. But where were we?'

'I.P.'

'I.P.! He was such a comfort to them that night, to the couple returning home jangled from an ugly fight. They found him asleep on the sofa, *Midnight's Children* on his chest, the dregs of a drink on the coffee table. He jumped up when he heard them come in, and, even in his sleepy state, sensed their tension and did all he could to disperse it. He saw that his brother-in-law was distraught and sat up late with him talking of, what, you know?'

'Of what?' she says, indulging him.

'Of the Russians! Such a subcontinental thing to do, no? To bury what is difficult and painful in cerebral things. To let the intellect soak up the blood from a fight. This is what we do. Not because we lack sensitivity, but because we lack the right language for emotion. English has such a jealous hold over us, but it is a hard and brittle thing in our hands. It doesn't suit the easy melodrama of our natures. And it has a way of making matters of the heart seem at once inert and deeply shameful. So what do upper-class Indian men do when they are too wretched to do anything else? They talk of the Russians! Of Dostoevsky and Belinsky, of "cultural schizophrenia" and "the lackeyishness of thinking". Ah, Gauri . . .'

'What is it, janum?'

'That they should have got I.P.!'

'Don't!' Uma hissed, into the diesel-infused darkness. She sat there frigid, statuesque in shawls and silk. Her features, etched angrily onto the thin plate of her face, shone in the orange light, bullet-sized and burning in the dash board. Toby removed his hand and, in a gesture that was like a sigh, draped it over the gear shift. Priti's voice, light and airy, broke in from the back, 'A heater. How quaint, my dear. I haven't seen one in years. I don't think we have them in Bombay any longer.'

The Bombay/Delhi rivalry! That was all pretty Priti had picked up of the tensions that arose that night. And it insulated her from the ugliness of the truth, which, in any case, she was in no position to understand. She had remained light and insouciant throughout. Pretty Priti till the end. She saw the job of defending her husband as nothing more than scoring the odd point for the Bombay team.

Hirachand was grimmer. He knew what had been at work that evening; he understood caste and its prejudices. He knew he had been the victim of that one caste prejudice that people still felt free to express openly: the prejudice against the bania. This man, whether he came in the form of a merchant, a moneylender, a trader or businessman, an industrialist or tycoon, was a central feature of social organization. And all society's tension, its edge, as it were, came from the existence of this avatara of money. A man to whom, beyond the usual accusations of cowardice, weakness and deceit, people even attributed colours and special textures of skin. 'Oooh that special bania blackness, blue blackness,' one might hear someone say, 'I haven't seen it in years.' Another might speak of his awful sallow colour: the unhealthy pulpy texture of his skin: the result, no doubt, of generations of vegetarianism. 'Mota lala pilpilla.' Even the Shudra, lowly thing, had pluck in him enough to spit on the name of the bania. 'Aggarwal, thooh! Gupta, thooh, Hirachand thooh . . .' It was as if the name itself – like Goldman, and all other names which contain gems and precious metals – was branded with caste.

Hirachand, playing at being the aggrieved party, and an insulted guest, kept up a forgiving and generous exterior, which only deepened the bitterness between husband and wife. Nothing like magnanimity to really drive the knife in! He pretended nothing had happened; and when, a little while before, Toby, shamed by his wife, had come up to apologize and to offer him a ride home, he gladly accepted.

In the jeep, making its way through deserted Delhi streets, over which there was the persistent crackle of fireworks, giving the city the air of the capital of an insurgency – Diyarbakir or Jaffna – the Hirachands kept up a lively banter. Their seeming happiness, when seen against the silence in the front, made Toby and Uma, more than the victims, appear the losers of the evening. Unfriendly Delhi people, stewing in their own bile.

'No, sweetheart,' Hirachand said, 'we have them in Bombay too. All diesel vehicles have heaters. Trust me,' he added leaning forward, and addressing Toby and Uma, 'my friend, at whose house we're staying, makes jeeps just like this one.'

'Oh, you're staying at the house of a friend,' Uma said automatically, 'you should have stayed with us . . .' And then she stopped herself.

'Yes, his family used to have the Willy's franchise in India. They're an old business family. The group has split and he got the raw end of the deal, but he's making a lot of what he's got. A great fellow, a real bloody Hindu nut. Loves America and Israel: the exact opposite of our Indian socialist mindset. Loathes the Gandhis, of course, and is obsessed – I mean obsessed – with ancient India. In fact, Toby, I think you'd find him very interesting.'

'Yes,' Toby said, with as much enthusiasm as he could muster. He felt Uma's gaze on him through the darkness and felt he must drink from the pool of yuppy happiness in the back.

'Oh, yes. Just the other day he was showing me this paper that a professor friend of his – a fellow called Choate – had written on the Indus Valley. Marvellous stuff. It basically proves that there had been horses in pre-Aryan India.'

'Horses, Hiru?' Priti's voice sounded musically into the dank interior of the jeep. 'So what, yaar? I mean, what's the big deal if there were horses?'

'You say, Toby saab,' Hirachand said. 'Tell them.'

'Horses,' Toby began mechanically, 'are the key to proving that there was no Aryan migration. If you can prove that there were horses in pre-Aryan India, then the whole idea of the Aryans having come from elsewhere falls through. Which, it seems, is a comfort to some. Though no one,' he said quietly, feeling Uma follow his every word, 'has done that so far.'

Toby knew the professor to whom Hirachand was referring; he knew, too, that he was a fraud who had tampered with his findings.

'But this fellow has! That is what I'm telling you!'

Toby didn't reply. The car sped on, over the Safdarjung flyover, past the hulking mass of the All India Medical Institute, heavy and Sovietic, the red illuminated letters of its sign, some unlit, of course, bleak in the foggy darkness.

'Sarvaujas Enclave?' he said.

'Yes,' Priti said, seeming to make fun of the care with which he had pronounced it. 'B-17, Sarvaujas Enclave.' Then turning to Uma, she said, 'Remember, darling, Mrs Randev in Welham?'

'How can I forget her. Awful little woman. What was that little doggerel she used to teach us about farting?'

'I remember! "Tarak padyam maha punyam, tooyen phus phus narak gayam." Ha, that was all the Sanskrit I ever learnt! Or wanted to, frankly . . . no? I hate all that chanting-shanting.'

'Oh, absolutely,' Uma said icily.

The car turned into the dark empty streets of the enclave. And yes, his mind made a cat's cradle of its name. Ojas: strength, vigour, energy, power: principle of vital warmth: from *vaj* like *vigēre*, vigorous; like *augere*, augur, augus-tus, *auxilium*. These things always spoke loudest to Toby, and most privately, when he felt threatened and unsafe. Hirachand began to direct the way. The numbering of the streets was so illogical that it seemed almost deliberate, as if part of a code.

The jeep came to a halt outside a bungalow with high walls and a gate of dark wood and brushed steel. A frosted glass plaque, brightly lit from behind, and painted thickly onto it, as if part of the inevitability of that evening, were fat black letters enveloped in an aureate mist: Maniraja. B-17 Sarvaujas Enclave.

That night on the way home Toby and Uma fought about the Indus Valley. That ancient and horseless society, with its undeciphered language and famous sewage system, came to inhabit for a moment the bitter tensions of their marriage. In this sense, in the way in which they can remake reality in their image, human relationships are like works of fiction, and often the more oblique the angle to the thing they have refashioned in their likeness, the sharper the reflection.

'Don't you see, Toby, don't you see?'

'See what, Uma?'

'He was trying to bring you in. He was trying to end the evening on a pleasant note, after you and that bloody fool, Viski, were so vicious . . .'

'I was not vicious . . .'

'You were. You say you're above these things. But what I saw tonight was the ugliest kind of casteism. And then just now . . .'

'But I responded to him! I listened. What more could I have done?'

'Sounded a little enthusiastic? A little less superior perhaps?'

'Uma, he was referring to the work of a well-known fraud. The man has tampered with seals to turn bulls into horses. A couple of scholars at Harvard have had to write an article rubbishing his findings. *Horseplay in Harappa*. I'll give it to you when we get home. Read it . . .'

'I don't give a shit. Don't give me this involved inside-academia cant. All right? No one knows – or frankly really cares – about these things. But they do care that people are courteous and don't humiliate their guests.'

'Look, what Viski did was awful. But I was not party to it. And, let me tell you, old Hirachand till he got it in the neck from Viski was no saint . . .'

'He's a guest! A guest for God's sake. *My* guest. What do you always tell me a guest is in Sanskrit?'

'Atithi.'

'Atithi, right. And what does that mean?'

'You know what it means.'

'I want to hear it from you.'

'He who has no date: who may come at any time.'

'And, when he does, you're expected, in this culture you claim to revere so much, to treat him like a bloody god. Not make him feel small for not being as erudite or refined as the Delhi drawing room set. Who, in my opinion, are the shallowest, most worthless people in the world. Someone like Hirachand, he might not be as full of manners as you lot, but the future of this country is his. And you, Raja saab, should get used to that, better start swimming . . .'

'Uma, what is this really about?'

The question almost brought tears to her eyes.

'I was so looking forward to this evening. For once some new people. For once something other than this small congested world of Delhi. And we drove them away! Sent them packing. So that we could all just rot here together. Oh, Toby! I didn't marry you only to become more deeply trapped. I married you because I thought you would help me get out.'

They had crossed the Safdarjung flyover. The car slowed and veered a little to the left.

'What are you doing? Smoking? Since when are you smoking?'

He did not reply. A match in his cupped hands turned his fingers red. They drove on in silence.

The fight that was one thing in the neutrality of the car became another thing in the familiarity of the home. Outside, it had been about two people – something they so rarely were anymore; inside, the family, the sleeping children, the adored little brother asleep on the sofa, *Midnight's Children* open on his chest, all became implicated, all factors. Uma, seeing this, felt grief. She felt it was this, the imprisoning security of this, with captivity as its other face, that she had warred against in the car. And Toby had been its defender. It made her feel ungrateful, and bad. Bad to her entrails, bad and wretched, for wanting to undo all this. She knew then – and later the thought returned to her – that she would never have the courage to break this circle of safety. But if it would open on its own, even for an instant – which it did – she would slip its noose.

I.P., on hearing them come in, rose and went straight to the bar. Eyes closed, juda sliding off his head, he returned, like a somnambulant, with two large whiskies.

'Nothing for me?' Uma said caustically.

I.P. now flared his eyes wide and blinked them confusedly at her. 'No offence, Mishi didi.'

'Offence taken,' she said and strode past him.

He searched Toby's face for an explanation but found only weariness.

'Brother-in-law,' he said mockingly, 'I've been having an interesting dream.' He rubbed his eyes. 'It was about Bhakra-Nangal . . .'

'The dam?'

'The dam, yes, temples of our modern republic. Didn't old Pundit ji call them that?'

'He did.'

'Well, in my dream – it was very strange! – I was part of a group of people, surveyors or somesuch, and we were on the lake formed by the dam's waters, a massive lake, looking for the source of the water into the lake.'

'But that lake is vast, I.P. It stretches all the way from Punjab into Himachal.'

'It's a dream, sir. A dream. But it had a very weird mood. Not like the dam was breaking or anything. But the wall of the dam cast this enormous shadow. No matter how long or how far we went, we could not get away from the shadow of the dam. The sun was high, but it was dark. And we were cold in our little boat. A wooden thing with a diesel engine. There was this endless feeling of anticipation. First to cross the line of shadow, and feel the warmth of the sun, then to find the source.'

At this point Uma reappeared briefly. 'I'm off to bed.'

'Good night,' the two men said, I.P. brightly, Toby cautiously. She gave them a wintry smile and closed the door.

Observing Toby's expression darken, I.P., trying again to distract him, said, 'Toby saab, I want you to tell me something: which country do you feel most resembles India? I mean which country's problems – not just poverty and illiteracy – but, you know, big problems, cultural and civilizational ones, are most like India's?'

Toby did not answer. He could not pry his mind away from what Uma had said in the car.

'Come again?' he said, after a long pause.

I.P. smiled.

'Which country reminds you most of ours?'

'Culturally speaking,' Toby said abstractedly, 'I'd probably say Russia.'

'Russia? Why Russia?'

'I'm not sure exactly why, I.P. But I can tell you that whenever I'm reading them, the Russians – Turgenev, Tolstoy, Dostoevsky; Dostoevsky, especially – or even the biographies of these great men, I'm forever writing in the margins things like, India! or ditto India! or just like India!'

'What sort of things?'

'All sorts of things. Themes of impostorship in Dostoevsky, imitation, an anxiety about foreign influence, this perpetual balancing of Slavophilia – of trying to be true to Russia and her soul – while at the same time assimilating ideas from Europe. "The riddle of the two civilizations", you know! And then there are other similarities: the isolated elite living at a great remove from the general population . . . Speaking a different language, chasing after European fashions . . .'

'But surely we're not the only people to do that.'

'Yes, but it is something apart here. The disdain we have for our own people and their beliefs . . .'

'The elite, you mean?'

'Of course, I.P.! Don't you think?'

'I suppose, but . . .'

'I was rereading *Demons* the other day. And there is this bit in it, where Shatov, an ex-liberal of some kind, says, "It all comes from a lackeyishness of thinking . . . there's hatred there, too . . . an endless animal hatred of Russia that has eaten into their organs." Incredible! I felt I could have replaced Russia with India and I would be here, in Delhi, among the drawing room set. The lackeyishness of thinking! What a phrase, I.P., what a phrase.'

'But what is behind it?' I.P. said enthusiastically, seeing that he had succeeded in distracting Toby. 'You think it's because of the English having been here?'

'No. It must be deeper than that. There's some great unsettled anxiety among the people, an ancient anxiety, about what is ours and what is not. An old friend of mine – a writer, Vijaipal . . .'

'Of course! Who doesn't know him?!'

'He used to talk of this fear among Indians of India being a nullity, of her having nothing of her own. And I think, in some respects, he must have been right. But, tell me: why did you ask me this question, which country is most like ours?'

'I suppose I wanted a historical point of reference, something to compare India with. Because, on its own, it is such a difficult place to form an idea of. It either exists for you instinctively in the form of tradition or one is bereft of it. And reading doesn't help much. Modern Indian literature – the stuff in English, at least – isn't really up to the task, is it? It doesn't give one an idea of, as you say, the soul of the place. And our history writing is either non-existent or written by foreigners: so, an Indian reading it in India is either an infidel or a savage. Not good for the morale, you know. It can feel pretty impenetrable, at times, India.'

'It is impenetrable. And increasingly so, as time goes on. Because the confusions multiply. And what the great critic Belinsky said of Russia is true of India too: he described it as duality, but it is really schizophrenia, cultural schizophrenia. Even the modern state is so imperfect an articulation of that old idea of India: so clumsy and insecure and violent, I.P. Terribly violent.'

The two men stayed away from the more delicate subject of the evening, Toby and Uma's fight, and the tensions it had raised. Yet I.P., in drawing Toby's mind away from what had happened, managed to console him. From the moment Toby entered the flat, he had felt his warmth. He had felt it in the way that I.P., without a word, fixed them drinks, then sought his opinion; he felt his great tenderness. It was as if he had read to the deepest vibrations of Toby and Uma's fight and made it his business to make Toby feel valued. To remind him of his worth. Then suddenly, almost as if he had seen something relax in Toby's face, a dilation of the pupils into their blue and yellow irises, he felt his work was done. And he wanted to go.

'Don't be silly. Stay the night. It's almost 1 a.m. Where will you go at this hour? To Fatehkot House?'

'I promised my friend, Thud, I would go to his birthday party . . .'

'Thud?'

I.P. gave a loud laugh. 'Vicky Thaddani.'

In the morning – Diwali morning – Deep Fatehkotia walked over to the flat, a lock of silver hair falling in a spiral over her beetled brow.

'And that was Diwali morning?'

'Diwali, yes, Gauri.'

They have come to the end of the long handsomely proportioned corridor with its dust-strewn floor of marble diamonds. A pair of glass doors give onto a badminton court, a fountain, a garden, some large trees. Gazing out at this scene, of which the dividing wall will make fast work, Skanda says, 'The strangest Diwali of our lives. One of those pale wintry days, when the sun has a sickly orange colour, the air is still and smoky, and there is an appalling winter haze, the kind I've only ever seen in Delhi. Every now and then an H-Bomb will go off. You know the ones I mean? Those deafening little fuckers with their thick green thread. Such a dense and moody day! It felt like nothing would pierce its pall, let alone the faintest of faint intimations that something was wrong.'

'Was there that?'

'Oh, for sure. People coming round at all hours. The furtive ferrying back and forth between the houses. The phone calls to everybody we knew. To police stations, to hospitals, to politicians.'

'What did everyone think had happened?'

'An accident, I suppose. I.P. had not showed up at Thud's and he hadn't come home. That was all anyone knew on that first day. And people just milled about with worried expressions on their faces. Which cleared only when they feigned normalcy for our sake. Then they smiled so brightly, and tried to sound so cheerful, that it struck an even more discordant note – made us even more uneasy – than their worry.'

'Us?'

'The children. Iqbal. Fareed. Rudrani. Me.'

'You were all together?'

'Yes, as we would be again during the riots. And there was that same mood: of a kind of deep placidity, almost as if everyone was on holiday, an air of board games and idling on beds, of closed rooms and waiting. Or that, at least, was how it seemed to us. Because there was nothing to be done, you know. But, all the time, mingled with that thick calm, like a stifled sob, there was this unease, this feeling that something was wrong.'

'Did you have a Diwali at all?'

'We did, a blackish Diwali at Fatehkot House. Eventually the day just seeped into night, and just before it did, my father said, "We must do the puja; we must bathe and light the diyas; there must be Diwali."'

'"Toby, how can you . . ." my mother said.

'"No, he's right," my grandfather said – the Brigadier loved my father – "we can't just sit here all night moping about. It's bad for the morale."

'And so there was Diwali. Everyone went home and came back an hour or so later, bathed and dressed. My father led the puja. One by one, the diyas in Fatehkot House came on. There was a bit of pataka action: rockets fizzling in old beer bottles; chakris spitting sparks; children using phuljaris to burn letters into the dark. And anars – my personal favourites! – foaming at the mouth, then burning themselves out to their core. The adults drank and played cards. So, yes, on the surface, there was Diwali. But, underneath, an awful anticipation. Funny, in fact, how certain festivals of family, of feasts and renewal, seem almost to anticipate calamity.'

'The expectation, you mean?'

'Yes. But, also, that encroaching sense of carnival. Of a dark element: of mala, Gauri! And take a look at this thread: *mélas*, Greek for dark and black and obscure, enigmatic; in Sanskrit, mala, which is dirty and impure; in Latin, *mălus* means evil; in English, the semantic stream broadens out into melancholy, Melanesia, malaise.'

'I like the way that physical things – like dirt and impurity, or blackness – become their associations. It's very suggestive.'

'It is. And it was what was in the air, preparing the scene for the arrival of the messenger. In this case, a drunken Narindar, who seemed almost to embody the hysteria that had lingered all day on the margins of that black Diwali. The hysteria that everyone had worked so hard to suppress. He was every bit the breathless wheeling madman, who, full of his news, breaks onto the scene of feast and festivity like a human bomb. The messenger, Gauri! "Who, almost dead for breath, had scarcely more / Than would make up his message!"'

'And what was the message?'

'I'll tell you, I'll tell you . . .'

A realization as heavy as the fall of evening began to descend over the Fatehkotias that, whatever else had happened to I.P., it was not an accident. An accident, by now, they would have heard of. Something less serious perhaps. He might have passed out drunk at the house of a friend, say; he could have left unexpectedly for Dehradun; he might have decided to take a beautiful woman fishing. All these things, though unlikely, were possibilities. But they would have been uncharacteristic; I.P. was not without a sense of duty. And, as much as he rebelled against his mother's wish to make a feudal out of him, he would have been mortified to cause her any distress. Especially on Diwali.

The other possibility was too grim to contemplate. Neither did it really inspire the imagination. No one could think what it might be. And, yet, it was this possibility – that something worse than an accident had occurred to I.P. – that hung over the latter part of the day.

At 5.30 p.m., just as everyone was getting ready for the puja, Skanda burnt his hand. He had been trying to put a chakri on his fingers in imitation of Vishnu's flaming disc. And suddenly, as the white fire of that burning coil began slowly to unwind, it scorched him. There was no one around to hear his shrieking and, in his panic, he couldn't get the thing off. At last it was Narindar – getting ready to take off for the evening – who heard and, running up, tore the lethal little wheel from Skanda's hand.

'I'd better take him to Dr Arya,' Toby said to Uma a few minutes later. She was still in her blouse and petticoat and stared in horror at the pouchy pus-filled blisters spreading like a rash over her son's hands.

'How did he burn them . . .?'

'Main Vishnu banna chahta tha . . .' His sobbing voice, thick with tears and panic and blame somehow, filled the apartment.

'It's nerves,' Toby said over him to Uma.

'From what?' she cried, her partially made-up face distorting her expression, making it seem clownish.

'They can sense it. Rudrani's been in a state all day too.'

'Uffffff!' she replied, turning back to the mirror, and feeling in that moment overwhelmed with the emotion she had been suppressing all day. If she had so much as let the phrase, *Oh, I don't know what to do*, enter her mind, her tears would have forced their way out. She banished them, with an anger that felt like strength, and reshaped them into, 'I don't know what to say! Yes, take him, I suppose.' Which sounded colder and more heartless, but she felt she was obliged to project strength in compensation for the weakness of the men around her.

The strength of her personality put a strain on the relationship between father and son. They felt, with the exception of when Toby was teaching Skanda Sanskrit, a great awkwardness around one another. It was not edged with something unpleasant, but was more akin to what two strangers feel, when, in those first moments of entering a lift, they wait uncomfortably for its motion to impart upon them a sense of purpose. It was not that they did not love each other; it was that they did not know how to speak to each other when she was not around. Their entire communication was shaped around her existence. And later, when she would not be there, they would both feel a degree of resentment for the dependence she had instilled in them.

Skanda later remembered that visit to Dr Arya's clinic, which was in a south Delhi house, with sliding doors and a rusting slide in the front, as one of the few times he had been alone with his father. And, if it was uncomfortable, it was not because it felt bad or good, but because it felt like nothing. It felt insubstantial, a dream, with that same sense of being present and not present, of being ferried along from sequence to sequence, but possessing no power to influence the course of events. The arrival; the waiting; the plywood and brown Rexene examination bed; the painted alphabet on the wall; the diagnosis; the prescription; the stop-off at the chemist; the little brown paper bag, with creams and a mild painkiller. Did they talk? Did his father try to console him? The impressions were so distinct. The empty roads; the setting sun; his father, with his floppy hair and whitening sideburns, at the wheel of the jeep. He even remembered the red burgundy sweater, with its leather buttons, that he wore that day. And yet, just as in a dream, the vividness of the images bore an inverse relationship to the substantiality of the experience. The clearer the pictures became, the more it felt that none of it had ever happened.

They made a quick stop at the flat. Uma, now fully dressed, waited outside with Rudrani, who wore a shiny blue salwar kameez, and a Doon School visor over her chaotic curly brown hair.

'I can't get her to take it off,' Uma said, in reply to the question in Toby's face.

'Leave it, leave it,' he said, and smiled, swinging her into the back.

'Where's Narindar?'

'I thought you gave him the evening off.'

'No. He was meant to come and help out at Fatehkot House. I told your parents.'

'How strange. I haven't seen him since he rescued Skanda.'

'He's very restless, that boy. I tell you, if he wasn't Labu and Sharada's son . . . Champ, you want to let your mother get in the front?'

'No, no, leave it. We'll make a concession to his poor burnt fingers. Wanted to be Vishnu! You're really the limit, Skandu. What next? Jumping from buildings like Hanuman?'

Rudrani laughed uproariously in the back.

'Shut up!'

'What? Who are you telling to shut up? Your mother?'

'Her, obviously!'

'Setting your tail on fire?'

Rudrani, at that age, when nothing was funnier than different iterations of the same joke, laughed still louder.

'Swallowing an ocean of poison? Where does it end, Skandu?'

And suddenly it was all real. The sound had been restored, the magic element put back into life, which now again was more than a mute reel of pictures. His sister's laughter; the jeep setting off on the short journey to Fatehkot house; his mother's voice in the back; his father at the wheel. The family was complete; a thing of flesh and blood again, an organism. So, there was no other way to put it: she, and she alone – Uma – had the power to make their life feel real.

At Fatehkot House the older cousins were setting off patakas in the garden. An H-bomb smoked now under a tangerine tree laden with rotting fruit. A man on one of the slim ledges of that large forties house laid clay diyas in a line. Dim electrical light was visible in the double doors and windows whose gauze screens were bent out of true and in places thick with grime. It felt, even by its own gloomy standards, like a house in mourning.

The decision to have Diwali had been made a few hours before. And now there was Diwali.

'Oṁ śrīṁ hrīṁ klīṁ mahālakṣmyai namaḥ . . .' The words rang out; a smoky fire was lit; and Skanda, ever protective of his father in relation to Sanskrit, came and sat by his side. Others gathered behind them.

'I say, fellow! Very nice to have our own in-house pundit.'

Viski made the remark as a joke, but, in the new political climate, it acquired an edge. He seemed half to mock the Sanskrit prayer. It was a language, which, in any case, had the potential to cause embarrassment among those whose sacred language it no longer was. It had an in-built air of authority, which, like some old law or the deposed monarch of an *ancien régime*, it exerted blithely, regardless of whether those in earshot respected its authority or not. And it had an odd way of stirring in people mixed feelings of reverence and rebellion.

Especially among the Sikhs who found themselves besieged that winter: the face of terror, in a way that would not have seemed possible after 1947. True, the idea of persecution had never left them; it was almost an article of faith. But it was also true that persecution, in the past, had always had a specific context, and the persecutors a specific faith, namely Islam. So, in 1947, when their persecutors were Muslims again, the Sikhs, at least on the level of historical memory, had been prepared. What they were not prepared for, once a curtain came down, in the form of a border, on that bad time in 1947, was persecution from Hindus. And, after the violence was over, it was not so much outrage at its perpetrators that the Sikhs expressed, but outrage at themselves, for not having seen it coming. 'We never thought . . .' a taxi driver later said, and broke down before he could complete his sentence. 'We never thought it would happen again. But just let them come now; now, if they come, we'll be ready . . .'

But, of course, they never came again.

Prejudice in polite society – and the Fatehkotias were nothing, if they were not that – did not come to the party dressed as prejudice; it came as humour. And that night, almost as if in anticipation of what had happened to I.P., there was a lot of humour of this kind.

'I say, fellow! Very nice to have our own in-house pundit,' Viski might say. The Brigadier, reading to the depths of the place from where the joke had come, might add, 'When I was a junior officer, and posted in U.P., there had been a riot of some sort. The army had been called in to put it down. If I remember right, old General Kumaramangalam was our commanding officer. I said to him, "Sir, was it Muslims?" And he says – though he was a Hindu himself, but a pukka angrez, you know, an Etonian, "No, no! Bloody Hindoos!" Bloody Hindoos!' the Brigadier repeated, and everyone laughed.

Their jokes contained a trace of racial superiority, for, in this country where the general population had until 1947 been ruled by foreigners, the Sikhs were like people who had broken from themselves. They were Hindus remade, free of all that they felt had made the Hindu ripe for enslavement, and they were never more contemptuous of anything – the British and the Muslims, they could handle more easily – than that old Hindu past, the past of ritual and magic, on which they had turned their backs.

The puja over, Uma retreated to I.P.'s old room, where she dealt privately with the pain of her homecoming. The room was full of I.P.'s things: his trunk from school – black and battered, under the bed, with his number – 250-J – painted on it; a stack of Tintin and Asterix comics in a bookshelf; some novels of Evelyn Waugh, to whom he had introduced her. Many Russian novels published by Moscow's Progress Publishers, who had their bookshop in the People's Publishing House in Connaught Place. Books, a narrow bed, a polished desk, a terrazzo floor with no carpets, and so little else. All the sad gentility of post-colonial life was to be found in the room. It was like a microcosm of their cultural world. Of the inherited British cities, with their dreary bougainvillea and empty streets, to which, like shabby annexes to a grand house, there had been the addition of colonies. Colonies that had come to fill in the empty spaces of that pale hard land dotted with tombs and mosques. Beyond that, a near perfect erasure. Nothing, save texts and literature, from which, in any case, they were cut off, to say there had been a past at all. That there had not just been nothing before. It felt small and inconsequential, their claim on the land, easily reversible.

If men's stories tell you anything about how they see themselves, it is significant that the Fatehkotia stories were all about violence and futility. Wars they had not meant to fight, but into which events had dragged them; blood they had not meant to shed. They were like people encircled by history. Never actors, always acted upon. It produced in them a kind of fatalism – a belief in magic, almost – as well as some measure of guilt. Their misfortunes – and there had been quite a few since the Mutiny of 1857 – all felt to them deserved. Corrective, even, especially where the Brigadier was concerned. His stories were almost always self-indicting and he was only too ready to embrace as historical justice every calamity life sent his way. Even now, with his son mysteriously missing, and the events in Punjab, out of no fault of his own, closing their circle around him, he took the line of a man deserving of unhappiness.

He wore a peach-coloured turban and a grey herringbone jacket; the Brigadier never wore Indian clothes. And he stared, with a kind of amazement, at the domestic scene around him – daughters and grandchildren milling about; wife, worry written into her face, having dinner served; servants coming in and out with ice and soda. It was almost as if he didn't believe that he had engendered it. He didn't feel responsible, didn't feel attached. The idea of place had been disrupted for him so early in life by the Partition; and, he had, in embracing the nomadic nature of army life, re-enacted that original disruption. He lived with a deep feeling of homelessness, and, seeing perhaps in his son-in-law a fellow alien, he would always say to him, in the tone of a man forced to repair a car he had not intended to buy, or caught in bad weather on a holiday he had not wanted to go on, 'You know, Raja saab, we're not even *from* here.'

'How do you mean, sir?' Toby said, smiling.

'Well: there's this rhyme we were all taught as children, a bit of oral history: "Ghaznion chade warraich, leke lakh sawar . . ." Do you understand? It means: from Ghazni rose the Warraich: we are Warraich; that is our clan . . .'

'Tad tad tambe tarti . . .'

'Oh, you know it? How wonderful! How do you know it?'

'Sir, I've heard it from you.'

'Yes, yes. Tad tad tambe tarti. It means the earth shook with the sound of hooves. Guru banaye Sardar: the Guru made us Sikhs, you see. But we were probably, in all likelihood, Muslims from Ghazni. Never from here at all, you see!'

Muslims from Ghazni! In India, where the great majority of people – even Muslims – could be scratched to reveal an underlying Hindu, often cognizant of caste, the Brigadier loved the shock value of this little remark. He might as well have been saying the Fatehkotias were not, in fact, mammals. It was the kind of statement that has special resonance in those places where the tensions of a great historical upheaval, like the Islamic invasions, though papered over, can still be felt. And where the authenticity of origins – "I'm actually one-sixteenth native American, didn't you know!" – has become fraught with significance: an expression of legitimacy, a way of asking to whom, after all, does this land really belong? In India people fell over themselves both to belong and to not belong, as though balancing legitimacy with a feeling of historical defeat that belonging would implicate them in. That defeat made India feel like a beautiful, but heavily mortgaged house, where to own the house was to own the defeat.

The Brigadier that night, as if acting out of some primal need for oral history, wanted to explain how he had come to occupy the patch of land on which he stood. In tracing the line back to his ancestor, M– Singh, and his terrible role in the Mutiny of 1857, the Brigadier seemed almost to prepare himself to face the justice of his present situation.

'Bad business, Raja saab,' he said, casting his mind back to the events of years ago. 'A very bad business.'

'1857?' Toby said, as if picking up the thread of an earlier conversation.

The Brigadier nodded, but felt perhaps that Toby mocked him. Because he now took a different approach into the story of his ancestor's collaboration with the British – those *services rendered!* – in the capture of Bahadur Shah Zafar, the last Mughal emperor of Delhi, and his sons, in 1857.

'The thing I can't get over, Toby saab,' he said, 'is that I, who am his descendant, have come to live on that very stretch of land where all that terrible history occurred. There's no reason for it, you know. It was a wilderness, barren scrubby land, when old M– Singh crossed it. There would have been nothing here at all. I mean, M– Singh, on receiving intelligence that the princes were hiding in Humayun's tomb, was coming from what is now the old city. The land in between was uninhabited virtually. But look at how things have come around: two points in a story, the old city and the tomb, with a stretch of a few miles of desolate land between them, and history has filled in the spaces that lie in between. And I, who descend from M– Singh, live – as a consequence of a separate upheaval – almost equidistant today from the two points in that 1857 story. Strange, no?'

'But sir . . .' Viski inserted, pouring his first drink at the Brigadier's cabinet, which, with its mirrors and heavy crystal decanters, was a little nod to the style of the old days. 'M– Singh didn't actually kill the princes, did he? Not by his own hand?'

The Brigadier craned his neck to see his other son-in-law, dressed that night in a maroon turban which matched the maroon satin cuffs of his bandgala. Then, as if something in his appearance dissuaded him from answering the question directly, he performed a little sleight of conversation. He made it seem as if Toby had asked him a different question – ah, the deceptions of old people! – and then went on to answer it with redoubled energy.

'It was September, you see, Toby saab. The mutiny in Delhi, at least, was over; the city had been recaptured, but it was still smoking from the siege. Brigadier Nicholson, I think, lay dying. Or had just died. I forget which. Now the day before, 20 September, they – Hodson Bahadur and his lot – had captured the Emperor of Delhi from Humayun's Tomb. And they had granted old Zafar his life. So, perhaps, I don't know, did my ancestor perhaps feel that the same terms would be granted the princes? Perhaps he did.'

He peered into Toby's face, looking, if not for sympathy, then for, at least, a little understanding. Mistaking Toby's attentiveness for something cold and unforgiving, he said, 'They were very bitter, you know . . . *we* were very bitter, us Sikhs. Only ten years before there had been the Anglo-Sikh wars. M– Singh had fought in those wars. There was a terrible feeling of betrayal among the Sikhs, a feeling of having been betrayed not just by their own leadership, but also by the rest of India, especially by what is today U.P. In fact, it was the very same army, now in revolt, that had defeated the Sikhs ten years before at Ferozeshah. Strange line of thinking, no?'

'What?' Toby said. 'That a British army made up of one's own countrymen, albeit from a different region, defeats you in battle! Then, ten years later, that same army revolts against the British and you, in seeking revenge against the army, but not interestingly its officers, join the British in suppressing the revolt?'

'But, Toby saab, this is what I'm saying: you have put your finger on it. This is India. This is our mentality. "Our great mutual distrust of one another." Is that not your phrase? Why do you think we have been conquered again and again? Our suspicion of each other is so great we cannot help but be ruled by foreigners. We trust them more than we trust ourselves. Don't you see? Why do you think we have these clowns now, the Nehrus and the Gandhis? Because they're the closest thing we have to our own homemade foreigners: Scotch whisky bottled in India!'

'I say!' Viski said, and gave a loud laugh. He pulled at his moustache and drew his bow-shaped lips back into a grin. The Brigadier looked at him as if he were a madman.

'But you were saying . . .'

'I was saying that just the day before – 20 September 1857 – the Emperor of Delhi had been granted clemency. So M– Singh must have felt the same would be done with the princes. How was he to know that his superior officer, old Hodson Bahadur, had other plans? How was he to know of his nefarious agenda? Tell me: how was he to know? And I've read – it is unconfirmed, an oral tradition, but recorded nonetheless – that M– Singh did what he could for the little buggers. Once he knew they were going to be killed like dogs in the street, he warned a couple of them. During the siege of the Tomb, I think, he saw two princes hanging about and he said, "Why are you standing here?" They said – terribly innocent, young fellows, you know! – "Hodson Bahadur has told us to." M– Singh glared at them and said, "Have mercy on your lives. When he returns he will kill you; run in whichever direction you can. And khabardar: dam na lena!"'

The Brigadier, though he was fully aware of Toby's deep knowledge of Sanskrit, always paused to explain its vernacular to him. '"Mind you: do not stop even to take a breath!" That is what he told them. Then he turned his face away, and let the little buggers escape. When Hodson came back a moment later and found them gone, he was furious. "Where have they gone?" "Who?" "Who?! The princes who were standing here." "Princes? What princes?" "You know perfectly well what princes." "I haven't seen any princes." That kind of thing,' the Brigadier chuckled, drawing out this one redemptive detail in an otherwise bad story.

Deep, who had been listening at a distance, but pretending not to, now sabotaged her husband's story. 'But later there was no sign of all this mercy/shercy. When they were being stripped naked at Khooni Darwaza, and shot dead in the street, the descendants of Taimur and Genghis Khan, murdered before a mob on the outskirts of Delhi, then he didn't seem in the least bit bothered, your M–Singh. He took the ring and ran,' she said, and let out a clear peal of laughter.

The Brigadier listened with anguish to his wife spoil his story, then winced painfully.

'What ring?' Toby asked.

'Oh, it's nothing!'

'What nothing?' Deep said. 'Treasured heirloom. The one bloody thing you lot managed to hang on to, even when you lost everything else. Nothing, my foot. The signet ring of the Mughal princes. Ask him, it is in their family.'

Toby turned to the Brigadier who gave a sad acquiescent nod.

'I say, sir,' Viski thundered, 'nothing to be ashamed of.'

'No, no. It was a bad business. Very bad.'

Deep, seeing him cast down, and recalling perhaps the heavier events of the day, said, 'Come on, now. Come outside. They've come. The girls' guests. Mrs – pfffff! – Arjun Singh. Ishi and Mishi think she might be able to help with . . .'

Her voice trailed off; she didn't know what she was meant to help with. Because she didn't know what had happened to her son and could not bear to imagine. Toby, seeing that the storytelling had helped the mood in Fatehkot House – for what else do old families do when they're in trouble but sit upon the ground and tell stories – tried to return the Brigadier to the story of his ancestor. 'Finish what you were saying, sir . . .' But the Brigadier didn't want to now.

They refilled their drinks and went outside.

A fire had been lit in the garden. A furtive slow-burning fire that crept along the reddening bellies of the large logs in the grate, and whose orange glow pressed darkly into the pleats of the women's saris. The fire, its light reaching no higher than their waists, gave the women a large and stooped quality. They stood around it like a line of caryatids in a temple warming their hands. Occasionally the fire would swell, and then, in the expanded circle of its light, a ring would flash, lips and teeth would gleam.

Mrs Arjun Singh's voice, clear, newsy, full of a singsong authority, dominated the conversation. She was a handsome statuesque woman whose forbidding appearance and sternly cropped hair belied her true nature which was gossipy and lascivious. Her husband, Arjun Singh, though a dour-faced fool, repressed and serious, was a close school friend of the PM's son, part of the change of heir in Delhi that had occurred a few years before, after Mrs Gandhi's younger son was killed in a flying accident.

An age of influence had begun in the capital, for the new heir and his mother had very different leadership styles. Mrs Gandhi – it was true – had at times been a paranoid vindictive despot; she had broken treaty with the princes, she had invaded defenceless Himalayan kingdoms;

she had introduced crime and sycophancy into the soul of politics in Delhi. It was hard to imagine a more destructive ruler. But she had been an adult throughout. And, in her own mad way, she had known what she was doing. Her son's rule, even in its regency, was something apart. He was to prove that, if there was anything more destructive than the knowing harm his mother did India, it was the unknowing harm he and his public school friends would do the country.

There were other differences too. Mrs Gandhi had waged war on the Delhi drawing room. Its frequenters lived in constant fear of raids, of alcohol and foreign currency restrictions; they had hardly been able to travel. And, though many things could be said about the government Mrs Gandhi ran, few could say it was comprised of the drawing room set. Her son, owing no doubt to the deep disdain for India that had taken root among his generation, made it clear from the very start that the drawing room, with its ethnistas, deracinees and Oxbridge Lefties, would not just play a more important role in government; it would be the laboratory of government. From this pool of pseudo-intellectuals and dinner party celebrities, the future prime minister of India would draw his most trusted advisers and cabinet ministers. Each of whom, even before he was PM, were informed that their presence was required in Delhi, and obeying the call of their country – as Arjun Singh had done – they left their jobs at private firms and came to his side. Their wives, society ladies, whose only talk until then had been of holidays and duty-free goods, peppered with the odd gentility, were put to work too. Little cultural committees were created for them to head; offices and government buildings found for them to decorate, dying rivers and soon-to-be-extinct weaving traditions for them to save. These women made it known to those less influential than themselves that, if their husbands had the future PM's ear, they had his wife's. Of these ladies, none was more influential than Mrs Arjun Singh. She was by far, and without a rival, the most intimate friend of the soon-to-be prime minister's wife. And it was for this reason that Kitten Singh brought her to Fatehkot House that Diwali.

Her presence there, on that night of festival, inspired something of the wonder of a visiting deity mixed in with the real and practical utility of a doctor paying an emergency call. Her nearness to power, expressed now through a small and revealing detail, reluctantly disclosed – 'Arjun cannot join us, unfortunately; he had to go to Safdarjung Road' – now through that closed and slightly beatific expression that people in power acquire, reassured the Fatehkotia women. They no longer felt so exposed as they had all day; their brother's situation, though yet unknown, no longer seemed so desperate. It was now for the first time openly conjectured that he might, in these bad times, have been picked up for being a Sikh. The conjecture was not aired with anything resembling outrage; Mrs Arjun Singh expressed it with that mixture of regret and inevitability with which we speak of the weather or a flat tyre. 'The climate,' she said, 'was now very bad. But if anything *untoward* had happened to I.P., she would do everything in her power to make sure they knew that he was not one of those Sikhs.'

'Those Sikhs?' the Brigadier asked with genuine curiosity.

'You know, sir, the bad ones, terrorist-types.'

In the silence that fell over the garden, Isha looked sternly at Viski. But he did not say a thing. Of late, almost as if he had been brought into line with the way people now spoke of the Sikhs, he had come to dislike the sound of his dissenting voice. It made him feel like a bore and an activist; and, like many people who try to fight an emerging status quo, no matter how ugly it is, he felt himself subdued, not by arguments, but by its casual tyranny. It is easier to fight the knowing bigot than it is to fight prejudice in the mouth of a child or the throwaway remark of a society lady. And Mrs Arjun

Singh, who had expressed a distinction that was now everyday more commonplace – the distinction between good Sikhs, our Sikh friends, and the bad ones – hardly even noticed the discomfort she caused in that Sikh household. In her view, and many would agree, she could not have said anything more innocuous.

Everyone stared at the fire, which now hissed. The flames had left deep red welts on the logs and the ash formed a precarious jigsaw pattern. As everyone's gaze was fixed on the fire, a drop splashed. Then another, flattening the ash. And yet another.

'Oho!' a cry went up.

'Let's go inside.'

'Rain on Diwali? Never heard of such a thing.'

'Pundit ji,' Viski said, 'is it inauspicious for it to rain on Diwali?'

Toby smiled. 'I haven't the slightest . . .'

Mrs Arjun Singh, who had come to please, seemed particularly upset, like a goddess no longer in her element.

'I should go,' she whispered.

'No, no,' Kitten Singh whispered back. 'It'll look bad. Stay for one drink, then we'll both go.'

In a land where there is no such thing as neutral rain, but always only good or bad rain, everyone, once they were safely inside, judged this particular shower severely.

'A storm would have been one thing. But this . . .'

'Just enough to spoil everyone's fun.'

'To put out all the diyas and make the patakas go phus.'

'A real little English drizzle. Pissy rain.'

'I know what I.P. would say,' Deep said, with the faintest catch in her voice. And, in just mentioning his name, she, like a conductor resurrecting a major strain, or a sūtra-dhāra in a Sanskrit play pulling hard at the narrative thread, returned the drifting conversation that evening to its central theme. '"You're welcome hither,"' she said into the silence, and gave a wild and wayward giggle.

It so alarmed the Brigadier, the pitch of her laughter, the nerves and hysteria tugging at the cords in the throat, that he said, 'I think I had better take her up. She's been awake for over thirty-six hours.' But, like a child, exhausted and elated, she didn't want to go up.

'No,' she cooed, 'I haven't finished. "You're welcome hither,"' she chimed, a half-mad cuckoo in a clock. The Brigadier rose.

'No,' she said now in a thick voice, 'Here it comes: "Nor no man else. All's"' – and now she raised her voice into a windy howl, so that she sounded liked a witch in an amateur production of *Macbeth* – '"All's cheerless, dark and deadly."'

Then, having said her bit, she gave a little bow, somewhat in the direction of Mrs Arjun Singh. There was still a harassed spring of silver hair – it had been there all day – hanging off her head. She said, smiling beatifically, 'My son loved Shakespeare.'

'*Loves*, Mama!' Isha and Uma said in one voice.

She smiled gaily at them as if to say, *Let be*.

Then, turning back to Mrs Arjun Singh, she added, 'And Lear, especially. Lear was his favourite.'

The Brigadier had her now by the elbows; and firmly, he led her upstairs.

Mrs Arjun Singh, having got much more than she bargained for, and having brought nothing resembling beneficence, also rose to leave. Kitten Singh accompanied her.

'I shall do my best,' she said, to those who remained. 'Please don't lose heart. Everything will be fine. I must go now.'

And then, as if as an afterthought, wishing to remind them of who she was, she added, 'Arjun must be home by now.'

'Look at these swines,' Viski said, as the car with Kitten and Mrs Arjun Singh drove away, leaving red light streaming over the wet drive, which, in places, was daubed black with petrol stains.

Toby, his face faintly flushed in the light of the departing car, said, 'I know what you mean, naturally. But why now, in particular?'

'Just listen to them. *Those* Sikhs. Bastards! The witch's son, the dead one, was in school with me, you know. And he came to see me one day now aeons ago, wanted my help in persuading my father – *prominent member of the Sikh community* and all that – to support a certain village priest, called Bhindran-*whale*, if you please!'

Toby laughed.

'In return, he would offer me some land trans-Jamuna, at a very affordable price. *Hello, fellow*, I thought, *OK!* I'll ask my father, but can't guarantee he'll consent. He's been an Akali all his life, you know. And he may not agree with everything the Party says and does, but he'll have them over these swines in Congress any day.'

'And so what did he say?'

'He told me to bugger off. He said this little Congress scheme to out-Akali the Akalis in Punjab by propping up this village priest will backfire on the Congress and I should steer wide clear of it. And look: seven years later, Bhindran-*whale* dead and gone; the Akal Takht destroyed; Punjab in flames. And this is just the beginning, if you ask me. Just the beginning. I tell you, I don't know why we stay, Toby saab. I don't know about elsewhere, but Time, here, certainly feels circular. We just go round and round, with not so much as a hint of progress. You still have it easy,' he said, cupping his hands and lighting a cigarette. 'You can leave. And you should; you must. Take your children, your wife, and bas, get out. Nothing's going to happen here. Not for decades. You can take it from me in writing. What does Ismail always say? "Everyone must get their chance to fuck this country once." And now, this Congress lot, they're having theirs.'

'But you can leave too, Viski. You're rich enough, God knows.'

'Money's not the issue. I'm a provincial. Isha too. We wouldn't be able to hack it. The loneliness would kill us. But you and Uma, you are both, in your heart of hearts, cosmopolitans. Sophisticates. You would bloom in the West. This place – don't think I can't see it – is strangling you; it is strangling your marriage.'

They were standing like that, in the light of a small encaged bulb, staring out at the now empty drive, when, at the far end, there was a sudden disturbance. A figure, barely distinguishable in the light rain, had appeared at the gates and was pulling furiously at them, nearly wrenching them clean off their hinges. His small pale fists, bloodless with his exertion, were planted firmly on the gate's iron bars. An awful slurring cry, desperate and persistent, rose from his throat. The gate, as if sucked in and out by a great wind, shuddered and whined.

Toby and Viski had not come halfway down the drive, when the watchman posted at the gate, wrapped up to his eyeballs in woollens, came hurriedly out and opened the chain, which slithered to the ground with an affrighted clanking. The gate's panels parted and, coming fast onto the drive, knock-kneed and wild-eyed, seeming almost to have been spat out, there appeared the crazed and wheeling figure of Narindar.

His shirt was torn; his face badly bruised; he could barely speak. His eyes, so dull and adolescent normally, flashed in his head. Gleaming drops of rain clung to the sparse stubble of his thin, unshaven face. The white of his vest was exposed and wet and thinly concealed a line of dark hair, plunging deep into the ravine of his chest.

'Narindar?'

He looked at Toby, his wide eyes a reddish white, and, ignoring all the customary greetings, threw himself into his arms. He was reeking of alcohol and a stale stench came thick off his body.

'Maharaj, maharaj. Forgive me . . . forgive me . . . please, I beg you, forgive me. Oh baba saab, oh baba saab. I couldn't do anything for him. Forgive me.'

'Baba saab?' Viski intervened. 'What about baba saab?'

'Baba saab, baba saab, you don't know. Oh! I can't tell you what they did to him.'

He screeched and tore at his shirt. Viski could see that his hysteria was, in part, designed to deflect from his own guilt.

'Baba saab?' Viski said sternly, but Narindar could give no reply. Tears choked his words. With every outburst, he fell back into Toby's arms and stroked them with his little hands as if trying to comfort an animal. His facial muscles, no longer in his control were so tremulous, his fear so great, that he seemed almost to smile.

Viski took him calmly from Toby's arms, held him with one hand by the neck, as if inspecting him, and slapped him hard.

The effect was magical; the hysteria vanished; he was suddenly calm. In a measured and sober voice, he told them everything. That I.P. had been picked up the night before; that he had been rude to the police and they had taken him to Tughlak Road Police Station. That he was being held there and beaten brutally; they were trying to make him confess to being part of a conspiracy to blow up the Bhakra-Nangal dam.

Then he said something which anticipated all the ways in which I.P. was safe, unscathed, in a sense; and all the other more powerful ways in which he would never be safe again. He judged the effect of the words perfectly, as no doubt the perpetrators would have judged the effect of the deed. He said they, the policemen – and he knew this because he had seen them fill the clear glass bottles with his own eyes – had made I.P. drink their urine.

*

The reason the Brigadier found the story of the princes painful was because he saw in it a shade of the martyrdom story of Zorawar and

Fateh, the two younger sons of the tenth guru, who, aged nine and seven, were brought as prisoners to the court of Nawab Wazir Khan. There, they were offered death or conversion. They chose death, but it did not come swiftly. They were bricked up alive. A wall, silent and deadly as a flood, rose around them. And, with every added line of bricks, they were asked to recant their faith, and every time, as SikhiWiki will tell you, they said no. The wall pressed close against their bodies, its musty breath stifling, till eventually the masons entombed the little boys, who, throughout, recited their prayers and hymns. That was how they met death, calm, clear-eyed, Sikhs to the last.

It was the mood of this story, which every Sikh knows by heart, that, in the Brigadier's mind, had merged with the story of the princes on that afternoon in September 1857. There were obvious differences. The princes were older; they had actually been part of the uprising, part of its planning; and they were not bricked up alive. They were stripped and shot. But the Brigadier, with his weakness for historical parallels, and for seeing in the pain of his enemies his own pain, could not get away from recognizing an identical element in both stories. The same pathos, and pity, the same wretchedness, the same frightening inevitability of the boys who must die for who and what they are.

And perhaps it was this – the special futility of historical justice in a land where history has no meaning – that made him finish the story of the princes once the news of what had happened to I.P. spread through Fatehkot House.

'I find it very moving,' he said to Toby, 'that they should have sought refuge in the tomb of their ancestors. And when they were denied the terms granted their father the day before, their little rath emerged from within its enclosure. The full glory of their past, the Mughal past, was there behind them and they, in a little rath . . . a cart, you know?'

'Yes, I know what a rath is, sir.'

'So, there you have it: a cart crammed full of the last descendants of conquerors and emperors. Of men like Babur and Akbar. The tomb, with its white dome, in the background. This is what history comes down to in India, Raja saab. Squalor and degradation! Their ancestors broke the nerve of a great civilization, and now, in turn, their nerve was being broken. And make no mistake: that is what was happening. The Angrez sent in no more than two officers! Two Englishmen, Hodson and his lieutenant, plus 100 or so native men. The princes had, by all accounts, 3,000 inside the tomb, and another 3,000 in the environs. All armed, mind you. But they could do nothing. They just stood and watched as their princes were carried away. You know why? Their nerve was broken. And once that happens – I've seen it myself on countless occasions – no amount of arms or munitions will help you. Have they gone?'

'To the station? Yes.'

'Will he be all right, you think?'

'I'm sure.'

'He's very proud, you know. Much prouder than me. I saw '47. I know how one's people can turn against you. He doesn't. He's been told he's a Sikh, he's been told to hold his head high, that Sikhs are not afraid, if they've done something to humiliate him . . .'

'He'll be fine, sir. I'm sure of it.'

'Will they have him out tonight?'

'Tomorrow, latest. They're speaking to everyone. From the DIG to the PMO. Arjun Singh himself is helping.'

'Damn fool man.'

'Yes, but powerful.'

The Brigadier's lip curled into a smile. 'All bloody crude power. Tarzan power. Will you have another one?'

'I . . .'

'Have one, Raja saab. We, also, need some little sustenance. We, who are not powerful.'

'Let me do it.'

The Brigadier handed him his empty glass. Then, as Toby was walking over to the bar, he said, 'I want him to leave, you know. *If* he comes out . . .'

'Of course he'll come out.'

'If he comes out, I want him to leave. To go away. I'll miss him; he has an inheritance here, ill-begotten as it may be; but I want him to go. He has a fine nature, you know; I want him to go somewhere where he can realize its impulses. Let him line up with the peasants outside the embassies and go to some place, where even a peasant might make something of himself.'

'But, sir, your wife, Uma . . . ?'

'They'll survive. But I.P., if they've dishonoured him, he won't.'

It made Toby uneasy to hear him speak like this. Neither the Brigadier nor anybody else had been given the details that he and Viski had heard; and yet, the Brigadier, as if intuitively, kept bringing the conversation back to the subject of humiliation, of dishonouring, of the breaking of nerve . . .

'Why are you so sure, sir . . . ?'

'It's what they do, Raja saab. They're little people who've suffered humiliations, they wait all their lives to get their own back. And now, it's open season against the Sikhs. They know very well – they would have been told – that no one will be punished for doing harm to a Sikh. You think they won't make use of this opportunity. Of course, they will! Thank you!' he said, taking the glass. 'And you?'

'Is there any soda?'

'In the purple fridge by the bar.'

Seeing Toby looking around for an opener, the Brigadier said, 'Here, give it to me.' Then, putting the bottle between his legs, he pried the cap open with the edge of his kara. It made a loud and satisfying noise.

'Sir!'

'I.P.'s little trick. He taught it to me. "What else is religion for?" he used to say. Silly fool.' The Brigadier chuckled. Then serious again, he said, 'I despise it, you know, religion.' He touched his hand lightly to his turban, then trailed his fingers along his beard. 'I grew up with these things. I never questioned them. They became, without my knowing it, a part of who I am. But I put no store by them. If I.P. said tomorrow that he wanted to cut his hair, shave off his beard, I would be only too happy. His mother, that's a different matter; women need these things. But not me, Raja saab. How come you didn't go with them?'

'I thought I should stay with you.'

'That's very kind. I'm very grateful for your company tonight. I'm not an intellectual, you know. Not like you and I.P. But I like to think of myself as a thinking man, as someone with sensibility.'

'You are, sir. Very much so.'

'Thank you. Thank you for saying that. But I wonder, Raja saab, will it be OK? Even for you, I mean. Will it be OK?'

'For me?'

'Because you, you *are* an intellectual. And not just an intellectual, but devoted to the thought and learning of this country. Will they not hate you for it, our people? For reminding them of what they want to leave behind. Will they not make you feel so small and worthless that you will want to leave?'

Toby looked confused for a moment, but then the Brigadier said something that revealed the true direction of his thought.

'My daughter, she is a great pragmatist,' he said. 'There is a lot of passion and romance in her too. But, at bottom, she's a pragmatist. Not as much as her mother, but a pragmatist nonetheless. What is right in her eyes – what is moral, even – is simply what is, not what should be.'

Toby laughed. 'Sir, that must be one of the best definitions of a pragmatist that I've ever heard.'

The Brigadier smiled. 'I told you I'm not an intellectual, but I like to think of myself as a thinking man. And, besides, stupidity, I'm sure you'll agree, is not an absolute value, but a deficit.'

'A deficit?'

'Yes: the gap between what one is fit to be doing and what one, in fact, does. Take the witch, for instance. Had she been a housewife, no one would have thought her stupid. Nor her son, had he remained an airline pilot. But put the same person in a job that is ill-suited to them, like that of the PM, and they suddenly seem completely bloody daft. People who are right for what they do never seem stupid. Don't you agree? I was a soldier, and, for that, I think I had brains enough.'

'Yes, yes.'

Then, as if his emotion was working its way out in the form of a willingness to face all life's cold hard truths, he said, 'Perhaps you'll leave too. Perhaps you'll take the children and my daughter, and go away. To England perhaps, where they value you, value your work, where you might live the life of the mind.'

'That's the second time this evening that someone has urged me to leave India.'

'Well, Raja saab, one is concerned. One sees what's happening, you know. Not always easy to put into words, but one sees.'

'What is happening?'

The Brigadier looked long at him. At the face in which, more and more, happiness was indistinguishable from sadness. A face where all expressions of joy had come into the service of concealing sorrow.

Then, changing the subject, or enlarging it perhaps, he said, 'It was late afternoon when they arrived back, Hodson and the princes. M– Singh was with them, of course. A crowd had collected at a gate on the outskirts of old Delhi. They pressed close on the horses of the sowars, and assumed every moment a more hostile appearance. "What shall we do with them?" Hodson said aloud. To his lieutenant, or to M– Singh perhaps. I don't know. But he answered the question himself. "I think we had better shoot them here; we shall never get them in." With this, he halted the guard, put five troopers across the road, behind and in front, and ordered the princes strip. Of swords, of arm bands *and* – this is what came down to us – of signet rings . . .'

'Sir, behind every fortune . . .'

'No, no, listen. Once their personal effects had been removed, he declared them fugitives before the crowd, murderers of innocents, women and children, and ordered them back into the cart, where he shot them, by his own hand, with a Colt revolver. And, with this small act of vigilante justice, he brought to an end the Mughal dynasty in India. Dusk fell, the city smoked; the bodies were left on display outside a kotwali in Shahjehanabad.'

At this the Brigadier rose and walked over to his cupboard. He returned a moment later with a green satin pouch which he handed to Toby.

'Open it,' he said.

It contained a large ring of dull smooth gold. The stone was a murky yellow diamond in the shape of a heart. Shattered and full of cobwebs.

'It's a large stone,' the Brigadier said, 'but worthless. Save for what historical value it has, it's absolutely valueless.'

'It's a terrible story, sir.'

'Yes, but I say this not because worse has not happened elsewhere, but because here, in India, it is all unprocessed, all undealt with. But it is there, somewhere, in the blood and memory of men. The past. And in this form, undealt with, it is, if anything, more dangerous. Who was it who said, "The past has to be seen as dead; or the past will kill."'

'A very good writer, sir, a very good writer indeed.'

'Well, let's not make things heavier for ourselves than they already are. Just remember – and I say this with Skandu as much in mind as you, for his nature is identical to yours – in certain places fineness of feeling is indistinguishable from weakness.'

'But how did it manifest itself?' Gauri asks.

'Oh, once these things find roots,' Skanda says, 'once a person becomes aware of an intrinsic weakness in their partner, the manifestations show up everywhere. In the smallest things – from his decision to stay with the Brigadier that night – to much bigger things.'

'Such as?'

'His general state of calm. Which to her seemed like resignation and helplessness. His concerns, his occupations, even his touch and smile came all to seem to her like manifestations of that same weakness. And she felt her system revolt against it; she could hardly bear to be near him. It was Darwinian, Gauri: what began to happen in their relationship after I.P. It may seem strange to you: nine years of marriage suddenly up in smoke over something that, horrible as it was, was, in the end, external to their marriage. But these things have their own logic. Sometimes an event like this, an intrusion from the world beyond, can make apparent the flaws within.'

Gauri has come outside. She trails her fingers along the rough red surface of the wall that has carved up the house on Curzon Road. It has followed them invisibly, like a lost river, in their progression through the house, appearing now framed in a teak doorway, now climbing the shallow stairs of a pillared entrance, now bursting out into the open to cleave in half what had once been large terraces. At the back of the house, it comes again into full view. After partitioning the badminton court at the short service line, it runs along an area where the earth is bare and cold and wet. Then, as if acknowledging a claim on the earth greater than its own, it peters out in haste before the giant roots of a pilkhan. In the fog and murk of that cold December night, under whose canopy Delhi's fragmentary history, its past and present, is brought together, Skanda and Gauri glimpse a narrow opening in the wall.

It is three feet wide and some five feet high. A doorless doorway in the wall. And drifting through it, like the unwieldy fog, which squares itself up on passing through, there is the murmur of voices.

'I think we may have found your party, Skanda.'

And, mad as it seems, she is right.

They must have come to the wrong side of the house. The decayed side: the side that is yet to fill with the energies – and airiness – of a new time.

Twice a year there is a distracting wind in the north. Once in March, when, after Holi, it bears along the summer, and again, in October or November, when, soon after Diwali, it contains a chill. It was there on the morning of 31 October 1984. One could feel it in the smooth-floored corridors of the medical institute. In those heavy passages, painted in two tones, brown and yellow, in two textures, oily and chalky, over which it seemed the thickest Nehruvian sleep lay, the unruly wind created a mood of restlessness. Beige-brown curtains, drab and hung from dented aluminium rods, flapped wildly in their metal frames; the open panes, dusty and spattered with brown paint, which gave on to balding rectangular gardens, creaked against their stays; now and then, a nurse, gliding down these empty stretches of corridor, with their white doors and fire hydrants, would lightly touch her nurse's cap, perched primly on a thick head of netted hair.

A wind-blown day of flapping curtains and sudden bursts of sunshine. Was there any escape from its mood? Was there any way a silently seething couple, awaiting admission to a patient's room, could not be affected by it? Dark shapes flitted across the smooth sun-washed surface of labyrinthine corridors. Toby and Uma waited for news of I.P. from behind a privacy screen.

I.P., before anyone had seen him, had made a strange demand through his doctors: he would see only Toby. And, when he was discharged, he wanted to go, not to Fatehkot House, but to Toby and Uma's flat. That was where he would spend his convalescence.

'If he knew how little you had to do with his release, he might perhaps have thought differently.'

She stood in a shaft of flickering sunshine, gazing out at the hospital grounds whose neglect spoke of a winter deeper than the one that was approaching, and on whose damp and litter-strewn surface, a tatty sheet of dew glistened. A bitch, udders full and exposed, warmed herself in the sunshine. Toby, entranced by the visual power of the scene, of his wife, dressed in an aubergine sari with little white diamonds, standing in a column of municipal sunlight, her back turned to him, tried to immerse himself in the moment, tried not to let its impressionistic power blow away the reality.

'It's not what you think, Uma.'

'What do I think, Toby?' she said with an acidity that contained a note of surprise, as if she didn't believe he had ever known what she was thinking.

She swung around briefly, as though to catch him out in his distractedness.

'It's not some expression of how he feels about you or his mother or anyone else, it's just sometimes . . .'

'Sometimes?'

'The humiliation, Uma. Sometimes it's easier to bear in the company of people who . . .'

He fell silent.

'Who what? Who don't judge? Who are accepting of weakness?'

'This is not about us, Uma,' he said automatically, without thinking of the implication of what he had said.

'Isn't it? Aren't I being painted again as the tough little bitch, who no one will go to when they need comfort, and you, ever generous, ever compassionate, ever able to take the long view.'

'But he's staying in our flat . . .'

'Because you're there.'

'Uma, you're falling into a trap.'

'What trap?' she said with genuine curiosity.

'What happened to I.P., to your brother, is not meant to happen to anyone. People cannot be expected to have a response. There is no question of strength and weakness here, Uma. It's the state we're talking about. It can destroy anyone. It has that power, a power given to it in trust. If it misuses that power – or uses it casually, to harm people at will – no one can be expected to be brave or cowardly before it. There is no question of humiliation.'

'You're contradicting yourself. You said a moment ago—'

'I know. I was saying it because it is my guess that that is what I.P. is feeling. That was why he sent for me. That doesn't mean he should feel it.'

'I want to get away from it, Toby. From the heaviness of it all, from the boredom. When I think of Skandu and Rudrani, I think how will they escape the gloom of this time, how will it not enter their soul, and stay lodged there inside them . . .'

'They're very sheltered, Uma . . .'

'Who will shelter them from this?'

'We will. We'll tell them that their uncle is unwell, and staying with us for a few weeks. What is there to that?'

'It's not so easy. These things have their effect. And they've been witness to it all.'

'To what?'

How much she wanted to say: To my growing unhappiness, but she said instead, 'To I.P.'s disappearance, to the worry in everybody's faces, to the wrangling to get him out. *You* were not witness to it; you were consoling my father; you were being philosophical or whatever it is you are . . .'

'Uma—'

'But *they,* they saw it all. And it will leave its mark. You see, for you, Toby, none of this is real.'

'None of what?' Toby said, with exasperation.

'Delhi. India. Whatever. For you it's all just some pale impression of the grand idea you have in your head. All just some thin and "imperfect articulation" of that other place.'

'What place?' he said, with curiosity.

'I don't know! Somewhere else. Some place of sages, of semi-divine beings, of Gandharvas, and Kinnaras and Apsarases. And whatnot, Toby! Someone says H.P. to me and I think: Oh, good old Himachal Pradesh. Mountains, hill stations, busloads of tourists. Little H.P. Tourism guesthouses with white bread and weak tea. But you, you're thinking, hima: snow, cold, frost; must be related to *hiems* and *hiver* and hibernate; and a | cala, that's a non-goer, immovable, and like na | ga, means mountain. Snow mountain. How pretty!'

Toby smiled. He thought, *For all the bad blood, how much I still love her.*

'What's wrong with that?' he asked finally, fighting off the approach of something querying and philosophical in his voice.

'Because for you the modern country doesn't exist. Not the place that, on a whim, hauls in your brother and thrashes him within an inch of his life. *That* India doesn't exist for you. You don't see it; you don't expect anything of it; you have nothing invested in it. It's just something going on in the foreground of your grand, grand background.'

'It's not true: I *do* see it. It just doesn't speak to me.'

'It *shouts* at the rest of us, Toby. For the rest of us it is the only India there is. A shoddy little shit-hole, by turns violent and crushingly boring—'

'But why are you saying all this? Why now?'

'Because I'm fed up with how easily you seem to bear it all. And I want to rub in your face the fact that you can bear it because you live in a fantasy world. A place that exists in your head, and in your head alone. And there is no escapism – you complain about Hindi movies! Ha! – no escapism more complete than yours. My brother, he wants to see you right now, and not his family . . .'

'I am his family.'

'His blood family. Because he wants you to help him escape too. He wants you to make a little room for him in the cocoon.'

'Uma, what would you have me do?'

'Give him a little dose of reality.'

'Don't you think he's had enough already?'

'Give him more. Make him understand who has worked tirelessly to get him out, tell him about his mother, his half-crazed mother, who hasn't slept or eaten in a week. Tell him about the phone calls and the waiting, the running from this politician to that bureaucrat to this policeman, tell him about the cups of tea with callous stupid women. "You *must* understand: he was *very* rude to them, dear." Tell him what a shallow and casual thing evil is in this country. Tell him about his sisters, who have their first streaks of grey from worry for him.'

She lifted her hair near her temple and it was indeed grey.

'Isha has the same thing.'

'So? What does that mean?'

'It means we worry, Toby. It means we strive and feel fear; we get angry; we cry and grieve, we love . . .' she said, as if asking a question. 'We live in the real world, not in our heads. I want Skanda to live like that too. I don't want him to be part of some effeminized elite.'

'Is that what you think I am part of?'

She paused. The doctor had appeared from a door behind the privacy screen. He was a man of medium height and sallow complexion; the sharp cut and tension of his moustache seemed to make up for something flaccid in him; there was, halfway up his white doctor's coat, a yellow stain near the button. An expression of great agitation was apparent in his small sunken eyes.

'Is something the matter?' Uma asked, observing his expression. 'Something wrong with my brother?'

The doctor looked blankly at her, then some irritation showed in his face, as if, in the middle of an important consideration, he had been disturbed with a matter of little importance. Addressing himself to Toby, in deference, no doubt, to his being a man, and a white man, at that, he said, 'No. Mr Inder Pratap is fine. Ready to be discharged. In fact, I would take him home this instant, if possible.'

'Why? What is the problem, doctor?'

'Some complications have arisen. *Not* with the patient. With *our* . . . how best to say it? *Our facility* here. It would be much better if he went home as soon as possible.'

'Can I see him?'

'Yes, yes, by all means.'

He stepped aside. Then said, 'I'll organize the paperwork. It will be just a few minutes.'

'I'll handle that with you, doctor,' Uma said meaningly. '*While* . . . Let my husband see my brother. Toby, I'll meet you downstairs?'

Inside, past the privacy screen, and the white door, the little room was flooded with sunshine, a steady stream of pale golden light. The room overlooked the main intersection outside – in those days there was no flyover – and provided, in a city where one was rarely high, a glimpse of the Delhi skyline. A pale green expanse, pierced now and then by a tomb, a tower, a Sovietic pile, over which there hung a thin mist. I.P., with his face turned to the window, seemed, with eyes open and intent, a little swollen, to be studying the view from his room when Toby came in. His solemn face, bathed in sunshine, made for an odd contrast with the foolery of the hospital gown he wore, and over whose low rounded collar some thick chest hair peeked. He didn't turn around when Toby came in – not even when he said, 'Hello, I.P.' – but his lips made as if to smile, then, freezing in a wince, were at rest again. Toby interpreted the silence as voluntary. But he was wrong, when he drew up a chair, and came to sit at his bedside by the window, I.P., with some strain, lifted up his lip in explanation. For an instant, the sunlight that flashed in bedpans, and gilded the metal frames of hospital beds, blazed along the line of steel wire, as thick as a zip, that had been used to bind I.P.'s jaws together.

Toby did not flinch. He caught his reaction in time, and converted it into an exaggerated and mocking curiosity.

'Going to be a hell of a job preventing the kids from calling you Jaws.'

I.P. shook a little with laughter.

'Or Hanuman!'

I.P. looked questioningly at Toby.

'Yes,' Toby said, encouraged to have I.P.'s attention. 'He cracked his hanu trying to reach for the sun. Saw it rising in the forest, thought it was a fruit – and *woosh!*'

But I.P. was not listening. He was searching his bed for something, and looking distractedly out of the window. Toby could not divine his meaning, and was about to accept defeat, when from somewhere deep within his sheets, I.P. triumphantly pulled out a small notebook and a pen.

'Voilà!'

'Indeed!' I.P. scribbled and showed Toby, who laughed.

Then he wrote, 'Two things . . .'

'Go on,' Toby said.

'1,' he wrote, 'What the F— is a hanu?'

Toby smiled and came over. Taking the pad from him, he wrote: 'Jaw, chin. Hanuman = (big)-jawed.'

I.P. took the pad back and wrote, 'nice!'

'And two?' Toby said, his own interest now aroused.

'2,' I.P. wrote, glancing out of the window as he scribbled, 'is a little more urgent.'

'What?'

I.P. pointed agitatedly with his pen out of the window. Toby looked down and saw for the first time what I.P. had been staring at. Not the Delhi skyline. Outside the hospital's wrought iron gates a crowd had gathered. Ordinary office-going men, in baggy dull-coloured trousers and Terylene shirts, who had parked their scooters on the side of the road, and stood, grim-faced, awaiting some kind of news. There was also among this crowd – on its periphery, in fact, Toby could see now – a couple of foreigners with video cameras. An armed guard. Photographers. Some people taking notes.

'What the hell is going on?' Toby said, barely aloud.

When he looked around, I.P.'s eyes danced.

'You know?'

I.P. held his gaze and seemed even, though his lips did not part, to smile. Then he took his notebook and wrote, 'The witch is dead. ☺'

Downstairs, Uma, in her battered black Fiat, tried with great difficulty to bring the car around. But every time she did, a lathi-wielding security man, or else another kind of man – in a baggy black faux-leather jacket – would stroll up to her and tell her to move off. It was the strangest thing. When they arrived, a few hours before, she could have parked right in front of the black metal gates had she wanted. But in the time it had taken her to go upstairs, fill in the paperwork and come back down, a crowd had gathered outside the hospital. At first, she had thought: Some old neta must be sick or dying. But as she drove around – she was forced to circle the hospital – the crowd grew larger, and grimmer. The odd foreigner with a heavy camera on his shoulder stood among security men, intelligence men and ordinary citizens. By a mysterious process, each one of them discovered within seconds what was now drawing them there. They ceased to do what they were doing, and joined the crowd with a solemnity and seriousness that contained in it a note of menace. Their watchful faces, though varied, somehow suggested kinship, like a band of conspirators.

What the F— am I going to do? she thought. *Just keep circling the compound till they come around? How will I see them in this crowd? And what is it about? Why are they all standing here?*

Automatically, as if the thought had passed from mind to body to machine, she slowed the car. She was on the edge of the crowd. Her window was open. She could hear the murmur of men's voices. She heard one say, 'She's been shot.'

In that instant, Uma knew everything. She – and moreover everyone around her – knew everything. Who. Why. How. The consequences. It was as if something that had been brewing in men's minds for months had, by an act of collective will, become suddenly manifest. Now the wrought-iron gates of the hospital flew open. A cavalcade of white Ambassadors sped out. In the half-curtained windows, the awaiting mob picked out family members, saw the shock written into their faces. A sigh of grief no longer than a breath, a brief exhalation, went through them and before she was out of earshot, Uma heard someone say, 'She's dead.'

Later she wished she had stopped the car. She felt sure that, before she drove around again, she had seen Toby and I.P. appear at the entrance of the hospital. Who knows? Here, the mind is wont to make mistakes. She probably didn't. It was probably her regret and guilt that afterwards set to work rearranging the chronology of events, punishing her for what she could not have helped, but that – had she been able to – would have made so great a difference. Whatever it was, she found herself in the extraordinary position of having to take another round of the hospital, having only heard what she just had, having guessed at the consequences. And it was in that round, channelled back into the oppressive ordinariness of traffic, that all that was bad – and later seemed avoidable – occurred.

Toby and I.P. had seen the cavalcade too. From the moment they had left I.P.'s ward – Toby wheeling him along – they had found themselves in proximity to a terrific internal tension in the building. Large corridors that, till a moment before, had seemed so sleepy and deserted came alive with a furious and urgent energy. Everyone, from the peons they passed to the nurses to the doctors, had the self-important air of people entrusted with a national secret.

As Toby and I.P. made their way through the hospital, they were more than once asked to stop and wait. The building trembled to the vibrations of the great and terrible event that had entered its system, and brought all its parts into a jangled and dissonant harmony. But then, just as the energy had spread like hope, it now turned caustic. With the same fury that it had come into the building it now receded from it. The nurses, doctors, patients, paramedics and plainclothes policemen with walkie-talkies followed it out, as if following an empty promise of deliverance, to the front of the hospital, where they stood, in a lobby of fluorescent lights and potted plants, their faces stricken with grief. There was a flurry of slamming doors and screeching tyres. A moment later a tearful cavalcade of white Ambassadors streamed out of the drive of the All India Medical Institute.

I.P.'s mood, which had been jubilant in his room, when he first suspected the news, grew heavier as they made their way out. He sensed his isolation; perhaps he already had an intimation of 'consequences' and felt something of the solitude – *and threat* – of a man whose team wins the cricket, even as he finds himself in a town filled with supporters of the losing side. Victory might have been his, but there was no triumph, and the thing that had seemed to him a moment ago so good and true and just – the cutting down of a woman who had cut down so many – curdled into a kind of shame within the vault of secrecy where he was forced to conceal it. Moreover, he felt – though in his visor and sunglasses he was hardly identifiable as a Sikh – people around him, as hope turned to despair, probe him for his reaction. He felt a scrutiny from the eyes that were following out the cavalcade, as though they were taking time off from their grief to look askance at him.

The violence of a repressed society, though men may dress it up as anger or grief, has the quality of a celebration. Those who participate in it know that at bottom what they are feeling is release and euphoria. And, even before Toby had wheeled I.P. up to the gates of the hospital, even before they had witnessed the scene that awaited them, which was itself only an intimation of things to come, he saw a change in the man he was wheeling out. He saw in this man, newly acquainted with the nature of his place, fear, naked and instinctual.

I.P. began to shake and tremble in his chair. His hands clutched the rests, his head crumpled into his collar bone. At first he himself did not seem to know what was happening to him. They had not come halfway down the drive; nothing yet was visible; he was in the sun and open air for the first time. There was nothing to be afraid of, nothing but a clear and breezy day, cloudless. And yet, as if truly he could smell the thing that was to be feared, his nerves, at the sight of the crowd behind the iron rails, began to give way.

'It's just some people,' Toby found himself saying aimlessly.

'People waiting. We're going straight home from here. I'm just looking for Uma. She has the Fiat. Can you see her?'

I.P. nodded his head and tried to look too. But he could not tear his eyes away from the crowd, which, having only just parted for the cavalcade, was trying en masse to process the finality of what it now knew before anyone else in the city. This early knowledge of something for which there would be consequences made the people restless. They felt an obligation to retain their advantage: to act first, having been the ones who knew first. They felt the pressure of performing before the press whose attention, until then focused on the hospital gates, was now directed at the people who would set the agenda, who would say how it would be.

A riot requires an audience. Sometimes that audience is a crowd of reporters, sometimes the terrified residents of a housing colony, sometimes – and this is when the line between riot and pogrom blurs – that audience is comprised of representatives of the state. A cluster of policemen. A local politician. Whoever it may be, to every riot there is an aspect of street theatre.

But, as with all creative enterprises, the riot depends also on what is left unsaid. It is not – and can never be – an out-and-out conflagration. Never a war of all against all. A riot is suggestive. The silent street at the end of which waits a mob. The quiet afternoon, an afternoon like any other, on whose fringes the fires burn. The sleepy town, of bureaucrats, boulevards and bores, which on that day alone is animated by a darkling energy. The sudden bursts of violence. Intelligent violence, unpredictable, predatory, which, armed with voting lists, knows the addresses of its victims. The possibility of violence is all. And, sometimes, more traumatic than the actual violence of a riot is its power of suggestion.

Later, much later, Toby, in his more thoughtful moments, would wonder if they had done too much to shield I.P. from what happened over those few days in 1984. A futile regret, for given what I.P. had just been through, no one would have done otherwise. Yet Toby could not help but feel that too much had occurred off-stage, too much had been left to the imagination. I.P. saw nothing of 1984. Even the children saw more.

For no sooner had the crowd fallen upon its first victim – more a symbol than a victim, a human spark – than Toby swung I.P.'s wheelchair around. He would have caught nothing more than the sight of an old man with a white beard and white kurta sailing blithely into that angry crowd. He was pulled off his bicycle and beaten up, his mauve turban torn from his head and stamped on, his bicycle smashed up. But I.P., though there was no way to stop his ears, saw nothing.

When Uma was finally able to bring the Fiat around, she watched an old man pick up the wreckage of an Atlas bicycle and walk quietly away, his turban looped in his arm like a mangled wheel; there was the mob with its first taste of blood, newly aware of how hungry it still was; and, strangest of all, past the wrought iron bars of the medical institute, there was her husband with his back to the crowd, casting a shadow over the cemented earth. His hands rested lightly on the handles of a wheelchair, in whose brown leather seat a cowering man, with a beard and sunglasses, stared blankly up at the vast and unspeaking edifice of the medical institute.

It was a clear beautiful day of pale gold sunshine. In the distance, the occasional bang of a cracker could still be heard – from a Diwali a week old to the day.

They have found the party. It is just past the doorway in the wall, through which the pale smoky breath of the night comes in, uniting old with new, past with present.

Beyond are deep courtyards open to the night sky; there are pastels and tiles, and wrought iron balconies, and fairy lights in the trees. Aśoka trees – a | śoka, like the emperor for whom they're named: he because of whom there is no śoka, no sorrow; the same śoka, whose access had produced śloka all those years ago – rise high into the darkness. Laughter and chatter and cheer filters down into the well of the courtyard, amidst the sharp clicks and muffled thuds of pool balls above. Waiters in white, the blue crest of the Raj embroidered onto their jacket pockets, bring around heavy inches of Scotch on silver trays. Clear beakers of soda, soft kebabs and the faintly charred loins of lamb. There is, though this is yet only a guess, cocaine in the bathrooms and Manali Cream on the terraces. There are blue mosaic fountains which actually play and slim Latinate terraces from which pretty pregnant girls look down, sipping pale glasses of white wine, while their husbands marvel at the turn to which life has brought them. 'Serdy, never thought you'd get married, yaar; let alone be a dad!' Such airiness, enough to air out the gloom of that old bad time, leaving them not just without a past, but hardly in need of one. It is airiness in which one man with brilliantined hair might say to another, 'Don't feel like I'm in Delhi at all, m'fucker! Feels like goddamn Mexico!' Airiness and lightness and security and, *mashallah*, wealth – and security about one's wealth.

Delhi feels tonight like a place where there is now and nothing else. So intense is this feeling of now-ness, so aggressive almost, that it creates at that party on Curzon Road an air of embarrassment among the older generation. Viski and Isha's friends.

Skanda watches as the older men, in baggy starched shirts and stiff jeans, buckled too high, wander through the party of young people, putting in a leg where possible. They are a generation that has grown old just as change has made the world new. It must impart onto their old age, he thinks, a magical quality, elongating their lives and distorting their sense of time. They must feel their youth is even further behind them than it in fact is. And, given that for many the bad time in the country coincided with a bad time in their careers and marriages, this feeling that things are better and brighter just as they are older must sharpen in them that eternal sense of youth misspent. How guilty they seem, Skanda thinks, of their knowledge of the past. None among them would dare say to any of us who are younger, 'You, who are here tonight, you don't know what it was like, you don't know what Delhi was like.'

'I feel so old,' Gauri says, taking Skanda's hand.

'You? You feel old. Why?'

'Skanda, I'm the only woman here under fifty dressed in a sari.'

He looks, and sees she's right. The young girls are in black dresses, in leopard print, in ill-fitting trousers, expensive designer dresses in bold colours. A busy world of stripes and straps and buckles.

'It's interesting, no?' she says, clutching her evening bag nearer to her, and lighting a cigarette.

'What?'

'That in a place so familiar with the use of colour . . . we should get it so wrong when it comes to Western clothes!'

'Who are you looking at?'

'Everyone. That one,' she says, her dark skin radiant in the light of the match. 'Look. The one in the pink and pistachio dress. A horror! And what she must have paid for it! I can only imagine. Tch, tch, Skanda. And just the other day, in Gurgaon, I saw a woman and – my God, baby! – you should have seen her style!'

'How was she dressed?' he says abstractedly.

'Effortlessly! A mud-coloured ghagra; an off-white blouse, full sleeved; and from her head to her waist, edged with a rough border of silver thread, a sky-blue dupatta. A peasant, Skanda, with a coarse and lined face. And not young, mind you; she must have been pushing fifty. But so glamorous, so effortlessly glamorous . . .'

She suddenly stops herself and says, 'Who are we looking for? I mean are we going to say hello to anyone? Or are we just going to stand here, on the edge of the party, bitching out everybody that goes by?'

He laughs.

'I don't know. I don't recognize anybody.'

'What? You can't be serious. No one? Not a soul? Not your aunt, your uncle, your cousins?'

'It's been so long, Gauri. And we made a clean break, you know.'

'And they? Won't *they* be able to recognize you?'

'I'm not sure, no one's seen me since—'

'What about that one? She's been staring at you since we walked in. Look. Next to the one we were just talking about. There, she's looking at you again.'

'Who?'

She now points to a woman with a scarf round her head and a baseball cap.

'Chemo, I think, Skanda.'

He looks over and sees the woman Gauri has been pointing to. She is dressed in jeans, keds and a red brocade kurta. Her face is bloated; there are lines of bitterness about the mouth, and emotion in the eyes. He looks, and looks again, but there is no immediate recognition. Then an odd thing happens. In watching her recognize him – watching the eyes send their frantic message to the mind asking it to merge a face from memory, a boy's face, with the grown man standing before her – he recognizes her. It is his mother's sister. Isha.

She stands there stock still. A smile on her lips, her eyes glistening, as if, in that moment, she can see the arc of events spread out before her, like a child who, staring out of the window of an airplane, has a rare view of the curvature of the Earth.

She just stands there, in one spot, swaying slightly, her body rigid with a joy that is like grief. Then mutely, she flaps her hand in their direction, gesturing to them to come over. No sooner does Skanda take a step forward, shattering the reverie perhaps, making it all too real, than she is struck by the force of her emotion. She clutches the hand of the tall beautiful woman she stands next to, and, swinging round, collapses onto a flight of stairs next to her. There, with her palms resting on the edge of the polished wooden stairs, she lets her head hang down, so that all that is visible are her tense shoulders, the nape of her neck, the knot of her scarf and the creeping margin of chemo baldness. And she sobs so hard her whole body shakes and shudders. The veins in her neck swell, her seated heart knocks hard against its cage.

'My God! Mama,' the girl in the dress says, with airy agitation, gesturing at Skanda and Gauri to go away. 'What on earth has brought this on?'

She makes no reply. She just lets her neck sink deeper into the trough she has fashioned for it with her shoulders, and weeps with enviable abandon. She seems hardly to notice that they are there at all. It is only when Skanda and Gauri, yielding at last to the girl's entreaties for them to withdraw, take a step back, that they see how acutely aware she has been of their presence. Skanda barely moves when a hand shoots out from that weeping mass and grabs his wrist.

'My nephew,' she says through her tears, looking up at everyone except Skanda. 'My nephew. I'm so glad you've come. My nephew.' And she squeezes his hand.

'Nephew?' the girl, who, it soon emerges, is her daughter-in-law, asks.

'My sister's son!' she scolds, as if scolding herself for something. 'Mishi, Uma. Mrs Maniraja,' she adds with a sneer. 'Don't you know? Silly girl! My sister!'

The girl, taken aback by this assault, smiles weakly in their direction. While Isha, still holding on to Skanda, but refusing to meet his gaze, drains her drink and shakes the empty glass impatiently at her daughter-in-law. She takes it hurriedly and withdraws. 'Son's married a damn bimbo,' she slurs – she seems very drunk – and using her nephew to get up, but no more than snatching a glance at him, as if afraid she will use him up if she looks too long, she murmurs to Gauri, 'He is his father reborn.'

The thought gives her a fresh burst of emotion – in fact, from the moment she sees Skanda she is like a woman caught mid-sentence, a woman anxious to get something off her chest, but unable to find a way to begin. It is as if she wants to do away with the intervening time and go straight to the heart of some other more urgent time. Then, in a phrase she chances upon, she finds an opening. 'Such a victim,' she says. 'Your father, you know, Skanda. He was such a victim.'

Skanda looks questioningly at her – at this abrupt beginning to their conversation – but Isha does not notice.

The phrase delights her; it gives her confidence, if only glancingly, to meet her nephew's eyes. And, as if only now able to see the full implication of her words, she says carefully, adding to what she said before, 'He was such a victim of that time. We all, to some extent, were. But him more than most.'

She pauses. A thought has come to her on the back of that other one.

'But not your mother,' she says, with all the force of revelation, shaking her head violently. '*Not* her. She got away. And she never forgave us for knowing her in the bad years.'

At this point her daughter-in-law – Iqbal's wife presumably – returns. The fresh drink, the arrival of another person takes some of the edge off this one-sided and jolting exchange. Isha sinks her lips into her drink, and says with sudden formality, 'How is she, your mother? Did you tell her you were coming here tonight?'

'No,' he says, meeting her gaze frankly.

She grimaces, and turning to Gauri, says, her lips frozen in their bitter stance, 'You see, my darling, we are not forgiven. Still unforgiven. And for what? For having seen, for having known.'

Tears stream down her cheeks.

'Isha Massi,' Skanda begins.

'I'm sorry, I'm sorry. I'm spoiling it all, aren't I? You're coming here for the first time – what?! – in twenty-some years. And I'm spoiling it. I'm so sorry. You haven't even met Iqbal and Fareed yet. And your Viski Masardji. And I'm spoiling it. Forgive me. It's just I . . . I love your mother, you know. I love her. And Rudrani,' she chokes. 'Rudrani. How is she?'

'Very well, Massi.'

'In America?'

'In America.'

'Doesn't want to come back?'

He shakes his head.

'Won't put foot here, no? Like your father. Won't even come for weddings and funerals. There's something sick, I tell you,' she says to Gauri, as if addressing a foreigner, 'about this country. It kills the ones with the fine natures and leaves only the scum. They survive. The Manirajas of the world. They prosper, they thrive! The good ones either leave or die.' She says this and glowers at Skanda, whose face is passive, as if to say, *Don't you dare stop me tonight: I speak from the heart.* 'They flourish, the scum! And anyone with just a little bit of sensitivity, anyone who's got an iota of fine feeling,' she says, for Gauri's benefit, 'his father, my brother, I.P. – they flee or die.'

She closes her eyes and drinks her drink. Again she shakes the empty glass at her daughter-in-law, who takes it but does not move. 'My daughter-in-law,' she says, and grins inexplicably. 'Her name is Alaya. Haven't a bloody clue what it means. But that's India these days: pretty things that don't mean nothing.'

'It means ascender,' the girl says sternly. 'It's Hebrew.'

'Hebrew-shebrew. Do me a favour, darling. Ascend the stairs and get me another whisky. And I don't mean Viski. Don't like my husbando,' she says, wagging an unsteady finger in Skanda and Gauri's direction. 'Dirty little git. Slithering about with the chinky women in Bangkok.'

Alaya pales before this revelation, and Isha, seeming to enjoy the shock she causes, continues in this vein. 'Yes, darling. That is what he goes for. Welcome to the family.'

Skanda and Gauri laugh nervously. And this eggs her on; she seems pleased to please them, and is suddenly contemptuous of her daughter-in-law.

'Do you want to hear a joke?'

'Sure,' they say with some relief at the sudden levity.

'Confucius say,' Isha begins, in an appalling Asian accent, 'man who go sideways through door is going to Bang-cock.'

Skanda and Gauri – it must have been their nerves – find themselves laughing uncontrollably. Isha, delighted at the joke's success, seems suddenly at her ease with Skanda. 'My nephew,' she says proudly, clamping his face hard between her fingers, and kissing his cheek. Then, glimpsing Alaya, still standing there with an empty glass, she barks, 'Go on, ascender. Ascend the stairs and get your mother-in-law a bloody drink.'

'Mama, should you . . . with your . . .' she says.

'With my what? My cancer?' She turns to Skanda and Gauri, and says, with exaggerated courtesy, as if excusing herself for having a bad throat, 'I'm dying, you see.'

'Mama, you're not dying!'

'Maybe I'm not. But I feel like I bloody am. A mutilated thing with a chopped off breast. I'm as good as dead. But none of that tonight. My nephew is here and I'm going to drink my bloody liver out. Alaya! Pffff! Your father,' she says, as if one thought excites the other, 'always knew what everything meant.'

'Oh, Isha Massi . . . may I call you that?' Gauri bursts in.

'Did you hear that . . . she called me Massi! Your girlfriend? Very pretty. But thin, so thin. Darling, you're not eating enough . . . Of course, call me Massi. I am your Massi.'

'I was just going to say: he's exactly the same, he knows the meaning of everything too. He won't shut up.'

Isha claps her hands with childish excitement.

'Really? You know Sanskrit too?'

'Not as well as Baba . . .'

'Don't be modest, baby. You know quite a bit.'

Isha clutches his hand. She can hardly listen through her emotion.

'Come upstairs,' she says at last, 'I want to show you a picture of them from the old days, a picture I took. *From the old days.* I used to be a very good photographer, you know.'

Halfway up the stairs, which she negotiates with difficulty, she swings around and says, with that irrepressible candour of hers, 'What happened with I.P., you know, it destroyed your parents' marriage. It all began with I.P., the rot. Do you like the new house, by the way?'

Before he can answer, she says, 'The gloom is gone!'

A very different kind of party is in progress upstairs. Younger, loucher, but more adult somehow. In a line of long thin-paned windows, clusters of dark mango leaves are visible, their veins gilded with streetlight. Pinkish halogen lights burn behind a bar of glass shelves; their shadowy reflection blazes dimly in the brass studs lining the green leather arms of a sofa. From the pool table at the centre of the room the low murmur of voices spills over like mist off a stage. The room is a holding pen for other rooms, for terraces and balconies, for bathrooms. And it is here, in this place so thickly absorbed in the present, that Isha, a half-crazed Katerina Ivanovna, comes hunting about for the past.

Her arrival causes some little stir. It feels as if friends and wives have been quick to spread the word to the brothers hosting the party, Iqbal and Fareed, that their mother has broken bounds.

One senses she has done this before, chosen a night like tonight, when hope is high and the memory of bad times more distant than ever, to resurrect the deadest of dead pasts. She comes, with Skanda and Gauri following, somewhat brazenly into the room and makes straight for a table near the sofa. After groping about in the darkness for a moment, she turns on a switch and a bright pool of light falls over a table with many framed photographs. The light coming on like that, in the dark room, gives people a shock, and they recoil, as if only now certain of a rumour that has been doing the rounds in the darkness. A few prettily made-up girls sitting on the sofa smile nervously.

Isha, oblivious to the reaction in the room, runs her finger over one picture with a silver frame. Skanda and Gauri, believing perhaps that it is the picture she has brought them up to show them, draw nearer. But they soon see that it is someone else. A black and white picture of a very beautiful woman with a boy. She has a heart-shaped face, a deep widow's peak, and dark lips and eyes full of laughter. She is dressed in what looks like a maroon or red salwar kameez, cut squarely at the neck, a chiffon dupatta hangs lightly off the springy mass of her hair. She stands behind a sofa, leaning over the boy, who is in school uniform, with his long hair in plaits and white ribbons. He holds a school book in his hands, but looks adoringly up at his mother. Gazing at the picture, half-tenderly, it seems, Isha murmurs, 'Bitch!'

Then she turns to the sofa where the girls sit. Her eye, trailing its length, rests on the girls whose faces are buoyant with collagen; their lips glossy; their cleavages deep and draped in chiffon. Her gaze sharpens, seems even to burn slightly; she considers them as if they are a stain on the leather; then finally, when they do not get the message, and smile nervously back up at her ever more lethal eyes, she says, 'Get up! Let an old woman rest her bones.'

The girls' gelatin lips part in white-toothed smiles of apology. They slide down the sofa, forcing one of their flock to rise. She stands by the arm, uneasily surveying the scene in the room. Soon the one nearest to her rises too, sending a seesaw of nerves sliding down upon the one who remains sitting. The two who are standing conveniently see someone they know by the bar and take flight. This is too much for the one who remains. She gives Isha who has just sat down heavily next to her a frightened look, a plea for understanding, and flees herself, leaving the sofa empty.

'Ha!' Isha says. 'We soon saw them off, the little sluts. Come sit down. And let me tell you. Where was I?'

Before they can answer, she turns her eyes, with their blank and loveless gaze, to the picture, which is in her lap now.

'Look . . .' she begins. 'Come sit down next to me. Why are you two standing?' Once they have sat down, she takes their hands in each of hers. 'Look. Even then you can see it: the poor git obsessed with her.'

Thinking, for some reason, of the photographer, Skanda says, a little distractedly, 'Which one?'

This makes her laugh. 'Exactly! Both, of course. She could do it to any man.' At this, Isha snips her fingers clumsily in the air. Then, seeing some confusion in Skanda's eyes, she says abruptly, 'You do know who this is, don't you?'

'No,' he answers.

She is incredulous. 'This – the little boy – is your uncle Viski. And this, this . . . woman is his mother.'

'She is beautiful,' Gauri says cautiously.

Believing perhaps that Gauri has offered this as an explanation for her power over men, Isha says, 'Yes, but that is not why. Many women are beautiful. I, myself, was not bad.'

'You're still beautiful . . .' Gauri starts.

She pats the air into silence. 'I know what I am. But *she*, she had something else. She had that strange ability only very few women have to inspire love in men and then systematically deny it to them. *Your mother*, Skanda—' she begins, then thinking better of it, says, pointing again at the boy in the picture, 'This poor sod, for instance, he wasted his whole life trying to earn her love. Sacrificed all the love around him, that of his children, that of his wife, for one little ounce from her. And, even that, she gave only to take away. It's one thing,' Isha continues, 'not to be a good mother to your children. God knows, I, myself—'

'Oh, come on!' Skanda says, hoping to stem the tide of remorse.

'No, no, I know. I can see these things very clearly now. And I have my regrets. But I never played with my children . . .' Sensing how strange this sounds, she rephrases, 'I never manipulated them, I mean. This one! They were like little chess pieces to her. Tick, tick, tick. Tick!' she says, moving a knight on an imaginary board.

'But why?'

'Because she could. Because she was supremely selfish. Because they – or Viski, at least – wanted her love, and she his money!'

'Isha Massi!'

'It's true, Skandu. Ever since she was thrown out of Curzon Road . . .'

'Out of this house?' Gauri asks, though she has been told.

'Yes! Well, the one next door.'

'We were just there, you know.'

She stares at them both in amazement.

'We've been lost for a while,' Skanda says sheepishly.

'But it makes perfect sense, baba. Don't you see? That's the only house you've ever known. Of course you went there. You virtually grew up there, after all. You must have gone automatically.'

'Were we there in 1984?' Skanda asks, thinking of Gauri's question earlier that night.

'During the riots?' Isha says with alarm.

'Yes.'

'No. No one was there. I mean people were there, but not us. It had become a fortress. No, you weren't there, not in '84. Why did you ask that? You were there a lot, though, for endless Holis and Diwalis. There, when your Viski Masardji and me had one of our big violent fights. *Swine*,' she says, with casual rancour, as if returned to the emotion of that night, 'he broke my nose. Do you remember that? I came running into yours and Fareed's room bleeding. And Viski, he was ready to beat me some more. And for what? Because I called his mother a whore. So? She was a whore.' She laughs out loud. A terrible laugh.

'I met your mother soon after it happened. She came to see me. It was just before we all went to Gulmarg for the summer. And she said – Viski must have gone whining to her – "Ish, did you call his mother (his late mother: she'd just died!) a whore?" I said, "I did. So? He called our mother a whore too." And your mother – she used to be so funny, Skandu: instead, of showing concern for her poor sister, still licking her wounds – she said, "Ish! What does it matter if he called Mama a whore? Mama, who's lived such a dreary life, she would probably be delighted if she knew someone had called her a whore. *His* mother, on the other hand – God rest her soul! – slept with half the Punjab. You can't go about – with her ashes hardly cold – calling her a whore . . ."'

Isha laughs uproariously and lights a cigarette; then, catching the bearer's eye behind the bar, she tinkles the ice in her glass, and mouths, 'Drink lao, fatso.'

Her mind, though in some ways puddled with alcohol, is, in other ways, flexible and capacious, able to keep many windows open at once, able to form surprising connections. She now says, 'But your mother, Skandu, was not like Viski's mother, who, though brave and beautiful and glamorous, was, at the end of the day, a fool. Her motivations were the motivations of a fool: lust, money, power. Your mother, though at times she chased these things too, chased them for different reasons. She had such a romance in her mind, about her life. She had such – I read this phrase once in a novel . . . must have been Dickens or Thackeray, James perhaps – *a talent for life*. Is it James, *Wings of the Dove*?'

He doesn't know, but he is deeply impressed. This generation, he thinks, this last little trace of colonial education in India, they are not so bad after all. They're on their way out now, and, when they're gone, no one will remember, in the world opening up, of collagen lips and blue glass malls, that there were once these people. These women, who, drunk and angry and bitter about life, could nonetheless, from the depths of some quieter India, where afternoons were longer, and reading deeper, throw a little Henry James your way on a cold December night, as easily as someone passing over a bowl of peanuts.

'But I was saying . . .'

'Her talent for life.'

'That's it. It was this she felt she could not betray. It was like a vocation to her; it was the only thing to which she remained true. She could endure any amount of hardship so long as she believed in the story she told herself about where her life was headed. And, with your father, it was this that began to meander. She was one of those women who need to be near things, you know, who need, in some way, for the times to be reflected in their lives.'

She says this and sits bolt upright. 'But, you silly fools, I haven't shown you the picture I brought you here to show you.'

Gauri smiles.

'No, no, no. I must show it to you. It was taken on the night of the 1st. I remember, I.P. had just come back. And the next day he left, left for good. Because, by then, the killings had begun.'

I, Padmi Kaur w/o Charan Singh aged 40 years, r/o A-4/165, Sultanpuri, Delhi do hereby solemnly declare on oath that:

1. On 1 November 1984, we were sitting in our house. Our relatives had also come because of the marriage of my daughter Maina Kaur. When we were taking tea, the police announced that all the Sardars should remained [*sic*] confined to their houses and nothing would happen. We got frightened. After some time the mob arrived, broke open our door and came inside. They caught hold of my daughter, Maina Kaur forcibly, and started tearing her clothes. In her self-defence my daughter also tore their clothes and also hit them. They tried to criminally assault my daughter. My husband begged them to let her go. The mob said that they would kill him. 'Koyi bhi sikh

ka bacha nahin bachega' (No Sikh son would be spared). They broke the hands and feet of my daughter and kidnapped her . . . confined her in their home for three days . . . I know some of the persons in the mob . . . Gupta has a kerosene oil depot . . . Mohan has a cow . . . They kept my daughter until 3 November. She has since fallen ill and has become like a sad girl.

2. After this the mob attacked my husband Charan Singh . . . my son . . . my neighbour . . . my brothers . . . These people burnt our house, they killed our men and criminally assaulted my daughter. The military escorted us to a camp set up near Sultanpuri and after that they took us to the Rani Bagh camp . . .

*

I, Nanki Kaur, w/o Late S. Gagan Singh, aged 50 yrs., r/o Kalyanpuri . . . do solemnly affirm . . . that on 1 November 1984 at 9 a.m. a mob of 250–500 came to our house. Immediately they started beating my husband with iron rods. He fell unconscious. The mob threw some white powder on him and put him on fire. His whole body was burnt except one leg and finger . . . I have received a total compensation of Rs. 3.5 lakhs for the death of my husband.

*

I, Monish Sanjay Suri, s/o Late B.N. Suri aged 29 years . . . do hereby solemnly affirm . . . On the evening of 1 November, I went to Gurdwara Rakab

Ganj about 4 p.m. on hearing there was trouble there. I was assigned to go there because I was a staff reporter with *The Indian Express* . . . The mob of 4,000 had tried to enter the gurdwara. They retracted when some men fired from within the gurdwara. After that at least two Sikhs outside the gurdwara were lynched by the mob. When I reached there I saw the bodies of the two men, both Sikhs, still burning on the roadside . . . Mr Gautam Kaul was conducting mourners at Teen Murti House when firing, killing and burning was taking place close by in the area under his charge . . . When he did come he stood to the side . . . he retreated instead of checking them . . . Leaders of the crowd seemed fully in charge . . . The police officer was obviously a passive spectator to commands by Congress-I leaders.

*

I, Randev (Viski) Singh Aujla, s/o Gyan Singh, aged 40 years, r/o 2 Curzon Road, Delhi do hereby solemnly affirm . . . that on 1 November 1984, at about 10 a.m., when I was in my office at the Raj Hotel, of which I am the proprietor, a Sikh police officer, with whom I am acquainted, came to see me. He was in a frantic state. He said, in the Punjabi language, ‘I have seen things, Sardar saab, that no man should ever witness.’ Then he laid his turban at my feet and begged my assistance. He said mobs were roaming the city killing, and burning alive Sikhs wherever they saw them. When I expressed my concern for my family, he said he would accompany me to my home on Curzon Road. We drove there in relative quiet, but, by the time we reached the Connaught Place area, I could see that parts of C.P. – parts that, I later discovered, were owned by me – were in flames. Outside my house a group of Sikhs had collected. One woman's skin and clothes were covered in a brown dust, as if she had been working in the fields. When I questioned her, she informed me, using again the Punjabi language, 'This is not dust. I am caked in blood, sardar saab, the blood of my family members.' The group of Sikhs wanted refuge in my house. I told them that I myself, after I had taken away my family, would be leaving. They said all that they wanted was the property; they would make a fortress of it. I consented to their wish and they immediately raised the Sikh battle cry – '*Bole so nihaal . . . Satzriakal.*'

Then my wife, who had already heard of the violence, emerged from the house with my two boys dressed as girls. She said she had spoken to her sister who is married to a Hindu of foreign appearance – H.H. Raja G.M.P.R. of Kalasuryaketu. She said we would be safe in their home. I consented to this plan, as their home was located in the same compound as my hotel. We were advised – both the police officer and myself – to travel in separate cars, and to be in the dickie, out of view. This was prudent advice, for, on our return, we were besieged by the mob. They wanted to know if there were any Sikhs in the car. My wife said, 'No, we are all Hindus' – and, fortunately, we were near the hotel by then, and the cars were able to pass, unmolested.

In the time that I had been away, a strange incident occurred. One after the other, the city's taxi drivers – a great majority of whom are Sikhs – had begun to arrive spontaneously at the hotel, seeking shelter. They had made a barricade of sorts around the hotel. When I emerged from the dickie of the car, they approached me, each with his turban in his hands. They said they were ready to fight to the death, protecting us and our property, provided I let them take shelter in the hotel and offer them any/all firearms, which they correctly presumed I must be in possession of.

Some among us were reluctant to take such a course of action, feeling we would be further endangering ourselves by doing so. But I – supported by my brother-in-law – gave my consent. The men were armed, the hotel and property secured and, given the state of lawlessness in the city during those first days of November, I believe it was this action that saved our lives . . .

*

Toby had seen the taxis too. It was his birthday that day – 1 November. A beautiful clear morning. The U-shaped street that ran around the public garden, connecting his block of flats to the Raj to C-Block on the other side, was freshly washed and the tarmac shone in the sunshine. He sat outside, reading the paper. He had just been with I.P.

His arrival at the flat the day before had created certain difficulties. The children, who had been told he was away on a trip, were eager to see him. Toby felt it was fine; that it would clear the air; but Uma felt it was too soon, that it would be frightening for them. And perhaps, she added, I.P. was not ready either. He had been put in Toby's study, a quiet windowless room, and had not stepped out once since his arrival.

When Toby, after knocking lightly, entered the darkened room, he found I.P. in a canvas chair under a pool of light. There was a tape playing softly. Nayyara Noor singing Faiz. Narindar had, unbeknownst to them, brought him some tea, which I.P. had partially drunk from a straw. And next to the brown ceramic mug, like an almost magical reminder of continuity, was *Midnight's Children*. Toby felt some shock at seeing it, casting its short bridge over what felt like an unbridgeable expanse of time.

Finding the book an easier point of entry into conversation than the usual small talk, Toby, gesturing to it at I.P.'s feet, said, 'Are you done with it? With the Rushdie?'

A smile appeared in I.P.'s eyes. Hunting about for his pad and pen, he scribbled, 'I've abandoned it.'

'Why?' Toby said, feigning amazement.

'Too long,' I.P. wrote quickly, and seemed to shake a little with laughter. Then Toby saw a slimmer book in his hands, which he recognized immediately.

'Ah,' he said, 'that! Well that won't take you long.'

I.P., marking his page with his finger, opened the book. He was at the end of the third canto. *The Death of Love*. Toby saw, from the faint markings on the page, that he had been trying to decipher the Sanskrit.

'Can you make any sense of it?' Toby asked, feeling a sudden optimism about I.P. 'Of the original, I mean?'

I.P. thought hard about the question, then wrote, 'The vocabulary, yes. But not how it all hangs together.'

'Yes,' Toby said, almost with a note of apology in his voice, 'you'll need to know something about the cases for that. There's no word order, you see. It has a very loose syntax. It was the one thing Panini didn't set down. "He goes to the fields. Fields to he goes. Goes he the fields to." All possible and impossible to crack without a knowledge of the cases. But I see you've underlined . . .'

I.P., who had been listening intently, put the nib of his pen to one of the circled words.

'Ambu | rāśiḥ,' Toby said, carefully voicing the aspirated ending, 'it means, quite literally, a heap of waters. The ocean, you see. Which in this case – for Kalidasa is the master of the simile, the upama – is being compared to Shiva's internal state.'

'Which is?' I.P., open-palmed, seemed to ask.

'Faint uneasiness?' Toby replied. 'Disturbance? He is unsettled like the ocean – ambu | rāśiḥ – at the rise of the moon . . .'

I.P., absorbing the comparison, wrote: 'Why?'

'Why?!' Toby exclaimed with a little rhetorical flourish.

'Why is he disturbed?' I.P. wrote quickly.

'Good question: why? Well, because his eyes have just rested on Uma's face, and he has felt the first stirrings of desire. But he shouldn't be feeling any desire, you see. For he is jitêndriya: one who has conquered the senses. And so, in the sudden stab of desire that comes unexpectedly over him, he infers Love's mischief. That is why he is uneasy. And, presently, when he sends his gaze out in all directions, he sees Love standing there, poised to strike, the arrow called Fascination fastened to his bow. Love, on Indra's command, is ready to flame amazement. And for this, for the violation of Shiva's austerities, he will die. Shiva is moments away from reducing him to ash. Later we learn that Love does not, in fact, die; he is only rendered bodiless. But I like to think – though there is nothing to support it in the text – that Shiva is, in some small way, also mourning the death of Love, that part of his uneasiness comes from his pain at what he is about to do.'

Scolded so often by Uma for these tangents, Toby suddenly stopped himself. '*But read on.* It's a very exciting moment.' Then remembering what he had come in for, he added, 'What's your plan? Do you want to stay in here awhile? Or shall I put a chair for you outside? It's a beautiful morning.'

I.P., as if guilty before Toby, for neither being able to appreciate what he had just said nor the beauty of the morning, wrote simply on his pad, 'In here, for now.'

When Toby asked I.P. about whether Skanda and Rudrani should be kept out of his room, he seemed visibly pained by the question. His lips tightened over the metal in his gums, causing him to wince. Then something boundlessly sad – and final, somehow – appeared in his eyes, and he scribbled, 'Forgive me. Not yet.'

'Don't be ridiculous!' Toby said, 'Nothing to forgive. The little monsters . . . they can see you when you're better.'

At the mention of this word – 'better' – both men felt a peculiar discomfort, as if something had been said that neither of them quite knew the meaning of. It made Toby feel an impatience that was not unlike what he felt when, while teaching Skanda, something particularly intractable came up – a rare aorist, an irregular form, an untranslatable enclitic particle – whose surmounting would depend only on time and practice. Leaving the room, Toby realized his impatience was nothing but the desire to make I.P., as if by an act of will or force, whole again.

As he was slipping back out into the flat, I.P. shuffled his feet and held up his pad. Toby craned his neck to see. 'Happy Birthday, Raja saab!'

'Birthday-shirthday. Thank you for remembering, brother-in-law.'

By the time he came out of his room the first of the calls had begun to come through. Rumours of violence in the city. The first to call was Chamunda. 'Well done, you guys,' she squealed, down the phone to Uma. 'Well done! But now please be careful. Ismail says there's going to be a backlash.' Then Nixu Mohapatra to say his sister, Gayatri, was unexpectedly back in town and he was having a dinner for her. 'But Nixu,' Toby said, 'Mrs G was shot dead yesterday.' 'So?' Nixu returned, 'Are we in deepest mourning?' Then, gradually, the calls became more serious. Mahijit Marukshetra called to say that there had been violence in Marukshetra. Toby's sister, Usha Raje, whom no one ever heard from anymore, called twice from Los Angeles. Once the day before to confirm – before the state broadcaster was willing to – that Mrs G was, in fact, dead. And now again to say that the American news was reporting riots in Delhi, and showing images of Connaught Place in flames.

'What worries me,' Uma said, letting herself fall into a chair next to the telephone table, 'is that I can't get through to Fatehkot House.'

'What do you mean?'

'It just keeps ringing and ringing, Toby.'

'Should I go over to the hotel? Viski might be there by now. Or they might have some news, at least.'

'Please do that.'

She rose; lit a cigarette; she was dressed in an old kimono he had once bought her. And, looking at her, he felt a pang of guilt, and knew why: he was enjoying the crisis, for the closeness it created between them. It was so long since she had confided in him, or needed him for anything.

At the hotel he found he had narrowly missed Viski. The general manager – a south Indian – told him about the policeman, about Viski leaving in a hurry. He said he would return soon. But the details worried Toby, and walking back to his flat, his mind retrieved the little snatch of poetry from earlier that morning: 'a calm, faintly disturbed, like the ocean at the rise of the moon'. The image, though a nocturnal one, fitted the present. It seemed to capture the unease of that radiant morning touched by some darker element, as with those days when the sun and moon appear together in the sky. Or when there is, like a catch at the heart, a sudden dip in the sunshine.

He had just come back to the flat; Uma was in the bathroom. He sat down to wait for her to come out and found himself trying, under changed circumstances, to resume the routine of the morning. He had just picked up *The Hindustan Times* – the headline read, 'Indira Gandhi Shot Dead' – when the taxis began to arrive.

They had the air of able-bodied men coming to sign up for a war effort, or donate blood, or desert the army of a leader who had turned tyrannical. There was that same solemnity of purpose; that same quiet resolve; that same hint of fear, masked – or banished – by the sanctity of a higher cause, to which, in some private moment of reckoning, they had committed themselves completely. Stern Jat Sikh faces, bearded and lined, the eyes vast and liquid, faces that even in good times had a kind of latent thunder about them, but which now seemed battle-ready, seemed to exude a terrible strength.

They came through the iron gates in ones and twos, then in a steady stream of threes and fours. They gave a little nod of satzriakal to their red-turbaned tribesmen and coreligionists who manned the door of the hotel; then, stepping out of their taxis, and following the example of the oldest among them, they removed their turbans and placed them in a row on the marble staircase of the hotel. And, without a word to each other, they stood in silence, seeming to await orders. Their faces were expressionless, but for what Toby thought – watching this spectacle – was the faintest trace of racial pride. A quiet acknowledgement that if they were to lose this fight, it would only be because they were grossly outnumbered. And yet, as many of them would later say, this was how it had always been with the Sikhs.

By the time Isha's car came through the iron gates, the black and yellow taxis had formed a barricade of sorts, looping two or three times around the hotel. And then all of what had been tentative and provisional coalesced.

Isha's car drove in just as Uma came out of the house, freshly bathed.

'Oh thank God,' Uma said, as she saw the car door open, adding quickly, '. . . Toby you'll have to go and check up on the parents . . .' And then, as if she had used up all her pragmatism, she collapsed into her sister's arms. Isha's two boys – dressed as girls – crawled out of the car with embarrassment. The driver hurried around to the back to open the trunk to reveal Viski. Who, from the shame and discomfort of the journey, or from perhaps having had some time alone, or from the experience of having people witness him get out of the dickie of his own car like a fugitive, had worked himself into a rage.

'Get in the house,' he yelled at his wife and children. Isha, now responding to her sister, was in tears too, and was saying, 'You should have seen them! Choodas, thooh, Uma! Scum of the earth. Coming with their kerosene rags up to the car. "Where are the Sikhs?" Thin, reedy little bastards who, under ordinary circumstances, would not dare meet the eyes of a Sikh let alone raise a hand . . . saying, "Sikh kahan hai. Sikhon nu mar dalenge."'

'Get in the house!' Viski yelled again.

The two women gave him a stricken look, though the boys, now having recovered a little from their embarrassment, seemed intrigued by the scene, even a little amused by the outpouring of emotion, by their father's escape in the trunk of the car, by the men, with their turbans in their hands, now approaching from the porch of the hotel . . . And there were as many conversations as there were things happening.

'Narindar, Skanda aur Rudrani kahan hain . . .' Uma began, and switching to English, said, 'Toby, you have to go to Fatehkot House . . .'

One of the taxi drivers approached. 'Satzriakal, sardar saab . . .'

'Satzriakal,' Viski said.

'I'll go right now.'

'No one should leave . . .'

'It's fine, Viski,' Uma said. 'He looks like a foreigner. No one will touch him . . .'

'What did they say?'

'Asi tayyar'an, sab de sab . . .' the taxi driver said.

'Viski, what do they want?'

'Wait a minute! For God's sake, Isha. Let me hear what they're saying . . .'

Then, after a moment's pause, 'They want us to shelter them, here, in the hotel. They're ready to give their lives . . .'

'Are you mad, Viski? What can . . .' she struggled to find a number, 'fifty . . . a hundred . . .'

'I think it might be close to two hundred.'

'Still! Against a whole city . . .'

'I'm just—'

'Do shut up, Toby. She's right. It's insanity. The moment they discover—'

'They're going to come here, anyway. It's the most well-known Sikh property in the city. They've already burnt what we own in C.P.; they'll come here next. Our choice is either to be prepared for them, or to sit cowering in your flat, and hope for the best. This way there's a chance . . .'

'What? That they'll get scared and go away?'

'Bhenchodh! I know what this kind of mob is made of. If one of these men – *one*, I say! – appeared among them with a weapon, they would melt away. The only reason . . . Don't give me that bloody look, you know perfectly well I'm right – and I'll scream it from the bloody roof of this hotel – the only reason they've dared to be so bold is because they know they have the blessings of the government . . . !'

In the time this conversation was happening, Toby had brought the jeep around.

'Take the Fiat surely!'

Ignoring her, he said to Viski, 'Arm them. Let them defend the hotel. Nothing will happen.'

'Toby!'

'Have you spoken to the parents?' Isha interrupted her.

'No, nobody's picking up the phone . . .'

'I'm going to Fatehkot House now,' Toby said and drove away.

The news must have been communicated to the taxi drivers, for even before he reached the exit gate on the other side of the U-shaped lawn, he heard cheering and clapping. Then – low and threatening like a first roll of thunder – he heard a lone voice cry, '*Bole so nihaal!*'

Which, in turn, was returned by a growling wave of '*Satzriakal.*'

*

I, Deep Fatehkotia, w/o Brig. Jitender Singh Fatehkotia, aged 56 years, r/o Fatehkot House, Delhi, do solemnly affirm that, on 1 November 1984, we were in our home when a mob of some twenty arrived. A Christian neighbour, Henrietta, had seen them in advance and came to warn us of their approach. She said she had smashed the name plate outside our house that read 'Singh' and advised we take shelter in her house. But my husband, Brig. Jitender Singh, outright refused this course of action. He said, 'If we are to die, we die here, in our own house. Not in the street, burnt alive by a mob of choodas.' He brought out his Westley Richards from his cupboard and sat down to wait for the mob. Soon they arrived. They had crude weapons, iron rods, tires, jerrycans of kerosene. My husband came out onto the balcony, fired once into the air, and warned them that the house was full of armed men and that his next shot would be a killing shot. This deterred them and they withdrew. But – we later learned, from our servant, Gopal – they had gone away only to come back in larger numbers. By this point, I had been able to persuade my husband to take shelter in Henrietta's house. This was wise, for later, when the mob returned, they set fire to our marital home, Fatehkot House.

A little while afterwards my son-in-law, H.H. G.M.P.R of Kalasuryaketu, arrived. Gopal, my domestic, told him where we were and he bundled us into his jeep and took us to his flat, which was a short distance away. There we were united with the rest of our family – my son and other daughter, our grandchildren – who were also seeking shelter there.

*

Later, when some had died, and others moved away, there were very few people willing to remember the 1st, as it had actually happened. An interim of some twelve hours, which though rounded off by despair on both sides, was for those hours a period of unashamed happiness. A small and irrational shoal of time, in which everyone present knew for those few moments a great feeling of joy and human warmth. So anomalous a memory was this, gnawed away at by tragedy on both sides, that in the minds of many it did not survive. It became a casualty of narrative. And those in whom the memory did not survive, those who would come to be persuaded it was chimera, later thought nothing of telling those in whom the memory remained that, 'No, you are sadly mistaken: charming as this notion is, of a night of respite from the awfulness of that time, it is a child's fantasy: 1984 was unremittingly awful.'

The mood that day began to change as soon as Toby arrived back at the flat, with his in-laws in tow. And it suddenly dawned on everyone that they were safe, all safe. Then came the first joke, once everyone was indoors and the doors were locked. Not so much a joke as an observation, but it made everyone laugh nonetheless. It was Isha who said, 'But, Papa, you look so elegant!'

Everyone looked, and everyone saw it was true! The Brigadier was in a double-breasted blazer, with brass regimental buttons, beige trousers and, rising proudly out of a spotless white shirt, an emerald green scarf.

'I say, sir!' Viski exclaimed. 'Well done!'

'Thank you,' the Brigadier said, with some embarrassment, and looking slyly at his wife, who was in her usual salwar kurta and sneakers, muttered, 'Didn't want to die looking like a rag, you know.'

Then, amid the laughter, Toby appeared out of nowhere – the pantry, it seemed – and said, 'What will you have to drink, sir?'

The Brigadier looked at his watch and something occurred to him.

'Isn't it your birthday today, Raja saab?'

'It is,' Toby said.

A murmur of 'Oh, Happy Birthday, Toby!' went through the room. The children, frantic with excitement and finding themselves all together in the consoling presence of their grandparents, began to sing. And if, at first, an effort was made to stop them, it was quickly overruled. The Brigadier added to the mood by saying, 'Well, in that case, I'll have vodka. Lord knows, I deserve one.'

And soon there was vodka, then talk of a cake. Deep Fatehkotia – whose chocolate biscuit cakes were legendary – began asking her daughter if she had any Marie biscuits. Games of some kind had begun, unruly and rowdy ones, issuing from imaginations newly inspired by the morning's events. There was something that involved hooping a hula-hoop around a victim. Which Rudrani, being the only girl, found she was made too often. A manic and ranging energy spread through the flat, making the time go by more quickly. The mood of the adults and children seemed to merge. Their whispered conversations shed their air of confidentiality. Soon Deep Fatehkotia was reading *The Swiss Family Robinson* to the children . . . And the Brigadier, sipping vodka from a dainty glass while glancing at the newspaper, found he needed more light.

Darkness fell.

The lamps came on. The bar was laid. There was talk of dinner; and Isha, now making herself a drink, asked Toby if he had a backgammon set . . . Or a game? Trivial Pursuit, say.

'In my study.'

He said this and now a hush came over the room. For, of course, though no one was saying it, there was something not quite right about this scene. Something off, something heavy and lingering.

I.P. had not set foot out of his room all day and no one – save Toby – had been allowed in to see him. He must have known that the whole family was together in the flat. But no one – not even Toby – felt they could tell him why. Not after what had happened.

'What if you were to say,' Isha whispered, 'that it was your birthday and you were having some people over?'

'It would embarrass him,' Toby said.

'Tell him the goddamn truth . . .'

'Viski . . . !'

'I mean what is this pussyfooting around one's own brother? He's a Sikh. A Jat. He can handle the truth; he would prefer it to all this . . . *Excuse me, please . . . I hope you don't mind* . . . All this walking about eggshells, minding our Ps and Qs. Let him know that what happened to him is bloody nearly about to happen to the rest of us . . . Speaking of which, I'm going to go and check on our barricade. I say, tell him the truth.'

The Brigadier seemed to read his paper more intently; the women traded uncertain glances; only Deep Fatehkotia, with something sad and hopeful in her face, held Toby's gaze. The children, in turn, fastened their gaze on her, waiting for their story to resume.

Before the tension could break, the door of the study opened. And I.P., a shawl draped over his shoulders, came out to join them, holding in his hands a battered blue box. *Trivial Pursuit*!

‘So it was OK, then? All OK, in the end? A happy time.’

Isha, with the picture of Toby and Uma in her hands, glances bitterly at Gauri; there is something sneering in her eyes. Then she drinks her drink, and looks long at Skanda, as if to say, *you tell her*. It is late, 4.30 a.m. The central room, with the pool table, is mainly empty. But outside, on the terraces and balconies, there is still the murmur of late-night voices.

‘What a great picture,’ Gauri says, taking it in her hands.

‘I took it,’ Isha said slurringly. ‘I could have been a good photographer, you know. But nobody became anything back then.’

‘Look. There’s even the picchvai of the white peacocks, with Krishna as the single blue peacock.’

‘Where is that picchvai?! So beautiful, among the most beautiful I’ve ever seen.’

‘Still in their flat. In exactly the same place. In fact, seeing this picture, it’s as if nothing has changed in that flat in twenty—’

‘Thirty.’

‘Thirty! Thirty years. It’s a great picture, Skandu,’ she says again, ‘so much of that time. And they make such a handsome couple.’

‘They were, they were!’ Isha says.

The picture produces a kind of wonder in Skanda. Which comes solely from the fact that he has not seen his parents occupy the same physical space in almost two decades, not since the night the Mosque came down in 1992.

As the memory of them together faded, Skanda and his sister had always said that nothing would be more miraculous than to see their parents together in the same room, breathing the same air. That would never be possible now, Skanda thinks. In fact, gazing still at the picture, he marvels at how their ever having been together had come to seem fantastical, like the merging of two famous but discrete stories into one.

And what does it show, the picture? It shows a man of European appearance sitting on a faded sofa with one leg thrown over the other. He wears black shoes with thin soles that are exposed and badly scuffed. He has Indian features with Western colouring. He wears jeans and a thick woollen Nehru-collared waistcoat over his shirt. There is something quiet and contented about him; he seems in a state of relaxation or calm – hard to say which – that is indistinguishable from fatigue. Next to him is a woman of darkish skin, her hair short and shiny. She wears a pale coloured sari, lilac or mauve maybe; even green perhaps. Her bones are fine and prominent, especially her collar bone, which seems to sprawl like a large necklace; her expression, open mouthed and staring directly at the camera, is unreadable.

Skanda tries to identify what it is that makes the picture a picture of its time. The lack of clutter perhaps. The feeling of a world pared down. The switchboards; the plastic ice bucket; a single bottle of White Horse whisky on a round wooden table; an aluminium tin, containing Deep Fatehkotia's chocolate biscuit cake, all speak of a vanished simplicity, of a time when, it seemed, there were just many more empty spaces than there are now. Spaces to read in, to have long conversations in, to have dinners that went on without care for the hour; but spaces also in which a riot or an industrial disaster could occur and the noise and commotion of the present were not there to sound an alarm. A time when bad things occurred and silence, distance and empty spaces fell like a muffler over them. A time of culpable boredom.

No, Gauri. Not all OK. Not a happy time.

It was of Time – of Kāla – that I.P. had been thinking while he was away from the others. His mind came to it in a roundabout way.

Except for Viski who had returned from the barricade with news that all was well, that the 'troops' were drinking whisky, and eating chicken curry, and playing cards, and that there had been not so much as a stir on the front line all day, the others in the room, with the exception of Toby, of course, were almost frightened of I.P. He had the air that night of the solitary – an air, in some ways, fierce and intimidating, of a man who has seen too much. Something dark and glittering in the eyes, something weary in the gait. And then that awful silence, which even upon fools can impart gravitas: but which, with I.P., because it was involuntary, and enforced by steel, gave him something of the dread aspect of those people who commit acts of violence against themselves. The trepanators, the body piercers, the heavily tattooed, the sadhus who run tridents through their faces and tie bricks to their penises.

He met everyone – touched his parents' feet, ran a hand over the head of the children – but he did not really meet their eyes. And it was this, his shame, that later, when they were drinking whisky together in the kitchen, caused so much pain to his sisters.

'What does he have to be ashamed of?' Uma said, working herself up.

Isha shook her head and said, 'This is it. This is what happens in these places.'

'What places? Why do you keep saying that?'

'I don't know! These places where the state is so violent, so unthinkingly cruel. And the society – us, Uma! – we have no response. We are just left shamed before it. It is not violence we understand.'

'Is there any violence one understands? Do you understand what's going on outside?'

'Oh, 100 per cent, Uma. That violence is naked in its motivations. I understand it completely. And, awful as it is, it does not produce shame. Anger, hatred, the desire for revenge, yes. But not shame. It is this violence that comes through the filter of the state that is demeaning, that produces shame and helplessness.'

'You know, Ish – everyone's always told you, you were stupid, just as they told me I was ugly – but that is the best thing you've ever said. And if we're not too hung-over tomorrow, try and remember it. Write it down. Tell it to I.P. It will help him.'

But there would be no tomorrow, not in the sense that she meant it. For I.P., as Deep would later say, was already gone. 'I could see it there and then. He was there, with us, in the flesh. But in spirit, he was already gone.'

Once he had greeted everyone he came and sat next to Toby. The family had tried to fill the awkwardness of his arrival with redoubled cheer and festivity. The children – though they loathed the game – had fallen upon Trivial Pursuit, for the sole delight of opening up the quadrants of its delicate board, for the fun of the different coloured pieces and the little corresponding pies, which only fitted in a particular way. Teams were being made; there was a full dinner being cooked in the kitchen; Narindar, with his special feeling of kinship for I.P., after laying out mattresses for the children in the drawing room, brought him a ready-made drink, with a little straw on a tray. Which made everyone laugh – the sight of I.P. accepting the drink and taking the first sips. He laughed too; and, for a moment, it seemed that what had happened to him was being assimilated, that the family, each in their own way, was confronting it and moving past it. But the laughter, as soon as it was gone, produced in him a corresponding sadness. And pain: as if equal to his physical injuries, there were psychological ones, that could no more bear laughter than his real injuries could bear exertion.

It didn't help that there was so much comfort that night, such intimacy, such a rare and exquisite feeling of human resilience, of the riot pushed back to the far reaches of everyone's mind, the way an unexpected downpour can push back the noise of a city. For it was nothing I.P. could feel part of. It made him feel his outsiderness more acutely; it made him feel he would never be whole again; and that rather than be reminded of his exclusion, in the company of people who wished to include him, he would go somewhere where no one would ask that of him, where, among strangers, his estrangement would go unnoticed.

As with many men, especially those raised in colonial countries, where the language of emotion and instinct – Hindi or Punjabi, say – is denied a certain class, and has been replaced with the formality of English, I.P. tried to understand what he felt, which was a thing with emotional charge, in purely intellectual terms. He seemed to want to crack it open like a puzzle.

The game had begun, when I.P., sitting opposite Toby, leaned in to show him something on his pad. Toby looked and saw it contained the record of the morning's conversation, 'I've abandoned it / Too long / The vocabulary, yes. But not how it all hangs together / Why? / Why is he disturbed? / In here, for now / Forgive me. Not yet / Happy birthday . . .'

Waiting for his reaction, then seeing his puzzlement, I.P. glanced at the pad and snatched it back hurriedly. He turned the page and showed it again to Toby.

It read, 'Kāla. Time. The Great Healer? SKT: Kāla. (1) Time, in general. (2) Time, as destroyer of all things: Death.'

'Yes!' Toby said, with exaggerated interest – he, of course, knew Kāla meant both Time and Death.

'Oh I know who this one's for,' Uma's voice cut in, and reading the card in her palm with care, she said, 'Whose first screen words were "Gif me a viskey ginger ale on the side, and don't be stingy baby"?'

Toby tried to deflect his embarrassment – Uma had taught him not always to seem so knowing – by drawing attention to the question. But I.P. was insistent and was urging him – over cries of 'Greta Garbo' and 'Viski, you ought really to have known that' – to turn the page. He did and it read, 'Sanskrit: *kal*, to calculate or enumerate. Latin *calen-doe*; Hibernian *ceal*, death and everything terrible. Cf. Latin *kalendarium*, account book.'

And then a question from I.P., 'Related?'

'Yes, very much so!' Toby said. 'You've made what I call an etymological poem, in which one creatively supplies what etymology only hints at. Yes, they are absolutely related. For at the end of all our calculations comes Death. And, in that sense, the word Kāla contains in it not just the notion of Time, but also that of its passage, the count of days, as it were, at the end of which Death waits. The ideas collapse into each other, you see . . .'

'Oh, here's one for I.P., I think: "What fruit was embroidered on the handkerchief that led to Desdemona's death?"'

I.P.'s eyes glittered feverishly. He scribbled – 'strawberry' – on the pad and showed it to Toby, who answered on his behalf. Cries of 'Pie!' rose from the people playing, but I.P. was not interested. He turned the page and now tapped Toby's elbow. 'And Kalā? Art. But which can also mean a division of Time. Is it related too?'

Toby laughed. 'To Death, and to Time, and to Calculation. No, no. That would be asking too much. That all those things should share a thread with Art! In any case, kalā means Crafts rather than Art in a unified sense. But, yes, were it true, it would give a whole new meaning to the consolations of Art . . .'

Toby could not gauge what comfort – or conclusion – I.P. was drawing from all this. It seemed as if some emotional need was finding the wrong outlet. At the same time he did not want to discourage him. Seeing his disappointment, Toby said, 'You know, some things, I.P., must just be allowed to run their course. They belong to the realm of feeling. They can't be solved like an equation. They *need* Time—' Toby stopped mid-sentence. I.P. looked crestfallen. 'What are you searching for?' he said.

I.P. thought about this and wrote at length, 'I don't know. A way for things to add up? For meaning, in the literal sense, to impart meaning in the abstract.'

'But that's a wonderful thing to say,' Toby said, looking at I.P. in amazement. 'That's almost all that needs to be said.'

But I.P. was not satisfied.

Iqbal, 'Would a pig have been able to swim if it had fallen off the Ark?'

'We're out, I'm afraid. We're just going to chat for a bit.'

There were groans of irritation from the adults lost among the excitement of the children having, at last, found a question they could hope to answer.

I.P., in the meantime, had written simply, 'What is the word for history?'

'In Sanskrit?'

I.P. nodded.

'Itihāsa, of course. And it's a compound: iti-ha-āsa: The Way indeed that Things Were.'

I.P. seemed, in his eyes, at least, to smile.

Then he wrote, 'How did you manage to stay above it all?'

'It was never open to me to get sucked in, I.P.,' Toby began. 'My father, you know, was older. Much older. I hardly knew him. He died when I was eighteen. And he was very disillusioned at the end. He didn't really know what to do with himself after Independence. My mother was a nurse. I was raised in boarding schools and colleges abroad. I was part of a grand family and all that, with a great legacy and tradition, but I was also, in an important sense, not part of it. Not part of its attitudes, at least. It was never open to me to adopt the politics of any particular group. I was an outsider, I.P., with a longing for India. With a need for it almost as intense as the need for self-realization. And Sanskrit – both as a language and as a little bit of old India preserved in amber – answered that need. It gave me a way in.'

'But what has it really given you?' I.P. wrote with fresh urgency.

'It hasn't *really* given me anything,' Toby said. 'It's like what Wilde says about Christ, comparing him to a work of art: "He does not really teach one anything: but by being brought into his presence one becomes something."'

'But what if it's all futile?' I.P. wrote.

'What?'

'What if this place is never able to appreciate what you become?'

'All acts of Love are like that, I.P. It is the risk we take. But, regardless of outcome, there is a record. And, I assure you, what we do out of Love in our life gets notched up in that column of the good things we've done. It's why I sometimes feel that Kama, the god of Love, is known also as Smara, which, like the Latin *memor*, means "memory" or "remembrance". Now try beating that as a good example of meaning in the literal sense hinting at meaning in the abstract.'

Their conversation – its urgency – had distanced the others in the room. The game of Trivial Pursuit had run out of steam. The children were falling asleep on the mattresses laid out for them; Rudrani had already been asleep for hours. The Brigadier and his wife had gone into Toby and Uma's room, which had been given to them. The Fatehkotia sisters were in the kitchen with a bottle of whisky. And Viski? Outside, smoking a cigarette.

I.P. was calmer and there seemed something resolute about him now. He looked long at Toby, then, seeming to weigh his options, he wrote, 'If I decided I wanted to leave. As soon as tonight, even. Would you help me?'

'Where will you go?' Toby said, in a voice that was something between a laugh of incredulity and a gasp.

'Anywhere,' he wrote. 'Nepal. Sri Lanka, at first. Just to wait it out. And then somewhere else.' He was about to hand Toby the pad when he took it back hurriedly, adding, 'Somewhere without itihāsa.'

'America?' Toby said, his voice still ringing with incredulity. 'Australia?'

'Even less,' I.P. wrote, and underlined, 'New Zealand. Canada.'

And then he looked at Toby with an expression – with that same boundless sadness – that said he had never been more serious about anything in his life. It was an expression at once imploring and desperate, seeming really to be asking Toby for help, in a way only Toby was in a position to understand. And, on receiving some unspoken word of acquiescence, he wrote quickly, 'I don't want anyone to know. Not even Uma.'

Toby, in what was like a sigh of grief, said, 'How will you manage, I.P.? You're in bad shape.'

'I'll manage fine.'

'Do you want me to come with you? I can.'

'No. I need to be alone. I need solitude.'

'And what? You want to leave now? Tonight?' Toby said, exasperated at how fast the conversation had come to this.

'In the morning, maybe. I think it would be best.'

'It's still so unsafe, though.'

'It won't be. Trust me,' I.P. wrote, and seemed to give Toby some hint as to his plans.

'You have your passport and things?' Toby asked, hardly able to believe what he was saying.

I.P. nodded.

'And what about tickets? Foreign currency?' Toby said, with increasing desperation.

I.P. gestured to Viski, coming in through the front door after his cigarette.

'I say, fellows! Should we have another one? I don't think our lot are going to get any sleep tonight.'

I.P., fastening his gaze more tightly on his brother-in-law, wrote, 'He can help. He owns a hotel.'

The bathroom door in the flat was open. A needle of light broke in over the floor strewn with triangular chips of white stone. Somewhere it illuminated the squalor that, as with railway stations in certain cities, gathers in that passage between the bathroom and the kitchen. A stained bucket, a broom, a rag, a wooden crate of Campa-Cola. Skanda, desperate for a pee, stumbled sleepily in the direction of the open door. The room was filled with sleeping bodies he had to pick his way past. He was especially afraid of his aunt, Isha, who slept lightly. He managed this feat, and had come past the minefield of bodies into the passage where the light from the bathroom door came in, when he froze.

His first impression was of a blazing white sink full of hair. Of long wet ribbons of black hair falling lightly into a gleaming ceramic bowl. And later, even when everything else had faded, this would be his one enduring memory of 1984: a bathroom sink full of hair.

His hands, which still hurt from his burns, groped back into the darkness behind him and closed gently over the cold iron handle of a gas cylinder. A perch of sorts now given him, he sat back and watched the scene before him. The barefoot man, in a thin white pajama, standing with his head over the sink, knotting his fingers around the wet strands of hair, drawing out gleaming ribbons, and cutting. Snip, snip, the tapeworm hair broke free, and fell backwards into the sink. It seemed, at first, alive, rigid and tense. Then, like a wilting flower, its crescent body suddenly drooped. Skanda watched with complete absorption.

There was an expression of elation on his uncle's face. The half-crazed look of a man cutting himself free. He cut at the strands of thick black hair, as if they were bonds that had manacled him. And it was amazing, the joy – when he knew it was short enough – with which he combed his fingers through his hair, looking, as if for the first time, upon his face. In the mirror, a trace of vanity flickered in his eyes, for now that the hair was gone, he saw the face of a handsome man. He flicked his wrist, getting rid of what little strands still clung to his hand, and held his wired jaw clamped between his fingers, almost as if it were someone else's.

He had just begun to clip away at his beard, when Skanda, trying to make himself comfortable, pushed back up on the cylinder. It made a terrible grinding sound, iron against stone. I.P. froze, then was at the door in a flash, a finger pressed to his lips. Skanda would have screamed had I.P. not quickly slipped his hand behind his neck, and, without a word, ushered him into the bathroom whose door he pressed shut with the help of a red bucket. Once inside, he took him by the shoulders, lowered the toilet seat and sat him down. Then he put his finger to his lips again. And smiled.

Skanda nodded, and made a little hand gesture of his own. A thumb pressed against the inside of his little finger. I.P. threw his head back and laughed mutely; his eyes danced. He raised the lid of the toilet, as if to say, *go ahead*. Skanda peed like a girl, silently against the bowl, as his uncle shaved for the first time in his life. He watched the face appear from out of the hair: the fine bones of chin and cheek, the prominence of the lips, the eyes set free of their clownish mask. Never had a man looked so emancipated; *and*, at the same time, in some essential way, emasculated. A man reborn, with all the inevitability of death that needs must always accompany such a rebirth.

The pre-dawn quiet of the flat fitted the mood of conspiracy that had grown among the men. The black Fiat, with I.P.'s luggage already in it, waited outside, the engine on. I.P., his hand resting lightly on Skanda's shoulder, moved like a ghost out of the flat, leaving behind him the sleeping bodies, as someone might leave, with a mixture of sorrow and determination, their dead at a scene of devastation. They met Toby and Viski just past the front door, in an anteroom of sorts. And there, for a minute, the two men who had not yet seen I.P. looked for the first time, in the half-light, on his metamorphosis. Their faces, discernible even in that silvery gloom, were like mirrors to I.P.'s own internal state. There was joy in them, something of the fast-footed spirit of renewal, airy and resurgent, rising up out of the charred and still smouldering remains of a former life. But, naturally, there was sadness too. The conflicting emotions made the two adults' eyes glitter in the coffined darkness of that tiny room where the men stood. Three men and a boy.

Toby glanced at I.P., then questioningly at the room behind. The room where the family slept, and from which I.P., had, only a moment before, made a thievish departure. I.P. resisted Toby's suggestion – and Toby would not have pressed the matter – but then suddenly he yielded. And, more stealthily than he had left the room, he stole back into it. Like a man returning to a burning house, not from some lofty sense of duty – not, for instance, to rescue a child – but for sentimental reasons, to save an heirloom or a relic, say. Down the long axis of the flat, past the sleeping bodies, and through a door into Toby and Uma's room, the waiting men watched I.P., in a gesture at once breezy and full of reverence, make as if to touch the Brigadier's feet. Then his shadowy form seemed almost to recoil and he repeated the gesture at the beige and socked feet of Deep Fatehkotia. Did they stir? Maybe. Viski swore later that he saw the Brigadier – from whom his own wife had inherited her light sleeping – open his eyes, smile and before I.P. could see him, pretend to sleep.

Outside, Viski handed I.P. the tickets, narrow and slim, with blue and red coupons, plus Raj envelopes fat with foreign exchange, rarer than gold in those days. He came up with them as far as the barricades. Watching him get out, and rouse the army of taxi drivers, seeing the black iron gates shudder and open, I.P., for the first time, became aware of the man he had become. A man without a visible identity. An unreadable smile appeared brighter in his eyes than on his lips. It seemed to contain all the scorn of the world.

The gates were open. On one side stood a taxi driver, in a vest and blue-green checkered tehmat; on the other, Viski.

'I say, sir,' he hollered into the open window, 'you are now leaving the immunity offered to you by the Taxi Drivers' Republic of Khalistan. Bon voyage, I say, fellow!'

With this, he gave a little snap salute, and clicked his heels, and the car rolled out into the joyless morning of a city preparing for another day of riots.

On Curzon Road, too, a sooty dawn rises pink over the house. It appears at first blackly in the trees, as if behind a screen, then brightens in scrappy snatches, restoring to the branches their texture, and to the twisting leaves their rich green colour. A conversation is under way, in which public school manners, worn and trusted, conceal deep tribalisms.

'Sogdia, fellow!' Viski says, looking with something like dismay at the brightening sky. 'From the grasslands of Sogdia and Manchuria. It is from there that we hail.'

'Sogdia, sardar saab?'

'Silk road, fellow. There was never anything in this mosquito-ridden swamp. And the Brahmin, let me tell you, he knows it. He knows the place is a big fat zero and that even *his* culture has come from elsewhere . . .'

Viski waves at the pale yellow parapet through whose thick clover-shaped apertures the morning seeps in. The men who stand around him – one young, one old – understand him to mean a place beyond the girdling mountains to the north.

'That is why he would always make his peace with the invader. Ha! He had much more contempt for the poor sods below him than they did. He'd been denying them their humanity for centuries. What did he care if he had to do it now in the name of some new Brahminism. Islam, Empire, Socialism, Globalization. There's always a new Brahminism, fellow, always a new way to suppress the soul of people. And the people, you know, they fall in line.'

'Sardar saab,' the older man, with a round face and a dense fuzzy white beard, says, 'I hope you'll agree that it was us – the Sikhs! – who always held the line, who stayed and fought. Those coward Hindus never did anything to defend this place. It was us who resisted the invader. Us, who fought him, and died. And once they had broken through the Jat Sikh resistance . . .'

'They found a country,' the younger man says, 'with her bloody legs open.'

The men laugh and the burning ends of their cigarettes play in the dismal light, bringing upon this scene of smoking Sikhs an air of conspiracy.

A younger man, unturbaned, joins them. And one feels, immediately, a pressure at the edge of the tribal circle. The conversation dies; and privately, it is understood that its resumption will depend upon what highly particular configuration of region, religion, class and caste the new arrival answers to.

The young man has barely greeted the older men when a voice further away calls out to him, 'Dadu, m'fucker, come here, spliff's smoking . . .'

'Serdy, wait, yaar. Grown-up-shrown-up conversation going on and all.'

'Don't let us hold you . . .'

'No, no, sir. What he's calling me to do I can do anytime. But it's not every day I get to speak to such . . .' He stumbles, he fluffs, 'Dignified . . . learned . . .'

'Oye! Cut the crap!' the voice calls.

'Shuddup, serdy!'

A red fire burning close to its base illuminates, for a moment, the craggy front of Viski's face. The glow climbs its furrows then, as if defeated by the steepness of the gradient, it shrinks back down.

'Were you in school with the boys?' Viski says.

'Sir, yes. I was with Ik-Ball, your son, I mean Iqbal, throughout. Both in Tata House and then in Oberoi.'

'Oberoi's not a real house,' the older turbaned man inserts.

'Sir, it was to us. We were in it!'

The men laugh.

Encouraged, the younger man says, 'You know, sir, it was me who gave your son his name . . .'

'Really?' Viski says, 'I thought it was me.'

'I mean, sir, his school name. Ik-ball. One-Ball. You see, one day he came back after his medical, you know . . .'

'Yes, yes, after old Goel was done fondling his balls.'

'Exactly! And he says, to the whole house, "Hey guys, how many balls are you meant to have?" So we laugh and say, "Two, buddy." And he's like, "Shit, serdy, I only got one." After that, sir, you can guess: he was not just Iqbal, but Ik-Ball!'

Gusts of laughter go through the little group. Heads are thrown back and fresh fires lit at the ends of cigarettes.

Then, with no warning at all, the young man whose name is Dadu – and who is clearly very high – dives down to touch Viski's feet, causing him to jump back in alarm.

'What . . . what . . . son? What are you doing?'

The man looks him in the eye. 'Bas. I've been wanting to do that for a long time. Now it's done. That's all.'

'But why?' Viski says.

'I just wanted you to know that I know. And bas. It's done.'

'Know what, son?' Viski says.

'Bas,' he says resolutely, though his voice – he is fighting to keep his composure – is thick with emotion now. Then, as if he can only by some mode of deflection express himself, he turns to the youngest in the group of men, and says, 'This man, standing here, let me tell you, serdy, he's our fucking Schindler. In 1984 . . . His mother,' he says, his voice now wild in his throat, 'when they were – bhenchodh! – putting tyres around Sikhs and setting them alight, she put sindoor in her hair, made herself a goddamn Hindu, and went from camp to camp, helping us. Great bloody family. Family of Sikh heroes.'

It is not the first time something like this has happened to Viski. But never perhaps so late at night, never so unexpectedly. He stands there for a moment like a man who's been struck. It is left to the others, who, having received so forceful a confirmation of the new arrival's identity, to comfort him. At length Viski puts his hand on his shoulder. Then, for his chief emotions are ever anger and laughter, he says, 'On a lighter note . . . Let me tell you a story from that time.'

Dadu rubs his eyes and Viski begins: 'Once it was over – the violence, you know – my boys, Iqbal and Fareed, they had a bit of trouble in school.'

Dadu, still snivelling from his outburst, looks with wide eyes up at Viski.

'You know the usual teasing,' Viski continues, and grins. 'Heckling. Fareed was younger and had a worse time of it. So, one day, soon after it all happened, he came home in tears. One of the boys had said to him, "You're a Sikh. Sikhs are killers. Sikhs killed Indira Gandhi." That kind of thing. Now it so happened my brother-in-law had come over for lunch . . . A very fine man. The old Raja of Kalasuryaketu. He has, in fact, only just passed away . . . I recently had word. But anyway, so, Fareed comes home in floods of tears. And old Toby saab hears what has happened to him and he takes little Fareed on his lap. And he says, "They said that to you? Tomorrow you go back to them and say, 'OK, fine, we killed Indira Gandhi. But who killed Mahatma Gandhi?' And so, Fareed, armed with this retort, goes back to school the next day, and again the heckling begins. But this time our Fareedu's prepared. When someone says, you killed Mrs Gandhi, he says, "OK, fine, we did, but who killed Mahatma Gandhi?" *Gandhi ko kis ne mara?* The boy who's teasing him says, "I don't know? Who did?" And our little Fareedu says,' Viski thunders, giving a clap of his hands, his eyes brimming with laughter, '"Neither bloody do I!"'

At this point Isha rushes out onto the terrace, still enshrouded in fog. 'You swines, you're still at it. Look who I have with me!'

The incident Viski described had occurred a few days after I.P.'s departure. Skanda had been present too. But first there was the drive home with his father, through the city of charred shop fronts, blackened cinema halls, graveyards of cars and taxis, whose carcasses lay in the street, their paint browned and blistered from the fires. The riots were by no means over, but a thirst had been slaked and an ugly sense of release now began to creep over the city. A photographer from the time described it – the mob's expression the day after – as the expression of men who've just finished playing Holi. Men fulfilled, gratified, men, who, though they are tired, their eyes feverish and rheumy, find it in themselves to keep going.

I.P. had seen them too. And when Toby said, 'We're going to miss you so much, I.P.,' he had taken out his notebook and written, almost with a wish to wound, 'I can't wait to be on the other side.'

Father and son had watched him disappear into the musty interior of that old airport, leaving behind him, as easily as he left behind the smell of wet cement, of urine and yellowing paper – the smells of the modern state – his past in India. It was hard not to be moved. Hard not to see it for what it was: the reprisal, cold and unfeeling, of the individual against the society that had tried to break him. He had a great wish in that moment to let India hang, to leave India to the Indians, as it were. And as the inky stamp came onto his passport – 2 NOV 1984 – his only regret was the decorum of it all. He wished he could have let that oily official at Immigration, boredom and sloth and greed etched into his face, know that he was not just another traveller, not just a man leaving on a short trip, but a man leaving for good. A man going voluntarily into exile, with nothing but hatred for his country, and who, if given the opportunity, would gladly have put a stake in her heart.

Toby knew, already in the car home, the final and shattering blow I.P.'s departure would deal to his marriage. In big and small ways, he could sense that it was emblematic of their own private calamity. He could almost hear the words that waited for him: 'There's nothing to feel proud about, Toby. Nothing honourable in what you've done. You enabled a man to escape. That is all. And there is no pride in escaping. I.P., in his heart of hearts, would have known that. That is why he didn't ask us . . .'

It was the tragedy of their marriage – of all failed marriages perhaps – that so much was known, and nothing could be done.

They drove home through streets flooded with morning light. The sun's indifference gave the impression of a world forsaken, of petty men left to their petty hatreds.

'So, Skandu,' Toby said, as they drew nearer the flat. 'You think you will carry on with your Sanskrit?'

'Yes, Baba. Why?'

'No. I was just thinking: you have so firm a grip on it now.'

Skanda did not reply.

As they approached the barricades manned by the taxi drivers, Toby said, 'So, then, you will have *this*, at least.'

'This?' Skanda said.

'The language, I mean. Sanskrit. Even if the rest of it goes' – he gave a joyless laugh – 'belly up. You'll have this, from my side, I mean . . .'

He glanced at his son.

Skanda had not understood. But it caused him no alarm: he was used to not understanding all that his father said.

Skanda wants badly to go home, but Viski is very drunk and will not let anyone leave. He has ordered 'Gangnam Style' be put on repeat, and leaping up, still dressed in full turban and bandgala, like an old pasha, he wags a furious finger at the rest of them and mouths the words of the song. He has brought over an old Englishman, with a tired and cynical face, whom he calls the 'Ashtray', to sit with Skanda. He insists that he knew his father. But the Englishman does nothing but smoke and drink, and has a terrible hacking cough. Then, looking at Skanda with confusion, as if some explanation is due, he says, 'It was actually your stepfather I used to know, though I did know your father a little too. I was a regular at your house once your parents split. Old Maniraja had me set up a foundation for him, but when things got too hot after the Mosque came down in 1992, he dropped me. *Threw me*, as the Americans would say, under the bus.'

Isha has removed her scarf and is sitting back in her chair, running her hand pleasurably over her bald head. From time to time, she slurs, 'Very glad you came, baba.' Then she squeezes her eyes shut, as if embracing him with them, and looks just like a newborn baby. Someone called Dadu is rolling a joint on the glass and wicker table. Morning light, though still unable to pierce the curtain of fog, seeps in. But every time Skanda catches Gauri's eye, hinting that it is time to leave, Viski is upon them like a hawk.

'Do you know what this man's name is?' he asks them, gesturing to the Englishman. 'Choate. Ben Choate! Unfortunate name to have in India, I say! Bloody fraud scholar. Not like your father, Skanda.'

'Really, Viski!' Choate says weakly in his defence, coughing as he speaks. 'How many times are you going to make that joke? I mean, really!'

Viski looks long at him, then at Skanda. 'They used to send us very fine Englishmen once upon a time,' he says, as if speaking of a brand of cigars or a rare and special kind of cloth. Then he chuckles to himself. 'But there is such a thing as jahaalat. Ignorance, you know. And sometimes people come at the wrong time and the society is unable to see their worth. Have I shown you . . . ?' And suddenly he is up, and begging he be given a few minutes to find something.

'Don't be silly, Viski,' Isha says, 'they're leaving.'

'Two minutes,' he says, with the desperation of a man needing to pee, and is gone.

In the meantime Iqbal, who has been standing at the parapet smoking, comes over. They had met some minutes before, but parted after a brief greeting, from embarrassment perhaps that two first cousins should know each other as little as they do. He is tall and handsome and bearded, with the somewhat hawkish features of the Frontier. He says, 'I can't believe we're cousins, yaar. It's been . . . what . . . I think my last memory of you was Gulmarg. 19-80-whatever, yaar. Fuck! How've you been, bro?'

The memory is clear in Skanda's mind too. They are standing outside CM1; the adults are inside the cottage with his mother; Iqbal takes out the blade of his Swiss knife and offers to kill the man who has just attacked his mother. 'I'll go right now and cut him up. Nobody can do that to my massi, and get away with it.'

Skanda is about to say something further to Iqbal, when Viski returns. 'Look, look at this.' He holds in his hands an old Penguin edition of his father's most famous book, *Three Sanskrit Plays*. The pages are yellow, the cover soft and black, with a russet image of an apsara on the front.

'This is out of print now,' Skanda says, for want of anything else to say. He has only one copy himself, which he had bought once at a second-hand bookshop in Holborn.

'Read the inscription, read the inscription,' Viski urges.

Skanda opens it. It reads, in his father's small fine hand, the black ink now brown:

My dear Viski,

Literature is a product of language. Its medium is words, as colour is that of painting, stone of sculpture. And language is the product of society. Language is a social activity. Stone and colour existed before man, and will ['will' was added as an insertion] exist without man. But language and literature, more than any other Art, are directly related to social life. This is [and he had drawn one: a long black one, across the page] a clear line.

Affectionately,
Toby
3.XII.1984

'I remember him giving it to me,' Viski says. 'We were sitting in the coffee shop of the Raj. It was the day we heard of the Bhopal gas tragedy. Awful bloody end to an awful year. A year of blood and gas.'

'1984?' Isha says, as if she hadn't heard.

'1984? Of course 1984. Annus Horribilis. We sat in that coffee shop, drinking bloody cold coffee with ice cream. And your father was saying that he was going to Kalasuryaketu for a while; that things were bad between your mother and him, but that they would come right; I'll never forget that phrase: "they'll come right". They never did, of course. Who knows why? She was a strange woman, your mother . . .'

'Eh, eh, eh. Watch yourself,' Isha says.

Viski bites his tongue comically and winks at Gauri. Then, serious again, he says, addressing her now, 'She blamed him terribly – I don't know for what? – for I.P. leaving. No one else did. Even old Deep Fatehkotia, God rest her soul, who blamed everyone for everything, never blamed your father for I.P. "He's in a much better place," she would always say, as if he was bloody dead. And, in a sense, to her he was.'

'What a time that was, I tell you,' Isha says, her legs up on the table, her hand resting flatly on the crown of her bald head. 'So hard to know what to do with it. Just feels like dead time, you know. Not lost, but dead.'

'Hey, serdy,' Dadu says to Iqbal. 'Spliff's smoking, brother.'

Round about now there is the first real brightening of the day. The sun, at last, rends a coin-sized hole through the fog. This new assault, of direct yellow rays, casts the terrace scene of drinkers and smokers freshly into damnation. Skanda looks imploringly at Gauri. They make to leave and this time nobody stops them, in their hasty exit from that divided house on Curzon Road.

It is one of those mornings when redemption, if there is to be any, lies in the continuation of morning rather than in sleep. There is an air of late-morning sunlight, of coffee, of dust dancing in a beam. They come in and seem to go their own ways. Skanda, long addicted to the comfort of radio, searches for his iPad. For the NPR app that, disembodied and distant, has been so consoling to him over the past six months. Soon it is playing.

Gauri, who has been lying on the sofa, her exposed belly burnished in the sun, rises and wanders up to the sideboard. She trails her fingers along the pot-bellied urn, with its ruff of blue polythene.

'Baby,' she says, and he likes that she says *we*, 'we must do this soon.'

'No hurry,' he says. 'My mother tells me they don't go off.'

She smiles, then comes back to the sofa and lies down. 'I'm going to have a little sleep right here.'

'All right,' he says, 'I'll join you in a second. I want to check email.'

His father's study. As ever, in deep shade. There is an email from Theo Mackinson. Skanda, having decided to take time off from university to devote himself exclusively to his translation, now occasionally photographs difficult sections of The Birth, and sends them as an attachment to Mackinson, who, though on holiday, always replies promptly. The verse in question is the moment when Rati – Love's wife – on seeing him incinerated, swoons and faints. And now rising, she says, 'Ayi, lord of my life, do you live still?' For she sees on the ground before her – and here Skanda had had trouble: puruṣ' | ākṛti.

Mackinson has glossed it in his email as 'the outline of a man'. 'But what?' he asks, pleonastically. 'What, Skanda Mahodaya, is there' – and he can virtually see him grinning as he asks the question – 'in the outline of a man? What does Rati see?'

Bhasman, Skanda thinks, and observes the case agreement. 'Ashes! She sees ashes in the outline of a man. Ashes of the fire of Shiva's wrath.'

Mallinatha – the great Mallinatha! – glosses, 'The sense is: that there is no man.'

For Love, it is implicit, had ceased to exist.

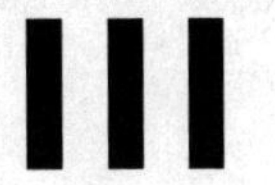

The lounge of the private terminal in Delhi. A place of beige leather sofas and cappuccinos, set deep in that world where a seeling modernity has yet to close over the land, and where in the empty spaces that lie between the elevated roads and the coloured glass buildings there are still, like insects taking shelter under the veined roof of a leaf, the encampments of families who built them. Black pigs still thread their way through the weeds, there are still patient lorry-loads of labourers, waiting among the dazzle of the new cars, for the lights to change. One India, dwarfed and stunted, adheres like a watchful undergrowth to another India which, in very physical ways, as with the roads that fly up out of the pale land, or the chunks of monorail that rise up from the ground like the remnants of an ancient wall, or the blank closed faces of the glass buildings, wishes to shrug off its poorer opposite: to leave it behind; to shut it out; to soar over it. One man, above all, captures the mood of this time: the security guard. In him, this man of expectation – a man not rich himself, but standing guard at the doorway to a world of riches – it is possible to feel the boredom and restlessness of a world that inspires ambition, but cannot answer it. Skanda watches him watching the lounge, with eyes glazed and yellowing from undernourishment.

A favourite phrase from college returns: *Quis custodiet ipsos custodes?*

The blaze is back. It is a year since his arrival in Delhi, a year to the day since his father died.

There is some commotion at the back. A plump man, dark and moustached, who must think he is waiting for Maniraja, rushes up.

'One minute, one minute,' he pleads, as if asking permission to pee. 'Chief is coming just now.'

Skanda does not expect this. He knew Maniraja and his mother were flying in together, but he does not expect to run into him. He is unprepared; a childhood dread comes up in him, an emotion that must have some deeper cause, but feels always like the dread of stilted conversation. Of never having anything to say. Too late to slip out to the bathroom now. The commotion is too near; and somewhere, in that eddying crowd of people, in that parade of briefcases and Louis Vuitton shoulder bags – the retinue of drivers, fixers, secretaries – a set of eyes has surely already seen him. Then the crowd parts, and he appears, with his slow gliding step, his silvery hair, his air of distraction, which, even as a child, had seemed to Skanda like the caricature of a businessman's busyness.

But his impression of Maniraja is not to be trusted. He can still see, too clearly, the man who first entered their lives. The man of astrological rings, albeit very expensive ones, of gold chains buried in a thick bed of greying chest hair; the man who made 'awry' rhyme with 'lorry', and broke the silence of the 'c' in 'scintillating'. The man who never dropped the 'so' in I don't think so, even when it was followed by a clause: 'I don't think so we can make it to Delhi today.' And though fragments of that man remain in the statesman-like figure now approaching him, it is the transformation that is staggering. Skanda has never known a man to grow more between the ages of forty and sixty – an age when men notoriously stagnate – than Maniraja. Not just in superficial ways; in profound ways, Maniraja seems to have absorbed the idea of self-improvement. Had he been a different man, Skanda would have admired him deeply. In fact, one of the reasons he resents Maniraja so much is that he makes him aware of things in himself that he despises in others. He makes Skanda feel like a petty snob: a man who, far more than the object of his derision, is himself diminished by his attitude. And, whenever he sees reflected in the admiring faces of others the man Maniraja has become, Skanda is reminded of his own defective vision, of how little he can see him as others see him.

'Hello, my friend,' Maniraja says, seeming, in the weary solemnity of his tone, to be consciously making time for Skanda while letting him know he knows it is their first meeting since Toby's death. He is dressed in dark jeans and a youthful shirt whose hem hangs short over a new paunchiness; he has his devices in his hand. The weight surprises Skanda, for Maniraja had always paid assiduous care to fitness; he had discovered it well before anyone knew the concept in India; and had, in those days, when people cared only how food tasted, paid visits to doctors in places like Austin, Texas, to meet with the father of aerobics and learn more about the workings of such things as the glycaemic index. So, the sudden fat, all unhappily concentrated, in the Indian way, around the belly of this small-framed man, seems to mean something, seems to speak of a greater change in attitude. But Skanda cannot say what; and, quickly, the thought is subsumed by another, no less surprising: his awareness of how long he has known Maniraja. Twenty years, almost. He is amazed that their relationship, even after all this time, is still so dependent on Uma for the most basic flow of conversation. There is still the crushing awkwardness of even two minutes together.

'Hi, Mani. Glad to catch you.'

'Yes, yes, my friend. I was just telling the girl that we must now, in a very clear and systematic fashion, set aside time for each other. Otherwise, schedules being what they are, too much time flows under the bridge. And one has reached that age, you know,' – here, he lets out a wet burst of raucous laughter – 'when time is finally a scarcer commodity than money.'

Skanda feels a familiar deadness come over him. As an adolescent he had mistaken Mani's way of talking for pedantry – and it had always shut down his mind. He sees now that Mani is struggling, in this rigid and unfeeling tongue, to condole with him.

'I was telling the girl the other day . . .'

Girl?! Had he missed it the first time?

'Which girl?'

Mani laughs. But it is not a joke. Which girl?

'The one on the plane,' he says, gesturing towards the tarmac.

'The air hostess?'

A look of dismay appears on Maniraja's face.

'Your mother!'

'My mother? A girl?'

'Why, what's wrong with that? I think she's still a girl.'

'If you say so,' he says, feeling teenage embarrassment engulf him.

Ever one to take things literally, Maniraja says, '*I say so*. I was telling her that this experience of death must be gone through. It is a new experience for you and her. I had it very early, you see: I lost my father, when I was still a young man. Death is part of life.'

'I know,' he says, trying to hasten through this ordeal. 'I lost my grandparents.'

'Yes, but that is something different. A parent is different. Even the girl – you wouldn't know it – she feels it too . . .'

'Yes, truly, Mani, you wouldn't.'

'No, you wouldn't.' Then, looking long at Skanda, he says, 'I want to show you something, my friend. Tell me what you think.'

Maniraja now indicates that they should sit. His retinue, forming a line and watching from a distance, falls back.

'H2 ka briefcase dena, Major saab.'

Major saab, a short stout man, with a handlebar moustache, sifts through Maniraja's half a dozen briefcases with ease. Each has been labelled: LV1, 2 and 3; H1, 2 . . . He hands Maniraja a soft bottle-green Hermes bag from which Maniraja removes two or three beautifully published books, in pale shades of orange, yellow and brown.

'In India,' he says, 'we have many words for this colour. For this yellowish-tawny-brown . . .'

'I know,' Skanda says, regretting the sharpness of his tone. 'It was my father who taught my mother that.'

Maniraja does not react. He does not have to; his name is on the insignia of the books; it is his library now. MCL. The Maniraja Classical Library. Skanda, of course, knows the books. But Maniraja is at pains to point out the black margin that has appeared on their cover.

'All the books this year, in honour of the passing of the founder of the library,' he says, careful not to mention Toby by name, 'including your translation, will be published in this fashion. Open it, open it. Look.'

He takes the book from Skanda and flips to the dedication page.

It reads, 'To the memory of H.H. G.M.P.R of Kalasuryaketu, Founder, 1940–2013.'

Skanda knows no cause for the terrible pity he feels. No cause, save the morbid feeling of embarrassment he has for his father. How he would have hated to be remembered in this way! A leaf out of Maniraja's book, a frontispiece to the project that he had envisaged . . . And yet Skanda finds himself powerless to protest. His mother and this Claudius, they have a way of recasting the world that is watertight; there is no room to slip in an objection.

'It's very nice,' Skanda says, and closes the book.

'How is your translation coming?'

'I am into the last few cantos.'

'Ah, and will you translate the later cantos?' Maniraja says knowingly.

'No,' Skanda replies firmly, 'only the first eight are Kalidasa's.'

'So, *The Birth of Kumara*, but there is no birth . . .' Maniraja says, and chuckles.

'Exactly. And there is something suggestive in that, something subtle.'

Maniraja's laughter vanishes.

'The girl tells me,' he says – now returning barb with barb – 'that you are yet to immerse your father's ashes at Prayaga.'

'I'm waiting for my sister,' he lies.

'Well, don't wait too long.'

'Why? The "girl" must have told you: ashes don't go off.'

The conversation is over. Both men rise.

'What brings you to Delhi, by the way?' Skanda asks.

'Politics, my friend, politics. Sometimes we, men of commerce, when it is asked of us, must play different roles. And this Italian bitch – this Whorebassano, you know!' he says, relishing what seemed to Skanda like a borrowed play on words, 'she's done this country a lot of harm. She must go.'

'So . . . ?'

'We want to put together a plan. A blueprint for a new and muscular conservatism. Something that will straighten the backbone of this country. But it is not easy. This place is so scared of winning, Skanda. It is very hard to make India believe in herself. But let's see. If Modi comes in, there's some hope. It won't be any thanks to your mother's friends, I can tell you. That chhakka Nixu Mohapatra has sworn never to join him, and that fool Chamunda thinks he's her rival. I tell you, we've been unfortunate in our elites. In other countries, the elite throws up the odd star; but, in India, it's just been downhill since Nehru. Chalo, we'll see. I'm meeting a few people.'

Then, contemplative, he says, 'I chose to live here, you know. I could at any moment have sold out; I could've bought a ten million dollar apartment in Manhattan, put my money abroad and lived comfortably. I didn't; I dedicated myself to this country, to its future. But, Skanda – I don't know! – this should be our moment, a moment that comes but once, and we've let it pass us by. People think it's an administrative issue, a question of policy and reform, but it's not. It is cultural; these things are inseparable from history. And there's an effeminacy about this place that I don't understand, an unmanliness that runs in our blood.' Then he stops abruptly, and, pointing at a corridor that leads to the rest of the terminal and the tarmac, says, 'But why don't you go through? The girl's waiting for you.'

'Is she really not planning to disembark?'

'No. She says she hates this city. She has her magazines, her iPad, her DVDs. And she has Suzie coming.'

'Suzie?'

He smiles.

'The pedicurist.'

The sun beats down on the tarmac, forcing a wobbly vapour to rise from its petrol-stained surface. In the distance, he can make out Maniraja's jet. A glistering tube, with a discreet crimson line along its flank, and a diamond on its tail.

GULMARG
(1984–89)

The separation had been like a long illness. A dull persistent ache. Uma knew – people told her – that she had to wait it out; to see it through to the end; that one day, she would wake and find herself whole again. But, so long as it was with her, the feeling of illness, it seemed there was nothing powerful enough to flush it out. Nothing that could rid her of her tiredness, which seemed to come from deep within her body, and which, like a beneficial enzyme, protected her from herself, limiting her range of intensity, disabling her capacity for strong emotion. So, no less than keeping her from the world of laughter and light and joy, it also insulated her from a sorrow too keen to bear.

A period in her life had begun that was like a second youth. She was living with her parents again; or rather, they, until Fatehkot House was rebuilt, as a block of flats this time, were living with her. Her husband was gone. Her children, more than at any other time in her life, seemed to be like someone else's, like nephews and nieces for whom she felt a great affection, but felt no real sense of responsibility. They came to her with their stories of school; with occasional anxieties about clothes, a frock that was too tight, a sweater too itchy. But she did not dress them in the mornings; she did not oversee the making of their tiffin; she did not give permissions. In fact, where the latter was concerned, and where, in the past, she had always been so diligent – and Toby so lax – the very request for a permission, to spend the night out, to go on a school trip, produced in her so vacant and wandering an expression that the children themselves stopped asking. It seemed to frighten them, that faraway look of hers. They went straight to their grandmother, onto whom many of the more banal aspects of their upbringing had devolved.

She told herself they did not think anything was wrong. Because, in some respects – and children can be shallow, in these respects – when it came to an impromptu bedtime story, or a sudden act of generosity, a Nirula's pizza, an Atari set, a chicken and cheese grilled sandwich at the Taj, she was more willing than ever before. She was, and she was only dimly aware of it, more and more like Toby. The source of all the nice things in their lives, and no responsibility. Their father, they believed – and they were partially right – had gone to Kalasuryaketu to work on a translation. *Three Additional Sanskrit Plays*. A companion volume to his much loved *Three Sanskrit Plays*, of which the new edition had only recently arrived from England.

The third play in the planned new volume was Bhavabhuti's *The Last Act of Rama*, which takes as its subject Rama's return to Ayodhya and his renouncing of Sita. Their reunification after a long sorrowful separation. Viraha. Toby had told them all about it, with that special genius he had for making things which even to adults would have seemed obtuse and remote simple for children: 'It is about two people, Ram and Sita, who love each other very much, but who, for reasons beyond themselves, are forced to separate.' She had, naturally, seen the barb, seen the parting shot. She knew, too, how much Toby liked life to be an exercise in meta-references. Left to him, that is all their life would have been. One long elaborate exercise in self-referentiality, turning in on itself, churning its guts, gorging on its tail.

And it would have been enough for him. He had once said – and she clung to it as the intellectual basis for their separation, 'I don't know why people feel that if this is the only life, then it follows that one must be hedonistic, or live hard. I should think that if this is the only life, if really and truly there is this and nothing else, then one can relax, squander one's life with impunity, spend it reading, sitting in a chair, or learning languages. Wait it out, you know. Treat it like a throwaway thing. One-use-only.'

'Toby, that makes no sense.'

'Do you remember when we were with the kids once, at that aquarium in Baltimore?'

'Yes . . .'

'And we bought Skandu that little plastic stick, which, if you cracked it, would glow in the dark . . .'

'Yes, he loved it.'

'He did. But do you remember what he asked us?'

'No.'

'He asked us how long it would glow for. Whether it would glow ad infinitum, or whether – and this was nice – it could be turned off, to glow again on another day . . .'

'Toby, what has this to do with anything?'

'It has everything to do with everything. *Because* – do you remember? – once we told him that that was it, that once he'd cracked the thing, it would glow till it ran out, and never glow again, he was instantly contemptuous of it. He threw it aside. We tried to explain to him that he should cherish it in the moment, enjoy the glow while it lasted, but it was no use: he was no longer interested.'

'Toby, are you saying that that is your attitude to life?'

'In a sense, yes,' he said, and grinned.

A joke, but it chilled her. It was a confirmation of something she had half-suspected. And she remembered it through the separation, because in these moments, when the framework of a shared life comes apart, one's emotions are unreliable. They are, like a swimming pool in spring, full of cold and warm currents. One has to be careful not to be taken in by occasional bursts of tenderness; not to mistake these short-lived conflagrations for real fire, for love again. In these moments, one needs, as protection, a rationale for the separation, something immune to strong emotion.

And she had hers. She missed Toby terribly; he had been witness to so much in her life; in fact, it was her missing him that was the cause of her convalescence. But never, in all this time, did a counter-argument emerge with power enough to overturn her decision. She never found a reason persuasive enough to make her want to be with him again, except for those that grew out of moods and sentimentality.

One thing, however, was real: not a reason, but a fear. Her fear for her children.

She told herself that, in the long run, once the initial shock had worn off, it would be better for them too. That it was better – everyone said so! – that they see their parents apart, and happy, than together and miserable. Which is what, in those final months, they had been. Rudrani was younger and saw less, but Skanda, on virtually a daily basis, was exposed to the toxicity of the dying relationship. And he had, in one instance – she could not wish it away – been witness to an incident he would never forget. That one scar, she had given him – there was no escaping it – and she was pretty sure it was permanent. It was what had brought the curtain crashing down on those last days of anguish.

The family was at the dinner table. I.P. had been gone a few weeks. Toby, turning to the Brigadier, said, 'Sir, you won't believe who came to see me today.'

The Brigadier, compressing his bearded lips, wet with droplets of whisky, looked over at his son-in-law. The light from a wicker shade fell in a bright pool over the red and white chequered oilcloth of the dining table.

'A fellow called Choate.'

The Brigadier laughed. Then, with some delay, Skanda laughed. Rudrani had not understood, and feeling left out, looked to her mother, who mutely wagged a disapproving finger at her. Deep was in the kitchen.

'What did he want, this Choate? Does he have a first name?'

'Ben.'

The Brigadier roared with laughter.

Skanda, complicit in the joke, and scornful of his sister's inability to grasp it, laughed too.

'He wanted,' Toby continued, 'my patronage, if you please . . . Some businessmen in Bombay, a fellow I used to know, put him up to it . . . *For* – it beggars belief! – a *holocaust* museum.'

'Dada,' Rudrani said, 'what is hollow-kos?'

Skanda didn't reply.

The Brigadier said, 'A Holocaust museum? In India? Bit strange, no? What next? A Civil War Memorial? A mausoleum to those who fell at Sebastopol? A parade marking the end of the Franco-Prussian War?'

'No, no, no sir,' Toby said, laughing. 'Not that Holocaust. Holocaust with a small "h".'

'Baba,' Rudrani said pointedly, 'Skanda doesn't seem to know – but what is a hollow-kos?'

'My darling, it was the extermination of the Jews by the Nazis. Millions died. But the reason Nana and I are laughing is that the man who came to see me today wants to open a holocaust museum documenting the killing of Hindus by Muslims.'

'Go on!' the Brigadier said. 'Is that right? But the man must be a damned fool. A real Ben Choate. There are no numbers, no evidence;

it would have happened – *if* it happened – over hundreds of years. What would you exhibit in such a museum? It can't be compared . . .'

'I know. I was appalled. I tried to tell him what insanity it was.'

'Dangerous insanity.'

'I even asked to meet his backers. Because, you know what this sort of man is about, sir? Cynical. Full of a foreigner's disregard. He comes into a place he knows nothing about; finds some banias, with a bee in their bonnet about Islam, and, suddenly he's convinced them to put up the money for a holocaust museum, and to make him the director, no doubt.'

Uma, silent throughout, now said, 'I don't see what's so wrong with it.'

Toby looked at her across the pool of light on the table and, sensing her aggression, did not respond.

It was her father who said, 'It's madness, Mishi . . .'

'Mishi?'

'Uma.'

'Mishi! Mishi! Mishy-mashy!' Rudrani shouted, finding it endlessly amusing that it had once been her mother's pet name.

'It'll criminalize the Muslims of this country. It'll leave the blame at their door, for a killing in which they had no part. A killing, which I might add, is undocumented. You can no more have a museum like that than you can have . . . I don't know . . . ?'

'One in the Levant documenting the people killed in the Crusades?' Toby ventured. 'I know. I tried to tell him: the Holocaust, both in its execution, and the ideas behind it, was a modern thing. And the Germans kept scrupulous records.'

Uma fell silent.

The kitchen door swung open, and Narindar, followed by Deep Fatehkotia, emerged with dinner. Cutlets, chips, peas.

'Well!' the Brigadier said, and drained his drink. An air of normalcy returned to the table.

Toby, though addressing himself to the Brigadier, tried secretly to placate Uma. 'But, sir, I fully support the desire to want to face the past. No matter how distant it is. After all, it is only as near or far as it feels. Look at Iran; Karbala might have happened just the other day. And that was 1,500 years ago. But you can't graft the modern past, with all its needs and anxieties, onto the distant past. It will only leave you more confused. And angry. Historical understanding – I think it is one of the South African writers who says this . . .'

Suddenly there was a loud crack, and 'Fuck!'

Uma, for some time now, had been playing with a loose strip of Formica on the edge of the dining table. It was noisy and Toby had looked over at her a couple of times, but had not said anything. She had now broken it and a tiny fragment of wood, he could see, was lodged painfully under her nail.

'Are you OK . . . ?'

'I'm fine,' she said, sticking her finger in her mouth.

'Go on. You were saying,' she said indistinctly. 'The South African writers . . .'

'No. It's fine. It was nothing . . .'

'No. Go on, please. I don't want to break your flow. I was listening.'

He began nervously: 'Coetzee perhaps . . . I can't quite remember. I think he says – and they, sir, you can imagine, know a thing or two about history! – that a historical understanding must, in the end, be an "understanding of the past as a shaping force upon the present".' Uma, having removed her finger from her mouth, now squeezed out a tiny bead of blood from under her nail. Toby could not help but stare.

'Go on,' she said, with a suppressed shout in her voice.

'And, in this sense,' he said – but the air was heavy – '"our historical being is part of our present." Which is why, I feel, the response cannot be borrowed from other places. It must spring naturally from the circumstances of that particular place, for it to bring real closure.'

'Yes, but these things take many forms, Raja saab. Not all cultures are the same.'

'Oh, I agree, sir,' Toby said, relieved to have his father-in-law's voice in the mix. 'Take the blacks in America. What a moving response they have had to their experience of the past. In recent times, with men like Baldwin and Ellison, it's taken a written form. But its soul was music. "Trouble in mind *and* . . ."' he began, smiling at the children.

They knew the song. They had heard it played, the Sam Cooke version – almost to the point of erasure – on their father's tape deck. They knew the words and could sing along at their father's prompting. 'I'm blue,' they sang back. And when he gave them their cue about laying one's head on that lonesome railroad track, they knew what came next. Loudly – and in unison – they begged that 2:10 train to ease their troubled mind. The Brigadier, though he did not know the song, was delighted and laughed out loud. Deep Fatehkotia, the food now all on the table, and steaming in the light from the lamp, put her hand on her husband's shoulder, tapping it in time with the children's singing.

Uma sat away from the rest. Skanda, seeing her isolated, could not help but reach out and take her hand, forgetting it was injured. On being touched, Uma let out an awful moan, hardly commensurate with the pain. Then silence. The next thing Skanda knew his mother was lurching across the table towards him and, like an animal driven to madness, she sank her teeth into his arm.

That was December 1984. The 2nd, to be precise. Afterwards – once the grandparents had managed to clear the scene away, in tears, in bandages, in bedtime stories, bringing with the benefit of their age, some comfort, a cooing assurance that things were only slightly out of true, and would soon be put right – Uma and Toby sat alone in the drawing room for the last time. He had given her a rasai, which she had wrapped about herself, and a stiff drink. Her hysteria gone, there was little doubt, in his mind, who suffered most; but, more importantly, who had been the true target of her rage. In what was almost an automatic response to what had happened, he put in place preparations for his departure to Kalasuryaketu the next morning. Even as they sat there, in that front room, he waited for a lightning call to go through to Laban. There was something cold and decided and final about him that night, perhaps at having glimpsed for the first time the depth of her animus for him.

Later she recalled, in those moments, when he had been full of his own quiet and wintry anger, that he had been attractive to her for the first time in years. At the end of a cycle, she felt herself released of a number of violent emotions that, without her knowing it, had for a while now defined her. She was more than their sum for the first time in a long time. She felt borne in on her something of the philosophical temperament that had always come so easily to Toby. She thought she could almost see around their situation. And she wondered – such a relief to be able to see the world again as others see it – how he saw things, how he saw her, how he thought of the little experiment their life together had been.

A kind of transfer took place, an exchanging of roles. If so far it had been Toby who was always able to take the long view, always able to see life in philosophical terms, and not in the mean light of a personal joy or dissatisfaction, it was in Uma that this faculty seemed now to grow.

Every failed marriage has its victors. There are those who walk away from its ruins with its vitality, its lessons, its experience; and then there are those who are undone by it, who are left with futility and nothing else. It did not seem that evening that things would go in

Uma's favour. She was wretched and full of shame – a danger to her children. She sat there with her rasai, clutching the whisky with both her hands, her toes gnawing at the rounded edge of a cushion. Toby, in contrast, though feeling a grief too deep to reach, was calm and businesslike, sitting with his legs crossed by the wicker telephone table. Nobody witnessing this scene could have anticipated that it contained in it the seeds of the man's diminishing and the woman's renewal. It seemed so much the other way round. But, as time went by, it became clear that it was Toby who was the real casualty of their marriage: Toby who would later behave in a petty way about money; Toby who would remarry first, and hastily; Toby who would find his heart empty of anything but the most arid love for his children. Most of all, it was Toby who, never so blind as not to see his own diminishing, would be filled with bitterness for the man he became.

That night, as if too timid to inhabit some future and yet unimagined life, they clung to the old configuration. They were more husband and wife to each other than they had been in years. They filled the new silences with that mixture of banality and tenderness that is the stock-in-trade of married life.

'Will you be taking the train or are you thinking of driving?'

'I'm not sure. Let's see what Laban says.'

'He hasn't called yet?'

'No. There seems to be some trouble with the phone.'

'Do you have critical editions of the texts you're working on?'

'The plays?'

'The plays.'

'Yes, but I might ask you to send me a few commentaries in a few weeks. Parts of the Vishakhadatta are confusing.'

'I've never liked him, I must confess. I've always preferred Bhavabhuti.'

'Bhavabhuti is a very great playwright. The jewel in the court of Yaśovarman.'

'Tell me. What is it the Tamasā says about rasa?'

'Oh, you remember that! She says, "What a course this story has run . . ."'

'I envy you seeing the Tamasā tomorrow; I love that river. I've put the Samsonite out, by the way. It'll be easier; it has wheels.'

'Might be too big; I'm not taking much.'

'How long do you think . . . ?'

She was cut off by the phone ringing. Toby picked up the pale green receiver. But the voice coming through its dust-encrusted holes was not Laban's; it was the operator, informing them that the call couldn't be put through; the lines were jammed; there had been some trouble in Bhopal.

The next day they heard about the gas. Methyl isocyanate, the somnambulist murderer, seeping out of the Union Carbide plant into the lives of sleeping people. But first, as if in response to the period of uncertainty that lay ahead of them, they made love one last time.

He left the next day without saying goodbye to anyone, except his brother-in-law, Viski, for whom he inscribed a copy of the new edition of *Three Sanskrit Plays*. It was not the usual unthinking inscription; he took some trouble over it. He was, more than at any other time in his life so far, intensely concerned with what his work, and especially his engagement with language, had amounted to. The visit from Choate – the talk of a holocaust museum – had disturbed him more than he was prepared to admit. He felt a reckoning of some kind, a reckoning with the past – the very past he had devoted his entire life to – was on the horizon.

The form it was to take was very far away from anything Toby envisaged, but it did not, in his mind, absolve him of responsibility.

Now I am become Death, the destroyer of worlds. But he had it wrong, Oppenheimer. Kāla, here, was Time, Time grown old. And kṣaya was not so much destruction as it was decay. I am Time grown old, decayer of worlds. The difference was tonal, the Christian finality of one versus the Hindu inevitability of the other. *All that lives must die, / Passing through nature to eternity.* And yet he was not able to treat as inevitable what he saw happening to old India: how does one stand back, when the knowledge to which one has given one's life is weaponized? *My dear Viski, Literature is a product of language. Its medium is words, as colour is that of painting, stone of sculpture. And language is the product of society*. That's right; that's the difference, isn't it? Language is a consensus. *It is a social activity.* It cannot stand aloof from men. *Not like stone and colour, which existed before man and exist – will exist*, he inserted – *without man.* That's it: we brought it into the world, the material of literature. We imbued it with meaning, we gave to its sound a hidden resonance, a deep tissue. A music that seems to contain our past. Isn't that what we feel when the śloka rises, that there is, though undecipherable to us now, buried in its anuṣṭubh meter perhaps, some historical memory to which we crave to give utterance?

But what if there is other music, competing with the music to which our idea of the past has become fused . . . what if there is an overlay of other sounds, like a muzak in the foreground, and it drowns out the secret music we want to hear? My dear Viski, when there is this, we are like people who stand with bated breath on the bank of some ocean or river, waiting for a voice to come off the water, and speak to us, but we hear nothing. Nothing but dissonance and the dispiriting sadness of an irrecoverable past. *Language and literature, more than any other Art, are directly related to social life. This is* – and he drew one across the page – *a clear line.*

In his heart he sensed the reckoning that was coming. And well before the great passion of his life would take the form of men in saffron cracking open, like an egg, the dome of an old Mosque in Ayodhya, he was sick with worry at the way the things he loved would one day be used. He wanted to clear his debts, his conscience, to explain himself, to say – like Virginsky in *Demons* – '"This is not it, this is not it! No, this is not it at all!"'

That day – the day Uma arrives in Delhi, with the inevitability of the heat returning – was to have been set aside for Gauri. It was the day Skanda was to meet Kartik. It is a point of friction between them that he has, despite Gauri's urging, never met her son.

Sensing his reluctance, she says the night before, 'What are you afraid of?'

'The timing,' he replies easily.

'But is there ever a good time?'

'No. But there are bad times,' he says, and laughs.

'I don't know if this is any worse than another. He has his holidays. And besides, at this stage, you're just "mummy's friend" coming for lunch.' A look passes between them. Something probing, something half-hopeful. Skanda does not respond and Gauri, as if suppressing the little expectation that had arisen momentarily in her, says quickly, 'Why? Do you think he'll sense something? Do you think he'll know? *Did you know?*'

'Did I know?'

'Did you know – the first time you met Maniraja – that he was your mother's . . . well, beau,' she adds coyly.

'No, I didn't know that till much later,' he says, casting his mind back, and finding it – his memory – fragment fast into the broken lines of a German expressionist painting. 'The sequence is unclear in my head. I know I came to associate it with many things.'

'Like what?'

'Like with a violent fight between Isha and Viski. With my father's marriage to Sylvia. With going to London alone for the first time. But, most of all, with my mother's vulnerability in those days.'

'Your father,' Gauri inserts, 'married Sylvia *before* your mother got together with Maniraja?'

'Yes.'

'But you didn't mind that?'

'No. Not as much.'

'Why?'

'I don't know. It's the way of the world, Gauri.'

'Sounds bloody unfair to me.'

'Perhaps. But the two things – the two relationships, I mean – had a very different character. My father's, though it came first, felt so much more like a settling for less, a scaling down of hope. It was pitiable, an act of desperation. My mother's . . . well, what can I say? There was something of the "rank sweat of an enseamed bed" about it?'

'Skanda!'

'"Honeying and making love . . . stewing in corruption."'

'Stop it!'

'"Frailty,"' he says – then stops laughing, and recalling what he just said about his mother's vulnerability, realizes he has imparted onto the lines a new meaning. '"Thy name is woman."'

'Pig,' she says, studying the changes in his face.

'I don't know, Gauri,' he begins again, with exasperation. 'These things have an embedded logic. That summer in Gulmarg; the bad night at my aunt Isha's; my father's wedding in London: throw these things up in the air and, no matter how they fall, they always add up to the same thing, they have only one inevitable outcome: Maniraja.

It just could not have been otherwise. They conjured him up, those events; and if there had not been a Maniraja at hand, we would have had to invent one . . .'

'Silly fool,' she says turning over in bed – for it is late. 'Do you, at least, remember meeting him for the first time?'

'Yes.'

'And?'

'And what?'

'What was your first impression?'

'I'd rather not say. I'm a bit embarrassed of it now.'

'Come on . . . you were a child, Skanda.'

'I remember thinking,' he says, and stops.

'Skanda!'

'I remember thinking that I had never met a man like that in my house before.'

She looks long at him, then says, 'Do you remember when it was, roughly speaking?'

'Of course,' he says. 'I know exactly when it was. It was 1989. How could anyone forget that year.'

'Why? What's the big deal about 1989?' she says, now sleepily.

'Gauri, what are you saying? A huge year. Everywhere. The end of that Stasi night in Germany, the war in Afghanistan, the Mandal commission in India: everywhere events *whose beginnings did not know their ends*. The twentieth century was never as over in 1999 as it was in 1989.'

She is not listening. He thinks she's asleep and, turning off the light, is about to go to sleep himself, when she says, 'And your mother? Was she single that whole time?'

'Yes,' he says, 'for a long while.'

'That must have been hard. Socially, I mean.'

'It was,' he says, then after a pause, adds, 'But less hard than when she found someone again.'

'Huh?' Gauri says into the dark.

He laughs. 'She used always to tell me, my mother – it was one of her great throwaway remarks – "Darling, we have just as much to fear from the people who can't handle our success as we do from those who can't handle our failure".'

The women who came into Uma's life with Toby's departure brought friendship, support, ways of healing. But there was, she sensed it even then, something parasitical about their sudden arrival. They seemed in some ways like people who reverence the thing – make a god of it, even – that they fear most. The thing being, of course, marital collapse, the loss of the man, abandonment, the shame associated with the breaking of the conjugal bond. They came, Uma knew, to stare in fascination, as crowds in a poor country come, when a rich man, who till then they had believed to be above death, is killed in his expensive car.

Built into their wish to help was an equally powerful impulse for Uma to stay as she was, to never quite recover, to remain the totemic victim of marital failure. Uma, now frighteningly available, was someone to be watched. And these women formed a protective girdle round her, which was meant at least as much to protect the world – that little world! – from her as it was meant to protect her from the world.

Of the women who came into her life during this period, one of the few to truly wish her well was Priti Hirachand. She was a woman to whom life had given so much that it produced in her a gratitude akin to nobility. It could be said, in the thanks she felt she owed life, that she was superstitious in her obligation to be the agent of happiness and pleasure in the lives of others. That she understood these things in very limited ways – to mean little more than Cartier watches, holidays in London, toosh shawls, love affairs and parties – was not her fault. In that socialist winter, with only the faintest hint of thaw in the air, everyone's idea of contentment, their sense of what happiness consisted of, was a superficial thing. Pretty Priti – remember! – had come of age at a time when the airlines were the only way for a girl of her class to see the world. That now, with even the slightest easing of the regime, her husband's biscuit fortune allowed her to travel freely, to move easily between London and Delhi, to stay for months, during the summer, in a suite at the St James's Court Hotel: well, it felt to her like life itself!

A Time of Things was at hand and, for that generation, who had never tasted real Italian food, who had never drunk anything other than French table wine, whose entire idea of the world came from a few foreign newspapers and magazines smuggled into Delhi a week late, the whisper of change in the air excited in them deep material passions. It was impossible not to want to cast off the genteel poverty of Mrs Gandhi's era for the wonderful optimism of what seemed to lie ahead.

It was at this stage just a change in mood, in sensibility even, and, as such, it expressed itself anecdotally. Businessmen, whom nobody had even known in the old days, let alone invited into their drawing rooms, suddenly found they were welcome in Delhi. Slowly, very slowly, Money found it was welcome too. The nature of corruption began to change. Having once obstructed business, it now enabled it. One sensed from the new discourse, as with something hard and sensual in the voice of a woman considering an affair, that a country, too good too long, enshrining Gandhian austerity in a sticky web of Nehruvian red tape, was on the verge of cutting itself free. On the one hand, there was glasnost and perestroika in Moscow, speaking even then not so much of change as of moral and ideological collapse; on the other, the spirit of Nehruvian austerity was undermined at home by arms scandals and malicious gossip that the prime minister's wife had a taste for expensive things, now sable coats and Charles Jourdan shoes, now toosh shawls and stolen antiquities.

Priti Hirachand, though she would later be a casualty of that time, was also the first creature thrown up by its effervescence. An early Aphrodite. Long before Kitten Singh was installed in a flat on Eaton Square, long before the new London was to come into being, of *Four Weddings and a Funeral*, of restaurants and rich Russians, of an easy prosperity and a deserted Belgravia, London, the city-state, long before all this, it was in Priti Hirachand's voice that it was first possible to hear the brassy chime of moneyed Indians abroad. There was something bountiful and generous about her, effusive to the point of being unnerving. It was, for instance, not uncommon – if she liked you – for you to receive the next day, as a token of her enthusiasm, a little piece of jewellery in a felt bag with a golden H on it. A ring of dull beaten gold links; a serpentine bracelet with rubies for eyes; a pair of cuff links with an H of dusted emeralds. To speak of vulgarity when it came to her was to expose yourself to stating the obvious, so much so that you would only come off a little duller for it, and she much brighter.

She called one morning in March giddy with excitement. She was having a birthday party for her son, Krish.

Krish was an overweight boy with deep dimples, whom Priti dressed in tweeds and referred to quite seriously as 'The Biscuit Prince'. The Biscuit Prince was Skanda's age and on his way to boarding school in England. Priti was throwing him a Ninja Turtles party in London and wanted Skanda to be there. She was calling from the Hirachands' permanent suite at the Taj. Her voice was full of careless luxury; a mixture of languor and pride; for, as much as Indians enjoy the riches and comforts of the West, there is no one they wish to impress more than the people they have left behind. It is the one loyalty that never deserts them. And Uma could sense – in the way Priti spoke – the deep satisfaction she must have been feeling at returning, full of tales of other places, to the city of her childhood, and drawing open the gauze curtains of her suite onto a skyline that must have gone through her like a breath of familiarity, the skyline of tombs and trees.

'What do you mean "spoil him", Uma?' she said. 'You think I spoil my Krishy? Not at all. He's being packed off to boarding school, and he's barely twelve. Just like we all were. Didn't do us a jot of harm, did it? But I want to give him a little something before he goes off, you know, a birthday *slash* going-away bash. We've turned a section of Claridge's into a warren of tunnels and sewers and what-not. You should have seen their faces when we first arrived. "Ninja Turtles, madam?" they said in those stuffy voices of theirs. And I said, "Yes, you better believe it: you're working for us now, buster." Colonial-shalonial; look who's giving you a run for your money; Empire strikes back and all that. I mean, darling, between us and the Arabs we practically own Mayfair. I haven't seen a white man there who isn't a chauffeur for years!'

A clear peal of laughter came down the phone and Uma could not help but smile. She had this way, Priti, of always making the excesses of her life seem like part of some elaborate scheme for historical justice, as if she was rich not so much for her own reasons, but so that she could redeem her country's reputation for abysmal poverty.

'And don't worry about costumes,' she said, with sudden seriousness, as if only now seeing Uma's reasons for not wanting to send Skanda halfway across the world for a birthday party.

'We have the lot. Donatello. Michelangelo. Raphael. Leonardo.'

'Oh, they're named after Renaissance artists, these turtles of yours? How nice!'

'What, darling?' Priti said distractedly. 'It'll be good for him, Skanda, he's been through a lot lately. And, you know, they adore each other, Skanda and Krish.'

This was an embarrassing lie; on the one occasion they had met, they had loathed each other on sight. And when Skanda had taken to calling Krish 'Krish-mish cake', Toby had had to be sent in to retrieve the situation.

'No, Preets, I don't think I can. He has school. And, besides, I'm a little strapped for cash. Toby's been behaving very strangely on the money front.'

'Really? I would never have thought . . .'

'I mean he does the bare minimum. School fees, etc. . . . But nothing else. He's closed our joint account. He doesn't reply to any requests of mine for money. I've been living off my mother and Isha, actually.'

'That's so strange. He was always so generous, Toby.'

'I don't know. I think he thought the separation would be temporary. And when it turned out to be more permanent, he just went off. It's not that I care about myself so much, but it's wrong to punish the kids.'

'How terrible! It's always the ones who claim to be, you know, *raffiné et cultivé*, who turn out to be such rotters. And the ones we were taught to think would have bad values, hearts of solid gold!'

'I don't know,' Uma said. 'People in pain can behave in strange ways.'

'But still! Why don't you let me give him the ticket? I'm practically his godmother; I'm allowed.'

'No, no. They've travelled a lot, these kids. There's no harm in them roughing it a little now. And, as you know, we never went anywhere till we were well into our twenties and working for the airlines.'

'That was then. Now is different.'

'Still. Besides the summer . . . When did you say it was?'

'15 June.'

'The summers are always tricky. Between Toby wanting them in Kalasuryaketu . . . plus I've just accepted Isha's invitation for us all to go to Gulmarg . . .'

'Gulmarg?'

'Yes. You know, they have that friend, Tariq Mattoo . . . They've managed to get his wonderful cottage, CM1. I haven't been in years and . . .'

'I thought you said Skanda had school.'

'By June, school's out.'

'Then, darling, send him to London. Because we might be coming to Gulmarg too, right after that. I'll bring him along.'

'Really?'

'Yes. Kitty Singh's been on my case. She wants me to come and stay with her. She also thinks she has CM1, by the way . . . I tell you, you Delhi ladies, you're always in each other's hair. And, you know, how much harder she has worked to get that cottage than Isha. She has, you know, rather a more intimate connection to Tariq Mattoo.'

'I do know. Nixu calls her . . .'

'They're coming too, I hear. Nixu and Gayatri.'

'Yes. It should be lots of fun.'

'What does he call her, Nixu?'

'Helen of FICCI.'

Priti gave a shriek of laughter. 'Federation of Indian Chambers of . . . ?'

'Commerce and Industry.'

'Oh, darling, it's too good. But this is why she's been on my case, don't you see?'

'She wants you to help her be unfaithful to that poor husband of hers yet again?'

'Poor Tunnu, the turd. But who can blame her? That little garden gnome of a man. And she has many flaws, old Kitty-Kat, but she's not an unattractive woman!'

'Not at all. But then why marry him?'

'Moolah, of course. But tell me about yourself. What are you going to do?'

'About Toby?'

'Yes, about Toby! And money, and security. We're too old to be out on our butts again, you know, Uma. Worst comes to worse: you divorce him and get a part of what he owns. Understand? Aren't there flats on Cheyne Row and palaces on the banks of temple towns?'

'They're all in trusts and off-shore companies, and things like that. Trusts controlled, in part, by Usha Raje. His declared income is near to nothing. And besides, you know how long these things can take in India.'

'Uma, be careful,' Priti said, with sudden gravity. 'There are only two kinds of women at our age: those who have prepared for the second part of their lives, and those who haven't. And, with every year, the gap between them gets wider, harder to bridge. There was that mid-to-late-twenties moment – remember! – that we all went through, and there's the now-moment. You don't want to end up flat and alone, believe me. If you lived in Bombay, I'd say it was still OK. But Delhi, it's still semi-feudal, still an overgrown village. It will make you feel your vulnerability. These bitches – the Kitty Singhs of the world – they will make you feel it.'

'What would you have me do?' Uma said, laughing off the alarm in Priti's voice.

'Find someone. It's been – what? – four or five years. It's high time.'

'Maybe Priti, but these things don't happen by magic.'

'They happen if you're open to having them happen. If we had youth and beauty on our side when we were young, we have availability now.'

'Priti!'

'I mean it.'

'Well, I'm available. What do you want me to do?'

'To meet a friend of mine who's coming to Delhi and staying next door to you at the Raj. I want you to have him over for dinner or something. Kitty's been plaguing my life – she wants me to introduce him to her; everyone does; he's hot shit these days – but I'd much prefer he meet you.'

'Why do you think he wants to meet me?'

'Let's just say, I know. He met you once before. Years ago.'

'Does he have a name, this friend of yours?'

'Mani, Mahesh Maniraja,' she added, with a question in her voice.

The name meant nothing to Uma. It entered her mind practically free of association, an outline, for her to fill in as she would. She had hardly any memory of the man she had met at the height of the Emergency, when she was passionately in love with Toby. And she had only the vaguest impression of that bungalow in fog with its high walls and gate of dark wood and brushed steel. A frosted glass plaque, lit brightly from behind, and the fat black letters that read, Maniraja, B-17 Sarvaujas Enclave.

Did the memory of her unhappiness with Toby that night lie buried somehow in the returning echo of that name? Had she not at the time thought of that modern house into which her friends had disappeared with something of the longing with which the citizen of a closed society might look upon the gates of the embassy of a better and freer country? Had it not filled her with a feeling of lack?

Perhaps. But it did not come to her with any association as direct as that. In fact, a great part of the appeal of that name for her, when she heard it down the phone that March morning, wrapped up ever so slightly in the warmth and freshness of the changing season, was that it felt utterly new.

'What will you do?' Gauri asks.

They are in the flat. It is the morning Uma is due in Delhi. The question feels loaded. Skanda's love for his mother, as if it is an extension of his father's, needs always to be checked, always to be balanced against what she is prepared to give back. There is a perpetual danger of the scales tipping too much in her favour. And Gauri's tone, the alarm with which she asks, 'What will you do?' . . . It is as if she is speaking to an addict in danger of relapsing.

The day begins with an exchange of BBMs. 'Janum, in Delhi for the day. Mani has some work with Modi. Lunch? Longing to see you.'

He already has lunch plans with Gauri in Gurgaon, arranged weeks in advance.

Gauri, still half asleep, says, 'What, baby?'

'My mother.'

'What about her?'

'She's going to be here, in Delhi, today.'

'Oh,' she says, now sitting up herself. 'But that's wonderful. Why don't you ask her to join us for lunch?'

He weighs the unlikelihood of that happening with the feeling that it would be good for his mother, or for their relationship, at least, to ask anyway. People must own their demurrals.

He writes, 'Gauri wants to know if you'd like to join us for lunch at hers,' and a moment later, despite her having been told on a number of occasions about Gauri, his mother replies, 'Gauri?'

'My girlfriend.'

Silence.

Her dismissal of his emotional life – her sublime lack of interest in anyone he's with – is among their ancient problems.

'Darling,' she writes, 'I really don't want to leave the plane. I have all my magazines and DVDs here. The pedicurist is coming. But please thank Gauri from me. Another time.'

'She says thank you,' he tells Gauri. 'But she doesn't want to leave the plane.'

'What, the whole day?'

'She has her magazines.'

'Oh,' Gauri says, with something like wonder. '*What will you do?*'

He considers not going, but he is tired of these negative stances, tired of having nothing but 'no' on his side. And, besides, not doing these things, he knows, affects him much more than it does his mother. There is no point in fighting her autonomy. One might quibble and say, 'Well, could she be so, if Maniraja did not bankroll it?' But that would be churlish. The world is full of people bankrolled to their eyeballs who are not autonomous.

And this is the point: he admires her autonomy – in his best moments, he aspires to it. But his is not like hers: his is like his father's: it needs an object. The language. His mother needs nothing but herself.

Still, she must have felt that Mani had eroded her autonomy, for Skanda recalls her saying to him once in relation to Maniraja, 'For so long, you see, it was I who had the power in the relationship. Because if there was one thing I learned from your father, it was never to fall in love. Toby never fell in love; he never gave himself completely; it was never the centre of his being. He had that quality certain artists and writers have where no matter how loving or generous they can be on the surface, there's a part of them that belongs always to their vocation. And some of that must have rubbed off on me, because, in those early days, it used to drive Mani mad. It was he who pursued me, you know; he who wanted me to move to Bombay; I was quite happy where I was. For a long time, that was our dynamic: him pursuing, me reluctant. It gave me the illusion of power,' she had said and laughed.

That voice of hers, Skanda thinks now, hard and cynical, full of laughter, it had never been her voice before. It was new. It was the voice of the Louis Vuitton years. Of private planes and compromise. Of Maniraja and Bombay: the voice of safety.

But, as much as she had been full of lost illusions, his father, working by a different logic, was also making his peace with safety. He was also ridding himself of illusions. His idea of love, no less than Uma's, was a thing in flux.

Summer approached. The light on the Tamasā grew white and still, the surrounding land drier and more bleached, even as the jade of the river, with every passing day, grew a deeper and deeper green.

It was the year of the Kumbh and Toby – as he had done twelve years before, in 1977, when Mrs Gandhi used that vast congregation assembled at the Confluence to announce fresh elections – had driven down to Allahabad with Tripathi for the Basant Panchami, the fifth day of the Hindu month of Magha, and, according to that calendar, the official beginning of Spring. Toby was in time for one of his favourite rituals. The 'dhūni tap:' the austerity of smoke – and it was more powerful than he remembered it, seeming almost to enfold the onset of the heat.

It began one morning after many days spent at the camp, drinking chai, and smoking chilams with Babaji. Babaji, who went between long periods of listlessness and sudden activity, where he would polish the chilam's stone with a red rag and furiously rearrange the few objects that lay scattered about him – a green-handled knife; tongs; a Vicks inhaler; a packet of Rothmans; a box of chandan; a prayer book. Then, with no warning, he would launch into long tirades about Ayodhya, where the demand for a temple at the spot where

Ram was said to have been born had revived in recent years. The contested site, on which there stood a sixteenth-century mosque, had been closed for decades. But, in 1986, the Rajiv Gandhi government, playing a cynical brand of minority politics, now giving to Muslims, now taking from them, had reopened it to Hindu worship, which, in turn, had reopened an old historical wound, and the air that year was tense.

'Why won't we have a temple there?' Babaji said to Toby, who, with eyes expressionless and glassy, stared blankly at the fire of burning cow patties from which a red and intensely hot glow was visible. 'We will have a temple there. Of course we'll have a temple there. Toby saab, you watch, we won't even have to break the mosque. It will fall by itself, and a temple will rise. You'll see. This is the power of faith. This cannot be stopped by any government.'

Toby continued to stare at the fire: a long slow-burning blaze, which crept into the bracketed structure of the patties, and appeared wavy and mesmeric in those easy-forming shelves, on which it was still possible to see the imprint of hands. *For by the fire of the idea of the abyss, it is said, there are destroyed beyond recovery the five factors of ego-consciousness.* Babaji nervously adjusted the coffee table book that a French photographer had made of his ashram, and which he used as a backrest, and turned to Tripathi.

'You've been coming here for over a decade, Tripathi. Have you ever seen me indulge in politics? Why should I indulge in politics? I'm a sadhu. I don't care for politics. Have you ever seen me angry? I'm a sadhu, I'm beyond anger.'

Both statements were wildly untrue. Babaji was intensely political, and given to outbursts of anger, directed mainly at his sous-sadhu, a roguish and slim-limbed ascetic, known in the camp as Chottiya, who, after a stint with hard drugs, smack mainly, had ended up in the care of Babaji. He was wild-eyed, with a deranged and gap-toothed smile. He liked to sit for long hours, in nothing but yellow sunglasses and a matching yellow loincloth, massaging himself with an electric masseur.

Sylvia – the girl from the Sachler, who, on Toby's request, had been given special permission to stay at the camp – had, when she first saw Chottiya running the bright plastic instrument over his long black legs, asked, 'Is he shaving them?'

'She wants to know what you're doing,' Tripathi said, jumping his eyebrows at Chottiya. Who, as if bowing to some cultish requirement that sadhus be fierce, flared his eyes, then grinned maniacally. 'You can tell her that even the chela needs a chela.'

Babaji's black lips parted in a smile; a chuckle rose from deep inside his damaged lungs.

'A battery-operated chela,' he said, 'I like that.'

Then, turning again to Toby, he said, 'There will be a great movement, you watch. The country will rise. A new temple will be built. For too long we've tolerated the desecration of our places. You see that, over there?'

'See what, Babaji?' Toby said, though he knew exactly what. 'We're in a tent.'

'That damn fort. Hanging over our heads. Akbar's fort. Why do you think he built it there?'

'To protect an important trading station on the doab. Why else?'

'Rubbish. Nonsense. He wanted to show us we were nothing. You know very well how long this place has existed. You know that there would always have been an embankment here. Otherwise, it would have flooded; it's a flood plain. He built it because he knew, as you do, that it is on record that people have been bathing here in the month of Magha for – this is recorded history, Toby saab! – at least fourteen centuries. And this rite, the dhūni tap, that you will witness tomorrow, how old is it, Toby saab? Tell them. I know you know. Go on, tell them: how old is it?'

Sylvia, her green eyes and pale features glowing in the light from the fire – and for whom Babaji's latest outrage had been rapidly translated by Tripathi – looked at Toby now with an expression of admiration.

'It was the Śākyamuni Buddha,' Toby said at length, and with a sigh, 'from whom we have a mention of the dhūni tap.'

'Twenty-five centuries!' Babaji said, giving a wet cry of astonishment. 'That is our tradition. That is what they set out to destroy. But it didn't get destroyed, did it? *They* were destroyed instead. We have endured.'

'Tell me, Babaji,' Toby said finally, and with great irritation, 'you go on about this bloody temple now, in Ayodhya, in a place you claim to be the very spot where Ram was born. Why is it you've never mentioned it before? Tripathi and I have known you, as you say, for over twelve years. You've never so much as uttered the word Ayodhya. Now suddenly you can speak of nothing else.'

At that moment, a visiting sadhu from another camp, a stout old man, jaunty and jovial, with thick bifocal spectacles and a little silver trident lodged in his jatas, entered Babaji's enclosure.

'Jai Shri Ram!' the men thundered at each other.

The greeting enraged Toby. 'Jai Shri Ram,' he imitated, 'what the hell is this? Like a bloody brick over one's head. Jai Shri Ram! Just listen to the violence of it. Jai Shri Ram! May as well say bloody Heil . . .'

Then catching Sylvia's eye – she was Swiss German – he stopped himself. The sadhus, hearing this outburst, chuckled among themselves, and began talking sadhu politics: which businessman was patronizing which sadhu, which bit of land had been bought by whom . . . Toby turned to Sylvia.

'The greeting at the Kumbh,' he said, 'for decades has been Sitaram. Very simple, very musical. A long Sita, a short Ram. Sītā-rām.

But, ever since this damn movement for a temple in Ayodhya began . . . *Jai Shri Ram! Jai Shri Ram!*'

The sadhus looked over and smiled.

Babaji said – and Tripathi translated – 'It means Victory to Lord Ram! It is our way of expressing solidarity.'

Sylvia looked at him with that mixture of alarm and perplexity that comes over us when we try to translate the chauvinisms of an alien culture into our own terms. Then, with a tenderness that went right through him, she looked at Toby.

He had watched as she endured every aspect of camp life. The bucket baths under taps, in a cemented area in full view of everybody; the corrugated steel sheds, with a fly-infested mud pit for shitting in; the sleeping on the floor with half a dozen strange men; the blaring religious theatre that went on all night; the long repetitive cycles of chilams, of tea, of visits from other sadhus.

For Toby it had all been part of his recovery. Even the long drive up from Kalasuryaketu had soothed him. The U.P. of his childhood. A place of fields of unripened wheat edged with flowers; of pale sky and kilns, and canals; of scorched elephant grass; of the sight of brightly dressed women, always in threes, working in the fields; of the bunch-backed rear of an old mosque; of the earth blackened with the deep shade of heavy trees, where, occasionally, there might be the little whitewashed grave of some local saint. All this had to some degree taken his pain from him. But surely this was more than this slip of a girl, wanting nothing more than to improve her knowledge of Indian languages, had bargained for?

He felt her attraction for him. He knew it was founded on who he was, on his achievement, his lifework and scholarship. And, at a time when his self-confidence was badly wounded, it flattered him deeply, this attention. But it also made him feel guilty. Not because he felt he owed Uma anything – no! – but because – as much as he was able to appreciate the appeal of her attraction to him intellectually – he could not return it. It made him wonder what kind of man he was. Someone drawn perhaps to those people who held him in contempt, who wounded him, who showed a philistine's disregard for the things he loved most: was that what excited him? And why, when confronted with a beautiful young woman, devoted to all that he was devoted to, did it leave him cold? Well, not cold. But if he was to share it, her interest in him – and this was not a route anyone should have to take – he would have to think himself into feeling attracted to her, just as one day he would have to think himself into being in love with her.

She had come from the Sachler with a clear brief. An old student of Toby's – an American called Arthur Kidd, rich and retired – wanted, out of his great love for the language of his college years, to do something for Sanskrit. But he didn't know what. That was for Toby to figure out. He wanted him to head the project, and the money was considerable. Had Toby been in a better position in his life, it was the project of a lifetime. But she had come, this Sylvia, at the most difficult moment in his separation from Uma. When, having equipped himself to deal with something short-term, something put in place to salvage the relationship, he now found, with all the sick-making feeling of a premonition, that the separation was permanent. He knew this, not from anything that Uma said, but rather from the dull charge of his own suffering, its low-grade intensity, which, as with certain fevers, seemed to hint at something more serious than the usual cycles of flus and viruses.

He did not want to let go of the man who suffered. The suffering, he felt, kept the place of love in his heart. And, as long as it remained . . . as long as *he* remained a man enduring the pain of viraha, he felt his love for Uma – and the hope of their being reunited – would remain too.

The appearance of Sylvia in his life was distressing, precisely because it raised the possibility in his mind of moving on. It also made him confront the fact that Uma had perhaps never been the right person for him; that someone else, nearer to him in interest and sensibility, could give him a more nurturing relationship, a feeding relationship. But well-reasoned as this notion was, it had no hold on him. He was pained by the idea that he should sacrifice the man he was at present, a man in pain – but one, who, on any given day, he would have preferred as a dinner companion – for someone wiser, but infinitely more dull. He had no interest in this future person, this man, who had the good sense to love – not well, but wisely – the right person.

His ideal of love, helplessly romantic, was modelled on his first love: his love of Sanskrit. There had been nothing practical or sensible about that; he had simply fallen in love; it had required no mental effort. During this period of separation and recovery, Toby, with long hours on his hands in Kalasuryaketu, gazing out at the depleting expanse of the Tamasā, and the dazzling heat, had on many occasions thought of the people who had come before him, his antecedents and rivals in love: the fallen heroes of Sanskrit.

At the top of the list there was William Jones. Toby imagined the great philologist coming to Calcutta in 1783 to take up his position as a judge. At that stage, he had displayed hardly any interest in Sanskrit at all. In those first letters – in the memorandum composed aboard the *Crocodile* – there was not so much as a mention of the language. It was all Persian this, Persian that; Persian, which Jones knew, and had translated out of, and considered among the grand languages of the world. Sanskrit, when it came up, was only a means to the jurist's end of codifying Hindu laws. And, when finally he expressed some interest in the language – arising, no doubt, out of an insatiable linguist's appetite for any new language – he was blocked at every step by the Brahmins. They told him, when he asked after something called nāṭakas, that they were works full of fables, and consisted 'of conversations in prose and verse, held before ancient Rájás in their publick assemblies, on an infinite variety of subjects, and in various dialects of India'. One sensed – just as they later refused to teach him the language – that the Brahmins were doing what Brahmins do best: hoarding knowledge. Finally he met – and it was Toby's friend, Michael Coulson, who told him this – one 'very sensible Bráhmen [*sic*],' who told him that these nāṭakas were, well, an awful lot like those things which in the cold season in Calcutta went by the name of 'plays'. That was how Jones discovered the existence of Sanskrit drama, in general, and Shakuntala, in particular. By pure accident.

Everything at that stage had the feeling of an accident. But they each excited Jones's interest and Toby noticed creeping into his letters things like: 'Daily Studies for the Long Vacation of 1785: Morning . . . one letter; Ten chapters of the Bibles; Sanscrit grammar. Hindu Law, &c . . .' Or, a little while later: '. . . I would rather be a valetudinarian all my life, than leave unexplored the Sanscrit mine which I have just opened.' Or – the following year from Calcutta – 'By rising before the sun, I allot an hour every day to Sanscrit, and am charmed with knowing so beautiful a sister of Latin and Greek.' The signs are all there and, of course, Toby recognized them: Jones was a man falling in love.

What a dangerous love it would prove to be, for it was accompanied – and the theme runs right through the letters – by an ever greater concern for his health, a fear of the climate that would eventually kill him.

> We talk of the year 1790 [he wrote to Miss E. Shipley from the banks of the Ganges] as the happy limit of our residence in this unpropitious climate . . . God grant that the bad state of my Anna's health may not compel her to leave India before me! I

should remain like a man with a dead palsy on one of his sides: but it were better to lose one side for a time than both for ever.

Prophetic words, but it was Anna who would live, and Jones who would die. Jones who – wanting only to make enough to be his own man in England, £30,000 – seemed almost marked for death. There was something unspeakably moving, Toby felt, about those last eight or so years of Jones's life: the years of immense intellectual discovery when, working round the clock, there was, ever-present in the background, Death. But it could not stop him: driven on by the sheer excitement of what he had found, he carried on working, using his every reserve of strength. The days must not have had hours enough! And for a sensibility like his, informed, on the one hand, by the myth of the Tower of Babel, on the other, by a debt to Greece, the discovery of Sanskrit would have been like coming upon the fount of language itself.

The similarities between Sanskrit and the other classical languages Jones already knew would have astonished him. He must not have believed what he was hearing. A voice neither active nor passive, called the ātmanepada? Well, he knew of such a voice, of course, because he knew of the middle voice in Greek. A dual number? Again, that was nothing new; there was one in Greek. Verb formations he recognized easily to be aorists; paradigms with identical cases; the locative absolute: vartir api dīpe naṣṭe dhūmitā bhavati: when the lamp has gone out, the wick becomes smoky and blackened. How long would it have been before he was reminded of the ablative absolute from his school days: *Ovidio exule, Musae planguntur.* With Ovid exiled, the Muses weep. And would he not have paused at this word naṣṭa: to destroy: and thought to himself, *Noceo*, *nocere* – to injure, to harm – *nuocere* in Italian, *nuire* in French, noxious in English?

They would have come flying at him, these resemblances.

And, when finally he makes his great conjecture, the cornerstone of comparative philology – delivered before the Asiatic Society in Calcutta in 1786 – it is made, as with certain mathematical discoveries, even before the proof exists. It seems to break from Jones with all the tragic force of a discovery that he must have sensed would be his death:

> The *Sanscrit* language, whatever be its antiquity, is of a wonderful structure; more perfect than the *Greek*, more copious than the *Latin*, and more exquisitely refined than either, yet bearing to both of them a stronger affinity, both in the roots of verbs and in the forms of grammar, than could possibly have been produced by accident; so strong indeed, that no philologer could examine them all three, without believing them to have sprung from some common source, which, perhaps, no longer exists . . .

A common source that may itself have decayed: the spring of all language run dry: it must have been so beguiling an idea! It must have spoken to him of a lost wholeness, a dream of underlying unity, that we, as human beings, are never quite able to let go of. It was what Toby's imagination had seized on too. That, and the fact that as cultural decay in the East deepened, Toby saw that India was increasingly unable to converse with herself. 'It is hard to realize,' Coomaraswamy writes, 'how completely the continuity of Indian life has been severed. A single generation of English education suffices to break the threads of tradition and to create a nondescript and superficial being deprived of all roots – a sort of intellectual pariah who does not belong to the East or the West.'

Coomaraswamy! Another of Toby's heroes. Even more than Jones, the Ceylonese art critic – perhaps because he was half-Asian and, like Toby, half-European, and perhaps because he, had he wanted, could also have lived a life of leisure in the West – had been a model for Toby. Few stories were nearer Toby's heart than the one Vijaipal once told him of Coomaraswamy in 1917, when he was forty, offering to donate his entire collection of Indian art to the newly opened Benares Hindu University. His only condition was that they institute a chair of Indian art, and make him the professor. 'And what did they say?' Toby had asked Vijaipal. 'They told him to go away,' Vijaipal had said, and begun to laugh cruelly. 'They told him to take his art collection and go away.'

The story had been told as a cautionary tale, a tale that was meant to jeer at Toby's innocence when it came to India. It was meant to remind Toby that India would always let him down. And though he recognized that, of course, he could not help but be moved by the sacrifices that were part of the life of pure intellectual endeavour, the life of the mind, even when – *especially when* – things ended badly.

It was like the story of his friend Michael Coulson, one of the finest Sanskritists of their generation. He was a professor at Edinburgh and had completed work on a number of very good translations; they had all found publishers, but the publication had been indefinitely held up. In those days a publisher could sit on a book for years. The waiting was terrible. And it was not the only kind of waiting Coulson had had to endure. Some years before, he had met someone and fallen in love. A relationship had blossomed and the man had promised to come to Edinburgh. Coulson, leveraging one hope against the other, had suffered the disappointments in his professional life by clinging onto this one hope in his personal life. Then, on a grey and depressing day in Edinburgh, the call had come to say the man would not be coming. Not then, not later, not ever.

Coulson lost his nerve. Or, depending on which way you look at it, he found it. When Toby asked his colleague at Balliol, reporting the sad news of Coulson's suicide to Toby over the telephone in

1975, how Michael had done it, the man had replied – and Toby never forgot, for it was phrased in a way that seemed to contain the essence of the story, 'He opened his veins in the bathtub.'

Michael Coulson. Ananda Kentish Coomaraswamy. William Jones. These were the men, the martyrs – witnesses, in the true sense – of Sanskrit: the men who had helped shape the character of his love for the language, and that mixture of futility and devotion it inspired. It was no surprise then that Toby's notion of romantic love would be an extension of his love of Sanskrit. It was why that morning at the Kumbh, a morning of clouds and light rain, as the dhūni tap got underway, and he had admitted into his heart for the first time the prospect of a sensible love, something more pragmatic, he had the terrible feeling of having betrayed the person he was.

He watched her watch the rite. The sadhus, after the sacrifice, gathered in the courtyard. With their two steel vessels, their measure of white cloth, and iron tongs. They each made a ring of burning cow patties around themselves. And they each settled down at the centre of their smoking circles in padmāsana. Then, when the smoke began to rise, they draped the white cloth over themselves, and became like rocks in a school play. There was a light drizzle, moistening and slightly besmirching the white shrouds of the sadhus. 'The fierce pupils motionless, their brightness slightly lessened, their eyes, directed downward, and focused on the nose, the eyelashes stationary, the stilled eyes stilling the brow . . . they were like clouds without the vehemence of rain, like an expanse of water without a ripple, like lamps in a windless place.'

Sylvia was transfixed. But Toby could think only, *Look, how affected she is by it all; Uma never cared for these things. And I showed her so much more than this.*

Outside, Babaji, covered already in ash, was having Chottiya mark his forehead with broad streaks of yellow, sandalwood and saffron, at the centre of which came a single red flame. The markings of the sect. Everyone was preparing for the procession to the river and the amāvasyā bathing.

'Tell me again,' Sylvia asked, 'amā means?'

'Together. And *vas* . . .'

'Ah, yes, you said: like our German *wāsan*, *ge-wesen*, *war* . . . Amazing. The being together?'

'The dwelling together, yes. Of the sun and the moon.'

Their affair began on a soupy moonless night once they were back in Kalasuryaketu. Toby remembered every detail. Sharada and Laban, as they had once been before in another time, laying drinks outside.

He was reading; Sylvia, in the light from a battery-powered tube light, was working through certain verses of The Birth. Every now and then she would interrupt him with a question, usually from the commentary, and he would help her easily. He no longer had even his children to teach, and, though he didn't say it, it was a pleasure for him to teach again.

Looking up from the text, she said, 'I don't want to rush you. But have you thought more about what you'd like to do with the Kidd endowment?'

'I have. I'm actually seeing Tripathi tomorrow to discuss it. We need to do something that would be significant here as well as abroad.'

'But, Toby,' she said with stress, and with that illusion of fluency foreigners derive from the use of adverbs, 'I *absolutely* agree.'

'We'll think of something. I have a few ideas. I don't know if you've ever come across the Loeb library . . .'

At that moment Sharada came out to where they were sitting, her face lined with anxiety, to say that Rani saab had called.

'From Delhi?' Toby said, betraying the blind hopefulness of his condition.

Sharada nodded, almost wringing her wrists with concern.

'I'll just be back,' Toby said, putting down his book and drink.

'Sure,' she replied, and did not look up from her work.

Gata eva na te nivartate sa sakhā dīpa iv'ânil' | āhataḥ:
Gone, indeed, is that friend of yours, and he will not return, like a lamp snuffed out by the wind. Rati – Love's wife – addressing Spring, after Love is incinerated.

The telephone in Kalasuryaketu was in the manager's room. A small musty cupboard of a place, with an unsteady plywood desk and a green metal Godrej cupboard. The door of the little bulb-lit room was open and Sylvia, even with the deep breath of the river, and the orchestral cry of insects, could hear snatches of their conversation. *Sentence-sounds*, Frost called them, believing that the music of human speech had semantic force. And here the music was jolting, abrupt, cold and sarcastic. He came back a few minutes later, Toby, visibly withdrawn and irritated.

She was too polite to ask if everything was all right. She saw him return to his reading – Proust, of all people! – but he was too distracted to continue. He put the book page-down on the flagstones and hunted around for something on the floor. Cigarettes. She passed them over without a word. In that act of attentiveness to him, it was as if she had asked him a question. And he was relieved to have been asked it. Almost throwing up his hands while at the same time lighting his cigarette, he said, 'That was my wife. Calling to see if I wanted to pay for my son to go halfway across the world for a birthday party.'

'How old is your son?' Sylvia asked.

'Twelve!'

Sylvia smiled.

'And when I said no, *obviously, no!*, she had the nerve to accuse me of punishing the family, because our relationship – hers and mine, that is – was on the rocks.'

Sylvia wanted to react, but felt that strong and feminine pressure, deeply tactical, not to say the slightest bad word against Uma.

'Children,' she said cautiously, 'can sometimes be very persuasive. And they don't always understand distances.'

'Rubbish. It's not him who wants to go. He loathes the little snot whose birthday it is. I had her put him on. Oh, no! It's my wife – consorting now with the yuppy crowd – who's put him up to it, who feels there's nothing a twelve-year-old needs more than to go to Ninja Turtle parties in Europe. Ninja Turtles! What kind of people are these? I ask you. Renting out Claridge's for a children's birthday party. Offering to fly people over . . .'

'How did you leave it?'

'I put my foot down. That's how I left it.'

Even as Toby said the words he felt some uncertainty at the pleasure his indignation gave him. Of course he thought Skanda had no business being sent to London for a birthday party, but he knew, too, that he was enjoying his outrage. His hurt feelings, which had created a more or less permanent ache in him over the past few years, were replaced by something exultant and self-righteous. How good it felt to say *no* to Uma. But no sooner had the thought entered his mind than he was struck by a feeling of pity at the slow death in him of the person who loved Uma, a version of himself that he was extremely fond of. For as much as men like Jones and Coulson, the Sanskritists, had been living models of his ideal of love, there was one man, who though not real, had exerted an almost equal degree of influence. Swann. Charles Swann.

Toby had first read Proust in his twenties. And then – save for Marcel's obsessional love of Albertine, which never seemed believable to him – he had loved it all: the nobility of Saint Loup; the haughtiness of Charlus; the social decline of the Duchesse de Guermantes. Balbec, Combray, Paris in the war years. The extraordinary description of Madame Cottard fighting sleep at a party at the Verdurins. He had loved the music of the language. The tendrils of prose, opening out slowly, like clouds of colour in clear liquid, into long relative clauses: the predications buried deep within the sentences, so that the reader felt almost, from the effort of keeping everything in mind, that the truth of what was said was being drawn from him, the reader, rather than revealed to him by the writer. It had been one of the most profound reading experiences of Toby's youth. He had returned to Proust many times in his life, but never so much with the urgency that he returned to it now, never so much for Swann, in general, and for his capacity for love – infinite and self-wounding – in particular. The blindness of that love was as soothing to Toby as the drive up to the Kumbh through the landscape of his childhood. It seemed in some deep and meditative way to work him through every motion of his own suffering for Uma, while at the same time, working it out of him. So that he felt at once both immersed in his pain; able, indeed, by giving it an intellectual dimension, to augment his agony; and yet, more able to bear it than before.

He felt the passages about Swann's suffering had been written with him in mind, decades before his birth. He went over them again and again. It is we, he thought, who make what we make of the people we love. *What is aught but as 'tis valued?* It is an act of the imagination, Love: mano | ratha: like a chariot of the mind or heart. But this time round I must make someone worthy, someone deserving, the object of that love. I must not make another mistake.

'Vartir_api,' she said, underlining the fine print of the commentary with her red pen.

He came to sit next to her. He could feel the nearness of her limbs through the muslin she wore. In his mind – for he wanted so much to love her – they were already making love. He could smell her on his lips; and his penis, cutting through the sharp reeds around the vagina, had already entered her. The deed was done. The habit of the sexual act, its repetitiveness, like a drill, would give him what he did not feel in the area of love. Soon, by the mere act of sex, he would be able to forget that their relationship would never be a passionate one, that he would never (not, at least, in the breathless way in which he had once thought of it) love Sylvia. And would it matter, really? Didn't all love end up in the same place anyway, in that sphere of domesticity and habit? Would anyone even be able to tell the difference?

'The locative absolute,' he replied, 'when the lamp has gone out: dīpe naṣṭe – *put out the light, and then put out the light* – the wick is smoke-blackened: dhūmitā bhavati. It's one of my favourite features of grammar, the locative absolute. With a simple change of case, word endings are freed of their normal function of connecting one word to another. Instead it becomes possible for an entire predication to be connected to another: to serve, in fact – as if cast into shadow by the locative – as the context for what follows. Here – because the past participle has this perfective aspect – it is past and present that are connected; one, coming like a train through a tunnel, to meet the other.'

'Like the past continuous?'

'Sort of,' he said, and felt disappointment. He could not help but think, *If I loved her, even her banalities would be beautiful.*

That night, with her asleep next to him for the first time, the name came to him. The Kidd Sanskrit Library. KSL. No sooner was it in mind than he knew what the books would be. He was able to imagine them down to the last detail. His legacy. He could see their tamarind tawny-brown covers, the Kiḍ written on the back in Devanagari. He could almost touch their cigarette-paper pages with the transliterated Sanskrit on one side and fresh English translations on the other.

All the great works of Sanskrit literature, he thought, *translated by the best scholars of our time.* He imagined all the people he knew, the Priti Hirachands and Kitten Singhs of the world, the Gayatris and the Chamundas. *They might not read it for fifty years,* he thought, *but they will buy it, for their children if nothing else, the way they buy them the* Encyclopædia Britannica *and the* World Book *today.* He would make it fashionable: it was all he could hope to do: to install it, like a Japanese washing machine, this moribund body of literature, in people's houses. *And perhaps one day,* he almost said aloud, smiling to himself, *one of these little Ninja Turtles will grow up and consider reading it. It won't be a renaissance, but it will be something.*

He put the light on; it fell aslant over Sylvia's bare back, where his eye fixed on a mole partially enveloped in skin. Again disappointment returned, deep and unreachable. He decided to finish the chapter he was reading. She stirred a little. He watched her with some mixture of curiosity and dismay. He was at the end of *Swann in Love*: 'And with the old, intermittent caddishness which reappeared in him when he was no longer unhappy and his moral standards dropped accordingly, he exclaimed to himself: "To think that I've wasted years of my life, that I've longed to die, that I've experienced my greatest love, for a woman who didn't appeal to me, who wasn't even my type!"'

It was in late April that Kitten Singh discovered CM1 was no longer hers. She was at the Steakhouse – of all places! – buying freezer-loads of supplies for Gulmarg when she heard. It was Mrs Arjun Singh who, inadvertently, told her. This revelation, detrimental to her hopes for the summer, came to her from a lofty mass of flowered grey chiffon, French perfume and sunglasses; and Kitten Singh was made to feel that this bit of news, shattering to her in every respect, was of no more importance to Mrs Arjun Singh than if a sweating block of Emmental, which she scrutinized with diamantine eyes, was, in fact, fresh or not.

Mrs Arjun Singh was not alone; the Mexican ambassador's wife, a large lady with reddish hair and moles, was with her.

'Christina, you tell me: does it look all right to you?'

'Rita, I'm no great expert. But' – she loved this little phrase! – 'I am not too keen on Emmental.'

'Oh,' Mrs Arjun Singh said, with some mixture of dejection and curiosity, as though about to hear something damning about someone who till then she had believed to be socially important.

'I prefer pecorino.'

Mrs Arjun Singh digested this information with hostility, then reminded herself that Christina was European – or kind of European – and that her knowing about these things was no more surprising than Mrs Arjun Singh knowing what quantity of dal was needed for the consistency of a shammi kebab to be right.

At this point Mrs Arjun Singh said, 'That Tariq Mattoo, I tell you, for a Kashmiri, he has such a quality of friendship! Can you imagine giving up your own house in Gulmarg in the summer, so that your old school friend can make amends with his wife.'

Here, Kitten tried to interrupt. But Mrs Arjun Singh did not let her.

'And my God,' she continued, fully enjoying the pleasure of the blow she was delivering, which had all the more force for seeming to come as if indirectly. 'You should have seen her. Poor Isha Singh Aujla! "I fell," she said simperingly. Fell?! With those bruises! Give me another one, darling! I wasn't born yesterday. We didn't know which way to turn. Don't you agree, Christina?'

'His cottage? CM1?' Kitten Singh finally inserted, trying in this tirade to snatch at relevant information. 'But he promised it to Tunnu and me months ago.'

'Check again, dear,' Mrs Arjun Singh said quickly, as if this was an incidental detail in a more important story. 'That poor woman, she wore it like a badge of honour. Gayatri Mann was there too. And she said, "Don't you love it, Rita ji? Only in Delhi would a woman, who's just been beaten up by her husband, feel sufficiently compensated – enough to tell people about it! – by a house in the hills!" I laughed and laughed! What was the phrase she used, Christina?'

The Mexican ambassador's wife, who was asking if the pork was safe, said carelessly, 'It's all so deliciously shallow.' The women exchanged smiles. Christina began, 'But tell me – I'm not too keen on it myself – you feel safe, Rita, giving your children pork in India?'

'Bacon, yes. But not ham, Christina, nothing uncooked . . .'

Kitten Singh, from the deep shade of that Jor Bagh shop, suffered the special ignominy of someone whose disappointment was too small to consider. She gazed vacantly out at the day. The scorching wind-swept day, in whose thermal flurries little pirouettes of dust and dried leaves leapt up and died, as if to the tune of a hidden music. They made her longing for Gulmarg more acute, and her disappointment at being so newly unaccommodated keener. There was no point in fighting it. She knew it was all true. She had in the annual rush for cottages suffered a crushing and unexpected defeat.

That swine, Tariq Mattoo, had given her house away.

When she got home she sent immediately for Parmeshwari, the masseuse. A fat black woman from the south with the arms of a wrestler and a plait of wiry hair as thick as a tug-of-war rope. She went everywhere, Parmeshwari, she knew everyone, and she was – the Delhi ladies all knew it – a poisonous gossip. After each of her indiscretions, communicated to them invariably by a rival, they made resolutions never to have her again. But they were powerless to resist her. For she was the very soul of the city embodied. And there were few things in the world more relaxing than Parmeshwari's strong coarse hands ironing out the knots in your body, round hard nodes of stress and idleness, even as she delivered in a voice, cynical and bored, and calibrated to her oily progress over your body, the talk of the town.

The price of gossip was gossip – and where Parmeshwari gave she also took – but there was, they told themselves, something neutral and even-handed about her. She was – and this was so rare in a political city – nothing if not non-partisan.

That day however, with the evil talent of an astrologer, she made

Kitten Singh feel, and she always harmonized physical pain with bad news, both vulnerable and dependent.

She arrived in the middle of an ugly fight. Kitten Singh was bearing down on her husband, who she had sat down in a chair in the middle of the room, around which she circled kiteishly. 'I'll tell you what they're saying. They're saying Tunnu, the Turd . . . Yes! That is what they call you. All over town. Not the serd, not the sardar: the turd! The one that hangs about in the toilet bowl, when the potties are done, waiting for a strong hand to flush him down. You know why they call you that?'

Something like curiosity gleamed in Tunnu's haggard face, in which the grey of the beard merged with the sallowness of the skin. It enraged Kitten, the sight of those two searching eyes, in that gnomish face.

'Because you're a coward. You sit there like a question mark, in that chair, even as the whole damn town laughs at you. Tunnu, the turd, got flushed out of CM1. But not to worry: he'll show up somewhere else. Turds always do. That's in their nature: they lurk. And sometimes, you know, darling,' she added, with unexpected tenderness, 'when I see you out and about, standing at the edge of the party, with your little drink, while the real men are talking and laughing – with me! – I see their point. Even though I'm your wife, I have to agree with them. You do seem a little like a turd. A mild nuisance. Ever-present, but no threat to anyone . . .'

At this point she caught sight of Parmeshwari, who stood in the doorway, in keds and a cotton salwar kurta, as yellow as the laburnum. She had pulled the thick rope of her plait over her shoulder, so that it lay like a sleeping animal on the great expanse of her breast. And – casting her eyes with feigned innocence about the room – she inspected the end of her plait for split ends.

'Chalo!' Kitten said, with a mixture of dread and relief. 'It's you, at least, for all small mercies.'

Parmeshwari possessed certain essential traits of a consummate gossip, such as feigned boredom and pretend innocence, but the quality that gave her a distinct advantage over others in her tribe was her compassion. She had a way, no matter how wretched a scene she had witnessed, nor how damning the talk she had overheard, of making you feel that whatever it was that people were saying about you, it was no worse than what they were saying about each other. In this, she seemed really to be of a piece with the spirit of gossip in Delhi: it was a blood sport, but it was nothing personal.

In the dark, with her face pressed against a bed sheet, in which she could detect the stale jasmine of previous massages, Kitten heard her say, 'So, it's nothing. You should see what I do to my husband. You have to do it. It's for their own benefit, no? Am I saying anything wrong, Kitty Madam? You tell me.'

Kitten, hardly consoled that her domestic life resembled Parmeshwari's, mumbled something incomprehensible. Parmeshwari, driving her thumb up her calf, knew she had struck the wrong note.

'I was at Chamunda madam's the other day,' she ventured, 'and – my God! – you should have seen the kerfuffle there. That Ismail – Mohammadan, what else? – he has a mouth like a sewer. Bhenchodh, machodh, bhonsadi ka, every other word out of his mouth, such a fat insult, I tell you! And he's taken against the little boy, you know: Rani saab's little son, Bhaiya. Constantly humiliating him. "Oye, little Raja," – he does with his hands like this, like this,' she made a Venus flytrap of a flower with her fingers, and Kitten craned her neck to look, "where are the crown jewels?" And, phataak, he'll grab the little boy's balls in front of all the servants and guests. Can you imagine – old family servants, seeing their future raja humiliated in this way? And by a Mohammadan, at that? I can't bear to look. I say: build the temple in Ayodhya, and send them all to Pakistan! The lot of them . . .'

'Who?' Kitten said, raising her head.

'Mohammadans. Who else?'

'Oh,' Kitten said, and put her head down, a little disappointed that Parmeshwari had given the gossip this edge. Then, with that weariness with which society people respond to the mention of politics and art in their midst, never finding in themselves the courage to say, *We'd rather just talk about ourselves*, Kitten said, 'None of that talk here, Parmeshwari. This is a secular household. And we, ourselves, you know, are minorities.'

'Me too, I'm *sacular*,' Parmeshwari flared up. 'We've faced discrimination too. Injustice. What they call zulm. Why do you think I felt so much sympathy with Uma memsaab,' she said, 'when she threw her man out the other day – you know, that businessman fellow from Bombay, who everyone's running after – for saying wrong things about Sikhs? I remember 1984! Tssss! With my own eyes, I saw one man set alight. The smell of rubber! Hey Ram! A burning tyre . . .'

Kitten Singh rose up like a yogic cobra, her back glistening in the dark, her red nails lightly puncturing the cotton of the bed sheet. She had had just enough of people that day burying important bits of information in trivialities. '*Uma memsaab*, for your kind information, Parmeshwari, does not have a man. Her man is gone. You must have made a mistake. Or maybe you mean someone else, her sister perhaps?'

A look passed between them. There was, for a moment, something hard and defiant in Parmeshwari's eyes. Then – as if glimpsing weakness in her adversary's face and deeming the fight not worth the fighting – the masseuse unexpectedly withdrew the challenge from her eyes. And, more than when she had been adamant, it was in the softer light of this shrinking gaze, of mercy thrown her way like a one-rupee coin, that Kitten wilted, and knew the terrible information the maalishwali had let slip to be the incontestable truth. She had lost much more than a cottage to the Fatehkotia sisters.

For a while the massage continued as before, Kitten silent, Parmeshwari, magnanimous in victory. They spoke of other things. 'Ms Gayatri, one woman, who no like talking during massage.'

'Well, for some people,' Kitten said waspishly, 'the massage is enough. And besides she must think of her books.'

'Yes. Smart woman. Always thinking. "Back very bad from writing," she say me,' Parmeshwari said, driving her fingers into a hard and humpish area on Kitten's back. They alternated between Hindi and English. The air in the darkened room was heavy. An inch of blaze pressing against the margin of the curtains. It made Parmeshwari uneasy; she was, at the end of the day, a service provider; the gossip was for entertainment, it was not meant to spoil the air of a massage.

She tried some old tricks. 'Uma madam, she say Chamunda madam, she no do exercise. She have too much cellulite.'

'So?' came the response.

'Her boobs sag.'

Silence.

She tried a bolder line. 'But poor Isha madam. Feeling very bad for her . . .'

'I know, I know, Parmeshwari, her husband beats her. The whole town knows. So? At least she has a husband man enough to beat her.'

A sad stung silence prevailed. Parmeshwari, as if wishing to begin on a clean slate, asked Kitten to turn over, and set to work on the front of her legs. From that place of servility, she muttered, with the false modesty of an antiques dealer saving his best pieces for last, 'But she should not have thought of suiciding. That was too bad.'

In the quiet tension the darkness now acquired, Parmeshwari sensed that all perhaps was not lost. In between running her thumbs painfully along the tendon that girded Kitten's tibia, she glanced up at her from time to time, and saw her face twitch with interest. She seemed to be processing this new bit of information. But save for the silence and the twitching, she made no other response. Then, just as Parmeshwari, now kneading her kneecaps, had begun to fear that she had supplied yet another bit of stale gossip, Kitten's face shot up in the dark. Her eyes were wide open; there was tension about the mouth.

'She tried to kill herself? I didn't know that.'

Parmeshwari breathed relief. Things were beginning to turn around.

'Oh yes,' she said, 'her servants showed me the empty packets of the pills. Sobrium. Two dozen she must have taken.'

'They didn't work presumably,' Kitten said with something like sadness in her voice. 'I mean, we would have heard.'

'Huh?'

'I mean she survived.'

'Oh, yes! I mean: yes,' Parmeshwari said, apologetically. 'The servants said there was no effect at all. She just slept a little later than usual, and was very hungry the next day.'

'Those Fatehkotia sisters are indestructible,' Kitten said with distaste.

And now, consoled by this new bit of information, and no longer feeling Parmeshwari rub her defeat in her face, Kitten found herself listening, without discomfort, to the story of the new man in Uma's life, and how one evening, just a few days before, she had thrown him out of her house.

*

The episode in question had occurred some weeks after Uma's conversation with Priti. It was an unseasonably hot April. The laburnum on Amrita Shergil Marg was already in flower. Convoys of cars laden with food and supplies had begun to leave for Kashmir. A beautiful haunting heat prevailed over the city, driving people into their houses in the day, stirring up sombre dust storms of green and purple light in the evening, which, once they had passed, would bring the temperature down enough for it to be possible to eat outside. Some days before, an exterminating wind had begun to blow and the mosquitoes, which earlier would have made dinner in the garden impossible, were all dead.

Her children were not with her that night. Skanda was at her sister's; Rudrani, on the farm, with her parents.

The pleasure of being alone still felt new. Of driving home after aerobics at the Taj Palace; of a bath in a darkened bathroom, in whose mirror, she saw, as she dried herself, her bedroom framed in a slim column of lamplight. On an easy chair in the looming shadows of a large potted plant, there lay the bound proof of the new Rushdie – come to her via Gayatri via Zubin Mann. A blue book, with a red devil on the cover; the same devil that had, only a few months before, due in part to the foolishness of the Rajiv Gandhi government, driven the writer into hiding. The book was banned in India and this made the thrill of the proof all the greater. The book, the music, the exercise, the house to herself – they were all like little symbols of her autonomy, of a freedom that had come accidentally to her, and awakened in her an interior life whose secret pleasures were akin – if not greater, for they flowed directly from her – to those we feel at the outset of a love affair. In fact, truth be told, she felt this private thrill far more intensely for her newfound interiority, for the joy of being her own woman, than for the man who was coming to dinner that night.

Even as she went around helping Narindar lay a white lace tablecloth made by the nuns of the Presentation Convent over a wrought iron table, and lighting fanooses, it was with that feeling of self-possession that comes over us when, under the guise of doing things for other people, we, in fact, do things for ourselves.

Maniraja – his influence always at its greatest in hotels – had made a special request of the delicatessen at the Raj.

'I'm not happy till I see blood, darling,' he said, enjoying the effect of this remark on the young woman across the counter.

'Of course, Mr Maniraja,' she said, blushing at the over-familiarity. 'Rare? Medium-rare? Well-done?'

'Pink as your cheeks, sweetheart. But hurry, please. I'm late for a dinner.'

The girl laughed, reddening further. Then just as she was about to disappear into the kitchen, a sharp snap of fingers summoned her back. It was an old trick of Maniraja's: to hold his fingers up like a pistol in the air, and snap them loud enough for someone halfway across a large room to hear. The girl turned around with a look of puzzlement on her face. Maniraja laughed.

'Like this,' he said, repeating the gesture.

The girl tittered. 'So loud,' she said.

'What's your name, darling?'

'Pooja.'

'Pooja what?'

'Paranjpe.'

'Oh, very good!' Maniraja said, adding with pride. 'My mother was herself a Brahmin. A Thanjavur Brahmin.'

The girl gave a smile of embarrassment; the mild embarrassment of someone obliged to refuse entry to another on the basis of a technicality, for she knew – no less than Maniraja – that this was a club far more concerned with punishing transgressors and preserving purity than offering concessions to those with minor quantities of Brahmin blood, Thanjavur or not.

A few minutes later the girl returned with a small foil container.

'Open it,' Maniraja said. The girl scrunched her face, and shook her head violently, handing the container over to Maniraja, as if it were a bomb. Maniraja laughed uproariously. Then, he carefully unfolded the foil of the box, removed the lid, and inspected the morsels of steaming beef swimming about in their blood and juices. He took one in his manicured fingers, and making direct eye contact with the girl, put it in his mouth. She gasped with shock and covered her mouth with her hand, which made Maniraja laugh so much that a thin stream of glistening liquid ran out of the corner of his lips.

'I like my tenderloin,' he said, his mouth full of meat and juice and laughter. 'Like all good Hindus, I, too, love the holy cow.' The girl instinctively handed him a napkin. Maniraja showed her his cheek; and she, now bursting with nerves, flashed a look left and right, before quickly wiping the liquid from his face. Then, as he put the lid back on the box, and folded in the silver edges, he fastened his gaze on her. And, with eyes steady and meaning, he told her to write her extension number on the napkin she had used to wipe his face.

'What time does your shift run till?' he said.

'Till 1 a.m., sir,' she said.

'Good. I should be back before then.'

'Will you have some of your . . . ?' Uma said. In the candlelight, it was hard to see what it was. 'Beef, is it?'

'No, no. No, thank you. I didn't know . . .'

'. . . if there'd be any dinner?' she said and laughed.

Maniraja was about to reply seriously, then saw she was joking. A strange joke, strange in its tone. He looked with dismay about the garden.

She had not noticed the significance of the beef. She had simply accepted it, as one might a bottle of wine or some flowers, and served it along with the rest of the food. It sat there now, in its little foil box, among the larger bowls of dal and vegetables and meat. And in that form, lost among the rest of the food, the effect was lost too. It looked absurd. Maniraja, thinking back to his success with Pooja less than an hour ago, eyed it with displeasure.

Their conversation was stilted and laboured. Nothing came out right.

'I'm a political Hindu,' he said at length, looking briefly in the direction of the beef. His voice contained a hint of apology.

'Oh! . . .' she said and then did not know what more to say. 'What does that mean . . . ?'

'It means I'm not religious: in the sense, I'm an atheist . . .'

'My husband – my ex-husband, I mean – used to say all the Eastern religions were fundamentally atheistic.'

Maniraja minded the interruption. He looked at her with the irritation of someone forced to suppress his irritation, but she could not yet read the expression.

'I mean: I don't follow any rituals: no practice, as such. I eat beef with relish.'

'Oh, I wish I'd known!'

'No, no, that's not what I'm saying.'

'You are, after all,' she said this carefully, 'the go-ghna.'

Maniraja's face went blank. But he did not ask for an explanation. What he did not know did not interest him.

'My son . . .'

My son! My husband! What kind of woman is this, Maniraja thought.

'My son is always showing it to me in the Sanskrit dictionary.'

'Your son learns Sanskrit?' Maniraja said, not with curiosity but with something like confusion.

'Yes.' And, conscious now not to say 'my husband' again, she said quickly, 'But what's interesting is that go-ghna, which should mean simply noxious to kine, is, in fact' – and she said this with such care that it was as if, able to see her life for the first time from the outside, she was saying, *I was married to a Sanskritist once* – 'an irregularly derived compound, you see.'

'I've been working with some Sanskritists,' Maniraja interrupted, feeling perhaps that the conversation had gone too far out of his control.

'Yes, but wait: let me finish—'

'Let you finish!?' Maniraja flared up, as if she had touched a nerve, crossed some unspoken cultural boundary. 'I was the one speaking, if you recall,' he added, now more softly, seeming with trouble to control his temper.

Uma stared at him in surprise. At that moment – before her judgement clouded – she knew, at least, in respect to his view of women, exactly the sort of man this was.

'I'm sorry,' she said. 'Go on.'

'No, no. Please! *You* go on.'

'It was nothing.'

'I insist,' he said, reaching over for the wine; and, passing a scrutinizing eye over the label, poured himself some.

'I'm not sure what I was saying . . .'

'Sanskrit,' he pressed, and smiling, added, 'Your husband, your son.'

He was beginning to feel in control now.

'I don't even know how we got onto the subject . . .'

'I said something about my being a political Hindu, about eating beef and you said . . .'

'Yes. Go-ghna! Which is apparently an irregular upapada tatpuruṣa. So instead of meaning noxious to kine, it is derived as: for whom a cow is killed.'

Maniraja winced.

'And guess what that is? A guest! Go-ghna is a synonym for guest. *Now go tell the men in saffron that!*'

Maniraja was silent.

'Wine?' he said.

'Why not! In for a penny, in for a pound.'

They both drank in silence for a while. A warm breeze began to blow; there was the scraping of dead leaves over the dry earth; the candles in the fanooses guttered.

'Storm,' she said, draining her glass. 'Should we go inside?'

'Sure,' Maniraja said quietly, picking up the bottle of wine. Later she would know what this quiet meant, but at the time – new to him, new to the situation – she interpreted it as a version of what she was feeling. Which was desire.

Inside, among the shelves of old orange-spined paperbacks and the looming shadows of potted plants, Maniraja passed an eye, at once bored and probing, over every detail. The books. The bronzes. The stacks of old records and tapes. The entire recessed wall devoted to Sanskrit; his eye trailed the brown and gold surface of a many-volumed Mahabharata. He saw the Rushdie lying carelessly on the canvas seat. And it all, in equal measure, like the woman whose flat it was, seemed at once to repel and fascinate him. He couldn't decide if there was really something here, or if it was not just all terrible phoniness, if these people were not just third-raters, hiding under the veneer of good English. His eye rested on the picchvai of the peacocks.

Uma, whose eyes had followed his, said, from where she stood near the tape deck, 'Krishna with his gopis. What is it Coomaraswamy says' – and she marvelled that she remembered – 'that it is all an allegory. "The reflection of reality in the mirror of illusion. The reality is the inner life, in which Krishna is the Lord, the milkmaids the souls of men and Brindaban the field of consciousness."'

A smile appeared on Maniraja's lips. It seemed to be directed not so much at what she said, but at her tone, her way of speaking. It all seemed so fake to him. Her security, her comfort, her ease with English, like a kind of play-acting. And now this little remark about Krishna, as if these were things that could be discussed in this off-hand way!

Uma felt the force of his discomfort. It was why she had put on the music, in part to dispel the awkwardness that had been with them throughout. And now, looking at Maniraja taking in the room, she realized how closed he seemed to her. *I can't see the child in him*, she said to herself. Then the music intruded on her thoughts.

'He reminds me so much of the Sixties,' she said, 'Leonard Cohen. Of joints, and of sitting alone in one's room, listening to music, of finding hidden meanings in the words. This line about not being lovers like that, and besides it still being all right: it captures the mood of that time so much, doesn't it?'

'I wasn't listening to this kind of music in the Sixties.'

'What were you listening to?'

'To Bhimsen Joshi.'

'How sad for you!' she said and laughed. 'Did you miss the Sixties, then?'

'What do you mean "miss" them? I was in my teens when they began, so no: obviously I didn't miss them.'

She smiled and let the conversation drop. Grating as their misunderstandings were, there was something she liked about them. They made her, in some strange way, trust him. They answered a need in her for her country, which, when she met someone like Maniraja, she realized was as exotic to her as a foreign country. She had once been fascinated by Toby's foreignness, but now, this other foreignness, this local foreignness, held an even greater power for her. His authenticity, it was so real.

He rose and walked around the room; she followed him at a distance; he stopped at a picture of I.P.

'My brother,' she said, in reply to the question in his face, and added, 'He doesn't live here anymore. He left after 1984.'

He lowered his eyes in respect; and in that gesture, in that lowering of the eyes, in the sudden gravity, she realized that one of the things she liked about him was his seriousness. It was like an emanation of other things: of hope, of patriotism, of guilelessness. It put her at ease.

But the easier she became around Maniraja the more it seemed to distance him. He did not like her, peacocking about the room in a kaftan, a glass of wine in her hand, talking about art and music; it killed the woman in her, she seemed so poised and artificial.

He was a man with little patience for beauty. His own culture, intellectually speaking, was closed to him, his feeling for its objects of beauty inseparable from the vestiges of religious feeling. He might stand before a tenth-century Nataraja and be moved to tears but he would never have been able to distinguish the emotion the object engendered in him from his reverence for Shiva.

And, besides, it was not as if the aesthetic spirit that had made the Shiva had made the world Maniraja lived and worked in, the world he saw around him every day. His everyday world was, as such, the same as Uma's, an overlay of foreign things, and the spirit that had the potential to move him was confined to museums and archaeological sites. The loss of an idea of beauty – instinctive or cultivated – left him with a void, which unkowingly he filled with an excitable and prejudiced politics that felt almost like revenge.

He saw the world only through the lens of his politics. It reduced the complex world into a simple binary, in which people were either this way or that. Maniraja's only task was to establish where they stood on the things that counted, which was why conversation for him was either a heated argument or something dull and utilitarian. Uma's joke earlier about the men in saffron had set off certain alarm bells; the fact that she was reading Rushdie now set off others.

'So what year were you born in?' she asked, thinking back to their conversation about the Sixties.

'1947,' he said.

'Ah,' she said, 'another midnight's child,' and gestured to the proof of the new book.

'I don't read novels,' he muttered, and moved away.

Maniraja felt the conversation slip away from him again; he felt almost as if she were laughing at him. He wanted in some way to pierce the crust of her manners.

He was not a subtle man, but he had a gift for coming at things in an oblique and roundabout way. He was the master of the non sequitur; and presently, sitting down in the canvas chair where she had been reading, and placing the Rushdie in his lap, he simply said, 'Bulgaria,' and fell into silence.

She waited for him to say more, but he didn't. He just sat there basking in the narcissism of a private consideration.

'Bulgaria?' she said, at length.

He smiled, and ran his fine fingers over the smooth blue surface of the proof in his lap. For a moment it looked like he would say nothing more. Then, just as the theatricality of his pause had grown comical, he said, 'Yes. The Balkans. The Battle of Blackbird's Field.'

'The Balkans? The Battle of Blackbird's Field? Bulgaria?' she asked in complete bewilderment.

Maniraja looked wearily at her, readjusting the sapphire on his fingers. She was surprised at his vanity, his self-regard; she saw in it something of the ugliness of the Indian male, a creature stunted by the premature and too-emphatic applause of the women around him.

'Go on, Mani,' she said, with irritation. 'Bulgaria. Battles of Blackbird's Field. What does it all mean?'

Annoyance appeared in his face. He was like an actor who had been rushed along, his routine spoilt.

'Bulgaria,' he said, 'it may interest you to know, perhaps the liberal-shits did not tell you, has some very compelling similarities with India.'

'Oh?' she said, now genuinely mystified. 'Really? Like what?'

Her amusement irritated him further.

'Yes, really. For instance, they, too, had a Muslim occupation, you know. Several centuries long, like ours. Their culture was also the victim of Islamic aggression. They have also had to address the problem of a 10–15 per cent Muslim population, which, by the way, has declined steadily since the years of Ottoman rule . . .'

'*Address* the problem of a Muslim population? Where is all this going, Mani? How did we get here? Apropos of what?'

'You know how many mosques there were in Sofia in the nineteenth century?'

'No, but why don't you tell me?'

'Sixty-nine. Sixty-nine! And you know how many there are today?'

'No. But I'm sure you're going to . . . Mani, where are you picking up this stuff?'

'One! One bloody mosque. The Banya Bashi – built, naturally, on the bones of a church. But while we let all the mosques that have been built on the bones of our temples stand, the Bulgarians did not. In their national museum, the entire five hundred years of Islamic history is dealt with in one case: one glass case, containing a sword, a prayer book and a little bowl. That's it. It was as if the Ottomans were never there. Islam tried to stamp out their culture too, but it recovered. And there's the difference.'

'Mani, you sound crazed . . . I don't know what you've been reading . . .'

He misunderstood her.

'I'm crazy?' he thundered. He had a childish way of always returning unchanged something thrown at him. 'You're crazy!'

She didn't react. The situation forced her out of herself. In her mind it was almost tomorrow, and she was telling a girlfriend – Gayatri Mann or Priti Hirachand, say – about the calamity her date with Maniraja had been.

Her silence temporarily calmed him down. Now, he was rifling through his tan leather briefcase. He handed Uma a pamphlet which he'd retrieved from one of its interior pockets. It had a picture of a mosque with blood dripping from the dome, set against a twilit sky streaked orange and purple. Fat bold letters repeating the colours of the cover, and bordered black, read, '*The Indian Holocaust*, Ben Choate. The India Memory Foundation.'

'Mani,' she said, now almost from concern for him, and in a voice in which she detected traces of Toby's, 'this is a pamphlet.'

He seemed not to catch the pejorative colour of that word. For he said simply, 'There will be books soon, and movies. We're thinking of setting up a museum. The Indian Holocaust Museum in Somnath.'

'*You* are the people behind that museum?' she said in disbelief, remembering that bad night from so many years ago. 'But it's a joke, that museum, this foundation. This is not serious scholarship. No serious writer . . .'

'I can say you're a joke. Your husband's a joke. And when he was in trouble, who did he come to? Have your forgotten the Emergency? He came to me. Your whole class of liberal-shits, Congress cronies, all jokes.'

'Congress cronies, Mani?' she said, ignoring the remark about Toby. '*We*, and Congress cronies?'

'Perhaps you have not read Vijaipal. Perhaps he is a joke too?'

'Don't talk to me about Vijaipal. I know Vijaipal better than you. He is a friend of my husband's. And he may have some controversial views, but he does not endorse this rubbish. Vijaipal is a man of intellect,' she said, and threw the little pamphlet to the floor. 'Congress cronies?! Us? That is rich. Us, who went through 1984! Congress cronies! That's a good one . . .'

'Maybe you needed to go through it,' Maniraja said, with the miserable smile of a man losing control. 'Taught you a lesson the Muslims would do well to learn too!'

She held his gaze a moment, as if offering him an opportunity to retract what he had just said. But finding his face closed, her eyes trailed away, as if in sadness, and suddenly she leapt to her feet and strode across the drawing room, knocking her knee against the coffee table, but hardly noticing. 'Narindar!' she yelled. 'Narindar! Saab, ki gadi bulao.'

A moment later, she was at the front door, holding open its one narrow panel with her hand. The warm breath of the night blew through the flat. Uma, with her head down, arm outstretched like that of a traffic policeman, repeated again and again, as if afraid she would forget, 'Go. Just go. No, no. Just please go . . .'

Maniraja came up to the door. He said, 'There's no need to call the car. I walked here. I'll walk back.'

But at that very moment both of them found themselves standing squarely in the broad yellow beams of a car's headlights.

'Whose car . . . ?' Uma began, but was interrupted by the sight – the silhouette, rather, large and billowing – of a man leading a boy in their direction.

'Skanda? Hira? What . . . ?' she said, as the figures appeared out of the smoke and headlights.

'Satzriakal, bibaji,' Isha's driver said and handed Skanda over to Narindar.

'Satzriakal,' she said in confusion. 'What happened?'

'There's been some trouble at the house,' the driver said quickly, and with embarrassment. 'Saab and memsaab have had a fight.'

Skanda, his hand in Narindar's, looked long at the strange man standing at his front door, then he disappeared into the flat.

*

Mani walked back to the Raj, alone and wretched. *Such a bad evening*, he thought. *Bad, bad, bad*, he said, almost aloud, and put his hands in his pockets. He found he still had the grease-daubed napkin with Pooja's extension number written on it. *What time is it?* He looked at his watch and saw that it was 12.30. *Good*, he thought, and smiled inwardly, *there is still time; nothing is irretrievable.* He took a deep breath of the warm night air and quickened his stride.

*

A few days later, Uma went to see her sister on Curzon Road. She drove through the hard dazzle of an April day. It was a season that anticipated the great heat with a parade of flowers. The silk cotton, with its fleshy coral flowers and stony branches, casting long shadows over the ground, had come and gone. And now, as the days grew whiter, and the scorching breath of grīṣma began to blow over the city, a procession of flowering trees ushered in the season of death. There was the burnt orange of the gulmohar, the phantasmagoric yellow of the laburnum and the heartbreakingly clement lilac of the jacaranda; on the city's roundabouts, the thatched canopies of jarul were covered in bright purple blossoms. It was funereal, this solace of flowers, even as the frank gaze of the sun beat down on the land; and shadows grew short and inky, the cool of old houses bewitching and intense.

At the house on Curzon Road, the verandas shrank back into the face of the building, forming solid blocks of shade. Such heaviness, Uma thought, as she made her way through the house, its air tinged with the smell of old flesh, of widowed aunts, in white cotton and chiffon, retiring for naps; air in which there was always the faint reek of a meal having just been cleared away; air, dark and enveloping, where the hum of a refrigerator or the distant whirr of an air cooler was pierced, now and then, by the sad and aimless shriek of a koel.

She passed a garlanded photograph of Viski's late mother, who had died some months before – old Teji Kaur, with whom the sadness of the house on Curzon Road had begun, and who, in death was more trouble than when she had been alive – and entered her sister's part of the house. She found her sitting barefoot on the shallow steps of an internal courtyard, her hair wet. The radio – a Hitachi – played old film songs; in a narrow strip of shade, there were large ceramic vats of pickle, whose yellow and white glazing, faintly cracked, gave off a distant and impenetrable gleam.

'Shikanjvi?' Isha said.

'I'd love some.'

'Bihari,' she yelled back into the darkened house, 'nimbu pani laana.'

The formality over, she did not look up at her sister. She just sat there, twining her wet hair into a rope and making it drip onto the sandstone stairs. Then with a joyless laugh, she said, turning to face her sister, 'What do you think? Shall we say conjunctivitis? Or a fall?'

It was impossible to make out anything past the sunglasses. No swelling, no colour. Uma found herself peering blankly at their large lenses, tinted a shade of brown.

'I can't tell.'

Isha removed the glasses and gave a languid tilt of her head. For a moment, before the reality of it all sank in, Uma found herself staring blankly at the bruises on her sister's face. A graded range of red and blue and purple around the eyes. The colours, glazed with lotion, merged easily into one another. On the bridge of the nose, there was a round hard ball striped with a short rude gash. Then, it all coalesced, and Uma recoiled before the image of the hard blunt edge of a hand striking her sister's face, little flesh, much bone. She made a sucking sound and said, 'Tsssss! Put them back on, Ish.'

Isha did with a wry smile and, with something martyred in her voice, asked how Skanda was.

'Oh, fine.'

'Not too traumatized, I hope, at seeing his aunt beaten up.'

'No,' she lied, 'he'll be fine.'

'I kept saying, "Not in front of the children, Viski." But he wouldn't hear a word. He chased me into their room: "Whore this, whore that. Your mother's a whore, you're a whore, your sister's a whore." Animal!'

A moment of awkwardness passed between them and Isha came quickly to its source.

'I know what you're thinking. I know you're thinking, bad old Isha, she must have said something to provoke him . . .'

'No. Not at all. Are you joking?'

'I already had Mama here: "Isha, you mustn't rub salt in his wounds." Rub salt in his wounds! I'm the one with the bloody wounds. I'm the one who was ready to put an end to it all . . .'

'Isha, you can't talk like that. It was terrible what you did. You have your children to think about. How many did you take?'

'Fifteen, twenty. Ask Mama; she counted them the next day.'

'And?' Uma said, unable to conceal her curiosity.

'And nothing! I slept like a log and woke up famished. I had a trout for lunch at the Golf Club.'

'Isha!' Uma said, and began to laugh. 'What can I say? Mashallah, you've always had such a good constitution. Only you could have a suicide attempt that ends in a good sleep and a large lunch.'

Isha chuckled.

'What did you tell Skanda?'

'Nothing. That grown-ups fight, and sometimes like children.'

'Did he seem OK?'

'It's hard to tell with him these days. He's so quiet.'

Nimbu panis arrived in two dented tumblers of solid silver, oxidizing blackly, the ice melting on the surface.

'What do you want to do?'

'I want to leave. The boys are both at school; I want to get the hell out of here. I thought things would be better once that witch was dead. But they are, if anything, worse. At least when she was alive we could discuss the meddling of a real person, a thing of flesh and blood. Now we can't say a word about Santa Teji, our Lady of the . . . I don't know! . . . whores?' she said and laughed raucously, then winced.

'What's the matter?'

'Ribs. They hurt when I laugh.'

'Isha, my darling . . .' She seemed to be about to express sympathy, then, as if wishing instead to give her sister some hard practical advice – for violence of this kind was not uncommon – she said, 'Did you call his mother a whore?'

'Yes.'

'To his face? When he was drunk?'

'Yes.'

'Isha! You can't tell a man who's just lost his mother, a man who's drunk at that and who, for all her sins, worshipped his mother, that she was a whore . . .'

'He called Mama a whore!'

'Mama, Isha? Mama! Mama has lived so dreary a life that she would probably be delighted if she heard someone had called her a whore.'

Isha smiled.

'*His* mother, on the other hand,' Uma began – Isha was laughing now – 'as we well know, slept with half the Punjab. Calling her a whore, when she's not been dead three months, is quite another thing from calling Mama a whore.'

'She was a terribly destructive influence in our lives, you know that. She filled him with guilt for being the only one of his children old Papaji didn't disinherit . . . .'

'That maybe. But he loved her. And she had her moments. She was a tiger in '84.'

Isha lit a cigarette.

'So what? Are you telling me to hang in there?'

'No,' she said, thinking of how ill-equipped her sister would be to manage life alone, 'but I'm telling you to think carefully about it. It's not all that much fun, the single life. Toby . . .'

'Toby never laid a finger on you.'

'I know.'

'But you left him?'

'I don't know who left who . . .' She gave a sigh of irritation. 'Should we go inside? It's very hot here.'

'Wait.' She squeezed out a few more drops from her hair. They splashed on the red stone of the stairs, turning it a rich rust colour that, edged with escaping granules of dust, gave a tantalizing impression of cool and moisture.

'Summer,' Isha said bitterly, and rose to go in.

They sat in her dressing room. The day, beaten back behind double doors, made a squalid mosaic of the tiny squares in the mesh that the years had left unclogged. A fly progressed haltingly round the sweetened rim of the silver tumbler.

Uma shooed it off, and began, 'It's not comparable, Ish. Your situation and mine. You and Viski, violent as it was, had a fight. Toby and I, in the end, did not fight. There was not enough fight to fight, not enough passion. We just ran out. We were nothing in the end.'

She could have sworn she made the remark without a thought for Maniraja. But, after a moment's silence, Isha said, 'And that businessman? How did you leave things with him?'

She stared at her sister in disbelief. Their thoughts must have become entangled in each other's. She had told Isha about the argument, but not about the rapprochement the next day. Nor about the flowers; nor the note; nor the meeting in his hotel room that Sunday morning, before he went back to Bombay. She had not told her, because what had happened was too strange: she had no way to explain it, especially in the context of what had occurred the night before.

'We left things amicably,' she heard herself saying without mental effort. 'But – I don't know – let's see. These are not people I really understand.'

'We never knew anyone like that in the old days, did we? And, all that cant we hear about India being secular down to her villages. My foot! Give people half a chance to improve their lot, and the hatred and chauvinism comes free with the new refrigerator.'

Uma laughed. And then, as later she often would, she defended Maniraja. 'I don't know if it's hatred and chauvinism as much as it's . . .'

'What?'

'I don't know – Toby used to be quite sympathetic with it – he thought of it as the striking of a new equilibrium. He felt us lot—'

'*Us lot*? Excuse me?'

'The deracinated Indians . . . we use words like secularism to make people feel small about their culture . . . He thought it was snobbery by another name.'

'Toby was very naive about these things, Uma. Prejudice is prejudice, I say. But tell me: are we all still on for Gulmarg? I hope so. Viski – guilty as hell, no doubt,' she said, and removed her sunglasses theatrically, 'has gone and spoken to Tariq Mattoo and he's managed to get us CM1. Kitten Singh is furious, of course. Because it was meant to be hers. And she, as we well know, worked much harder for it. She was to have your friend, Priti Hirachand, coming to stay. She wanted to play the big hostess. Queen of Gulmarg. But these damn Fatehkotia sisters have come in her way. She's been bitching us out all over town. One's gone and stolen her house, the other . . .'

'Her man?'

'Exactly!'

'How does she know?'

'They're snakes, these women, Uma. This is all they do. Play one off against the other. Even Priti, you think she set up this meeting with this Hindutva-fellow from the goodness of her heart? Not a chance! They get married, these ladies, and then they become like madams to the rich businessmen. It's their cachet. If they can't sleep with so-and-so hot new tycoon in town themselves – or if he's done with them and wants to move on – then they position themselves as his agent to the next thing that catches his interest. Don't you see? It's a form of currency for them.'

'Isha!'

'I'm just saying: be careful.'

'Of what?'

Isha hesitated, then said, with a frankness that would one day be the end of their relationship, 'Of being passed around.'

'I'm not listening to this,' she said and made to leave. Isha caught hold of her hand, and looking in the direction of the gauze door, said, as if in apology, 'I can't wait to get out of this place, to leave this heat.'

Uma sat back down.

'Me too,' she said softly.

'And these months building up to it, they give one such a feeling of dread.'

'Toby used to say . . .'

'Toby, Toby, Toby . . . What's the matter with you today?'

'He's been on my mind lately.'

'Why?'

'I'll tell you in a minute, but let me first tell you what he used to say: he used to say that "us lot", we no longer have a feeling for the seasons in India.'

'Does that make them hotter?'

'Apparently so. He used to say that if you end up estranged from the natural world in your country then it comes to feel like a foreign country, its seasons alien, its extremities harder to bear.'

'Probably right, no?'

'I think so. He loved the change of seasons. He would always show Skandu and Rudrani those sections in the epics where the natural world and seasons were referred to. The epics, he said, were packed full – even at the cost of narrative – of the names of trees and flowers. And that just the fact that most Indians today don't even know the names of the trees or flowers is an indication of how much has been lost.'

'What kind of things?'

'Oh, I don't know. Shirishas. Shinshapas. Dhavas. Shalmalis. Kinshukas . . .'

'Never heard of them!'

'Me neither. Kinshuka, I know, is *Butea frondosa*. Flame of the forest. It comes up a lot in literature. But the rest, well, you know, I never paid attention to a damn thing he said . . .'

'But still. You must have picked up a lot just by being around him.'

'Not really. And what there is will go fast. Skanda is the one who will retain it. I see the signs already.'

'Of what?'

'Well, of someone compensating for his father's absence with the things he taught him, with Sanskrit. He never took it so seriously when Toby was around. But, now, it's as if he's using the language as a proxy, to fill a hole, you know.'

'You'll bring them to Gulmarg, of course?'

'Yes. Rudrani, I might send up with the parents beforehand. Skanda, I'll bring myself.'

'Why?'

'Because he has to go to England first.'

'Uma. Don't tell me. You're not sending him all the way for that silly birthday party. You'll spoil the market. What'll I tell my kids . . . ?'

'No.'

'Then what? Why does he *have* to go to England.'

'To attend a wedding.'

'A wedding? Whose?'

'His father's,' she said, and with a smile that seemed to heap scorn on the world, a smile the Fatehkotia sisters had between themselves perfected, added, 'Toby is remarrying.'

'That was our last summer in Kashmir,' Skanda says, looking out of the window onto the cemented surfaces of Legend, one of the many developments to emerge on this southern extremity of Gurgaon. The land around is full of what the Indian Society of Weed Science describes as 'aggressive colonizers'. And some of that aggression must have rubbed off on the people too, for Legend was built in alarming haste, even before there was a proper road. It is here, among these beige towers, with their traffic-island greenery and Tetris sky, that Gauri lives with Kartik.

Skanda, as if perturbed by something he sees outside, says, with sudden agitation, 'It's so hard to connect one time with another, this world with that world. The scale feels all wrong. The shape of things . . . What was the little phrase you read me the other day, Gauri?' he says, gesturing to the book on the coffee table, *The Masque of Africa.*

Gauri has marked out the pages she likes in the back. She picks it up and reads: 'And then I thought that his life had been too varied, full of unconnected or disparate parts, and he hadn't worked out a way to present himself. I suppose that meant he hadn't been able to make a whole of his experience.'

'That's it! You see, in life, a man we hardly know can break into a woman's bedroom in the morning, beat her up in front of her son and leave. Life owes us no explanation. If it sits badly with us, it's our problem. But if – decades later – we recall the event, as part of *our trying to make a whole of our experience*, it is not enough just to say it happened; not enough to say it was terrible; or that it left a scar on the woman and her son: not enough to say that, for her, it was a final confirmation of her vulnerability in a world she had sought always to escape . . . Or that, for the son, on the verge of becoming a man, it dealt a blow to his masculinity from which it would never really recover. A masculinity that, I should say, the sins of the father had already put in jeopardy. Not enough to say that, is it . . . ?'

'Not enough? Why?'

'Because I feel it doesn't work; it doesn't add up.'

'But doesn't it work, really?' she says, answering him with an impatience of her own. 'We know Kitty; we've met Tunnu. We know her trouble with the Fatehkotia sisters. Your mother made off with a man she was interested in, not once, but twice. Your aunt stole her house. And we can sense Uma's restlessness. What is so hard to understand?'

'The pettiness of it all. The meanness of the motivations. The more one seeks to explain it, the more it feels like a lost cause. And yet . . .'

'And yet?'

'It mattered so much, Gauri. It was a final expression of *the way things were*. It came out of nowhere. And that is the point: it was a world where ugly motiveless things could come out of nowhere, and be forgotten. A world where a man could beat a waiter to death for being rude to him and get away with it. A world whose behaviour was unregulated by the public sphere: an inward-looking and Hobbesian world. And it was always what she had sought to escape. On the night of her birthday party, her angst against all those women was nothing but a wish to escape them all. To get out, once and for all. It was all she had ever wanted. But my father was a false escape, a cul-de-sac: for he could live in the world and be apart from it. He had the life of the mind, you see. That was not what she wanted: she wanted the world, the real world.'

'And Mani gave it to her?'

'He did. But, at a price.'

'Of course.'

'But after Gulmarg she was willing to pay any price. It was so humiliating, so unprovoked, compared with what happened . . .'

'What was the provocation?'

'Something ridiculous. An argument or some such, a fight with Chamunda, perhaps – about how Ismail was treating her son . . .'

'You?'

'No, no. Chamunda's son. Bhaiya. And Kitty kept interrupting, till I think my mother told her to fuck off. And, so, she left in a huff, and sent Tunnu back the next day. How long is it before Kartik gets home?'

'Half an hour or so,' she says, looking at her watch. 'And your parents?'

'Not till after lunch. I just had word from Maniraja's office.'

'Do you want a beer?'

She returns with a Stella. He takes a deep sip and looks out again, as if in disbelief, at the scorching expanse of Legend. It returns him to his earlier train of thought. 'Yes,' he says, 'that was our last summer in Kashmir. Everyone's last summer.'

They went up in convoy. The cars wound their way through pine forests in which there were still melting moraines of snow. The forest, full of shadows, with its soaked pine floor, its mezzanine of fern, and its sudden swinging vistas of the flat valley below, left a cool and magical impression. The occasional view of the plains gave the passengers of the climbing cars the elation of having escaped a misfortune. It made Delhi feel like a place which a coup or a pandemic had made unsafe, and which had to be fled under the cover of night.

The green-roofed houses ranged around the meadow filled fast with the families of these refugees. They found each other again with the excitement of familiars in an unfamiliar place. There were cards, lunches, golf, tattu rides for children and fire-lit dinner parties, with whisky and kebabs and Trivial Pursuit for the adults, many of whom felt the thrill of certain émigré communities who – for the service it does their social lives – seem almost grateful to the calamity that has forced them from their homes. All that was commonplace in Delhi, the running of their houses, the entertainments of their children, the glimpsing of a familiar face at lunch, acquired a special novelty in Gulmarg.

But as much as the seclusion of the hill station, the privilege it implied, heightened their joys and pleasures, it also rattled their nerves. They were like people suddenly without an accepted idea of their worth in society, forced to make themselves over in a new place. Cars, cottages, clothes, even the tattu a child got: these things became a source of hysteria among them. They were oversensitive and excitable. The slightest put-down or barb that, at home, might easily have been brushed off came in that closed and crowded circle to acquire a sharper and deadlier sting. The air in Gulmarg, as is so often the case in those places where the rich gather, was chilled, fragrant and faintly poisoned.

On the day of her birthday party, Uma watched the rain through the thin-paned windows of CM1's enclosed veranda. A gallery of sorts, overlooking the meadow, bounded in by a slack loop of road. Golfers, walkers, bearded men with russet skin running alongside ponies ridden by children. She had a cup of tea, a rasai and a book, *Chronicle of a Death Foretold*. That was how she had spent most of the six weeks they had been up in Gulmarg: quiet, reading, withdrawn. She was almost thirty-nine – at the end of one life, half considering the beginning of another – and she felt the need to stand back for a bit. She felt the need to observe her own life and to let Gulmarg, like a framing device, serve as a vantage point.

It was especially nice to see Skanda and Rudrani from a distance, to watch them as if they were somebody else's children. Ha! At times, it felt as if it was all she had ever done: watch them from a distance. Rudrani, especially, was virtually her parents' child now. There was something robust and untroubled about her, something whole. On the night of the birthday party, she had elected to go with her grandparents to Pahalgam.

'Don't you want to be here for the party?'

'I'll be back tomorrow. That's when it counts, that's the real birthday.'

That self-possession, a kind of *emotional precision* almost: that was how Uma knew Rudrani was fine.

It was no less apparent than the instability she observed in Skanda. As a child, when he had been more at ease with himself, unafraid of his sensitivity and aloofness, he had, in some strange way, seemed more protected. But now, as he grew older, she often saw a kind of terror in his eyes. He was almost afraid of his emotions and impressions, unable to trust his view of the world. Manhood, the culture of being a man, fell like an ill-fitting shroud over him, seeming to muffle him.

Some of it could be put down to the awkwardness of the age he was at: the burst of height that gave his movements a broken and uncoordinated quality, like a horse who's lost his gait; the deepening voice that now had a grating and robotic quality to it; the pheromonal stench of pre-adolescence . . . These things, she was told – by Viski and others – were expected. But they did not affect Iqbal and Fareed in the same way; these changes were something apart in her son. They gave him an opaque and inscrutable quality; they made him unreadable. It was why the terror, when it appeared in his eyes, had such power for her. It was the last natural reaction left in Skanda, that look of naked instinctive fear that seemed to make his pupils fly back into the green of his eyes, like stones vanishing into the depths, meteors hurtling away into the safety of deep space.

There was something evaluating in his gaze. His eyes were full of memory. Too simplistic to say that, at times, he felt like a stand-in for Toby. And, besides, it was not just Toby she saw in those eyes; it was herself too. She saw something of Toby and their shared past. The scrutiny of his eyes, with their speckles lodged deep in their green liquid, like sand kicked up at the bottom of a pond, was like the scrutiny of the past on the present. She felt answerable to the arithmetic in them and though they seemed able to see her ever more clearly, she was less and less able to see past the one-way mirror of their gaze. There was an element in their relationship now – some dialectic of guilt and shame, of blame and responsibility – that she had not been able to name. It was new, and had only surfaced in the post-Toby years.

Skanda had come back from London full of an adult language, which, she guessed, was Toby's, but which he had nonetheless made his own. When she asked him about his father's second marriage, he had said, 'I think that it'll be a feeding relationship for Baba.' 'A feeding relationship?' she said, with the alarm we feel when the poise of someone we love sets us at a distance from them. 'In the sense,' he said, cool and analytical in the face of her hot distrust, 'I think Sylvia will play quite a nurturing role in his life.' 'And what? I didn't . . .' she shot back, falling straight into the trap. 'No, no,' he said, sensing for the first time an advantage over his mother. 'I just meant that she is of the same temperament as him; she shares the same cast of mind.'

The conversation died there, but she had felt its bite. And she had, with great prescience, seen in it the birth of an emotional mechanism inimical to their relationship: the more Toby disappointed Skanda – the more aloof and distant and self-involved he became – the more he came to seem like a hero to him. An unassailable ideal, the embodiment of vocation, something totemic and sacrosanct. Whereas she, the more she was present and real and engaged in his life – human, in a word – the more she appeared flawed and earthly: the cause of Toby's withdrawal from the world. Skanda, she felt, had already appropriated something of Toby's desire to be unassailable, to always be, as if out of a Sanskritic horror of contamination, above it all.

It was after London that she began to notice a growing rigidity in her son, a studied cool. She read its vibrations correctly: she saw that it was his way, in the absence of his father, of safeguarding himself, his way of becoming a man before his time. It was another reason she was happy to have brought him to Gulmarg. In the company of his older cousins – running about being stung by bicchu buti, hurling missiles at birds with the slingshots they had all been bought on the way up to Gulmarg – his reserve, which seemed so laboured, given his age, relaxed a little. He became less buttoned-up, more spontaneous; his language changed, the new diction fell away. He seemed for a while, at least, to become a boy again.

The rain, blurring the line between morning and afternoon, made her misjudge the time. She saw now that it was nearly 12.30. She went into the dark interior of the house, the floorboards sinking under her feet, and dressed for lunch in the pale light which came in through a gap in the heavily curtained window. Isha, the only other person in the house, entered as she was getting dressed.

'You're wearing a sari?' she said, opening the curtains to reveal a high escarpment, almost a wall, covered in shrubs.

'Well, I'm having lunch with Gayatri, who always does, you know, so I thought I might as well too.'

'Gayatri is a professional Indian, Uma. She wears saris on Park Avenue. You mustn't compete with her. It's going to be hell getting down there in a sari and heels.'

'No cars?'

'No. Viski and the boys have taken both cars down to Srinagar to get supplies for this evening. They'll only be back after lunch. Are Gayatri and that lot coming tonight?'

'I think so.'

'I'm in a bit of a bind about Kitten.'

'Why?'

'I don't know what to do about her.'

'How do you mean?'

'I mean: should we ask her? She's been poisonous about us both. I'm a suicidal wreck, apparently, and you're, well, just a slut.'

'That's very rich coming from her . . .'

'I know! But, there you have it. What do we do?'

'Ask her, ask her, Ish. It's too small a group here not to ask her. It'll be noticed. Don't let there be bad blood. Much better we neutralize her.'

'If you say so. It's your birthday. But I'm pretty bloody pissed off.'

'Never mind. There'll be so many other nice people; nobody will notice her.'

A film song began suddenly to play.

'Ah, electricity's back,' Isha said, and flipping an old-fashioned black switch, turned on a naked weak-rayed bulb overhead.

'You should take this with you . . .' She went out of the room and returned a moment later with a pair of sneakers and an umbrella.

A few minutes later, the sisters stood on the stone steps of CM1, dry under its deep eaves.

'So then,' Isha said wearily, hanging in the glass double doors of the gallery, 'if you see them at the Highland Park, Mr and Mrs Turd, ask them to come tonight.'

'Why would I see them?'

'You'll see him, I'm sure. Poor fellow. He's always there at lunchtime, crouched over his food in some corner, on his ownsome-lonesome, of course!'

'Why? Where's she?'

'She? Oh, she doesn't get up till one.'

The rain had stopped, and a few cautious spokes of light broke through the thick wandering clouds, distantly illuminating a crescent of meadow. Some unpainted sheets of corrugated iron blazed in the sunshine. Uma felt a surge of optimism: the sudden post-romance brightness of wanting to show someone something beautiful: and then it was gone, and she had a corresponding sense of vacancy.

She had found no way to assimilate what had happened with Maniraja that day. The nature of her attraction, its perversity, had always been a mystery to her even when she was young. But what happened that Sunday morning after their big fight was impenetrable even by her own standards. They had fallen into each other's arms the moment she walked through the door. They had had sex and she had drunk in his smell. The evil reek of his armpits, pressing its way past the tired curtain of cologne. It had been enough – combined with the power of rapprochement and the violent unexpectedness of the encounter – to give her the full shuddering ache and terror of an orgasm. He hovered over her, as her face was grazed by the scorching cotton of hotel bed sheets, and she heard muttered, with the airy and fanciful quality of a nursery rhyme, the words, 'My God, darling, you're makhan. Pure butter.'

Then he was gone, and she was left to balance the power of the morning's encounter with what had happened the night before. She was leaving for Gulmarg soon after and she had decided to think about it while she was away, to hold off his advances till her mind had cleared a little. As time went on, the dialectic of mind and heart produced a strange result in her. She still held on to the conviction that this was not the man for her. The argument stood, but what changed was that all the passion left it. It felt true, but inert: it had no power to animate her. Her passion, with double-dealing ease, went over to the side of wanting him, more than ever, to call. If anything remained of her earlier resolve to ward him off, it was just that she would not call first. It was not pride that made her act in this way, but the ghost of a self-protective instinct: for she still believed, in the rational part of her mind, so discredited by swelling desire, that he was not good for her, not right for her. In the face of her uncertainty, she found she slipped into passivity.

And yet, with every part of herself that was mysterious, that had the potential to stir the thoughts of others, she willed him to be in touch. He became the object of every horoscope she read, every coincidence she encountered, every little inkling she had that something was about to change in her life. She addressed herself to him in mirrors; she drove him into her dreams; she made him the invisible witness, as she did now, to the beautiful things she saw, the sun breaking over the meadow on a rainy afternoon . . . And naturally – anyone could have told her! – what she was doing, which excited the imagination's talent for filling absences, was a far more certain way of her falling in love with Maniraja than if she had just picked up the telephone and called him. But she did not see it that way: she thought of herself, out of a virtue too heavy to bear, as denying herself the thing she wanted. This penance had the effect of creating a new Maniraja, far removed from the reality of the man. A Maniraja of her imagination. The more she resisted him, the more perfect he became, the staler her reasons for resisting him became. And it was in part to fortify herself against him that she had chosen Gayatri Mann to have lunch with that day: a woman she associated purely with the intellect, a woman whom she knew would loath a man like Maniraja, and who, more than anyone else, would be able to reinforce the case against him.

She saw her, in a lilac chiffon sari, at a table by the window. Smoking, reading, sipping a nimbu pani. A small woman, with short hair, and a dark intent face. Black Gums, her enemies called her, for she could be vicious. But she was also – in Uma's view – among the most intelligent women she had ever met. Uma recalled the story Toby used to tell about her, 'I'd just finished reading *The Crack-Up*, the Fitzgerald essay, you know; and it has this very memorable line: "The test of a first-rate intelligence is the ability to hold two opposed ideas in the mind at the same time, and still retain the ability to function." Now, for some reason – one afternoon in New York or London, I forget which – I remember quoting it to them, Zubin and Gayatri; and Zubin said, "It's very good, but it's not his, is it? This idea? It feels like someone else's." And Gayatri – without missing a beat; I hadn't even thought she'd been listening – says, "It's Hegel: it's the idea of the dialectic." I was so impressed, I can't tell you! Because, of course, she was right. But to see one thing in the other like that, and so quickly . . .'

Uma and Gayatri had not always had an easy relationship, for Gayatri – unlike her direct opposite the fair-weather friend – was a tremendous support in bad times, but unreliable in good times.

On seeing Uma, she leapt to her feet, greeting her with that smoky rush of words, singsong and barbed, for which she was famous, 'Uma ji! Many, many happy returns. Is it today?'

'Tomorrow.'

'Well, Happy Birthday in advance. How are you? What a pleasure to see you. How well you look. And Skanda baba? How is he? And Rudrani?! Beautiful names. I see Toby's hand there, no doubt. Are they thriving, the both of them?! Please give them my love. I'm just in from New York. Zubin's off at some sales conference or the other. He just gave a big bash for John Richardson, who's working on a wonderful four-volume biography of Picasso. But, chalo, let's leave the West in the West, shall we? It's all AIDS there and nothing else. Terrible, terrible! Robert Fraser a few years back; Chatwin this year. It's like the plague in Thucydides. You remember Chatwin from that little dinner Nixu gave in the Seventies? I was at the memorial in February. Poor Brucie. How he used to love India.'

Uma nodded, managing just to insert, 'I know. I'm sorry also to hear about the trouble with Salman. Zubin must be . . .'

Gayatri did not tolerate the slightest incursion onto her turf. And if ever someone raised a subject that was clearly her territory – but was perhaps also in the public domain – she would cut them off, and say something so perversely contrary about it, so clearly opposed to all conventional opinion, that it was obvious her main objective was not to enlighten the person on this subject, of which she had intimate knowledge, but rather to remind them that it was not their place to have raised it in the first place.

'Well, Salman,' she said acidly. 'That's another story. And let me tell you: he had it coming to him: he knew just what he was doing with that crazy book. But leave Salman. Tell me about you. Or wait: let's order first? You know how these cretins are!'

The lunch room at the Highland Park Hotel was one of the most festive places in Gulmarg. The hotel had a little flag, which it hoisted every morning with great ceremony, and took down in the evenings. Mealtimes were fixed, as were menus, and a bell would ring at 3 p.m. to announce the end of lunch. The waiters, distinguished older men, with neatly trimmed beards and thick bandgalas, their brass buttons blazing, knew all the regulars, and welcomed them with that stern air of efficiency that, like a form of tough love, is the hallmark of those places that are supremely proud of their clientele, but where, out of the need to cope with the excitement of serving dazzling celebrity, a kind of reverse snobbery prevails. Movie stars and the wives of rich businessmen were ushered to their tables, as if they were children in the canteen of a boarding school, and questioned brusquely before an open notebook.

Abdul Rahman Mir – the oldest of this breed – appeared before them now, and having taken down their order like an inquisitor, he slapped shut his notebook and was gone.

For a moment Uma's eyes had a searching look; her smile fell heavily on the table; Gayatri made her anxious. She noticed the book she was reading.

'Ah, the Eliot!' Gayatri said, following her eyes intently. 'The essays. I haven't read them since Cambridge. Zubin's doing a new edition this fall. There's a wonderful one on *Hamlet*. I couldn't believe I'd forgotten it. He says, "the essence of the play is the feeling of a son towards a guilty mother . . ." But then – listen to this, Uma ji. Are you fine with nimbu pani, by the way? I don't think we can get a drink here for love or money – Wait, I need my glasses: can you imagine? How old we've become! When I was in Cuba with Helmut, I used to be able to read the numbers on his negatives. And, now, look! Sit, sit, sit.'

She reached for a slim pair of reading glasses that lay among the white table cloth and silver, and read aloud: 'Haan, toh: "Hamlet", he says, "is up against the difficulty that his disgust is occasioned by his mother, but that his mother is not an adequate equivalent for it." Isn't that nice? He says it "envelops and exceeds her". . . "becomes a thing he doesn't understand" . . . "and it therefore remains to poison life and obstruct action." Wonderful, no?'

She removed her glasses and, eyes smiling, she said, 'A better explanation for inaction I've never read. It's about those people who, afraid of action, look for reasons not to act. And we know so many, don't we, Uma ji? But enough with all this high-mindedness! Tell me about yourself. How is your heart? I saw Toby, you know.'

'You did?' Uma said, with some disbelief.

'Yes. I was at the wedding. How could I not have been, Uma! I've known him for yonks. Small squalid little affair in a registry, followed by a nice lunch afterwards at Claridge's. He's married a terrible little drudge of a woman. Mousy, common, something between an au pair and a nurse.'

At this she cackled happily, and was every bit Black Gums.

Uma felt as though Toby, this person she had known so well, had suddenly been taken from her and returned to the world, like a card, essential to a winning hand, thrown back into the anonymity of the deck. She tried as best she could to seem unconcerned, but wavered between curiosity and a wish to know nothing more.

Gayatri, for she was far from simply malicious, must have sensed how she was feeling and said, 'But you mustn't think about it, Uma ji. You're well out of that situation. Toby's at that stage in his life where his rage will now turn to bitterness . . .'

'Rage?' Uma said with surprise. 'And Toby? I've never heard those two words used in the same sentence before. What rage?'

'Oh, such rage!' Gayatri said, thinking nothing of lecturing Uma on her own ex-husband; and, as if wanting to erase the scepticism she saw in her eyes, she continued, 'That pure intellectual rage of the visionary or the utopian. Thomas More, Allama Iqbal, Adolf Schiklgruber: these are Toby's kindred spirits, his brothers in utopia. Don't go by the placidity on the surface, or the fact that his interests seem esoteric. He is boiling underneath. His is that withdrawal into the world of pure form, that heaven of theory, where the strengthening or weakening of every root can be perfectly determined, every verbal formation governed by laws: this is the hallmark of the kind of man he is. He ain't a Sanskritist for nothing. And it is, by no means, a private or benign vision. No! He would have this fierce system order the world, if he could. His dream of renaissance, Uma, is a frightening thing. And do you know what?'

'What, Gayatri?' Uma said, half-mockingly.

'He is about to come face to face with reality.'

'How do you mean?'

'You see all this time he's held us-lot in contempt. Deracinated, colonized, little brown sahibs, keener on Shakespeare than Kalidasa . . . And he's not wrong there. All the time, he's held out hope that some other truer, purer, *more authentic* India will rise, and push us out. Then, verily, we will see the coming of Ram Raj or whatever fantasy he's cooked up in that head of his. There'll be seminars on Tantric Shaivism and theatres full of well-heeled people applauding the latest rendition of Bhavabhuti: children in school will argue whether Vallabhadeva was a better commentator or Mallinatha: and in the drawing rooms of Delhi people will be made to feel small for not knowing the third person optative of the Class VII verb "*rudh*" . . .'

Uma laughed.

'You're mad, Gayatri.'

'I mean it, Uma ji. He has always harboured some little hope of a second Ayodhya rising up, like a city upon a hill, out of whatever churning is due our way. And here, again, he's not wrong. There will be a churning. This old order will not survive. And it is true: the people who come after us will have more regard for the things Toby has such high regard for. But if he thinks that it is Renaissance – *quattrocento* Florence-style – that's coming our way . . . Wow-zee, does he have another thing coming to him! Because he doesn't know rough till he sees this bunch. And what's more . . .'

Their food arrived. Uma looked at the dishes being laid out in the hope that they might bring respite from this tirade. But Gayatri seemed only to be warming to her subject. She tore up a naan in her fingers, as if to occupy her hands. When the waiter was gone, she began again, 'And you know what else? You know what Toby doesn't see? This new order – this bania century that is upon us – they will use the things of Toby's world – the epics, the poets, Manu, Ayodhya, whatever – and they will hollow them out of meaning. They will make slogans of them. That is what they want them for, as symbols of their rise, and nothing more. They don't want an intellectual rebirth; *that* requires hard work and labour; *that*, if it is taken all the way, can be a frightening thing. It can force you to confront things about your past that are uncomfortable. No, no, no, Uma! This lot, much more than us, wants the full tacky blast of modernity: the malls, the cars, the fat children shovelling McDonald's and KFC down their throats, the wives, dolled up like Christmas trees, in Armani, from head to toe. They don't want a renaissance, Uma: they want the West, onto which they will graft the little symbols of their culture, so as to give themselves the illusion of not having lost it. Here a little Indraprastha luxury mall, there a Maharaja Mac, Ram and Laxman action figures made by Mattel. And they will say proudly to you, these new Indians' – and, here, she gave a little nod of her head, and adopted an accent – '"Look, you see, even the mighty McDonald's had to Indianize itself before coming here." What they don't know – of course! – is that McDonald's, before it came to our beloved country, made a hundred such adjustments in a hundred such places: it was their express strategy to make these adjustments.'

'But, Gayatri, what has all this to do with Toby?'

'It has everything to do with Toby. Because when it happens our messiah-in-waiting will see that change has indeed come, but that he is no part of it. And there will be the extra pain for him of seeing the things he has treasured most in his life turn to dust before his eyes. There will be more Hinduism – oh, yes! – more temples, more jagrans; the air will be high with chauvinism. But Kalidasa will be just as forgotten as ever. No one will be any better able to decline Sanskrit nouns. And the study of Indian things will fall quietly – as so much else has – to the scholars in Europe and America. Toby's renaissance, in short, Uma, will be a big fucking dud. A lemon, if ever there was one, with no intellectual component! And what's more: when this lot gets rich: they're not going to build institutes of classical studies, oh no! They're going to pay for chairs in Oxford and Princeton, and send their children to those places. Who, when they return to India – with the veneer of Western education sticking thinly to them – will, if you swap America for England, be just like us, Uma. It'll be us all over again, but on a bigger scale, and a hell of a lot more vulgar, I can tell you.'

Her eyes gleamed. She sat back and lit a cigarette. In the window, the clouds had lifted, and the sun shone brightly over the mountains covered in old waxy snow.

Leaning in, the smoke tumbling out of her mouth, Gayatri said,

'You cannot manage the hopes and desires of people. You have to feel them as *they* feel them. And the trouble with dear Raja saab is that ideas move him much more than people. I met a man in London—'

'Bas, you've eaten?' Abdul Rahman Mir said, returning abruptly, and stared with dismay at the largely untouched food.

Uma smiled. 'We're watching our weight, Abdul.'

'We're old ladies now,' Gayatri added.

'Nonsense. You want old, he's old.' He gestured to a small man, with a pale pink turban and an ashen face, crouched over a bowl of custard. He didn't look up; he just sat there, filing away bright yellow spoonfuls of the dessert between his bearded lips, stopping only to wipe them from time to time.

'Tunnu,' Gayatri whispered, smiling cruelly. Then looking at the waiter, she said, 'Would you believe me, Abdul, if I told you that when I was a ten-year-old girl in Delhi he was not even born.'

'Mashallah!' the waiter said flirtatiously. A younger man had arrived at his side, and soon they were clearing away the lunch.

'You must remind me to speak to him before I go,' Uma said.

'Why ever for?'

'I want to invite him tonight. I hope you're coming.'

'Of course. The whole jing-bang lot of us. Wouldn't miss it for the world. So, you're having Kitty then?' she asked, making it clear she knew of the tensions that had emerged between the two women.

'May as well.'

'Quite right.'

'Is she talking very badly about me?'

'No. But I think she's trying to cause trouble. Putting in a little word here, a little word there. I think she's succeeded in part with Chamunda, at least . . .'

'Chamunda? How so?'

'Oh, she seems to have told her that you disapprove of the way that brute Ismail treats her son. Which, of course, we all do. But she's an insidious little thing, Kitty. She sets these things up to seem worse than they are . . .'

'Well, I hope Chamunda is not taken in. I mean, like you said, I disapprove . . .'

'I know! We all do. You know how these women are, Uma. It's a vipers' nest. In any case, it's all rubbish. What was I saying before . . . ?'

'You were saying you met someone in London . . .'

'Ah, yes! With Pretty Priti, at that ridiculous party for her son. Talk about vulgar! Ooof, and that obese child of hers, trussed up in that costume, looking like – I don't know! – a pig at a toga party. Toby – I know – was very upset with you for allowing Skanda to go . . .'

'Well, he was going to be there anyway. For his father's wedding. Why, did he say something?'

'Only in passing.'

Because Gayatri was an intellectual and not a socialite, she had a habit of approaching gossip in oblique ways – and it was, in a sense, more disconcerting, because she would say unsettling things, while seeming all the time not to care. But now, even by her own standards, she stretched the limits of credulity.

'Yes, so I was saying, I met this fellow in London. Businessman of some sort. One of Priti's finds. She was flirting shamelessly with him all night. But that's not the important part, not, at least, from a sociological point of view. The part that was interesting for me – and let me say, frankly, I loathed the man. He represented everything that is terrifying about this new axis between Temple and Corporation. Reminded me of just the kind of businessman, who, in the thirties in Berlin, might have thrown in his lot with Schiklgruber and the brown shirts. But what was interesting was that he, though he had none of Toby's learning, say, definitely had essence. Not an ideas man, but big on people. And he adored India, Uma. Not as a concept either; not as something it might be; but just as it was. His hope for it, ugly as his politics were, was quite moving. Quite affecting, I must say. I had, of course, to set him right about a number of things.'

Uma, though privately amused by this charade, played along. 'Such as?'

'Oh, everything. One of those people who approaches history already knowing what he wants from it. You know what I mean? He doesn't seem to want to understand the past as *a shaping force* on the present, but wishes rather to shape the past in the light of the present, and the future. I had to say to him, finally, you have it all wrong, Mr Maniraja . . .'

The name! It was said so quickly that Uma hardly had time to admit a thought into her head – a feeling into her heart – let alone respond. She had half-suspected what Gayatri was doing, but the actual mention of the name gave her an ache of remembrance, a chilling need for repossession. *That Gayatri had seen him, and she had not!* She felt Gayatri, even as her words continued unabated, scrutinize her face for signs of the instability she had sought to cause.

'. . . You're coming at it the wrong way, Mr Maniraja,' Gayatri said again, for extra measure. 'The past is not something that can be made to say what you want it to say; you have to let it speak to you, as it will.'

'And what did he say to that?' Uma asked, trying through her impression of casual attentiveness to seem unaffected.

'Oh, nothing. He was unacquainted with the art of conversation. His eyes flared up, went all white and goggly. And he accused me of the very same thing that I only – two seconds before – had accused him of. But that is immaterial. Indians, by and large, have no gift for conversation; their idea of listening is talking. They have absolutely no understanding of complexity. No shades of meaning: everything must be this or that. And this fellow – I don't know! – he'd read practically nothing, save for Vijaipal, perhaps. That was about it. Kept banging on about invasion this, feeling of defeat that. Sense of loss. I said, "But all that was hundreds of years ago. Everywhere's been invaded. Everywhere's had loss and upheaval. What's so special about you?"'

'And what did he say to that?' Uma said, clutching at the little phrase till she could recover her composure.

'Something quite nice, actually: the only thing perhaps that slightly endeared me towards him: he said, "history does not go quiet till you confront it." Toby, you see, would not have understood . . .'

'Of course he would have, Gayatri,' Uma said, with irritation. 'The remark is virtually straight from his lips.'

'Well, OK. Maybe he would have understood, but he would not have known what it felt like. The past, for him, was already quiet. That was why he could approach it so coolly.'

It was only once they had left the Highland Park that Uma realized she had forgotten to tell Tunnu about the party that night. It had begun to rain again. The looping road around the meadow was starting to run; the air was alive with the shrieking of tourists; horses, their thin bodies drenched, their quarters frothy, were being cantered hurriedly to shelter by their owners, who kicked them hard in their stomachs, with heels that were bare and cracked. Nosing their way through this scene of chaos was a line of cars. Their circuit of brake lights sent its ruby colour high into the misty air, so that it flushed the faces of low-lying fruit trees, many still in blossom.

The two ladies stood to the side of the collapsing road, their saris drenched and immobile, their hair clinging to their faces.

'Screw Tunnu,' Gayatri said, when Uma mentioned it, 'we got to get out of here. We look like a bunch of freaks, standing here all dolled up in the rain. *Two Lunching Ladies*, par Edgar Degas!'

'Should we go back inside?'

'Maybe! I'd kill for a fag.'

'But they won't really be able to help organize a car or anything. And we're already so wet.'

They were debating this matter when a car pulled up beside them. A window came down. A small bearded man, with a drawn and tired face, said with a smile, 'Bombay ka fashion aur Gulmarg ka mausam.'

'Tunnu! Thank God. How strange! We were just talking about you.'

'Tunnu! A saviour . . . We're having this thing tonight at the cottage, this little party for my birthday, and I want you and Kitty . . .'

In this way, the car halting along on that rain-drenched afternoon brought the two ladies to CM1, where fires were being lit, where men and boys had returned from Srinagar, and where preparations were underway for the party that night.

Kartik is back from his play date. Even before he enters the house – when he is still on the drive screaming at his mother to come and see something he wants to show her – he puts Skanda on edge. He is small and intense, with dark watchful eyes. His mother fears there is too much of his father in him. And it is easy to see why. He is a natural moralist. From the moment he sees Skanda, a grown man drinking a beer in his mother's house, his limbs stiffen. Something cold and rigid enters his manner. Skanda senses from him the pure hatred of the possessor. He comes in like a cat, following Skanda with his large eyes, while gliding swiftly towards his mother. His awareness of his own size and strength is acute, and it informs the mixture of fascination and repulsion he feels for Skanda. He wants him instantly to witness his dominion over his mother. He has a book and a Frooti in his hands.

'Who gave you that, baba?' his mother asks, seemingly oblivious of the tension between the men. 'Did aunty give you that?'

'No,' he says, and laughs.

'Who gave it to you then? I hope you didn't pick it up off the ground.'

He doesn't reply, but starts squeezing out drops of the sticky yellow liquid on the parquet floor. This is all for Skanda's benefit, Skanda knows.

'Kartik, stop that. Who gave you this Frooti?'

He turns to his mother and screams in her face, 'Aunty gave it to me.' Then he won't stop. 'Aunty gave it to me, Aunty gave it to me. Aunty gave it to me.' Again and again, while sprinkling drops of the yellow liquid on the floor.

'Stop that.' His mother says, and snatches the Frooti from him. He snatches it back, and the anger in him, for a moment, is direct, no longer disguised with laughter. He tears open the little box. Its silvery interior is crawling with black ants.

'Kartik! That's disgusting. Give that to me.'

Then he is laughing again. A crazed and grating laugh.

His father, when he was born, had told his mother, 'I've given you a son, the greatest gift a man can give a woman, from now on we will be celibate.' But celibacy interested him less – he was soon writing semi-pornographic poems to a colleague in the English department – than a systematic wish to shatter Gauri's self-confidence. He was unspeakably cruel. They would be out walking in the early days of their marriage – Gauri would be talking about this and that – and he would suddenly stop her and say, 'Can you tell me if I'm going to learn anything from what you're about to say next? Because, if I'm not, I'd prefer we be quiet.' If ever she went out, to a party, say, where there was drinking and smoking, she would return to find him meditating in the drawing room. 'Go to your room,' he would instruct her, 'You have polluted the energy of this house. I must cleanse it now.'

When Skanda first heard these stories, he was amazed she had put up with as much as she had. A full eighteen months under these conditions. 'Why?' he had asked her, again and again. And she had no answer for him, save for, 'I was thirty-nine. I got pregnant within weeks of meeting him. I was afraid I wouldn't find anyone else.'

At last the celibacy and the discovery of the love poems became too much for her. But she was surprised herself at how much she had been willing to bear. 'We were alone a lot in his university house. And, I suppose, in that isolation, it was easy to lose sight of how things were really meant to be.'

Kartik returns in shorts and a lime green T-shirt. He flips through the heavy pages of a spelling book. 'W for vhale,' he says mechanically, and at such a pitch that he seems determined for no one else to talk. His intelligence is forbidding. The kind of intelligence that will make school hard for him. He forms connections effortlessly across languages. On the 'K for Kite' page, he defiantly says, 'P for Patanga.' At X for X-ray, he says X for 'Skeleton!' Gauri has talked so much about him – his love of religious movies, his strange atavistic feeling for the sound of Sanskrit – but she has never once said how difficult he is. Skanda feels the pressure not to disappoint, for the meeting not to be a failure. It has taken as long as it has, he sees now, not just because he was reluctant; she must have been reluctant too: her son is a nightmare, like his father, and it must chill Gauri to see that, especially since the boy has not seen his father since he was one.

She leaves the room for a moment to get Skanda another beer. Kartik and he are alone together. And that is when Skanda, in his wish to please, makes a fatal mistake. He picks up Kartik and roughs him up a little, tousles his hair. There is a moment's pause as Kartik becomes aware of what is happening, becomes aware of the physical overpowering, then a shriek breaks from his lips. He writhes in his arms like a wild and possessed thing. He throws his tiny clenched fists at Skanda, bites his hands, kicks him wherever he can. His eyes are moist and black with rage. Skanda pretends to laugh it off, but it is terrifying. The pure violence of his emotion is terrifying.

Gauri hears the shrieks and comes rushing in just as he puts Kartik down. He runs up to her and starts beating her with his fists, kicking her shins.

And now the full moral outrage that he has been suppressing, his disgust at returning home to find his mother entertaining a strange man, comes frothing out of him. He stands by the door of the room, pointing a finger at them both. 'Tum gandi ho, tum buddhi ho, tum gaddhi ho.'

Again and again, every insult he can think of wrenched from his tiny lexicon like a dry heave. There is mania in him, but fear too. He seems as if frightened by his inadequacy, as if burdened by a responsibility too great for him to take up. But, at the same time, there is something enviably direct in this experience of fear; it produces anger; it brings him to his feet and hardens his fists. *It was never that way for me*, Skanda thinks, *never so direct, always hidden.*

There was a kind of acting that came easily to Skanda. The trip to London had seemed to require it from the very beginning, from the moment his mother, with an expression of suppressed amusement, had told him of its strange purpose to when, after a cycle with travel agents and foreign currency marketeers, she woke him one hot night in June for his flight.

Delhi airport. Their goodbye, self-consciously casual, among the high emotions of immigrant send-offs. He flew unaccompanied, and adopted an air of jaded familiarity in front of the British Airways air hostess, who was American, and fawned over him, bringing him toys, and food, attending to him during their various stopovers. Once in Dubai – which was dazzling – and again in Kuwait, which was dull, except that she – Dawn was her name! – pointed out from the air that the airport was made in the shape of a plane. Furlongs of amber dots, as if the crust of the earth had been punctured, to release the light within. Then the handover in London. London! Of which, later, his only memory was the smell of high-octane fuel in the cold morning air. These were his impressions and the stranger they became, the more he pretended they were ordinary. They became part of his acting: the air of adulthood he had assumed, and which seemed like nothing so much as treating what was new and unfamiliar as if it were old and known.

He did not feel the acting as fraudulence; he felt it as a responsibility to his mother. And, if responsibility was the foundation of being an adult, perhaps its first duty was pretending to be an adult. He saw, too, that it was only in the moments when he was found out – when someone commented, usually Sylvia, on the wideness of his eyes, or his unnatural silence – that he felt anything at all; it was almost as if the very business of feeling had become its reflection in the people around him.

On his own, he felt nothing. His interior life was consumed by the task of keeping its contents hidden from view. And, as he grew older, no question was more embarrassing than: what are you feeling? Or worse: what are you *really* feeling? Because, so often, the truthful answer was nothing, nothing at all.

Everyone, in a sense, was acting. His mother was acting at being cool. His father . . . well, that was harder to gauge. His father was acting at not acting: pretending to be natural. He certainly seemed to be acting at being a husband to his wife-to-be. But he seemed also to be acting at being a father to Skanda. Everything about the way he was, from his wish to make him breakfast to his taking him to Huntsman to be fitted for a suit, seemed laboured. Skanda knew, too, that all this acting was not for his benefit, but for the benefit of an invisible audience of one: his mother. He knew his father wanted him to report back on the kind of father he had been during Skanda's time in London. And, since such a report could only ever consist of tangible things, his father, who had never been a conventional father, seemed to externalize the notion of fatherhood, seemed to be ticking boxes that had never been there before. Breakfast, suit, visit to museum . . . It made their already stilted conversation more stilted.

It was only when his father was teaching him that Skanda felt he was still in the company of the man he had known. Then, everything else fell away, and he became as relaxed as he had ever been. It was also from this time that Skanda formed the deepest impression of his father's vocation and truly understood what he meant when he said, 'I am only a teacher.' Not in the sense of belittling the vocation, but making it clear that Toby was nothing beyond it. When he became the teacher, Toby's conversation grew more sophisticated, but it was also easier to understand. He dumbed nothing down, and yet what he said had a semantic force that was lacking in his day-to-day conversation.

They read every evening from a new set of books, a library of Sanskrit classics, that Toby was putting together. They were still in manuscript form but he displayed them with great pride, showing off their cover design and the Kiḍ in Devanagari. He wanted them to be published in shades of an orange-tawny-brown colour that he said was the most Indian of Indian colours.

Toby was so excited about the new books that they read together even on the day of his wedding to Sylvia. Skanda was leaving for India the next day and, after the lunch, they came home to the flat on Cheyne Row. It was a summer evening, and in the long windows of the flat the glitter of the river was visible, a leaden Thames. Sylvia was making dinner, and his father, still half in his wedding clothes, a glass of rosé at his elbow, was slightly drunk, slightly sentimental. In that frame of mind he always became, especially in relation to Skanda, concerned about transmission, concerned about passing on what he knew. He insisted they read, even if only a little. His thoughts were scattered, but it was in these moments that Toby was at his best, when the evening sun, passing over the landscape of his mind, turned unseen channels of water to molten silver. There was a reference to Yama, god of the underworld – or so Skanda thought. But it was in the dual. Yamau. 'Two Yamas?' Skanda said in confusion. He looked up to see his father's eyes full of a glassy ardour.

'Not that Yama,' he said with the excitement he felt when the language accidentally revealed – with something of the charm of a lifetime partner still able to surprise – one of its chief delights. 'Yama, here, is twin-born, twin, forming a pair; it applies to the god only as an extension: because he was one of a pair of twins. And it comes, the word, from a very old set of Indo-European sounds: aim-, aiem-, iem-,' Toby said, with difficulty, 'to mean similarity and resemblance. From where we have the Latin, *imago*.'

'*Imago*?'

'Like image. A likeness, a copy, an imitation.'

He took a big sip of his wine, and was suddenly playful: '"Accurate scholarship can unearth" . . . so on, so forth . . . "what occurred at Linz, What huge *imago* made / A psychopathic god."'

'Baba, what are you talking about?'

'You don't know that poem?' he asked him, as if trying to remind an old friend of something from their shared youth. 'The Auden poem?'

Skanda shook his head.

'Sylvia! What is the line from the Auden poem: "Find what occurred at Linz . . . what huge imago made . . ."'

Sylvia appeared from out of the kitchen, smiling, her pale skin beaded with sweat.

'Ooops,' Toby said, and, winking at Skanda, whispered, 'Shouldn't have asked her? Don't mention the war!'

'Toby!' Sylvia scolded. 'Don't put funny ideas in him. We are not *those* Germans.'

Skanda, though vague about the reference, laughed at their tone.

'"I and the public know,"' Sylvia began, as if asked to recite a poem before a group of visiting dignitaries, "What all schoolchildren learn, Those to whom evil is done / Do evil in return."'

Toby looked at Skanda, and expanding his eyes while turning down the corners of his lips, made the face of a man impressed.

'There,' Sylvia said, and swinging around, went back into the kitchen.

Skanda watched his father for a moment. At length, he said, 'Baba, are you happy now?'

Toby looked at him questioningly, unsure of whether he meant right now, as in, in that present moment, or more generally.

'I mean after your marriage,' Skanda clarified, using the word as if it were something clinical, and very far removed from what his own parents had been engaged in.

'Yes, Skandu. This will be a good relationship for me, I think. A feeding relationship.'

A moment of silence followed, then a sudden awkwardness. Skanda, like an actor pushed too hard, could no longer sustain the front of adulthood he had put up, and had no idea what to say next.

'So imago is image?' he said haltingly.

'Ah, no. Not here. Not in the poem, I mean. Here it's being used in the Freudian sense to mean an idealized mental image of someone, a parent usually. Especially an absent one.'

Skanda looked blankly at his father. 'What's Freudian?'

Toby seemed confused, then laughed, as if he could only now see that he was speaking to a twelve-year-old. 'It's a long story!'

That was London. A few days later he was in Gulmarg, and a very different set of demands were made of his newfound acting talent.

His mother was in a strange mood. At times she was distant and withdrawn, spending her time walking or reading, or just staring out of the gallery windows at the meadow. Other times there was something frantic and urgent about her; a hint of desperation; she wanted him around, as if in need of comfort of some kind. He sensed her instability and restlessness, and it alarmed him so much that he found himself compensating with an exaggerated composure. And though this annoyed her – 'Don't always be so buttoned-up,' she would tell him – he felt he needed to bring a measure of calm to her disturbance. She was also drinking more than he had ever seen her drink and then, her mood amplified, she became every bit the tragic heroine, full of bluster and indignation, at once pathetic and magnificent. In those moments, his acting talent deserted him and he just kept away. The force of her emotion frightened him. But the more agitated she became, the more she needed him – not Rudrani, just him. His presence was a palliative of some kind. For what, he couldn't say.

The night of her birthday party, she was frantic. She wanted a showdown. Skanda stayed away, spending his time with Chamunda's son – Bhaiya – whose troubles were so much more considerable than his own that it was a comfort just to be around him.

He was a little older than Skanda; at that age when the physical marks of being a man exceed the psychological; and it was this deficit between the child inside and the man outside that his mother's boyfriend, Ismail, had exploited all summer. The physical changes in Bhaiya – and Ismail watched them with the grim displeasure of a man seeing a puppy he has mistreated grow into a large dog – aroused an animal hatred in him. He was a small man himself, but fierce and abusive, and he seemed to take the changes in Bhaiya's physicality, the hardening of the limbs, the thickening of the voice, the knotty appearance of a lump in his throat and the wispy growth of facial hair, as a personal affront. He did everything in his power to humiliate him. 'Oh, here comes the royal oaf,' he would say every time Bhaiya entered the room. Or 'Oye, come here, Raja of Dufferpur.' It was as if he meant to discredit the appearance of manhood in him: to impress upon him that his becoming a man meant nothing.

The two boys spent a good portion of the evening outside, where there was a bar and a fire. It was a soft July night; at times clear, the disc of the moon brilliant overhead; at times, overcast and wet. A faint drizzle drowned out the noise of chat and laughter that came from the cottage. A parade of headlights, confusing the boundary between light and darkness, interior and exterior, made uneven and clumsy progress up the road leading to CM1. Sometimes their beams flashed wildly into places where there was nothing but earth and exposed roots, rock and grass, the piercing gaze, green, empty, intent, of some small animal.

Inside, a tired and ugly energy had come over the party. The children, all in their nightclothes, threaded their way through the party, refusing to go to bed. They were full of a frenzied wish to please and to surprise. But their jokes had a grating quality, and the less they amused, the more they repeated them, the louder they laughed. In one corner, Iqbal, who now many moments ago had made Nixu Mohapatra laugh briefly by saying, 'May I have a cigarette please,' had, on the partial success of that one joke, repeated it at least ten times in new iterations: 'May I have a cigarette please: may I have a whisky soda please: may I have a Bloody Mary please: may I have a vodka and bitters please . . .' On and on, with that indefatigable capacity children have for making lists, till finally, Nixu Mohapatra, who was trying to discover from Chamunda why Ismail and Tariq Mattoo were having so heated a conversation, snapped at him, 'Fuck off, you freak.' Iqbal wilted, then scurried off. 'Nixu, you don't talk to a child like that!' Chamunda protested. 'Monster,' Nixu said, and looked away. 'Now, tell me: why are they so het up?'

'Kashmir, I think,' she said, pulling her feet under her, and massaging their arches. 'He's accusing him of betraying the valley in the interest of cosying up to Delhi.'

'But that's no secret, surely! What's to get so excited about? After the '86 election, I would have thought everyone knew . . .'

'I know, but he doesn't like to hear it.'

'Hear what?' Gayatri said, coming up, dressed that night in a beige and gold sari, and sandals with socks.

'Have you become a communist, sister?'

'If you think I'm trudging up and down that hill in heels, you have another thing coming. Now tell me: hear what? What doesn't he want to hear?'

'What everyone knows: that he's a puppet of Delhi. And that when Delhi sinks, which is soon, he's sinking with it.'

'Poor sod. The pitfalls of the provincial politician, I tell you. Seduced by that great Gandhi charm. Father might have taught him a thing or two about these people . . .'

Iqbal returned.

'Gayatri Massi, Gayatri Massi, what do you call a pig with three eyes?'

'Go to sleep, you cretin, why are you still awake?'

'Tell, no?'

'I haven't a clue.'

'A piiig!'

'Ayi, these children,' she said and broke off, watching him vanish into the crowd.

'"Fuck me in the mouth, Mattoo." That's what my old pal Harappa would have said. Swine. Coward. Bloody two-generation old Muslim. I can fucking smell the bhenchodh Brahmin in you.'

'There's no point insulting me for that, Issu,' Tariq Mattoo said, 'I'm very proud of our Brahmin origins.' Mattoo was a large fleshy man with a hedonist's mouth. He was dressed that night in jeans, waistcoat and karakul. Ismail's attack on him brought a mild stoniness to his face, but it was clear it did not touch him deeply. His lips parted in a smile, to reveal a compact row of strong Vronskyish teeth. His eyes glittered. 'Ask Uma. Haven't I always – in my speeches – referred proudly to our Brahmin ancestry.'

Uma, lying back on the sofa, in a deep blue silk sari – one of the few things to survive Deep Fatehkotia's assault on her trousseau –

nodded and smiled. She was drunk and sentimental. She kept saying, 'Thirty-nine. My God! Not children anymore.' Then, aimlessly aggressive, she would add, 'I tell you, Ismail,' – or Tariq, or Isha, or Nixu, or whoever was listening – 'after thirty-nine, you don't want to put up with any more shit.' If someone, out of genuine curiosity, asked her, 'What shit, Uma?' she would smile and say, 'Bas, I've said it. After thirty-nine, you know who you are and you don't want to put up with anything. No more shit. God knows, I've put up with a lot in my time.' She was full of romantic ideas that night, of what it meant to be a woman, the passage of time, of suffering, real and imagined, of men she had known, of husbands, of children, of lovers, of movement and change, the impermanence of things. There was a throwaway quality in her voice, something sultry and cynical and indignant.

She was especially aggressive towards the other women present. The occasional glimpse of Kitten Singh roused her anger. Every time she would see her, dressed in her trouser suit, with a little woollen beret, her long straight hair ironed and open, her lips thin and red, she would whisper loudly across the room – to Nixu Mohapatra, say – 'Doors to manual.' And he might say in return, 'You would know, darling!'

Her animosity for Kitten Singh was an extension of the rich blustery feeling she had of being thirty-nine, and of 'no longer being willing to put up with shit'. By which she meant those people, women especially, who had inhibited her, prevented her from living as she would like to have lived. And perhaps she had already come to some sort of decision about Maniraja, because the sight of Kitten Singh, the rage it produced, seemed also to be a rage at a certain hypocritical element in the society – embodied in the person of Kitten Singh – that she felt she had unknowingly ingested and that had prevented her from acting in her own interests.

'I have no cause to feel guilt,' she told her sister, 'I won't live in corners. I'll live large.' No sooner had she formed the words than the room was full of her enemies, full of people who wanted to force her into corners, force her into living small. The origin of her mood – that little bit of grit that drunkenness can enlarge – was a wish for renewal. And, when she felt her sister's hand come lightly to rest on her shoulder, she clutched it, and, looking up at her with reckless amazement, said, 'Ish, I'm going to have a big fucking affair. And no one's going to stop me.'

Isha, responding to the angst in her voice, said, 'Of course you will. And why should anyone stop you?'

Uma smiled. 'You're wonderful,' she said, and her eye clumsily surveying the room, caught sight of her son, past the government-issue tables laden with half-drunk drinks and ashtrays. He stood with Bhaiya, plates and forks in their hands, wandering along the edge of the dining table. She suddenly felt a stab of pity. The alcohol had clouded her reasoning and she made no connection between the surge of tenderness she felt for her son and the declaration she had just made to her sister: she simply wanted to hold him close to her that minute. 'Come here, baba,' she yelled from across the room.

'I'm about to eat,' he said, exposing the face of his empty plate in explanation.

'Eat later. First come and give your mother a hug. It's almost,' she said, glancing at her watch, 'her birthday.'

Skanda looked at Bhaiya, then at his mother.

'Bring Bhaiya,' she said tenderly. 'Both of you come here.'

The boys smiled, and, with their plates still in their hands, walked across the room. Just then, Ismail, whose argument with Tariq Mattoo had continued unabated during Uma's changes in mood, continued almost as background, rose to go back to Chamunda.

'Bugger you, Mattoo,' he said, 'I've said what I had to. The rest is your choice. You want to do chhakkabaazi with Delhi that's your choice. But the next time you're out electioneering try to get one of your bloody constituents to teach you the meaning of a very important Urdu word: ghairat. Just ask them, for my sake: you like referring to yourself in the third person, don't you, you cocksucker? Well, just ask them then: "Tariq Mattoo wants to know what ghairat means."'

He got up and, in a few short fast strides, made his way across the room to Chamunda, his progress corresponding exactly with that of the boys coming the other way. He noticed Bhaiya and it brought a smile of boyish malice to his lips. His green eyes shone cruelly. He had not walked one step past Bhaiya, when, as if forgetting something, he swung back around, ducked, and, in a single movement of great alacrity, tore down his pajama.

The room froze.

Bhaiya, his dark cheeks flushed, stood before the party with the black nozzle of his penis visible from under the hem of a Thunder Cats T-shirt, his pajama lying in a hopeless heap at his feet. 'Behold the crown jewels, ladies and gentlemen,' Ismail said, and continued calmly across the room.

The sequence of what happened next was impossible to determine. A rousing murmur, appalled and muffled, as if wanting, by expressing its outrage silently, to shield the boy from further embarrassment, went through the room. Somewhere the words, 'Ismail, you swine,' were heard, and the crowd closed fast around Bhaiya's nakedness. An ayah, with a fast scurrying step, appeared from out of the wings to usher Bhaiya away. Skanda, his empty plate still in his hands, began to cry. And suddenly everywhere there were recognizable faces: Isha Massi and Viski. Nikhil, and the black-gummed Gayatri Mann. The Maharaja of Marukshetra with his brass spittoon. His whole childhood world swam around him. And his mother? She was sweeping across the gallery, a livid bolt of rage, and grabbing hold of Chamunda's wrist, she dragged her from the room.

•

Behind closed doors, the two women had an argument that was audible to others in the cottage; one of those cathartic fights between two old girlfriends who are finally able to express the litany of grievances that have arisen between them. From the level of 'Parmeshwari is telling all of Delhi you think I have flabby thighs' to 'I warn you, Chamunda, if you don't put a stop to Ismail humiliating that boy, I will take him away from you and raise him with Skanda.'

The others left them alone, but Kitten, in part aware that they were fighting over trouble she had caused, in part preying on intimacies, kept interrupting.

'. . . Kitten? What are *you* doing here?' Uma said.

'I just want to say one thing.'

'No. Please leave. This is a private conversation.'

And she did. But she soon returned.

'Kitten, I think I already told you: I'm having a private conversation with Chamunda . . .'

'It's not right for friends to fight. Come on: come out and join the rest. They're putting the cake—'

'Fuck the cake, Kitten. We're talking about something important. Please leave.'

Kitten looked to Chamunda who sat smoking in a corner of the room. 'She's right, Kitty, we need to talk. We'll be out in a minute.'

But there was soon a third interruption.

Uma was heard saying, 'I've already told you twice, Kitten, you silly cow: get out! We're having a private conversation . . .'

'Are you telling me to leave?'

'Out!'

'Throwing me out of your house?'

'Kitty, no one's throwing you out,' Chamunda said.

'Out, Kitten!'

'She is. Listen to her: out, out, out! I've never been so insulted in my life.'

'She means the room.'

The door slammed shut.

The women, whose fight Kitten Singh's interruptions had robbed of its edge, were between sobs and rapprochement, when there was a fourth knock on the door.

'*I'm going to fucking kill . . .*' Uma said, and wrenched the door open.

It was Isha. She said with a grin, 'You two, you threw Kitten Singh out of the house?'

'Not out of the house . . .'

'Well, she's gone,' she said, and laughed. 'Good riddance.'

'Was she upset?'

'Hysterical. Threw a huge tantrum. Sanu thude maar maar ke nikala si. It was like one of those fairy tales in which the evil godmother leaves in a cloud of sulphurous smoke.'

The women began to laugh.

3 p.m. – Legend – and Kartik is asleep.

His rage ended in farce. He made a barricade of pillows, armed himself against his mother and Skanda with toy guns and plastic maces. He was still full of fight, but breaking through his belligerence, Skanda could see, was an anxious wish to be reconciled with his mother. And unable to find a way to do so without losing face, he fell asleep, leaving the barricade unmanned.

'How soon do you have to leave?'

'Quite soon. They should be here any minute. Do you want to come?'

She smiles, and looks out onto the day blazing whitely outside.

'No. I better stay here with Kartik. I should be here when he wakes up.' Then, careful not to cause offence, she says, 'Do you know what set him off?'

'It was my fault. I was too off-hand with him. It would have felt threatening.'

'I suppose. He's grown up with a complete absence of authority. There's never been anyone in the house to discipline him.'

'Yes, but he must also be afraid for you; he must feel the need to defend you.'

'And the anger? Where does that come from?'

'From his incapacity?'

'Is that what you felt?'

'Very much so. Anger at my mother too, for endangering herself, for exposing herself to attack. She was so audacious, you know, so excessively bold that when someone came along to teach her a lesson, I almost felt it was deserved. And Kitten Singh, you know, was certainly not laughing. She went straight home, woke that poor husband of hers and set to work haranguing him all night. And for a man like that to do what he did, it must have been quite a harangue. She must really have worn him out.'

'Did he come back that night itself.'

'At dawn the next day, when everyone, except me, was asleep . . .'

They go outside; the bleaching sun is high; there is a tremendous feeling of nowhereness, here, within the islanded confines of Legend, with the land around still bare and full of weeds.

'Whose car is this?' Gauri says, looking at the silver Fortuner that has pulled up, a uniformed driver at the wheel.

'Maniraja's,' he says and smiles.

'Skanda,' she says as he gets into the car, 'you didn't mind . . . earlier?' Then she stops herself.

'No. Gauri, you must know: I, of all people, understand . . .'

She nods her head vigorously and he feels for a moment that she is about to cry.

'Will I see you later?' she says hurriedly.

'I hope so.'

Dawn. With mists still thick over the valley, a small figure, turbaned and haggard, his beady eyes bloodshot, made his way over the wet spongy earth to CM1. He had not slept a wink all night, and his ears still rang with his wife's abuse. He went in search of her honour, but he did not have the strength of voice or body to come for it in the day, in the presence of the waking world. He went instead to retrieve it as a thief, with everyone in CM1 – he sincerely hoped – still fast asleep. His mind fastened on a single logistical question: *How will I get in?*

He climbed the stone steps of CM1 and, trying the brass knob of the gallery door, found it bolted; but then, peering past the thin panes, frosted with dew, he soon had his answer.

Skanda, though he had been up late the night before, had never been able to sleep into the morning. Moments before, he had been amusing himself with a loose strip of plywood on the headboard of the bed he was sharing with his mother, snapping it up and down, till she ushered him out with, 'Baba, let me sleep. We were up very late last night. Why don't you go outside? Nana and Nani should be here soon.'

His feet had barely pressed against the floorboards in the corridor when he heard a familiar, 'Oh, Skanda, go back to sleep.' His cousins. Who, it always seemed to him, more than sleeping late, enjoyed boasting about it.

Outside, all around him were the remains of the party: ashtrays, powdery and full; clear glasses with the flat still remains of whisky sodas, some containing a stray cigarette butt, whose black nose dipped down, while its body swelled and thickened, the tipping paper gently peeling off. The morning broke weakly over the smells of stale smoke and flowers; the light was pale and diffident.

Tunnu had been trying the door, but, finding it locked, or perhaps glimpsing Skanda inside, had decided instead to rap. At first, Skanda was not sure he had heard correctly; the noise came from an anteroom beyond a thick curtain; his footsteps on the wooden boards were loud. But when he stopped walking, and the house regained its quiet, he heard it again, distinctly this time. He thought it must be his sister and grandparents.

He pushed aside the curtain and followed the rapping to the door. He was surprised to see an unfamiliar face. Still, a visitor was a visitor, and, if nothing else, it was an excuse to wake the others.

He turned the key in time with Tunnu turning the brass knob. The door opened with a shudder and the full freshness of the Gulmarg morning, of grass, dew and sunlight, poured in, overthrowing the stale air in the house. But Tunnu was not of a piece with its freshness. His face was drawn and lined, his features lost in the sagging mass of hair; and only the redness of his eyes, like two dying embers, brought anything that might be described as life to his ashen face. He was like someone fearful of the day. He entered with the haste of a man wanting to escape its light and freshness.

'Bete,' he said rapidly, 'where is your mother's room?'

'She's asleep,' Skanda answered casually, adding with annoyance, 'everyone is.'

'I know, bete, but where is her room?' Tunnu pressed him.

Skanda suspected nothing. He was pleased to allow into the house someone willing to wake the others.

'I'll show you,' he said, turning toward the large door that led into the internal corridor. The gloom closed around them and the two figures moved soundlessly through the darkness of the corridor.

At the door of his mother's room, the visitor said in a quiet, but friendly voice, soft and full of patience, his eyes shining, 'Now, go outside, bete. We have some grown-up things to talk about.'

Skanda nodded, put his head through the door and said somewhat triumphantly, 'Ma, someone's come.'

Then he turned around and vanished down the corridor.

He had barely made it to the main room, when reaching him past the vault-like hush of the house, he heard a harsh splintering sound. An upward movement, a snap. Immediately his mind made the connection: the strip of plywood I was just playing with has been torn from its place on the headboard. But why? That short cruel sound was followed fast by a volley of muffled thuds, incoherent conversation: 'Huh? What? Who?' '*Whore. Bitch. My wife.*'

Then they came, and they sucked the possibility of action from his body. He crumpled on hearing them, buckling against a wall in the outside room to his haunches, unmoving but for the violent and involuntary trembling that gripped his body. *His mother's screams*. It was as if he had anticipated this moment for years now; the moment of real physical threat to his mother; it was something that was built into the idea of his father's departure, always there in the background. But now that it was real, he found himself inert. Cowardice – for that was what it felt like – rose like a cold, silent flood. It was like drowning. With every cry that came from the bedroom, he tried to listen for some hint that the fight was turning in his mother's favour. But, though they were angry cries – and they would have been that way right to the end – they suggested no victory of any kind. The house was silent, the man emboldened and his mother's screams were growing hoarse. Where were the others? He was useless. Fine! But – oh, God! – where were the others?

He dragged himself to his aunt's room. It was across the corridor from his mother's, and, though Skanda himself could not speak, he managed to throw open both doors at once. On one side, the dark silent cavity of his aunt's room; on the other, a scene more terrifying than he could ever have imagined. A tempest of white sheets and morning light. A little man, like a spirit or djinn, his short wild shadow dancing against the wall, blue turban and hair unravelling about him, struck his mother again and again, now with the blunt end of his fist, now with the strip of plywood. Skanda saw the open gash on the headboard. And his mother, until now so strong and defiant, was a pathetic figure of rage and sobs, a battered woman. The image, as if closing a circuit in his mind, wrenched from him a shriek. For a moment there was no response. Then, as if the black cavity of his aunt's room had been a mute intelligence of some kind, watching and listening, but not speaking, it let spring from its unresponsive darkness, the enraged and running figure of his aunt.

She tore into his mother's room, not stopping once to take in the scene. Without a moment's hesitation, she caught hold of the little demon's beard and spat in his face. 'Go beat your whore of a wife, who sleeps with all of Delhi!' The petty demon shrank before her strength, and, even before she had taken the green plastic jug of water that lay at Uma's bedside, emptying its entire contents in his face, he was vanquished. He had become in a few short seconds the weak-voiced figure of moments ago and, his beast having deserted him, he could only mumble through his soaked beard, 'Teach your sister some manners next time.'

'I'll teach you some manners, you little fucking turd! Dirty coward. Beats a woman when she's asleep. Beat your whore of a wife . . .' his aunt yelled, and dug her hands into his shrunken body, throwing him to the floor.

Now others had appeared in the corridor – Viski, his cousins – but the object of his fear had been reduced to this tortured figure, dishevelled and deturbaned, collecting hair and cloth about him, while trying to stand up. There was little left for Viski to do. He grabbed hold of Tunnu's elbow and pushed him out of the corridor, causing him to become entangled in the long length of his turban. It was left behind, and Fareed and Iqbal took pleasure in gathering it up crudely into a blue starchy knot, and throwing it after him.

Outside, the sun burnt away the mists that lay over the meadow, striking each drop of dew with a fatal and bcguiling portion of light.

Skanda sat on the stone steps of the cottage with his cousins. They had gathered about him, in that instinctive, but inarticulate show of male affection, as presence and deed rather than word. Iqbal was saying, 'I wish to God I'd been awake. I'd've taken my Swiss knife, and before he'd even put one finger on Uma Massi, I'd've cut his neck, like the little chickens last night. I'll go right now and cut him up. Nobody can do that to my massi, and get away with it.' 'But, Iqbal,' Fareed said, after a moment of solemn, but awe-struck, consideration, 'the slingshot would've been better. You can't even reach his neck.'

'On my skates I can.'

'You'd've come on your skates?'

'Of course.'

'Over the carpet and everything?'

'Yeah,' Iqbal said, now doubtfully, 'and he's, by-the-vays, not so big, Fareed. He's a puny kind of guy. Not like papa. I'd've squashed him in my mutthi.' Then realizing the conversation had extended well past their commiseration with Skanda, they fell silent again.

Fareed asked, 'What I don't understand is how d'he get in, in the first place?' Silence. Iqbal, at last, taking as neutral a tone as he possibly could, said, 'Skanda opened the door.' 'Oh,' Fareed said, and they were quiet again.

Some distance away, at the edge of the garden, a conversation, in low murmurs, with the occasional raising of a voice, a word of abuse, took place between Viski and Tunnu. It was strangely peaceable, and it was wounding to Skanda. He was not alone in this feeling. When his aunt, after tending to his mother, came out and saw the men speaking, she threw open the veranda door and yelled, 'What is that man still doing here? What's happened to your famous Sikh courage, Viski? You stand there talking to a man who's just beaten up your sister-in-law?! Get him out, this minute, or I'll come down with a hockey stick. Do you hear me, Tunnu? Go back to your wife, or is your place already taken? Swine!'

Tunnu accepted the abuse, Skanda felt, for it came from a woman who was protected. And then, a few minutes later, he saw him, a free man, set out across the valley.

He did not know when Rudrani and his grandparents had arrived. Ten or fifteen minutes later? Or two hours later? The day, save for that one moment that had defined it, acquired a fluid formless quality; the hours seemed just to roll out; the sun to shine meaninglessly. He was wandering about the side of the house – he had been asked to keep away from his mother for a little while – when his grandmother approached. Always one to put the blame for misfortune at the door of the victim, she had a strange and hunted quality. It was as if she was afraid to be asked her opinion, as if she herself was guilty of the morning's violence. And yet she wanted to comfort Skanda. She approached him with a mug of milk and Bournvita. They did not speak directly of what had happened. 'You'll grow into a big, strong man,' she said. 'I can see it already. You're a talker, a true batuni, you might become a lawyer, or a diplomat, you should aim for the United Nations. Then when you're rich and strong, you can support your old, frail nani. Yes, Skandu? Defend her from all the bad men in the world? The goondas who want to push her over and snatch her handbag, no?'

'Yes,' he replied weakly.

She could always get her point across.

When at last Skanda saw his mother, it was with everyone else. She appeared on the veranda, in jeans, a sweater and large, purple-tinted sunglasses. The ridge of her lip had flowered into a ripe swelling, giving her smile the benign and comic aspect of the mentally ill.

She came and sat next to him and Rudrani. But of what had happened, she said only (and he knew for his benefit), 'What a shame your mama's such a deep sleeper, baba. That little runt of a man. Why, if I'd been awake, I'd have thrashed him myself.' Rudrani looked impressed, but Skanda did not believe a word she said. He wished his mother happy birthday and withdrew. No one could know the extent to which he now grasped her insecurity, she, who was manless and alone in the world. She whose husband had left her open to this kind of attack, and whose son was too much of a coward to protect her. Skanda later observed – on account of his shame, no doubt – that he was written out of the adult retelling of the story, which became one of envy and revenge, something that might have happened to anyone. The shame of it, which was the shame of vulnerability – the fact that it could have happened only to his mother, and no one else – was edged out. Friends, friends solemn and whispering, streamed in. Chamunda, Nixu and Gayatri, Tariq Mattoo. The story was repeated, clothed in detail, emotions relived, and the terror Skanda had known that morning became like the accidental by-product of some larger story. His emasculation was edged out; and he, on the verge of becoming a man – *vir* in Latin, vīra in Sanskrit – was left to deal privately with the meaning of that word.

That was their last summer in Kashmir.

They drove down to Srinagar a few days later by an alternate route. The trouble had already begun. There was talk of rioting and stone throwing on the old road. That summer, unbeknownst to them, hundreds of Kashmiri boys had crossed the border into Pakistan to receive military training. Tariq Mattoo's government would only barely see the opening of the new decade. But that was more than could be said for Rajiv Gandhi's; or, for that matter, the Berlin Wall.

It was 1989.

IV

The screen at the far end of the plane shows a flight map. A great golden disc, hollow at the centre, spins slowly over an astral view of India. The country of red earth and dark patches of greenery, India veined with rivers, and wreathed with mountains. The India of the opening of the Birth: 'There is in the north, the king of mountains, divine by nature, Himalaya by name, the abode of snow. Having entered both the eastern and western oceans, he stands like a rod to measure the earth.' A night sky over this peninsular view of India plunging into the ocean shows the curvature of the earth and *a whole silent heaven full of stars*. The graphics people at Maniraja's office have recreated classical India on the map. They have used all the old Hindu names for the country's rivers, cities, mountains and forests. Kannauj is Kanyakubja again – the hunchbacked girl; Delhi Indraprastha. Nothing remains of British or Muslim India. No Allahabad, no Bombay. The world – or a corner of it, at least – has been remade.

Skanda, gazing at the map, feels it contains something of the mood of the Messenger Poems, in which a lonely yaksha might charge a cloud, say, to take a message to his beloved halfway across the country; and the cloud, in doing so, will make a survey of the land. An assimilative mood, a wish to knit together and make whole what in reality is fragmented and beyond grasp. And this map would have made classical India real for Maniraja – as Sanskrit had for Skanda and his father – in ways that it had never been before. It must have given back, albeit thinly and nominally, what history had taken away.

Skanda is surprised at how much meaning it has for him, this ancient map, how many red dots on it have been part of the shape of his life. There is Kalasuryaketu, a tiny red dot on the blue vein of the Tamasā, where his father, before he turned his back on his country, had retreated with Sylvia. That was the real death: the death that won him a place in the poet's hell, reserved for those who 'died as men before their bodies died'. There is Ayodhya, of course, the cause of his father's leaving India, a fat red dot on the Sarayu. There are the southern hills, where he, Skanda, went to school, to escape his mother's new life with Maniraja. And finally – if we take some liberties – there is Indraprastha, abode of his memories. Which in the early 1990s, as with Paris before Haussmann, was still unstitched, still without arteries, still a place of colony markets, still a town so boring that there was nothing more exciting than to drive with your best friend to the crest of Raisina Hill, put your car in neutral and, with Lutyens' palace framed in your rear-view mirror, let it roll forward.

He sinks into one of the smooth seats of coffee-coloured leather, and looks out at the dead heat on the tarmac. The hostess hands him a glass of champagne. She looks familiar.

'Have we met before?'

'I am Pooja!' she says. 'Pooja Paranjpe. Don't you remember me? I used to work at the Hospitality Desk of the Raj.'

'Oh, Pooja, of course! Where is my mother?'

Before she can gesture to the partition, Uma's voice rings out, 'In here. Out in a minute. Suzie's just finishing drying my hair.' Then, after a long pause, she says, 'Are you alone, darling?'

'Yes, why?'

No reply.

'The queen of the unsaid', Rudrani calls her, along with 'Her Ecstasy', and 'stepmother', which drives her mad. Rudrani has never – not for a moment – romanticized their mother. Nothing about her has ever seemed tragic or pitiable. She sees her in clear and simple terms as selfish, manipulative and, most damningly, as someone whose worst moments are a form of vanity. 'If you could know,' she once said to Skanda, after one of Maniraja's uglier scenes, 'how complicit she is in her debasement, you would not feel a jot of pity for her. She loves it, don't you see? It answers a deep need in her for opera and high drama. It was what Baba could not provide, and she never forgave him for it.' Put in those terms, it seems true, but Skanda – and here perhaps lies his own complicity – never quite believed it, never as a conviction.

'Did you see Mani?'

'I did.'

'And? How did you find him?'

'*Healthy*, as they say here.'

'I know! And he used to be so fit, do you remember? Men, I tell you, I don't know what happens to them. They just go off after a while, don't they? Anything else?'

'Calmer.'

'Well, I don't know about that' – and now the plane sinks a little under the weight of her footsteps; Suzie's voice is heard; the partition parts and Uma appears.

THE MOSQUE
(1992)

The years after Gulmarg were her hardest in Delhi. The freedom she had glimpsed in the time after Toby had proved to be a dangerous thing, a shorthand for her vulnerability. And, as much as she tried, she was unable to recover the innocence of that earlier time. The city had shown her the insecurity of her position and she was like someone who, relishing the dark, is suddenly made aware of the dangers that reside within it. She was surprised to know how few defenders she had. There were many to commiserate, but none to defend as a brother, husband, or fully grown son might have. *It is in this way,* she thought, *through an experience like Gulmarg, that one is made aware of the feudal character of the place one lives in*. Beneath the token outrage expressed by friends and family, there lay – and she could see it in their eyes, placid, unshockable, desensitized – an easy acceptance of violence as the organizing principle of society. Though she was hardly conscious of it, it altered her idea of her independence, turning what had been a privilege into a lack, carving out in her a need for security that she had never thought to possess. And, though later, someone looking at her life might easily have said that that need had always been with her – that the insecurity Toby made her feel was part of her rejection of him – life, being an instinctive exercise, something through which we grope our way right to the end, the need never made itself apparent in the abstract till it was embodied in a person.

Mani, in those months after Gulmarg, was not a part of her life. Not for any lack of interest from him, but because she, acting as if out of an animal instinct, found herself incapable of responding to his advances, found herself wanting nothing more than to go to ground. So much of romantic life – and our willingness to admit it into our lives – is an extension of our self-esteem, our exuberance and energy. And, after Gulmarg, Uma's capacity for these things was severely diminished. This was why later she never came to associate her love for Mani with need, because, so long as she had really been *in need*, she had actively kept away. It was only when she felt well and strong, and had the courage to be in the world again, that she had allowed him back into her life.

After Gulmarg she wanted justice or revenge. She wanted to see Tunnu behind bars, publicly shamed; she wanted him to lose his position at the head of his companies. For a while she considered pressing charges. *Assault and battery. Forced entry* . . . She seized on these terms with that special comfort the legally untrained derive from legal jargon. When her friends – Priti Hirachand, namely – tried to persuade her of the futility of this course of action, making the case that the same society that had not expressed sufficient outrage for what had happened would also find ways to legally protect its perpetrators, she fought with them. She fought with many people in those days after Gulmarg. She fought with Isha for not walking out of a dinner at which Kitten Singh was present. 'Mishi . . . Uma, I mean: it was a sangeet: there were some two hundred other people there.' 'I don't care,' Uma answered her, 'you're my sister. You should refuse to be anywhere that will have people like that.'

The position she took made her own social life difficult, for Delhi was still a small town in those days, and how many parties could one walk out of! Her voluntary withdrawal from society, her isolation, increased her feeling of injustice. She felt she was being made to suffer, while her victimizers roamed free.

She could not remember when exactly this cycle broke – how many months it took – she only knew that it corresponded exactly with the coming of foreign television to Delhi, which began slowly, with the first Gulf War, when the most fashionable place in town became a disused discotheque in the Taj Hotel called The Number One. It was here that the ladies of Delhi would come to watch CNN. They had always seemed, these ladies, so cynical and knowing, so weary of the world. But, in The Number One, watching for the first time the green carpet of Baghdad be bombed by Scud and Patriot missiles, listening to the voice of Peter Arnett, an incredible innocence came over them. Their poise fell away, their stern faces softened and all their style, one came to feel, had been nothing but the sulkiness of deprivation. By the early 1990s, they were missing dinner parties – or arriving very late, at least – because they could not tear themselves away from *The Bold and the Beautiful* and *Santa Barbara*. As Gayatri Mann, who sensed perhaps the end of her own utility in these changes, said, 'Who would have thought that after wars and riots and emergencies, the thing to deal a deathblow to social Delhi would be American daytime television?!'

Uma went at first because it was a public place – of which, in those days, there were relatively few – and should Kitten and her husband have appeared, she could have left without a scene. A few times they did – or Kitten, at least – and a few times Uma had walked out. But, gradually, she began to notice that she made Kitten far more uncomfortable than Kitten made her, and she decided to stay and let her stew. Uma found that their old group of friends closed around her, and often her being there meant that it was Kitten who had to keep away. She began to come more often to The Number One. And it was there, one day, after many months had passed, that she saw Maniraja again.

It was dark in the old discotheque and at first she didn't recognize him. The city was flooded with Indians who had left the Gulf during the war and they sat – Nixu Mohapatra and her – with Ruxana Idriss, a tiny Indian woman, with bright intent eyes and short hair streaked white. She had a Kuwaiti husband, and the couple, together with their three sons, dressed often in 'Free Kuwait' T-shirts, were waiting out the war in Delhi. They came almost every evening to The Number One, offering, in accompaniment to the news stream coming off the large screens, a private commentary of lives disrupted and escapes through the desert at night into Saudi Arabia, even as Saddam's tanks closed in on the little oil-rich emirate.

Uma, newly returned to social life, enjoyed it all. The drama on the big screens, the news as entertainment, which seemed so unbelievable after a decade of being subjected to the tedium of the state broadcaster; the foreign ads, which put within reach a world hardly anyone was able to afford as yet, but whose very existence on those screens seemed to assure its impending arrival. It was an exciting time: a Time of Things!

Uma was talking to Ruxana's engineer husband, Hisham, about the special features of the stealth bomber, newly introduced into the war, when Nixu squeezed her leg under the table and whispered, 'Darling, don't look now. But they're here. The turds. *Les deux.* Ignore them. Please don't let it spoil your evening.'

Uma didn't look, but her good mood drained away. She had seen Kitten since Gulmarg, but not Tunnu, and the thought – nothing more, just the thought – of setting eyes on that little man caused the tendons in her knees to tremble and soften; her stomach churned painfully. Hisham's words, so fascinating till a moment ago, grew suddenly remote. A rush of emotion rose in her like a fever. Her mind swarmed with things she would say or do, if she found herself face to face with her assailant. She could almost have yawned from the strain on her nerves; she feared she would lack the impetus to do anything. And aware of this incapacity – and it was just that! – she thought, *How nice it would be to have someone stand between me and the world, to have a defender; I've never had that!*

Then she saw Maniraja.

She was still in that liminal state, still feeling the cold standing flood of a panic attack rise in her, when she heard Ruxana, in her clipped convent accent, say, 'These businessmen-types, I tell you. We may treat them offhandishly in our houses. But, look: here, in the hotels, they are the undisputed kings.'

She looked over and, in the green light of Baghdad seen through night-vision lenses, there he was. He sat at a round table with a few men who looked like they worked with him; there were a couple of bottles of Black Label on the table, and vodka, it seemed, in a large ice bucket; the manager of The Number One was tending to the table personally. Maniraja didn't seem to know anyone else there, but it didn't bother him. He seemed, she recalled thinking, perfectly alone and perfectly secure. It was an image that remained with Uma; and later, if she forgave him some of his worst behaviour, it was because she could see only too clearly that it came from insecurity, and rather than condemn him for it, she felt responsible. She felt that it was she who, by bringing him into contact with a world for which she felt nothing but loathing, had, in some ways, robbed him of his natural security.

None of this was in view that night; that night, as Ruxana pointed out – and as, to some extent, would always be true of those places where money and respect were closely linked – Maniraja was king.

Nothing, save the entry of a movie star or a politician, could have drawn the manager of The Number One away from his table.

To Uma, the sight of Mani, sitting alone with his business associates, an island of unfamiliarity in a stagnant sea of the known and familiar, was like a lifeline. A way out of some unique and interminable hell of singledom, late motherhood and a forties and fifties that had all the potential to be at once more active and full of promise than they had been for her parents' generation – Deep was an old woman at fifty! – while possessing, in equal measure, the danger of being bleaker and more directionless.

'Isn't he the same man, darling?' Nixu's voice came in. 'He's looking straight at you. And such DGs, all goggly-eyed. What did you do? Break his heart? What a pool of piranhas this Number One is; the turds on one side, and now this serial killer of an ex-lover on the other? Uma? Say something!'

She ignored him. She knew perfectly well what was at the bottom of the long cold stare, a little surprised, a little frightened, that Maniraja gave her, once they made eye contact. This was one set of hurt feelings she knew exactly how to deal with. And, excusing herself, she got up a moment later and walked over to his table. Maniraja looked away when he saw her coming, but she carried on, threading her way between the round tables, through this strange scene – never to be witnessed again in the city – of fashionable people congregating at an old discotheque to watch 24-hour news television.

He didn't greet her, but she pulled up a chair and sat down next to him. The manager automatically asked her what she would like to drink. And now Mani, unable to deny this courtesy even to his worst enemy, for he was pathologically generous, could not help but turn to her.

'Kya peeyogee?' he said, half-sneeringly.

'Main toh champagne peeyoongee,' she replied coyly.

He handed her the menu, and frosty again, said, 'You'll have to choose yourself. I don't know anything about champagne.'

'I'll have a glass of Dom Perignon,' she said.

A quick look passed between the manager and Mani, and he went off with a nod. Soon, a bottle of champagne was added to the ice bucket with the vodka. Uma drank the first glass almost in silence; then she asked for a second; and Mani, after studying the dark green label, carefully poured her one.

'Is it any good?'

'Very good. Have some.'

'I don't drink champagne.'

'Drink some tonight.'

He beckoned to a waiter to bring him a champagne glass. The man came back a moment later with a champagne saucer. Mani stared at it in wonder before pouring himself a glass. Uma was onto her third. And it was only then – quite drunk, and relishing the pleasure of making confidences to an old lover – that she told him the story of Gulmarg, told him why, in short, she had shut him out of her life. Mani was expressionless. He listened, as if he was listening to someone making a business proposal to him. But, from time to time, when she would look up, Uma saw, really for the first time, the outrage she had looked for and not found among her own people in Delhi; she saw something cold and threatening and unreadable in his eyes.

When the story was over, he said nothing more about it, but asked, 'And he's here, tonight, this man?'

'Yes.'

'Point him out.'

'Don't say anything . . .'

'Point him out.'

'Mani . . .'

'Point him out.'

Under the pressure of his words, she scanned the crowd. Tunnu, with his turban, was easy to find. He stood at some distance from a table where Kitten Singh, lips thin and painted, a large fake hibiscus in her hair, was entertaining a table of Delhi businessmen.

Mani looked long at them, then beckoned to his friend, the manager, and after a whispered exchange, the two men walked over. What played out had, in Uma's mind, the mute and comic aspect of an early Hollywood double act. The two men approached the table. Kitten rose and greeted Maniraja in her usual effusive way, when meeting rich men other than her husband. Mani seemed to accept the greeting; but, in the short exchange that occurred between them, Kitten's face lost all colour and her expression sagged. Then the three of them – Kitten, Mani and the manager – turned to look at Tunnu, who looked back at them with the innocent surprise of a small child unused to being picked for the team, finding himself picked first. He walked over with something like curiosity. The manager moved forward – some quick words passed between them – and slid his fingers behind the lapels of Tunnu's grey coat. But Mani, like a gangster showing mercy, stopped him. Some more words were exchanged; the alarm in Tunnu's face, as with the moody lighting of the discotheque, alternating between blues and pinks and yellows, changed to resignation, then to what almost seemed like gratitude. And now the manager slipped his arm into Tunnu's and led him out of The Number One. He looked tragically back at Kitten, who returned his expression with impatience before swinging back around to rejoin her table.

The scene was a perfect cliché. Mani's actions were often drawn from cliché. He was neither subtle nor unknowable, and, although he would never be able to surprise Uma – which, later, drove him to seek out women less mondaine – his predictability was a great comfort to her. She felt she could always see the shape of his thought and, where she lost out in excitement, she gained immeasurably in dependability. His betrayals were never of the serious kind. Uma knew that for all his moods and tantrums he was a man she could entrust her life to.

That night, as a feeling of jubilation overtook them, there were other clichés: more champagne; caviar and blinis; there was the bathtub of a penthouse suite . . . In the bright lights of the bathroom, she made a careful inspection of Maniraja's body. It was as if she wanted to understand what part of his physicality had so deep a hold on her. *His fucking cheapness*, she said almost aloud in her drunkenness, as her eyes followed the thin line of greying hair into the sallow chasm of his chest. They paused at the gold chains; she noticed the small bones and the surprising musculature around the stomach, which, in another time, she knew would have had the soft dimpled fatness of generations of vegetarianism; she held his erect penis in her hands. Long, thin, uncircumcised. The folds of foreskin glistening with precum. She observed the hair grow thin over the slim sinews of his thighs, the tiny calves, the small beautiful feet. She pressed her face against the bullet-black nipples and smelt his armpits. Their smell, even after a bath, was still there. His expression was hungry and open-lipped, as if he meant to inhale her. If she could only focus her mind, she felt she would be able to identify what it was about his physicality that held such power for her. But her intellect stalled at the attempt to express in words what must forever remain slightly mysterious. They fucked deep into the night.

In the morning, there was a last and memorable cliché. Her eyes opened to the rattle of a trolley, fat wheels over a carpeted floor; there was somewhere the sight of pale morning light coming in past gauzy white curtains, there was silver and orange juice and the smell of coffee; and Uma exulted in what must be one of the great underrated pleasures of our time: the pleasure of waking up in a hotel room in one's own hometown.

Uma is dressed in an aquamarine sari (Mani has forbidden her salwar kameez, which he finds unflattering); she has a towel about her neck and shoulders; her hair, which has been straightened, is light and freshly dried.

'We had a little scene just before landing,' she says, 'didn't we, Pooja?'

Pooja smiles shamefacedly. 'Yes, ma'am.'

'The champagne apparently wasn't right. Can you imagine? And this from a man who had never drunk champagne till he met me? Hello, darling,' she says, and clutches his hand. 'You look well.' Then looking closer, she adds, 'But thin! I wish I could be a little thinner too. I've just come back from Buchinger – boot camp, I tell you! – and I don't think I've lost an ounce. Can you tell the difference?'

'I don't know. I haven't seen you in a while, Ma.'

'I know, darling. But, you know – I didn't want to say it earlier; you seemed so content here – but this town, you know how I loathe it. My worst memories . . .'

Sensing how this must sound, she stops herself and says, 'Not with all of you, of course. But later. I don't know; I'm not saying it right. It's not even as if it brings back bad memories. Just feels like lost time, you know. Almost as if I never lived here.'

'You don't remember it?'

'Hardly. That's the strange part. I know I lived here; there's proof enough; but I don't *feel* that I did, not in my bones, you know. It was easier to come to see you when you were in New York. That, at least, was something new.'

The brassiness in her voice momentarily falls away, and she becomes as he remembers her.

'I loved your introduction to the Birth, by the way,' she says. 'Thank you for sending it to me. I read it on the flight over here. I want Mani to read it. Do you mind if I pass it on to him? It'll do him good.'

'Sure, Ma. But, you know . . .'

'What?!' she says, falsity returning to her voice. She knows exactly what, but she wants to hear it from him.

'There's no point. He's not much of a reader, and, besides, it's as Rudrani says,' he begins, regretting his tone, regretting the power of family to draw us into old patterns. 'Mani already knows all that he wants to know.'

'*Firstly*,' she says with irritation, 'that was your father's phrase; she's stolen it from him. And, secondly, it's just not true anymore. He's changed. We all have, but him much more than others. He's not the man he was when you first met him. He's improved; I've improved him. The prejudices are almost all gone. And he has other qualities, you know. A very caring side.'

'Financially, you mean . . . ?' Skanda says, and stops himself, but it is too late.

'No, not just that. It's not right of you to say that, but now that you have: let me tell you, that matters too. Your father left us flat. Not just me; all of us. Mani would never do that. But no: it's not just about money. Very wrong of you to say that.'

'I'm sorry.'

She looks out of the window, her expression blank and searching. Some men in blue jumpsuits pull away a red trolley whose tyres leave fat black marks on the tarmac. 'He's the only man,' she says at length, 'to have really made me feel he cared about me.'

And then, as if annoyed by something she sees outside, she adds with impatience, 'I only wish I had better handled his entry into our lives.'

And she was right. His entry into their lives might have been better handled. The year was 1992. It was the year the Ayodhya issue divided Delhi like a Dreyfusian knife, and their family unit entered its last cycle before disintegrating completely. It was a year of change. And Maniraja, with his suits, his foreign car, his way of always laying the removable face of his car stereo down on the coffee table next to his gold-rimmed spectacles, was so much of a piece with the change.

It was not simply that for the first time since 1980 there was no member of the Gandhi family in power. There were other things too, more tangible than politics, such as potato crisps and Lehar Pepsi, new cars in the streets: Maruti 1000s in the streets! This simple sedan did more to put an end to those socialist years in India than any announcement from Moscow, Berlin or Racecourse Road. At a time of migration to the city the Maruti 1000 put money and status firmly at the centre of the new mandala. The appearance of this car, with its stoutly beyond-reach price tag of some 3.8 lakhs, was like a reason to keep going. It was an ideal that, for once, people could actually see and touch, and show their friends, a hard concrete symbol of who and what they were, just as they were more unsure of it than ever.

That Time of Things made simple people of everyone, and Maniraja embodied its simplicities. He was the kind of man who always meant everything he said. A true literalist, there was never a gap in his speech between word and meaning. He spoke a language that was lacking in those shades of meaning that come usually to be part of its music. If listening to him speak, one found one had to concentrate hard, it was because the words were just words; they were not spoken with any feeling for sound or emphasis; and one could be replaced with another. His language, as with certain borrowed forms of art, was stripped of all possibility of liveliness and invention, of subtlety and humour.

This was especially true when he spoke ill of Muslims. And it was deeply shocking for Skanda and Rudrani to hear him speak in this way. They had been raised on the pieties of the Nehruvian state, of which, in that pre-Babri Masjid era, none was more sacred than secularism. In the world they grew up in, secularism meant much more than just a separation of church and state; it was a modern articulation of what many believed to be an ancient and emic idea of religious tolerance in India. An expression of the Indian ethos, even: of those great moments in her history when, faced with the choice between purity and synthesis, she had gone the way of synthesis every time.

So, when Maniraja, accompanied often by a Goebbels-like figure called Choate, whom he was paying to write pamphlets, and set up holocaust museums, first began to arrive at their house for dinner, and would say things like 'those Islamic shits' and 'Bhenchodh Mohammadans', Rudrani and Skanda felt they were confronting a man who their entire upbringing had been an inoculation against. They had no context for Maniraja, no idea of the extent to which he was a man of his times. They knew little about the movement for the temple in Ayodhya. Even if they had, they would certainly never have met anyone who supported the demolition of the mosque. Maniraja, just as he was their introduction to certain new technologies, was also the first man they met to hold such attitudes as these. And nothing could have made them feel the desecration of their father's home more acutely than witnessing his easy bigotry at their dining table.

These scenes occurred on a number of occasions and their mother played a very strange part in them. She seemed almost to be mocking Maniraja herself, especially when he spoke out of prejudice. In fact, if there was one thing for which the blame could be put squarely at Uma's door, it was that she discredited Maniraja, long before she let it be known that he was her boyfriend and she would be moving to Bombay to live with him. In the moments when Mani's presence was a cause of shame to her, either in the form of her own abasement or in the form of his poisonous prejudices, she seemed herself to be laughing hardest at him. And it was only later when Skanda was old enough to see how jokes can sometimes hide hysteria that he recognized his mother's laughter for what it had been: a form of self-defence. An encoded message that Skanda interpreted as, *Ma, for reasons of her own, must be with this man; and he's not all bad, but you mustn't take what he says too seriously.*

A typical dinner would go like this: they'd be sitting at table, and Choate would say, 'You know what's interesting: Oxford was founded – the university, I mean – the very year after *they*' – and everyone knew who *they* was – 'destroyed Nalanda.'

Choate had a heavily lined face with greasy blondish hair and hard blue eyes. He was the author of such books as *Awake, India!* and, of course, *The Indian Holocaust*. He spoke in roundabout ways, but he knew exactly how to work Maniraja, to rouse him on a level that seemed mysterious to an outsider. So, for instance, in response to this observation about the universities, he drew from Maniraja a painful shaking of his head, and the word 'See!' muttered under his breath like an invective.

'See, what?' Uma said languidly.

Maniraja flared his eyes, then saw she was being playful, and smiled contemptuously.

'Well, if your liberal shits don't want to see what is plain for everybody to see, I can't help them.'

Silence.

'It might have been a great university today,' Maniraja began again, and with feeling . . . 'with an unbroken tradition of – what? – how many centuries, Choate? When was Nalanda founded?'

'In the fifth century,' Choate said.

'There you are: a centre of learning fifteen centuries old. Think of the confidence it would have given our people. The feeling of continuity. But they went about it single-mindedly, destroying whatever they thought our people cherished, and giving us nothing back in return. Nothing!'

'The Taj Mahal's not bad,' Uma said and smiled, making the children giggle.

'Mosques and tombs! Nothing but bloody mosques and tombs. And none of it Islamic, by the way, all stolen from other places. You think the Taj Mahal is Islamic?'

'Is it Christian, Mani? Hindu? Jain perhaps?'

'Not bloody Islamic. Persian! Iranian! You think there was anything in bloody Arabia, you think those damn baddus, with nothing but sand and oil, could have built a Taj Mahal?'

'Mani, if what you're saying is that Islamic culture is a composite . . .'

'There's no such thing as Islamic culture!' he roared.

'If you're going to shout . . .'

'I'm shouting? You are shouting!'

This is how it would go. In the beginning, she was pluckier. She would fight back. But, later, as the scenes became more violent, she would just smile and look away. She would tell herself that it was a form of resistance, but, to those who loved her, it never felt that way.

-

The three of them – Skanda, Uma and Rudrani – did not discuss Mani's presence in their lives. Uma never described him as anything more than a friend; and the children, for fear perhaps of hearing the truth, did not probe further. It was only when a woman began calling their house at strange hours, soon after Mani had become a fixture in their lives, that this period of wilful ignorance came to an end.

More often than not she got their mother on the phone, and they would see Uma, standing by the telephone table in silence, as the woman spoke, interrupting only to say quietly, 'Please stop this! If you have a problem with your husband, you must speak to him. You can't call here.' They had sensed naturally that something was the matter, but they had not been able to tell what exactly, until – once or twice, when Uma was out – they had answered the phone themselves. At first, when the woman heard it was them, she just breathed noisily down the phone and hung up. But gradually she became emboldened and, on one occasion, while speaking to Rudrani, who was endlessly amused by her calling, she said, 'Tell that randi, your mother, that she will never have him. You hear? Rolexes, she wants? Well, Rolexes maybe she'll have, but never him. Go, go and tell her!'

But they didn't mention a word to Uma, though they did see she had a new watch.

It was a strange time; it was as if their mother was taking a kind of revenge against their family, almost as if she was punishing Toby by exposing his children to Maniraja. She also ended up doing Maniraja a great disservice, for, in not explaining his presence in their lives, she never made her children take him seriously. One felt almost as if she had abdicated her role in their family and meant now for everyone to be left to their own devices.

Skanda had, for a long time, been unnerved by Maniraja, especially during those dinners when he attacked Muslims. There was something disturbing about his tone and, though Skanda could not prove it, he suspected he was ignorant of the things he spoke so excitedly about. He never forgot his elation when he discovered for the first time that what Maniraja was saying was not just ugly, but wrong. Plain wrong.

He was almost sixteen at the time; his aunt Isha was present too at dinner. And this – the presence of others, especially those from Uma's old world – always brought out the worst in Maniraja, for as Rudrani liked to point out to her brother, 'Dada, you know what kind of man he is?'

'What kind?'

'The kind who thinks it's cool to make his girlfriend look bad in front of his friends?'

'Oh, and you've known many men like this?'

'No, dada. But I know one when I see one.'

Maniraja was speaking over everyone to Choate in a loud and boastful way about model villages they were setting up in the hills of U.P., where people would be taught – or *retaught*, as Maniraja said – to speak Sanskrit.

Skanda, in part because his aunt was present, and in part because of the recent telephone calls, was in a combative mood. And though Maniraja, especially in those days, spoke in a way that was impossible to interrupt, Skanda saw his opportunity and said, 'But, Uncle Mani, why are you setting up these villages?'

'Why?' Mani asked. 'Why are we setting them up?'

'Yes, why?'

'Because, son,' Maniraja said, 'language is a great source of confidence for people. Rob them of their language, and you break their spirit. So what we're trying to do in these model villages is to give people back the language of their ancestors.'

Skanda looked long at Maniraja, then he said softly, 'But it was never the language of their ancestors.'

Maniraja looked confused.

'Forefathers, son. The generations before them, before the coming of the invader, you know.'

'I know what *ancestors* means, Uncle Mani: what I'm saying is that their ancestors would never have spoken Sanskrit.'

And now Maniraja began to get his drift.

'Means?' he said cautiously, and laughed. 'What did they speak then? Swahili?'

Skanda could feel his aunt's and his mother's eyes on him. And channelling the ghost of his father, he said, using an old form of entrapment, 'Who, by your own estimation, do you suppose spoke Sanskrit?'

'In the past or now?'

'At any time in the history of the language.'

'It was the language of India. Everybody spoke it!'

Skanda held his gaze a moment longer, then began to laugh. He looked at his mother, and she, after a moment's hesitation, began to laugh too. Then Rudrani, and then Isha – though she was not sure why – also began to laugh.

Skanda, as if the fight was not worth the fighting, said nothing more. But his mother, enjoying herself, and amplifying something Toby had once told her, said, 'No, no, no, Mani. You're out of your depth, my darling; you've obviously never so much as opened a Sanskrit play. Or you would know, and anyone will tell you – Sheldon Pollock, for one – that, *it was never the language of the nursery, the bedroom, the field* . . . Its relationship to the local languages operating below it was always and only – even more so than English today' – and how she relished the use of this difficult word – 'one of "hyperglossia". Not simply a high language, my darling, but an über, über language: a language of the super elite, as there has never been anything the likes of since. And the peasants of Uttar Pradesh, Mani dear, did not speak Sanskrit – not now, not ever. They spoke no more Sanskrit than you do . . .'

Maniraja did not say a word. But, in the whiteness of those eyes and in those chapped slightly parted lips, through which a crooked row of tobacco-stained teeth was visible, it was possible to see the rage of a man whose past was lost to him, and who, out of that anger, would see destroyed not one or two or three mosques, but a thousand, before he found his way back to that elusive confidence he spoke so much about.

Looking out of the window at the low line of trees, standing at the base of an immense white sky, Uma says, 'This is the heat of my childhood. You lot are lucky. You've never had to experience it. In those days, we had air conditioning in only one room of the house, if at all, and power cuts all the time, and those slow dead hours. What a time!'

Suzie kneels at her feet, listening intently. Removing one of them from a red tub of warm soapy water and wrapping it in a towel, she says, 'I remember. It like that when I come here.'

Uma looks at her in puzzlement, as she removes her other foot from a red-soled Louboutin and places it flat in the warm water.

Then looking at Skanda, she says, 'Bombay is not like that. Save for the monsoon, the weather has no gravitas. There is always a breeze, always the breath of the sea; the nights are moist and smelly. There's something clammy,' she says with distaste, 'about the climate in Bombay.'

He can see what she is doing. When she does not like what has been said – and she did not like their earlier conversation about Maniraja – she changes the subject to something seemingly irrelevant, like the weather, but gives it the mood of what she is feeling, and then, when the time is right, she will return to the original subject obliquely. By saying, for instance, 'Charm. I suppose that matters a lot, doesn't it?'

Skanda waits for her to say more, but she just smiles at him, and lets her gaze rest on Suzie's scalp, on the neat parting lying like a caterpillar over the head of shiny straight hair.

'Huh? What do you mean?'

'Oh, nothing. I've just come to feel over the years that it matters a great deal, it's perhaps all that matters. People will always forgive someone with charm. Rajiv Gandhi had charm, and look: they forgave him everything. Rudrani has charm, too, when she wants to.'

'So do you, Ma. Great charm.'

'Thank you, darling. Your father had it too, of course, in bucketloads, which you have inherited. Toby was one of those people who made you smile the moment he walked through the door. Everyone was willing to do everything for him. It was a gift, really. It made people happy to make him happy. Not everyone has that,' she says pointedly.

And now he begins to see where she's headed.

'You mean Mani?'

'Mani has no charm. Poor man! Not one teeny weeny little ounce. And he suffers for it. He has no friends. I'm his only friend. He's forever telling me after meeting some old bore or the other, "I think he likes me." And I think: how pathetic! Who gives a fuck if he likes you? Do you like him?! But people who have no charm have to think of these things.'

'Ma!'

'What?'

'Let's please not make it seem as if all Mani's trouble boils down to his not having charm. He was also capable of some pretty ugly behaviour.'

'Never directed at you!'

He laughs. 'So?'

'So? *So* what people do in the context of love – *out* of and *because* of love – cannot be used as a just assessment of who they are.'

'No?'

'No! A big emphatic no. You can't run your emotional life following fixed rules, never giving second chances; the ones who do either end up alone or with someone many times their inferior, with a—' She stops herself.

'With a . . . ?' he says, unable to tell yet if this is a veiled attack on him or his father.

'With a Sylvia,' she says easily, and adds, 'The big relationships are like the big novels, messy, chaotic, imperfect. They operate by an emotional logic. You can't lay down guidelines for good behaviour, and expel anyone who doesn't follow them.'

'But when do you draw the line? When is enough?'

'When there's no feeling anymore, obviously. When love is gone,' she says, and peers vacantly into the eddying islands of soap.

Skanda is silent.

'Suzie?' she says, a moment later.

'Ma'am?'

'May I take a cigarette break?'

'You're smoking?' Skanda says.

'Only menthols.'

'Really? But you haven't smoked in years.'

'It's like riding a bicycle,' she says and smiles.

She slips her feet into a pair of Balinese slippers and they walk to the door of the plane, which Pooja opens, unfolding the rubber steps and letting in a great stultifying blast of heat.

'Ah,' she says, breathing it in, looking out in dismay at the day while lighting a brown cigarette. Her face, as the peace of the cigarette works its way through her, acquires a cool surveying quality.

Skanda, thinking still of what she said earlier, says, 'No, Ma. It is not just a question of charm. He was awful and you know that . . .'

She does not resist his words. Soothed by the cigarette, and enjoying the sudden focus on her life, she says, 'The trouble with Mani, the power he had over me – was that he was always willing to go to a place too ugly for me to follow him into. Those scenes! They defeated me; I could never compete with them.'

Watching her smoking at his feet, looking philosophically out at the sweltering tarmac, he says, 'How many do you smoke?'

'I don't know, darling,' she replies, half in irritation. 'I smoke them one at a time.'

1992. The year Uma moved in with Maniraja. The year Skanda went to school. The year Rudrani went to live at the newly built Fatehkot Apartments. And the year their flat became vacant, a memorial of sorts. No one had planned for it to be that way; it just happened. But, once it had, it was impossible to escape its significance. It just sat there squarely at the centre of their lives, a great breathing vacancy, empty and preserved, a physical expression of the hollowing out of the family unit.

Skanda, when he was home from school, would have liked to live there. But Mani, as an indication of his growing power over their lives – and in a gesture that Skanda always interpreted as malicious – asked that he not be allowed to. The reason ostensibly was that Skanda, in his holidays, at least, should be given a chance to get used to his mother's new life. But, strangely, perhaps because they knew what the answer would have been, nothing of the kind was ever asked of Rudrani. It was his mother who made the request, 'Please, darling. You'll be doing me a huge favour.' When he said, in return, 'Why not Rudrani?' she replied evasively, 'She's a girl; it matters less.'

But what exactly it was that *mattered* seemed to matter much more to Mani than to his mother. It was a mysterious request because already, in that first summer before school, it was clear from the way Mani behaved around Skanda that his presence made him uncomfortable. And yet he seemed to need him there, almost as if his dominion over Uma would be incomplete without Skanda.

Maniraja's treatment of Uma required witnesses. Again and again, he would request the presence of someone from the 'old days' – Chamunda or Gayatri, or Isha – for dinner at their seafront flat in Bombay, only to run Uma down before this person. Her past life – it was clear – made him insecure, and his method of conquering that insecurity was to debase Uma in front of people from her past. It was his way of possessing her.

The debasement took a particular form. And it was not always easy to know if it was something instinctive or carefully worked out. It could be described as a tyranny of his world over hers, but what it really meant was the privileging of all that was small and dull and banal over anything that had the potential to be interesting or amusing or subtle; and, as an extension, threatening. So, for instance, on hearing Viski and Isha were in town, Mani would insist they be called to dinner at once. They would arrive; there would be drinks; soon the easy flow of laughter and conversation would begin, a story, perhaps, told by Viski about his witnessing the assassination of a Punjabi politician in his adolescence . . . And, suddenly, seeing Uma begin to enjoy herself, to get a second drink perhaps, Maniraja would interrupt the conversation, and ask that she go to their bedroom to fetch him his eye drops.

Now? This minute? 'Please, darling,' he would say in a babyish voice, 'Mani needs his eye drops.' And she would go. In her absence, the broken threads of a conversation would try to reconstitute themselves. She would return with the eye drops and hand them to him. 'Darling,' he would say, his face souring grotesquely, 'not these; my Japanese eye drops.' Now there would be real awkwardness. And either to dispel it – or, as Rudrani would say, to make an exhibition of it – she would go again, with perhaps just a rolling of the eyes. Again conversation would resume brokenly; not a story, of course; but something small and polite. She would return with the Japanese eye drops. And Mani – for no tyranny is complete without repetition ad absurdum – would ask that she go back yet again, for the 13 per cent, and not the 15 per cent that she had brought. Now, at this point, if she was to say – and there were many to witness this – 'Fuck off and get them yourself' – there would be an ugly scene.

Or, Mani, having read in the paper that Zubin and Gayatri were in town, might – for he seemed really to seek out these people! – ask that Uma invite them to dinner in a restaurant, the Zodiac Grill say. If, by chance, they were not free, he would rub in her face that they had snubbed her. If they were free – and dinner was arranged – he would, with all the awkwardness of having a fifth person at a dinner for four, insist that some friend or professor or relation whom he had only the other day himself described as 'very boring', join them. Then, in the middle of a conversation about the Clinton election, say, which Gayatri and Zubin since they now lived in New York knew something about, he would loudly, across the table, say to the fifth guest, who until then had been sitting in complete silence, 'Thambi, tell us that poem of Thiruvalluvar.' And Thambi would begin reciting the alliterative verse of the classical Tamil poet, in Tamil, about the first rain. Then Mani would ask him to translate, and Thambi would say, '"The rain drips down, drippety-drop-drop, the first rain . . ." Leave it, Mani, it is hard to convey the beauty of the verses in English.' 'No, no, please go on. I insist.' Thambi would labour through with a few more lines, after which, Mani would smile, and turning to Zubin, might say, 'So, Mr Mann, have you thought of publishing Thiruvalluvar in New York . . . ?'

Whether it was eye drops or Thiruvalluvar – and later it seemed almost an admirable quality – Mani was completely unafraid of boring people. It was an aspect of his inability to listen. He was a man who treated what other people said as an interlude in which he could prepare what he would say when it was his turn to speak again. So much so that later, when he went on to meet a variety of interesting people – and he met many – Nixon, Gorbachev, in one of his first public appearances after the end of the Cold War – he could always only remember what he had said to them. Never a word of what they had said to him.

He was fascinated by little things about his person. That he had small very beautiful feet or excellent handwriting or that he liked his eggs a little burnt underneath and soft on top were subjects that he could talk about for well over half an hour. Eggs, it is worth mentioning, were an eternal source of tension in the life Uma and Mani made for themselves. Having perhaps never fried one himself – but applying what must have been some corporate desire for uniformity – he had a notion that an egg was spoilt unless its yolk fell exactly dead centre of the white. On an average morning he would send back some three plates of eggs, his temper boiling with every returned plate, until he got one – and he very rarely did, for, by now, the cook's hands had begun to tremble – with the yolk at the centre. Uma, naturally, was to blame for the shoddy operation she ran, in which a cook couldn't even make an egg properly. And again she put up with it, even when the people who loved her were driven away because they could not bear to witness it.

Why? Money was one obvious explanation that many, including Rudrani, offered. And it was a real consideration. Because Maniraja, for all his other faults, was extremely generous. There were cars and holidays and first-class tickets, expensive shoes and handbags; hideous but exorbitantly priced pieces of jewellery, such as the emerald tiara he gave her, with Uma written touchingly in rubies on the front. So, money could not be discounted as a motivation for why she bore it all; it was a Time of Things after a time of deprivation, and Uma was not immune to its appeal. But it never seemed to Skanda like an adequate explanation for why she stayed; not simply because what she put up with was not worth the money; but because, in those early days, at least, before habit and security closed her escape routes, she seemed really, with energy and conviction, to be in love with Maniraja. *Or*: in love with the idea of herself in love.

She had a way, Uma, when in love, of appropriating every aspect of her lover's world, of making its politics, its beliefs, its attitudes all her own. So, if as the wife of a Sanskritist, she was reciting ślokas and making opaque references to classical India, and lamenting the loss of funding for Indic studies in the West, then, as the girlfriend of a businessman, she became a full sethani, with a mouth reddened by paan and a bunch of keys in her petticoat, and strong views about Manmohan Singh's budget. And it was not as if the Sanskritist or the businessman asked these things of her. They asked them of her no more than a people one is travelling amongst ask that you take on the intonations of their speech and accent. But, not unlike certain travellers who do, travellers with a good ear and an active imagination, she found herself powerless to resist the allure of reinvention that love offered. It was for Uma the ultimate form of self-discovery.

When the door has closed again and the cool of the plane returns, Uma asks, 'It's strange that I'm here today of all days. A year to the day since Toby died, no?'

'Yes.'

'And? How do you feel?'

'I'm fine, Ma.'

'Good. I'm glad to hear it,' she says, with the casualness we adopt when we want to conceal our need to talk about things. 'He was very strange, in the end, your father; I didn't like his aloofness where the two of you were concerned; but that is not how I want to remember him.'

'How do you want to remember him?'

'Well,' she says – making it clear what she really has in mind – 'I'll tell you how I *don't* want to remember him. The way he was just before he left India in '92. So lost and off track, part of that ridiculous NGO crowd – Vandana and Dhanalakshmi: people who, by the way, he, more than anyone, used to laugh at in the old days. Racing off to Ayodhya like Rambo to singlehandedly stop the demolition of the Mosque. That huge fuss he later made with me over the Sanskrit Library. And it was him, you know, who asked me to step in when that fellow – what's his name . . . the American millionaire?'

'Kidd.'

'Right. When Kidd went into a coma, and his wife – God knows, I don't blame her! – put a stop to that project, wanted, as Toby used theatrically to say, "entomb it". Well, it was Toby who came to me, asking if Mani would support it. And when I arranged for that – and Mani was happy to do it, believe me: it was . . . it *is* a truly grand project . . . But what a fuss he later made!'

'Well, Ma, in fairness to him, he didn't know that the same money that funded the library would also fund the demolition of the Mosque.'

'It did not *fund* the demolition of the Mosque. It was paying for karseva . . .'

'Ma, that's ridiculous. The karsevaks demolished the mosque. Those men in the pictures, clambering on top of the dome of the mosque, with saffron flags in their hand, *those* are karsevaks.'

'But Mani didn't know that. When you're rich, you give to charities. You don't track every penny. I tell my Muslim friends this all the time . . .'

'You have Muslim friends?'

'Very funny. Many, in fact. And I tell them all the time when they go on about the Saudis funding the jihad: I tell them they're not funding the jihad; not, at least, knowingly. They're giving to Muslim charities; now if that money, after several degrees of separation, ends up buying a jihadi in Waziristan an apple, an AK-47 and a suicide belt, it's hardly their fault.'

Skanda laughs, and his mother, after peering into his face to be sure that the laughter is real, not rhetorical, laughs too. It is her great quality: she may strip the people who come into her sphere of their charm and humour – including Rudrani, who is ice cold with her – but she never lets go of these things herself. She is one of the very few people he can think of with whom it is possible to spend a day like this: on a stationary plane, with nothing but conversation to pass the time.

And, as much as life for her is blindingly real, she is never deaf to its laughter, big laughter, that makes life, if not less real, then certainly more expendable, a thing to be burnt rather than saved. Her approach to life is like the gambler's approach to money: he cannot do without it but neither does he hoard it. And it is an aspect of how close life still feels to her that death is unfathomable. She has, for instance – with regard to Toby – made none of the little adjustments we make for the dead; she has not unclenched her fist, as it were; she simply speaks of him (and perhaps always will) as if he is still alive.

'And he was wrong, let me tell you,' she says, the laughter in her voice suddenly falling off, 'your father. All that talk of fascism and the coming of tyranny: it was all rubbish. Vijaipal, when he came on TV the day after the Mosque was demolished, was right. "These are foreign words, fascist and the such," he said, I remember so well, "they have a specific historical context, related to the history of Europe. They should not be applied easily in India." And – what? – twenty or so years later – it's pretty clear that what happened in Ayodhya might have been a bad thing, but it was not the Beer Hall Putsch.'

'What are you getting at, Ma? What's bothering you? Why all this, now?'

'It's not bothering me. I just don't understand.'

'What don't you understand?'

'Why he had to take everything so much to heart, your father? Why did he have to leave India the way he did, never to return? Why did he give up on life? He became so aloof, even from you and Rudrani. Never helped with anything. Don't forget – much as you might resent him – it was Mani who put you through college; he was happy to do it, of course; but let's not forget who *funded* that, your little escape into classical India . . . Not daddy dearest, no. Mani!

And, believe me, there's a much clearer money trail to that than there is to the demolition of the Babri Masjid . . .'

'Ma!'

'What?' she says irritably.

'I don't know why he took everything so much to heart. Nobody does.'

'Well, then don't make it seem as if it was all in some way my fault . . .'

'Do you feel,' he says, asking a question that years of therapy has made possible, 'that I do that? That I make you feel you were responsible for Baba leaving India, for his disillusionment at the end of his life?'

'No. Not you, anymore. But your sister.'

And then, as if anticipating his answer, she adds, with her special taste for conflict. 'You too, in your way. Because you're full of sympathy for him, and none for me.'

The return of love made Uma unrecognizable to her children. But she seemed to them, in many ways, better off than their father. In her eyes, though dimmed, there was still the light of familiarity, there was still recognition; in Toby, it had gone out completely. When Skanda met him that autumn in Delhi, during his mid-term break from school, he was alarmed at how changed he was. Perhaps because they met at the President's Estate Polo Club, which itself was soon to close, or perhaps because they met alone, it left him with one of his strongest impressions of his father. And it was of a man in whom something essential had gone quiet.

It was September. The rains were gone, the sky was free of clouds. The sunshine dazzled, but there was still something moist and congested in the air. They sat out in rattan chairs in front of the old red club house with its sloping roof of corrugated iron. The rides were over and the two Sikh brothers, large Jat men, with whitening beards coiled neatly into knots at their chin, were calling in the horses. A single rider stick-and-balled on the great field under a pale sky.

They had just come back from a ride on the Ridge, and there was the sweet tired dirtiness of that post-riding hour still in them, the smell of sweat and leather on their red and faintly calloused fingers.

The quiet of the forest left them with some residual closeness. But, now out of those wooded trails, and in the big world again, Skanda was surprised to see how quickly it faded, how aloof his father, in actual fact, had become. Skanda had just returned from two months away at a new school, in a new place, halfway across the country, but Toby, until prompted, asked him nothing about it.

In the past, Toby's faraway quality had been compensated for by an amazing human sensitivity, an attentiveness and concern for the interior life of the people he loved, an ability to make you feel that his distance was but a stepping-back only so that he could see you more clearly. Nothing was out of his range, nothing too low, nothing too high; it was one of the most wonderful things about him, his talent for elevating what was low and ordinary, and simplifying what was difficult and out of reach. But now, that other component, that ability to join the human with the cerebral, was gone. And it gave to his high-mindedness a frazzled and wayward quality; his speech seemed to lack volume, seemed almost to have the empty urgency of static.

He had been speaking for many moments about the only two subjects that still interested him, the Kidd Sanskrit Library and Ayodhya.

'Mites, Skandu. Red mites. Gopas. Indragopas. Or, if you will, śakragopas. Monier-Williams incorrectly translates them as fireflies. Leuchtkäfer. But Onians is right, I think, in saying they are mites. Red mites. A hallmark of monsoon poetry, because, you see . . .'

'Who's Onians?' Skanda said, peering into his tea.

'Onians? Oh, a wonderful scholar at Chicago. One of the translators for KSL. She's done extraordinary work on certain stereotyped elements of monsoon poetry. Because, you see, in old India, the inventiveness of the poet was confined to what he did with certain fixed elements of poetry. He was not expected to invent new elements. He was expected to play with what he had. So, just as the

Western poet of a certain age had to show his inventiveness within the confines of metre, the Indian poet was limited not just by metre, but by theme and metaphor too . . .'

'Is it going well, your library?'

'On the scholarship and translation side of things, splendidly. Couldn't be better. But we're having trouble with our investors. My old friend Kidd is sick, and his wife – forgive me, son – is a bitch. Hates India, hates Sanskrit. Given half a chance, she would entomb . . .'

'Baba?'

'Skandu?'

'I have a girlfriend.'

'A girlfriend, really. Where? Skandu!'

'In school. She's called Aurora and – it's so funny! – she's from a place called Auroville . . .'

'I know Auroville, of course. Aurora! The dawn. What a lovely name. Cognate, you know, with the Sanskrit uṣas. She's all over the Ṛg Veda, your Aurora. Uṣas and sandhyā, the dawn and dusk. Where did I read something beautiful about them the other day? The new Calasso perhaps; it's not out yet, but he sent me some pages. "Uṣas and sandhyā, everyone wanted to couple with them, for coupling is the image of connection" – I'm paraphrasing, of course! – "and uṣas and sandhyā were the image of the supreme connection." Bandhu! Which, as you know, is related to the English bind, the Latin *fides*, *fidelis*. *Adeste, fideles, Laeti triumphantes* . . .'

'Baba!'

'I'm sorry. I thought you'd enjoy it. Is she pretty, your Aurora? Is she faithful? Aurora what?'

'Borealis.'

Toby laughed uproariously. And, in that moment, he was briefly himself again. Whole, not hollowed out.

'Aurora Vohra.'

'You're having me on!'

'I'm serious. Her father is Punjabi.'

'Good Lord. Not Pompy Vohra?'

'That's him. You know him?'

'I do. A very fine fellow. He was a professor of I.P.'s at Stephens. And then, yes! – you're absolutely right; I remember now! – he went off to live in Auroville. Very much part of that Sixties/Seventies moment. How extraordinary that his daughter should be your girlfriend! Have you told your mother?'

'No, not yet.'

And, suddenly, at the mention of I.P. and of Uma, a sadness came over Toby. But it made Skanda happy, for momentarily his father was familiar again. The disjointed broken quality was gone.

'How is that going, by the way? Uma and her businessman.'

He only ever referred to Mani that way.

'I hate him.'

But Toby, either out of principle, or because the pain was too great for him, refused to encourage Skanda. With his eyes blank in their sockets, the crow's feet ever deeper, he said simply, 'You mustn't say that. You must be a support to her. I ran into them, you know, some months back, in the lobby of the Oberoi . . .'

'Really?'

'Yes. It was a nice chance to catch up, for Uma to meet Sylvia, and for me to meet her businessman. He's not a bad sort, you know. The trouble with a man like that is he already knows all that he wants to know. But . . .' His voice trailed off.

'But what?'

'But not a bad sort. Not a bad sort at all. And you must be there for your mother. You're almost a man, now.'

Toby looked at Skanda as if seeing him for the first time, his height, his build, his green speckled eyes, his longish black hair. 'A very handsome man at that, I should add. She's a lucky girl, this Aurora. I hope you'll bring her to Kalasuryaketu. Pompy Vohra's daughter! Incredible! How strange life is, Skanda.'

Then, he said, 'I spoke to I.P., you know, the other day. I called him in New Zealand, just to fill him in.'

For a moment Skanda thought he meant on the changes in their lives. But no.

'On the madness over this temple. On these shiny-faced thugs in saffron, wanting to build a temple in the place where Lord Ram was born. *In a manger*, no doubt! Who are these people, Skanda? Crusaders? Mujahideen? Not Hindus, surely. Can you imagine? No culture in the world less anxious about place and time than ours. A *panchronistic* flatland, Deshpande called it. A sacred scheme that could be – and was – reproduced anywhere. Never needed an army, never an imperial project. But, despite that, it went everywhere, as far as Java, purely on the appeal and confidence of that culture. Never jealous, Skandu, never mean-spirited, never interested in stamping out the local culture that came under its great vault. Never Rome. And yet as grand as Rome: among the most effortless and peaceful transmissions of culture the world has known. And these greasy little swines in saffron will see it reduced to the mean objective of demolishing a mosque and building a temple. It's too squalid for words.'

Then – and only then – did he give some indication of why it hurt him so much. He said, 'And you know who their real enemy is, Skandu? Not the Muslims. They, poor fellows, are just stand-ins. Their real enemy is their past. They act as if they want to preserve it; but they want to destroy it, to remake it completely.'

'But why?' Skanda said, for truly he did not understand what his father meant.

'Why?' Toby said. 'Because it's inconvenient, no less than I am inconvenient. It doesn't tell them what they want to hear. But what they don't see is that their repackaging their culture in this way will not strengthen it; it will kill it. And what's happening in Ayodha in the name of Hinduism is far more alien to the culture of this land than that little Mosque.'

The road from the club, which was in a clearing in the forest, curled out into Willingdon Crescent. Soon neither club nor road would exist; or, if they did, they would be either renamed or relocated. Skanda would never drive down that road again.

A precise line of orange fire burns away on the margin of a sky to which colour is gradually returning. Her pedicure is done, her toes, their nails painted a bright red, are separated and drying. Pooja has brought them snacks – a stale mezze – which Uma does not like. When she is gone, Uma, suspicious perhaps of Maniraja's tawdry glad-eye, says, 'You know, this girl, Pooja, she has no language.'

He expects her to say more, but she stops there, as if wishing to be prompted.

'How do you mean?' Skanda says, wondering what Maniraja has said or done to cause this sudden assault on Pooja.

'I mean she has no language. Her English, well, you can tell what it is. But the interesting thing is that she has no Hindi either. I said to her the other day, "What do you speak at home?" She said, "English." Can you imagine?! The global pariah, your father would have said. And, on that front, I must say he was dead right.'

'In what sense?'

'In the sense that long before this new world of ours, of iPads and Twitter, came into being, he predicted a frightening loss of language for this country. A moment when, just as the need for expression would be greatest, the means of expression – language, namely –

would be at their most inadequate. And I'm afraid he was absolutely right. Well before the dots were as dispersed as they are now, Toby would talk of the need to be able to join them. It was one of the reasons he was so insistent about Sanskrit when it came to you.'

Then, after a pause, she says, 'And? Was he right? Did your learning Sanskrit make things easier? Did it give you an advantage of some kind?'

'It did. Yes,' Skanda says, embarrassed to be questioned so seriously by his mother. 'I suppose that in making it possible for me to see through language, it gave me a glimpse of an underlying unity, which, when things are as fragmented as they are, is a comfort.'

'A comfort? How?'

'Well, it's like a metaphor, isn't it? This shared history of sound and meaning – for how the world can be both various and one, impartite . . .'

'Impartite?'

'Indivisible. Of one essence, but distinct.'

'Really. How?'

'The way space in a jar – Coomaraswamy's metaphor, by the way, for ātman – is distinct, and yet indistinguishable from space without.'

She holds his gaze for a moment, as if seeing something that is beyond his grasp – an emotional judgement more important than his intellectual – then, releasing him, she says, 'You're so much like your father.'

And, as if taking pleasure in having made him speak seriously only to mock him, she continues, in a different vein, 'Well, you know what does it for me? This!'

She waves her iPad at him.

'This is what helps me make a whole of the world.'

'Your iPad?' he laughs.

'I'm not joking. This has helped me piece together my life more than any little ability to see through language . . . Time, distance, what happened then, what happened now – memory – it has simplified all those things: they've all just collapsed into one another. I'll give you an example,' she says, seeing something sceptical in her son's face, 'I.P. leaving. Such a big deal for me. I'd say the biggest thing that happened in my adult life. My brother – my little brother – leaving in the way he did. Those long years of his absence, the trunk call every several months. It broke me in half.' She narrows her gaze, as if to say, *I don't do emotion; this is the most you're going to get out of me.* 'But now? Now I FaceTime him, twice a week. And it's as if he never left. There are many things like that: all the pals from the old days. Nixu, Chamunda: I hardly see them anymore – they're both so busy with political life now – but we send each other direct messages on Twitter. Even Gayatri – despite being in a wheelchair – manages to send me the odd email. And Priti, if she wasn't so scatty, would do the same. Ditto certain historical events . . . take 1984. So much of what was sinister about it was the silence that fell over that time: now you can wikipedia 1984; you can see footage on YouTube. The past is not as obscure as it once was. Distances don't have the same meaning. Your father leaving India in 1992, never to return, meant something then, when there was one flight a day to London, and no mobile phones. But, by 1998, or certainly 2008, when there were seventeen flights a day to London alone, and Skype, and mobiles, and Facebook and whatnot, it meant nothing.'

'It meant something to him.'

'A tremendous amount. I know! Which is why your bringing him home was so important and your immersing his ashes . . . Have you done that, by the way?'

'Not yet.'

'Skanda! What are you waiting for?'

'I don't know, Ma, this has been a strange year . . .'

'We can give you a ride, you know, in the plane? Would you like that?'

'To where?'

'To Allahabad. Or wherever. I can ask Mani; it's no big deal.'

'No. No, thank you.'

'Well, it's your father, his ashes, do what you want. But what was I saying earlier?'

'His leaving.'

'His leaving, but not just his leaving. His whole approach to things, to history, to memory, to place, to civilization: it was of another time. He used to think people couldn't do without an idea of their past, without an idea of who and what they were. But I think probably they can. The result might not be spectacular. Ha, look at Pooja! But she doesn't seem on the verge of an existential crisis either, if you know what I mean!'

'What do you mean?'

'That perhaps people can get by with a lot less than we thought. That perhaps this thin overlay of global culture, a few malls, a few movies, a mobile phone or two, is more than enough for most people. Enough to get them through . . .'

'But there's more to life than just getting through.'

She makes a face, a faintly Gallic expression of indifference – a tant-pis! – and says, 'To you perhaps.'

Pooja has appeared behind her in the semi-darkness. She senses her presence and, turning round, says, 'What? Time to go?'

'No, not yet, ma'am. Chief has called. He's on his way back. Some traffic, he's stuck in . . .'

'How long?'

'Fifteen–twenty minutes.'

'Oh, OK. Fine.'

Pooja goes about the little cabin, turning on the lights, which create a magical and violet effect.

'Should I be on my way?' he asks.

'Stay a minute longer. What were we talking about?'

'About how nothing matters anymore.'

'Ah, yes,' she laughs. 'My favourite subject.'

'Do you feel at least that we should aspire to more? That the hope Baba expressed that night, before leaving the country, was valid?'

'The night after the Mosque came down?'

'. . . was *brought* down. Yes.'

'Why were we all together that night?'

'Ma, come on,' he says sternly, feeling in moments as these that Rudrani's judgement of their mother is correct: that she is complicit in what happens to her, and that she enjoys reliving those episodes that, no matter how wretched, give her the illusion of having lived hard. 'The Shivaji Sheraton? Have you forgotten?'

'Ah,' she says, jaunty laughter now turning to embarrassment. 'One of the many times I almost left Mani. Yes, of course, how could I forget: the Shivaji Sheraton!'

The Shivaji Sheraton was the airport hotel where Skanda and his mother stayed on the night Pompy Vohra came to dinner and Uma and Mani had one of their ugliest fights on record.

It had till then been an interminable winter, balmy, dull, full of awkwardness. Mani's insistence that Skanda stay with them in his holidays had meant that, though he was home, he was terribly homesick for his sister, for his grandparents, for his flat and life in Delhi. His mother and Mani lived in a modern apartment, placed at an awkward angle to the sea, which was visible – a greenish-brown causeway of water, often in retreat – through the gaps in the squarish buildings, their faces moist and blackening in the salt air. There was an odd feeling in that flat of being at once cloistered and exposed. The little air-conditioned space sealed with glass and glue, and then the street and surrounding squalor, where it felt as if an explosion or natural calamity had occurred and thrown everyone together, abolishing all personal boundaries, and creating an intimacy akin to that of a refugee encampment. It was an exhausting cycle of human activity: people bathing, cooking, washing, worshipping and mingling.

The air in the flat, too, went between cycles of tedium and tension. There were cyclical explosions at mealtimes, interspersed with long lecturing conversations, usually about politics. For Skanda there was the awkwardness of witnessing his mother adjust to this life. The little jogs along the sea face that she would accompany Maniraja on, the two of them kitted out in fluorescent clothes and insect-green sunglasses; making conversation with his friends and relations; dressing up for dinner in a sari, a bunch of keys in her petticoat; the sadness of the bedroom door closing at night. He felt like a dumb animal forced to observe the customs and habits of a species other than his own.

His sole comfort during this period was Aurora. Aurora of Auroville, Aurora Vohra. The Aurovilleans – and there was a small contingent at his school – were natural friends for Skanda. For one, they were often, like him and Rudrani, of mixed backgrounds. Two, there was, due to the experimental community in which they had been raised, a great reverence in them for Indian things. They had the most extraordinary names – Satyen and Samya Tait; Surya Burkhardt; Ribhu Gautier, Akincana Vohra. Skanda had, in fact, first met Aurora when she came to thank him for protecting her little brother from the Delhi and Bombay kids, who teased him relentlessly for his name and accent, calling him 'Kinky'. The Delhi and Bombay kids thought his name was a German name. But a | kiñ | canaḥ, which meant he who possesses nothing, was among the names by which Parvati referred to Shiva in the Birth. And it was an odd but revealing comment on the times they lived in that a half-German boy with that name would be teased to death in an Indian school for having it. Aurora and her brother had gone to Germany to be with their mother for Christmas, but she had written and called throughout the period when Skanda was in Bombay. And he was full of her.

Full of her beauty: she was almost as tall as he was, with clear blue eyes and dirty brownish blonde hair. She had that same mixture his father did: of strong Indian features – the largeness of the eyes, the prominence of the bones, the small mouth – combined with

European colouring. He was full of the way she spoke: she had this faint German accent, but spoke accentless and fluent Tamil. Full of her smell, too: she wore a perfume called Pleasures which that winter, he felt, had entered his soul. Full, most of all, of her intelligence: she would send him books and poems, journals she had filled in with photographs and letters to him, and on the first handmade page of which there might be, in blue ink, a little epigraph from a poem by John Wilmot, Earl of Rochester, 'Yet still I love thee without art / Ancient person of my heart.'

She was the kind of girl who, when you're older, and you meet others, you spend inordinate amounts of time casting your mind back to, in the vain hope of discovering if she was really as perfect as she had seemed or if it was your youth and inexperience that made her that way.

One morning – and this was just the kind of thing that amused her – she called from Bremen to say that her father, whom Skanda had never met, was passing through Bombay, and would he, Skanda, like to have dinner with him. Skanda agreed immediately, for in those early days of love, there is nothing worse than being unequal to a provocation. But no sooner had he put the phone down than he was faced with a difficult question. He wanted Aurora's father to meet his mother, but he did not want him to meet Maniraja. And there was no way in the petty tyranny they lived under for just the two of them, mother and son, to take Pompy Vohra out for dinner. When he mentioned it in passing to his mother, she said what he was afraid she would say, 'But call him here. Of course!' He tried to back out, but in his hesitation he let slip what his father had said: that Pompy Vohra had been a professor of I.P.'s at Stephens. No sooner had he done this than he knew that Pompy Vohra's coming to dinner now meant much more to his mother than it did to him. 'I absolutely insist,' she said. 'I think I even remember him. Give me his number, I'll call him myself.'

He did, and two minutes later she was on the phone to him, laughing and joking, completely at ease. When she put the phone down, she seemed almost surprised to see her son goggle-eyed with anticipation.

'What?' she said.

'What, what?'

'What nothing. He sounds terrific. He'll be here at eight.'

Mani's objections began even before he came home from work. Over several conversations he had with Uma, while still at the office, he seemed to take her through cycle after haranguing cycle, till she said, 'I'll cancel it, I'll cancel it. I'll call him this minute and cancel it.' But, just as she said this – even sometimes after she put the phone down – Mani withdrew his objection, and insisted the dinner go ahead. It was hard to know the origin of his trouble. Some wish to control, certainly, to have everything flow from him, seemed to be part of it. But there was something else. An anxiety, which, when glimpsed, almost made you feel sorry for the way Mani suffered over such little things. He was exquisitely sensitive. A highly particular configuration of class, caste, region, language – a lock of a thousand different keys – and everything chaffed against him. Everything made him feel raw and exposed. The world to him was a place full of slights and snubs and put-downs, and his only defence was to rage against each one.

The cook came in to take the dinner order, while Uma was on the phone with Mani.

'Kali dal, shammi kebabs, karara bhindi . . .' she said unthinkingly. But she had barely begun when there was a fusillade of hot words down the phone.

Skanda could not make out the nature of the objection, but he heard his mother say, some half a dozen times, 'No, Mani. I don't think Punjabi food is superior to South Indian. But he – our dinner guest – is Punjabi, and lives in South India; I thought it would be nice for him to have a Punjabi meal. That's all!'

Over this question of food a shadow fell over the dinner, and it was not till 4 or 4.30 that Uma had permission for it to go ahead. Then Mani wanted to eat at 7.30; otherwise it would interfere with his sleep and exercise, he said.

'Mani, we can't eat at 7.30! He's only coming at 8 p.m. . . . No, I can't ask him for 6. This is India; not America; you can't ask anyone for 6 . . . Mani, please, for God's sake: stop this. You're not even going to be home by 6 p.m.!'

Exhausting as these exchanges were to the outsider, Mani – and later Uma – hardly noticed them. They became part of the natural temperature of their relationship. Sometimes it even seemed – especially to Rudrani – that Mani, easily provoked and susceptible in the French sense of the word, more than Uma, was their victim: that their mother seemed almost to enjoy stitching him up. When he returned home from work that day, just as the view of the sea had become a dirty strait of choppy orange, Mani seemed not to be at all aware of the hysteria he had caused in the little flat. He seemed to look forward to the evening ahead, seemed relaxed, in a good mood; and, later, when Skanda – whom Mani had now, especially after a fight with Uma, begun taking into his confidence – would think back to that night, he almost felt pity for how wretched Mani's behaviour must have left him feeling.

Uma was in a flamboyant and unreadable mood, either on account of her son, who had witnessed just how difficult it was for her to have someone to dinner, or on account of her guest, in front of whom she wanted to be her old self for an evening. It was as if, with the acuity of children in a playground, she had gauged how easy it was to set Maniraja off, and, instead of pacifying him, as she often did, she had decided that evening to make an exhibition of his over-sensitivity.

She strode into the drawing room of the flat, just before eight, dressed in a maroon and gold sari. Then she made herself a whisky soda, a drink which she had mysteriously given up since meeting Mani, and came and sat down under a large and garish work of modern Indian art. A grand tableau of obese green women crouched on their haunches, keeping vigil over the body of a dead man.

At a few minutes past eight, when sky, sea and buildings were all one colour, a smoky blue dotted with a Braille of white and yellow light, the doorbell rang through the flat.

Pompy Vohra was a tall man, with a full head of white hair, and a dark youthful face. His skin, from perhaps a particularly violent outbreak of pox as a child, was scarred and pitted, and he had long gapped teeth, which along with his youthfulness gave his face an impish and mischievous quality. He was dressed in jeans, loafers and a light brown corduroy jacket. And he was instantly familiar to Skanda. It was not just that he reminded him of his uncle – less a physical resemblance than one of manners and style – it was that he exuded a certain calm, a repose, that, after his time with Mani, it had begun to seem inconceivable a grown man could possess. He was somewhere between a schoolboy and a hippy and he lightened the air in that flat in ways he could hardly have been aware of. Well, initially, at least.

His entry into the room coincided with Maniraja's, who came in wearing dark jeans, square-toed shoes, a slim expensive belt and a black shirt, across which – or rather, crouched in the left corner of which – there was an embroidered and brightly coloured Chinese dragon. Uma flashed him a glance, then looked at Pompy, who had brought her a present.

'A book!' she cried, and clapped her hands. 'You're clearly not from Bombay, my dear Pompy. We haven't seen one of these here in years. Or not, at least, in *our* crowd. Whose house were we at, darling, the other day,' she said, turning briefly to Maniraja, 'where there was an entire library of fake books? And the man said proudly, "I don't read books, but I like the way they look." You almost had to admire him: the sheer bald-facedness of it! What have you brought?' she said, taking the book from Pompy, who was already chuckling quietly while taking in the room.

He said, 'Given all that is going on in Ayodhya at the moment, a very controversial book, I'm afraid. But I'm a big fan.'

Uma, without bothering to introduce the men, took the book and fell into the sofa like a little girl who'd been given a doll. The men awkwardly took the initiative upon themselves. 'Skanda!' Pompy said, with great warmth. 'The rescuer of my son. How nice it is to finally meet you. My children adore you!' Then, by way of getting conversation going, he began to tell Mani the story of Akincana being bullied at school. He was only part of the way in when he was interrupted by Uma saying loudly, 'I don't believe it! I just don't believe it! My God,' she said, looking up at him. And suddenly – it was incredible! – she had tears in her eyes . . .

'This really takes me back,' she said, then stopped. 'I shouldn't go on . . .'

She flashed a quick glance up at her son.

'Ma, what is wrong with you?' he whispered hurriedly. 'Why are you crying? What's the matter? Are you drunk?'

'I'm not drunk, you stupid boy,' she said, rubbing away her tears. 'It's just – ah! – this book. I know him; I know the writer, you know. Vijaipal. He was with us all those years ago when I first fell in love with your father. It was the year of the Emergency. 1975 . . .'

At the mention of the year, a fresh batch of tears appeared in her eyes. She clutched Pompy's hand, and said, 'Thank you. Really, thank you. It means so much to me that you have brought this book tonight – of all books! . . .'

Pompy laughed. He seemed not in the slightest bit perturbed that his hostess, within minutes of his arrival, had burst into tears. The man who was perturbed to the point of being ill was Maniraja. He had forbidden Uma from having pictures of Toby in the house; and, in the past, even the mention of his name had caused terrible arguments. So much so that Uma had implored Skanda never to mention his father in front of Maniraja.

And now? Well, she seemed only to be warming up.

'What will you drink, Pompy?' she said, rising suddenly, and making eye contact with an ashen-faced Maniraja, added, 'I, for my part, am having a whisky soda.'

'Whisky soda for me too, please.'

'Have some Dom,' Maniraja said, trying to regain control over the room. He had opened the champagne especially.

'He doesn't want "Dom", Mani. Not everyone likes champagne. It was me,' she said slyly, as if in a Shakespearean aside, 'who gave him his first glass. Can you imagine? So rich, and never had any champagne – poor man! – till little old me came along. Whisky?'

'Whisky, please,' Pompy said again.

Uma walked over to the bar, apparently content to let the men stew in the discomfort she caused.

When she returned, Pompy and Maniraja were trying to establish some little rapport of their own. Uma, sensing she had made herself essential to their dynamic – and knowing, moreover, the social difficulty subcontinental men face in these situations – fell back and talked to her son instead. Seeing he had a drink, she said, 'I don't know if you should be having one. How old are you, darling?'

'Ma, you know perfectly well how old I am.'

'I forget. Was it '76 or '77? You came in such quick succession, you two.'

Then again she withdrew into a kind of a reverie. 'Do you think Rudrani would have enjoyed being here tonight?'

'I doubt it.'

Uma laughed.

'Why? Am I being very naughty? And your father? He might have enjoyed it.'

'No.'

'And you?'

'I'm OK. But please stop winding him up.'

'He's very nice,' she said, changing the subject, 'your girlfriend's father. I liked him the moment he walked in the door.'

'Me too.'

'So familiar, no? I miss that familiarity. They just don't get it here, in this town, do they? Or, at least, the people *he* knows,' she said, glancing at Mani. 'They're so one-dimensional. No fun in any of them, no real humour.'

The murmuring conversation the men were having acquired a serious tone. There had been crowds gathering in Ayodhya over the past few days and – though no one had seen the news yet – there were rumours that afternoon that the Mosque had been attacked. Uma heard Pompy say, 'Oh, no. I wouldn't say that . . .'

'Wouldn't say what?' she inserted casually.

Pompy, relieved at the intervention, said, 'I wouldn't say Vijaipal endorses the Ayodhya movement . . .'

'Of course he doesn't. Mani's never read Vijaipal; Mani reads pamphlets . . .'

'I've never read Vijaipal?!' Mani said, in a voice that was openly threatening. 'And you? Who have you read? I can say: you've never read Vijaipal. Never read anything, stupid . . .' Then he stopped himself.

'You could say that,' Uma said. 'But you'd be wrong, of course.'

She was not yet ready to draw him out; and, eyeing him, she said calmly, 'Name me one book of his other than the one I'm holding in my hands?'

'I don't have to name anything for you . . . This is not a class, and you're not the teacher!'

'Don't get excited, Mani,' she said, knowing full well that it would only excite him further.

Pompy intervened, 'You see, his model, in the end – Vijaipal's – is that of the European Renaissance. And so, in a sense you're right: a certain kind of violence, especially religious violence, he would recognize as resembling that of Shakespeare's time, say. But what he would be looking for – and, here, I'm afraid the men in saffron fall woefully short, Mani – is an intellectual element.'

'Exactly!' Uma said. 'Listen to him, Mani. Don't always be so blinded by prejudice. There's more to civilization than killing Muslims and demolishing mosques . . .'

Mani looked at her straight in the eye, his chapped lips quivering with anger.

At that moment, or one long moment later, the bearer opened the door to say dinner was served. And it was this man who received the full brunt of what Uma had excited. Mani, whose behaviour with servants was habitually vile, spoke to him in a manner that did more to diminish himself in the eyes of a man like Pompy than anything else. 'Eh, bastard, bhenchodh, interrupt when you want to, huh? Can't you see we're talking . . . ? Do you want me to rip your asshole out and garland you with it; you want me to do that?'

The man stood stock still in the doorway, shrinking from the abuse.

'We were not talking, Mani.'

'You . . . you just . . . keep quiet.'

Then he turned back and continued insulting the poor man.

On the way to the table, in the corridor, Pompy could not restrain himself. He kept saying, under his breath, but loud enough for Skanda to hear, 'Not done; just not done . . .'

The stage had been set for a fight. But, like those storms where rain is slow on the heels of thunder, it broke only after dinner, when everyone, especially Maniraja, was much drunker. The provocations of the evening seemed mutely to have returned to him over dinner, and become amplified under the influence of alcohol. He had tried brokenly to participate in the conversation, which was all Ayodhya; but, seeing Uma, irreverent and taunting, and making an exhibition of the fun she was having in Pompy's company, he had retreated into a long hostile silence. In these moments, it seemed to Skanda almost as if his mother by some strange inverted logic was punishing Maniraja for something . . . For what? His charmlessness? For the boredom of the life she led with him? Its security, its compromises? Punishing him, perhaps, for not being the big love of her life. And what made it all very sad was that as much as Maniraja could be controlling, and his behaviour crude and violent, of one thing there was no doubt: Uma was the big love of his life.

When they came out into the drawing room, Uma went straight for Vijaipal's book and, pulling her feet up under her, she sat down on the sofa as if meaning to read the whole thing right there and then. Mani tried to tell her to put it down and come and join them, but she ignored him. 'I want to show you something,' she murmured.

The men had just about managed to resume some kind of conversation, something about the advantages of American universities – of which Mani was a great advocate – over the English, when Uma, having found what she was looking for, interrupted them with, 'Ah, listen to this: "Over the course of a journey like this – eight months of travel across India – more people help than can possibly be remembered here. Still, the generosity of a few stands out . . . Padgaonkar . . . Ajay Sharma . . . philana dhimkana" – Ah, here it is – ". . . and my old friend, HH The Raja of Kalasuryaketu . . . over two decades of friendship, we have disagreed over many important issues concerning India and her past, and many disagreements still stand, but it is him whom I must thank for first helping me to recognize the futility in a political idea of revenge . . . and in the end, I suppose" – listen to this, Pompy, this is for you – "there are only two kinds of people: those who are of the intellect and those who are not . . ."'

With this she slapped the book shut with a pleasing sound, and, looking Mani in the eye, said, 'There you have it, my darling. Don't go about co-opting good writers for your shameful cause. Vijaipal does not support a political idea of revenge, in other words, he does not support demolishing the Mosque in Ayodhya.' Then, for good measure, as this was very much her style, she added, 'Got it, dumbo?'

But Mani had got it long ago, and now pronouncing the words carefully, for they did not come naturally to him, he said, 'Fuck you.'

Then he walked over to her and, snatching the book from her hands, sent it windmilling across the room. It fell face forward on the sofa, its flaps stretched uncomfortably back, its spine bulging.

India: Decay and Renewal.

Uma stared at him in cold silence, then at the others and said, 'In a country where Saraswati is a goddess, where there is nothing more sacred than the written word, you throw a book? Shame on you!'

'What do you know about this country? You know nothing about this country!'

'More than you, clearly,' she said, and smiled.

'Fuck you,' he said again, as if he had got hold of a mantra.

Silence.

Uma said, 'Well, all right boys. That's my cue. I'm off to bed. Pompy, it was lovely to see you. You remind me of my brother and of many wonderful things besides. Good night!'

With this she sailed out of the room to which she had brought such turmoil. Pompy stayed a few minutes longer, just so as not to seem as if he was leaving in a huff too, then he excused himself and slipped away, leaving Maniraja to a long session of remorse and confessions and drinking. He had switched to Black Label – his pre-Uma drink – and he kept Skanda up late into the night, wanting to impress upon him that he had not meant to offend his guest – 'I was honoured to have him here' – but that it was his mother, Uma, who was determined to create a scene. 'I don't know why . . . we were having such a nice evening . . .' he said again and again, borrowing a phrase that Skanda recognized as his mother's.

Skanda, enraged at the spectacle Pompy Vohra had been forced to witness, wanted to leave for Delhi that very night. He stayed out of concern for his mother, though, as it turned out, that was not necessary.

He had been asleep for barely a few minutes when he heard more shouting, the slamming of more doors. Their fight had resumed. Then, moments later, there was the fast patter of feet in the corridor, and Uma was saying, again and again, 'It's too awful, it's just too awful.' Silence followed; some moments of indecision perhaps; then there was a knock on Skanda's door. He opened it and saw it was his mother, her face still half made-up. 'I hate to do this to you, darling,' she said, 'but pack a small bag. We have to leave.'

That was how they found themselves at the Shivaji Sheraton, where – on CNN – they saw that the Mosque had been demolished.

It is dark and he is alone. The plane's engines whirr with new urgency. On the flight map, the golden wheel spins faster, and a broad lime-green arrow now leapfrogs between Delhi and Bombay. Outside, the heat of the night is still palpable: now in the bothered shiny faces of the men who come and go from the plane, now in the strangled quality of the amber lights, which seem barely able to pierce the density of the night.

Uma returns, freshly made-up. An actress in the bright cabin lights. The slackening of skin around her mouth and neck, where two parallel rills are digging in, the dark pouchiness of her cheeks, gives her newly painted lips a sternness that was not there before. Her hair is brushed, and her face, a throwback to the flying days, has a closed quality. *Change is real*, he thinks; *we must not expect people to speak as people they have ceased to be.*

'I saw Isha Massi,' he says, 'and Viski.'

'How nice for you,' she replies. 'You must see her. She's your aunt. See her all you want.'

He smiles. But she does not return his smile.

'She's also your sister and she seemed very sad that you don't speak to each other anymore.'

'Who? Her and me?' she says, buying time.

He nods.

'Ah, yes. Well . . .'

Silence.

'That's it?'

Irritation, as if he has just spoiled her make-up, appears on her face.

'I'm too old, Skanda, to be told what to do,' she says. 'I won't live with anyone's disapproval.' Then, as if what she has just said has accidentally become imbued with deeper meaning, she adds, 'I'm sixty-three. Sixty-four, this year. I'm not answerable to anybody. I've done the best I can. But now everyone must also do what they want.'

Her eyes, from under which she has recently had the bags removed, are hard and intelligent; they hold him just as long as is needed for him to know that what she has said must be applied widely. Then they are veiled again, and she says, 'Well, I'd better be off.'

Which really means that he, Skanda, had better be off.

Pooja, as if magically, appears behind her to say Mani is on the tarmac.

'Ah, good. Tell the car to wait, so that it can take my son back.'

He stands; she lets him come in for a parting hug; then, clutching his hand, she says, 'You must deal with Toby's ashes; it'll be good for you, too. He loved this country more than anyone I know, your father. His problem was . . .' She glances at the tarmac, where Maniraja has arrived in a convoy of white sedans. Then, looking searchingly at her son – there is a glimmer of something frantic in her eyes – she says, 'His problem was that he could see what no one else could see, but he also failed to see what everyone else could: what was plain to see. And then – what can I say? – one day he did.'

•

The night is heavy and sweltering. They pass each other at the foot of the stairs, Mani and Skanda, strangers as ever, exchanging a brief word of farewell.

Soon he is on his way back to the flat, driving through the velvety darkness, channelled along a network of elevated roads, whose amber tendrils peel fast off their central stem.

The television hung from the foam ceiling of the terminal in Bombay. Skanda and Uma, their boarding passes to Delhi in their hands, were among a group of passengers whose eyes were trained on the screen split in two: in one half was the Mosque in Ayodhya, prior to its demolition. Three domes, blackened and scarred, set against the pale blue of the December sky. It stood there, like a rock impeding the course of the river of young men bent upon its destruction. In the other, Uma stared with wonder at the changes in Vijaipal's person. He was in India promoting his new book and the interviewer was using it as an opportunity to ask him about what had happened in Ayodhya the day before. It was hard to know how much he knew. When the British-born interviewer asked him about fascism, he said, seeming almost to glance at the images of the besieged mosque, 'These are foreign words, Mr Datta. They have a specific context, related to the history of Europe. They cannot be used to explain what is happening in India today.'

Uma remembered him as a lean dark man, quite ugly. There was now something leonine and graceful about him. He was fatter; his eyes lidded; he had grown a beard, in which there were streaks of white. He had made something of a grey eminence of himself. What had not changed was his irritability. And when the interviewer, a youngish man in a blue polo neck, said, 'When you say we should go back to the past . . .' Vijaipal snapped at him, 'That is not what I was saying. That is not at all what I was saying. You haven't understood a word. I'm talking about a historical sense. Which, in fact, can only come about when you accept the past as dead. The last thing India needs is to *go back* to her past. Nor should she try to repeat it; that will only make things worse . . .'

Then he directed the interviewer's attention to a book he was holding in his small dark hands. A slim tamarind-coloured volume.

'The Kidd Sanskrit Library,' he said, 'a very grand publishing project – akin to the Loeb books – put together by my old friend the Raja of Kalasuryaketu . . .'

'Baba!' Skanda said.

'I told you, didn't I? He was a friend of Baba's. Now, shush: either listen or go and find out when this flight is leaving . . .'

Vijaipal continued, 'Paid for by an American, of course; Indians have no regard for these things. But what I was saying, Mr Datta, was that my friend Toby Kalasuryaketu, the founder of this library, is the man responsible for first helping me to see the futility in a politics of revenge. It was also, incidentally, the old Raja who introduced me to that beautiful opening canto of the Ramayana. The one, you know, where the poet from an access of grief, śoka – I believe the word is – derives the śloka, poetry, placing the idea of compassion squarely at the heart of Indian poetics. How strange then that, in the name of the hero of that same epic, the crowds gathered yesterday in Ayodhya to tear down that little Mosque! No, no: I'm afraid I cannot endorse it, Mr Datta. India must take as its maxim what old Raja saab had once told me it was his life's ambition to be: "A Hindu, without vengeance, and without apology."'

When Skanda returned from checking on the flight, he found Uma standing with her hand over her mouth, her eyes wide and intense. She stood among what was now a small crowd of people. The suspended screen floated above them, bathing their faces in its bright and garish light. It was the country's first televised trauma. And it showed them their place as they had never seen it before; it showed them faces they had never seen before. Shiny faces full of laughter and joy, in which the excitement of being on television, it seemed, far surpassed that of the great event they had inadvertently become part of. And they stared back, the faces, through this strange two-way mirror at the unknown millions who watched them.

'A dwarf nation . . .' Vijaipal was beginning to say, as the crowd advanced upon the mosque.

But she was not able to catch anymore, for Skanda had returned to tell her – and she heard it announced now over the commotion spreading fast through the terminal – that their flight to Delhi was boarding.

It was late afternoon and the light fell long over the land. Uma thought of the images she had just seen ricocheting – as they could only do now – among people, spreading alarm. And yet, though trouble was on the way again, for the first time on this scale since 1984, it was less scary somehow. It was as if a certain kind of negative space, a pact of silence, had been abolished. The realm of the unsaid had shrunk. It was from this sphere of unspoken things, where rumour was news, that, in the past, the greatest part of their fear had come. She realized she had no television memory of 1984; nothing except Mrs Gandhi's funeral. But she would never forget what she had just seen; and though it made what occurred in Ayodhya real in ways that nothing had ever been real before, it also made it less frightening. There was a safety of noise and numbers in this new and easily forming consensus.

'Look, Kāla | sūrya,' Skanda said, pointing at the setting sun.

'Ah, yes,' she said, thinking of the little town set somewhere on the expanse of their journey north. 'What is it, again? I once used to know. The final sunset?'

'The sun of Time,' he said, 'the sun at the end of the world.'

'How stylish! What a grand coat of arms to have!'

Then, looking out at the land, parcelled out in brown, and turning faintly violet, she said, 'I wonder where he is? Our Raja of Kalasuryaketu.'

At sunset Toby was on the outskirts of Delhi, in a wasteland of weeds and poisoned water bodies. He had been driving all day, running, he felt, from the bad news that followed him. He had been in Ayodhya till that morning, working alongside political action groups and NGOs. His friends, Vandana and Dhanalakshmi, who were part of one such group, had recruited him to help prevent the demolition of the Mosque. For among that sea of people determined to destroy the Mosque, there were many whom Toby knew personally. Babaji, of course. But others too. Teachers, religious and secular; local politicians, bureaucrats and collectors. This was Toby's world. The India from where the madness had come was not only familiar; it was the India Toby had banked on. It was the country he had believed, when empowered, would supplant a worthless and effeminized elite. It made what was happening much harder to bear. And it was not so much blood or riots that he feared; he had seen all that before; it was the corruption of his dream: the dream of renaissance turned to nightmare.

He had done what he could in Ayodhya the day before, but it had come to nothing. He had left the town at dawn the next day, sending Vandana and Dhanalakshmi ahead in a separate car. It was at a hotel on the outskirts of Delhi that he first saw on television what he had seen in reality. His old friend Vijaipal was being interviewed. He was saying, '. . . a dwarf nation . . . that is what comes of countries who sanctify history they don't understand, who invent enemies out of their own self-loathing . . .'

Then the television flashed to images of young men on whose mute lips he could read the cries of 'Jai Shri Ram!' They had saffron strips of cloth tied around their foreheads and their eyes were white with exhilaration. He saw them advance upon the Mosque and swarm its base. He saw them crawl, with whatever little instrument they could find, to the petalled summit of its dome.

His memory filled in the rest: he saw the white dust of the dome's demise rise from it like a sigh of resignation. He saw the rank red brick of its interior, akin to inflamed muscle, as it was cut open. He saw the faces of the men on its summit, smiling and happy, deeply content, coated in a clownish layer of fine white dust.

The day before he had called his travel agent, Kharabanda, to book some air tickets. He now called Kharabanda back and told him to issue them. He wanted to escape what he had just seen on the television, but it followed him. Everywhere he had stopped on the way, the news grew richer in detail. And the feeling of consensus it created, the consensus that had been a comfort to Uma, was oppressive to Toby. A triumph, not of will, but of some base and encircling energy that had singled him out for extinction. The voice of the collective! It had spoken at last, and there was media now to reverberate its echo. The soul of the country was articulate; it was a moment Toby, more than anyone, had waited for; but now that the voice had sounded, Toby found he did not recognize its timbre. It gave utterance to a rough and rapacious spirit, it contained a note of barbarism – it was not the voice of a country he recognized.

That night – 7 December 1992 – they all unknowingly converged on the flat in Delhi. The flat, which had become a void at the centre of their lives, and in which, already, the air had grown stiller, the switches faintly yellow, the electronics outdated.

It was Sylvia who arrived first. Toby had sent her down in advance with Vandana and Dhanalakshmi, the frontline in 'Civil Society Against Fascism'. The two women had thoroughly enjoyed their activism in U.P., and, after a few mournful moments in the car in the morning, they had returned to their usual chattiness and good humour. They sat fatly outside the flat, on the red sandstone stairs, their crumpled cotton saris pulled up, smoking cigarettes. When it began to grow dark, Dhanalakshmi turned over Vandana's plump wrist to see the time, and yelled into the house, 'Sylvia, darling, the morale is low, the troops are tired. What about a little drinky-poo?'

Sylvia, who was waiting for the arrival of a travel agent, said, 'I'm not sure what there is.'

'Take a look, darling,' Dhanalakshmi said bossily. 'Toby and Uma's house. There's bound to be some booze lying around.'

Vandana, a bully herself, said, 'Yes, go on, Sylvia, dear. I'll drink carbolic acid, if I have to.'

Sylvia emerged out of the house a few minutes later with whisky sodas for the activists, who, before taking their drinks, each removed their large red bindis, and laughing raucously, put them on the step next to them, like a piece of chewing gum they hoped later to return to.

Uma saw them as she drove in.

'Good God,' she said to Skanda, as the car stopped outside the arched doorway, 'what are those two fat cows doing here?'

The women, their saris hitched up to their fleshy knees, had ordered fresh drinks; they sat on the step, greedily eating nuts from a dainty silver bowl between them.

'Uma! My darling!' Dhanalakshmi yelled on seeing the car. 'What are you doing here? What a beautiful surprise! We weren't expecting you.'

'I wasn't expecting you either, Dhanalakshmi,' Uma said frostily.

'Darling, we're just back from Ayodhya! It's too awful, too awful for words. Those revolting little people crawling over that beautiful old mosque.'

'Le deluge, my dear Uma,' Vandana chimed in, 'le deluge.' Then she put her two fingers to her upper lip, in imitation of a toothbrush moustache, and said, 'Heil!'

At which point the two women fell over themselves laughing.

Uma was still under the arch of the doorway – Narindar was bringing in the luggage – when Kharabanda, a stout man with a fog-horn of a voice and a cream-coloured Vespa, pulled up. Seeing Uma and Skanda, he let out a cry of joy and bounded up past the women.

'But Rani saab,' he said, 'what are you doing here? I thought you were in Bombay. I have no tickets for you. Only for Raja saab and a lady . . .'

Then, opening the flap of one of the two Air France tickets he held in his hand, he said carefully, 'Ms Sylvia.'

Sylvia, who, on hearing the commotion, had come outside.

'Sylvia!' Uma cried. 'Thank heavens! What on earth is going on?'

The two women had met only once before, and Uma still had in her manner traces of that exaggerated warmth we show our successors in love when we want to reassure them that we are no threat to them.

'Oh, Uma?' she said, somewhat overwhelmed by the scene. 'And Skanda! But Toby never said a word . . . ?'

'He didn't know. We're here somewhat unexpectedly. But how nice that we're all together! What's this about tickets?'

'We're leaving for Paris tonight.'

'Paris? Why?'

Sylvia was about to reply, then seeing Skanda, she said, ‘Maybe, it’s better Toby tell you himself. He should be here soon.’

Uma drew a breath, as if trying, in the growing darkness, to absorb all the activity around her. The women on the step; the travel agent with the two Air France tickets; Sylvia; and then, of course, ever present in the background, the memory of her ugly fight with Maniraja – her thoughts of leaving him – all of which had given her her own reasons for being in Delhi.

‘Well, come inside then, you lot,’ she said brusquely, casting a quick eye over the onset of the December evening. ‘No point everyone sitting outside. We had better make a little party of it, no?’

It was dark on the Mathura Road. Not the darkness of night but that of a brown haze. A smog that swallowed the headlights of cars, and muffled the thunder of trucks. The yellow beams of the car smoked before them. Toby was surprised to see how ugly it all was. The flat land, the pools of poisoned water fringed with grass, the black earth, the outlines of factories and granaries, the narrow shabby houses with their unplastered flanks, the unevenly metalled roads, the paint refusing to adhere to its lines, the filthy air: *Why have I never noticed any of this before?* he said almost aloud. *Why does it seem so new, this ugliness?* And just then he was aware of something else too: the voice in his head, it was silent. It was for once not playing its little games. Not once in that long car journey across U.P. had it seized on, say, ‘rudra’ painted on the back of a truck and thought, from *rud*, to roar and weep, related to the Anglo-Saxon *reotan*, the Latin *rudere*. Not once had he in a small town – Kannauj, say – seen Lipika Salon, and thought lipika? Scribe or clerk, from *lip*, which means to smear or anoint, related to the Latin *lippus*, but more importantly, to the Anglo-Saxon *libban*, the English live and life.

It was as if a faculty of his mind had been disabled and a whole world of meaning had gone quiet. There was nothing now holding his India together. Squalor was just squalor, dirt just dirt, people just people . . . And India, for the first time, seemed to him devoid of an animating idea; it was just a place where a lot of people lived.

He thought of Uma saying to him, in another life, 'Someone says H.P. to me and I think: Oh, good old Himachal Pradesh. Mountains, hill stations, busloads of tourists. But you, Toby, you're thinking, hima: snow, cold, frost: must be related to *hiems* and *hiver* and hibernate: and a | cala, that's a non-goer, like na | ga, means mountain. Snow mountain. How pretty!'

But was that really the reason? Was the language all that had held the world together? Had that alone been the source of meaning? Certainly it was true that, in the past, he had not been able to share the pessimism with which Indians viewed their own things. Mrinala, to a society lady in Delhi, might have seemed a common name, an ayah's name, even; she might perhaps have preferred Zhyra or Kaireen or Alaaya; but he could not have thought of it that way. Not when he knew that it meant lotus-root, and that it was derived as that which is mṛṇyate, crushed, for the sake of eating; and, immediately, from the name alone, one had a sense of its fragility. Or, take śarīra: which might to some have been an ordinary word for the body, but Toby could never have seen it as anything but a reflection of the Indic world – its deepest values – for he knew that it was traditionally derived from śṝ, which means to break or destroy, and śarīra was nothing but that, 'which wastes away at every moment'.

So, it was true – he could not deny it – that his feeling for the language had now, for as long as he could remember, been part of his way of seeing, part of the way he configured the world. But had it blinded him to the reality of the place? Had it spoken of an interconnectedness so deep and attractive that it had negated the India that everyone else saw? Had it contained a hope of regeneration so compelling that he had been prepared to wait forever? And now that that hope had been extinguished, killed at the germ, had it made his world unbearable? Not because it was ugly or squalid, but because it was devoid of meaning? A grand and beautiful scheme, springing from the very essence of language, had fallen through. Or worse: it had been poisoned at the source and it made Toby doubt the things he once loved. *Decay is never benign*, he thought, *I have allowed myself to be duped by that greatest of great Indian lies: the lie of eternal India.*

Rudrani had been in touch through the day. He wanted to see her, and his ex-father-in-law, now very old and deaf, before he left. For a long time he had not been sure he would leave. But, when he saw the images of the Mosque under attack, he called the travel agent. Then he called Rudrani back to say he was leaving the country; not for good, he couldn't say that; but for a short holiday, and that he wanted to see her before he left. The last time they had spoken she had told him, 'The strangest thing, Baba: Ma and Dada are here, too, at the flat.' The Brigadier and she were on their way there now. He should come too. They would meet him there. Good, he thought, looking out from a PCO booth on the Mathura Road, shrouded in its thin mantle of brown smoke, it's right that we should all be together on a night like this. And, for a moment, speaking mechanically, he said, with the voice and sensibility of a man from another time, 'Darling, is there any champagne?'

'Of course not, Baba!' she laughed.

'Order some, please. Ask your mother to call Pappu, the bootlegger, and order some. And food?'

'I think Ma's organizing it.'

'Tell her to make sure there are some eggs in the house; I'll pick up some foie gras on the way.'

Champagne, foie gras: it was the last time these things would be rare or sought-after in India. Toby spoke already in a voice from the past. For a moment – for an evening, really – he was a version of the man he had been in the seventies, the man of linen suits and foreign exchange, who travelled with a large blue British passport in his pocket, and a bottle of whisky in his luggage. The man who felt it was better, if truly he was leaving India for good, to go first class to Paris, and decide the rest later.

That evening, the flat was alive again. Windows were opened, heaters were brought out, there were flowers in the vases and Narindar – on Uma's insistence – wore his uniform. Skanda came later to distrust his memory of that night, for though he did not know it then, it was the last time he would see his parents together.

There was a great quality of friendship between Toby and Uma that night, as if they both quietly acknowledged how long an association it had been. Uma, in the presence of Sylvia, seemed tickled at playing the role of the ex-wife. It must have appealed to her sense of the absurd. And it did not take her long to see the absurdity of their present situation, nor that part of it that was deeply moving to her: which was the shared despair, the loss of illusions public and private, that had brought her together, for the last time, with a man, who, more than any other, had been the witness to her life. A man, who, once the obligation to love him had been lifted, she felt boundless amounts of affection for. And concern! Especially when intuitively, she sensed his tragedy better than anybody else. In the past, she had thought Toby's view of India hopelessly romantic, but that night it was for India that she felt a chill, for any place willing to break the heart of a dreamer as ardent as Toby.

At one point the two of them – in between his making foie gras omelettes, and her helping lay the table – took some time out together, in private. That was when, Skanda later learned, his father had asked his mother's help in saving the Kidd Sanskrit Library. And though her own situation was as uncertain as ever – she thought she would leave Maniraja – she promised to help, promised never to let the project die or be 'entombed'.

Skanda's enduring impression of that night was not of his parents, but of his father and grandfather. Deep Fatehkotia, now too arthritic to leave the house, had not come. But the Brigadier, though he was very old himself, his eyes almost gone, his beard totally white, his mouth ever a little open, had made a special point of it. He had sensed his presence was needed. It was he, after all, who, from the depths of that bad time in 1984, had first advised Toby to leave India, and never return. And though no one had told him that Toby was leaving for good – no one knew! – he seemed to have guessed he was, and that was why his presence was required.

He spent the evening, a stiff whisky in his mottled hands, talking to Toby alone. He kept saying, 'So pleased you're leaving, son. You must,' he added, certain that everyone who left India went to the same place, 'give my salaams to I.P. He has become a policeman, you know, in Canada. Or New Zealand, is it? It is his little revenge against the world.' Then, as if he hadn't asked it until now, he said, 'Tell me, Raja saab: I see your reasons for leaving, of course, but why now?'

At first Toby, who wanted to make light of his departure, bluffed. 'Oh, I'm only going for a short holiday, sir; I'll be back soon enough.' But this brought an impatient and dissatisfied expression to the Brigadier's face, and, after only a short gap, he found a way to rephrase his question. 'Wonderful that you're finally off, Raja saab. I always thought this was no place for a man of your quality and intellect. But why not earlier? I mean: why now?' Again, and again, till Toby felt the truth of what he sought to conceal wrung from him.

'See, sir,' he said at last, almost from exasperation, 'the thing is – the reason I'm leaving – is that I fell in love.'

The Brigadier chewed his gums, unsure perhaps if he had heard right.

'Not with your daughter,' Toby said quickly, 'though I loved her too. Very much.'

'My daughter – ' the Brigadier interrupted, 'I don't know where she gets it from – has tremendous common sense. She is, I think I told you once, a great pragmatist. But you mustn't doubt, Raja saab, that under all this good sense – and I fear it won't bring her a day of happiness – there is a great store of romance. You mustn't think of it as having all been a waste. I can tell you: she doesn't. And this little bania she's found . . .' he began with contempt.

'It doesn't matter, sir,' Toby stopped him. 'What I was saying was that though I loved her very much, my great love was always this language, which I found as a young man. It seemed to me at the time to contain a whole universe of thought and feeling and sensibility. I believed it to be the most beautiful thing in the world . . .'

'I see,' he thought he heard the Brigadier say.

'This, I believed, must be what the poets of old had meant when they spoke of language as a deathless thing and gave to its most basic unit – the syllable – the word akṣara: that which does not decay.'

'Come again, son,' the Brigadier said, with renewed interest, '"akṣara" did I hear you say? What did you say it meant?'

'The imperishable: that which does not decay.'

The Brigadier's eyes widened.

'Lovely. Very lovely.'

'Yes. And what can I say, sir? I held out some little hope for it.'

'For what?' the Brigadier said with confusion.

'For the language, for the place. I suppose I felt that some particle of the spirit that had made it might fertilize a future time in this country. And that I would witness one of those moments so rare in history . . .'

At this point there was a disturbance at the centre of the room. Vandana or Dhanalakshmi – hard to know which – had, after saying, 'Let's see what those damn firangs are saying about us,' turned on the television and its light and noise filled the room. The novelty of it was still very real and the others soon gathered around.

'Bloody racket!' the Brigadier began and, inadvertently quoting Nehru, said, 'What were you saying? "A moment comes, which comes but rarely in history?"'

But Toby could not continue. He was too far from the television to hear, but he could see replayed the images he had seen that afternoon.

The Brigadier was urging him to go on, to finish what he had been saying.

'I thought I would witness,' he said at last, speaking as if out of a dream, 'one of those moments when genius returns to a place from which all memory of it had departed. But I was wrong, sir,' he said, his concentration returning, 'I see now that I was terribly wrong.'

The Brigadier's eyes shone. His mouth remained partially open. He gave Toby no indication that he had heard what he said. But neither did he ask his question again. His face came to rest.

This was the impression that Skanda, sitting at some distance from the two men, retained, of their faces flooded with the light from the television: the face of the older man, either from peace or indifference, was quiet and closed, the eyes marbled with cataract; the younger man's face was searching and quizzical, as if able only now to see to the heart of a truth whose simplicity – had it not caused him such grief – would have made him laugh out loud.

It is late when Skanda returns to the flat from the airport. This is the hour when he has used it most. It is at this hour that the sediment of years is heaviest – and here is a nice long thread: sīdati, in Sanskrit; Latin *sedere*; Lithuanian *sedeti*; Gothic *sitan*; German *sitzen*; Anglo-Saxon *sittan*; in English *sit* – the soft preservative darkness, keeping what has come, but willing to admit no more. And, even after a year of living in the flat, there is very little of him to be found in it. Whatever trace there is can be easily removed. He could pack his bags and, in less than an hour, the place would return to itself, with a sigh of relief no doubt, like an old person kept too long at lunch.

Its decay, acting as a preservative, has kept everything. The picchvai with the peacocks which seems tonight to glow with an interior light, a real *schöne*. The heavy carved sideboards. The balding discoloured carpets. The cream paint, once such an innovation, now brittle and cracking. The low-voltage lights, which seem always to know their place, and never to shine too brightly. His father's desk in whose deep grooves a thick gunk has formed, which he – while translating his poem – likes to drive a paper knife through. The thin sheets and rasais, which more than anything – for thread has ever been associated with narrative, and so with Time – seem in the loosening of their warp and weft to contain the underlay of past lives lived in the flat.

He wants to be near it all tonight, to have it close around him; to breathe it in, the air of the vacancy, to have it wash over him, and, for him to live sensually, one last time perhaps. What he does not want are summations, no tying of knots, no ceremony of farewells. *Let be.* Nor tonight does he want to think of what the vacancy at the heart of his life has meant. The passivity that made every effort of his a half effort; the feeling of dislocation that always overpowered him; the absurdity that broke the back of the relationships he entered; the feeling of drift that made only those situations he drifted into feel real. He has no answer for why he allowed his life to become an extension of his father's grief. Nor does he know how the tragedy of the language came to be mixed up, in his mind, with that of his father, or why his immersion into it had been a way of coping.

He had made the language the substratum of his life, a great chthonic city of ruined streets and public buildings, through which he could wander at will with the comfort of knowing that to this place, at least, no further calamity could come. Here, all that was to happen had happened. Ground zero. And, this was another nice thread: *khthōn*, like the Sanskrit *kṣam*: earth or ground, cognate with the Latin, *homō*: man.

He moves easily through the darker reaches of the flat, far from the round open face of the anglepoise lamp. The very darkness feels dated, feels like it has the texture of another time. All is familiar, all is known – a place without threat – and soon he is at his father's desk, before the cool astral glow of his computer. There is an email from Theo Mackinson.

Subject: Balliol this fall

Skanda Mahodaya,

I'm at Balliol this fall for my doctoral thesis on ring theory. Richard Lundquist, who I believe you know, and I were speaking about wanting to do something in memory of your father. Nothing too extravagant, but some kind of memorial that would acknowledge his great contribution to Indian learning, perhaps nothing more than a lunch on a Monday of your choice at the high table. I hope the idea appeals to you. Let me know what's possible and great good luck with your translation of The Birth. I look immensely forward to it. Hope you're thriving.

Laterz,

Theo

Balliol! The name returns him to Indic Mondays at the high table among numismatologists and walrus-faced Vedic experts. There are Apabhraṁśists and TamBrams, in whom an overlay of English manners disguises the secretly vocational nature of their interest; and then there are fair-haired Alexes and Juliens, who, with Greek, Latin, Hittite and Avestan already under their belt, go after Sanskrit with the addict's need for novelty.

He sits back and lights a cigarette, his father's chair sticky against his skin. So here it is, at last: a reason – and one only ever needs something like this – to break the cycle he's fallen into. He steps outside and is about to go back into the drawing room when he notices a slanted line of light from his bedroom, falling diagonally across the terrazzo floor. He pushes open the door and sees Gauri, asleep on his bed. A scrawny child-like figure in a faded T-shirt and pyjamas dotted with little yellow and pink flowers. She came! A feeling of great tenderness and pity rises in him. Not just for the gesture of solidarity, made so quietly on this hot night, but also for the lowness of expectation that they have maintained all year. The hope of romantic love, dead or asleep in their breast, like a faculty they no longer possess, a demand they no longer dare to make of life.

He is about to step back out, when he sees something on the bedside table, flapping away in the blast from the air conditioner. An A4 paper folded in half. A child's drawing in wild reds and yellows of an armed figure on the front. Some mixture of Rambo and a jihadi. Inside: 'Dear ~~Mr~~ Uncle Skanda, Please sori for my bad' – and, here, the mother's guiding hand clearly visible – 'behaviour today. ~~Love,~~ From, Kartik.'

He smiles, thinking of the resistance the author put up right to the end, at the card that was both an apology and a redoubled threat. But, when he thinks of the mother's labour in extracting this apology, of the anxiety that lies behind it, he has to steer his mind quickly away, for fear that it will flood his eyes.

Outside. He lies down on the large sofa whose peach flowers, like a memory of gaiety, have hardened with time, and are coarse against his back. The smoke, in its upward ascent into the high vaultages of the room, where a mute storm plays over a tableau of white peacocks, wanders carelessly over the margin of lamplight, so that its coils and tendrils are cropped and exposed. *I'll go,* he thinks, *why the hell not. I'll definitely go. And I'll take Gauri and the little terrorist, too. We'll drive up from London and stop at pubs on the way. Maybe we'll ask I.P. to join us. Maybe we'll shake this malaise once and for all . . .*

His eye, passing through the screen of smoke and light, stops at the urn on the sideboard, with its collar of blue polythene. And the moment he sees it he knows what he must do: knows perhaps also why he has waited so long.

ANTA

CF. GOTH. {ANDEIS}; GERM. {ENDE}; ENG. {END}

They – Skanda, Gauri and Kartik, Narindar at the wheel – leave Delhi by a new road, heading south in the direction of the rains.

The city is dry and exposed. Its streets, with their fine margins of dust, stare blank and open-faced up at the sky, as if seeking the answer to a question. And the sky, a sooty blue at that dawn hour, stares back, with no answer to give. It seems worn out by the futility of its own cycles, by the empty brightening and darkening of its dome. The tyranny of grīṣma is never worse than when it is at its most vulnerable. In the last week of its reign over the city, it has released the full force of its desiccating winds, its asphyxiating stillness, its blanching heat. But, as with those regimes whose catalogue of cruelties in the final days speak loudest of their impending collapse, it is at an end. The news of it has spread through the natural world, which prepares the conditions for its demise.

There is something of the death rattle in the dry wind that goes through the peepal, causing its leaves to clatter, leaves on whose dirt-encrusted surface one can already imagine the first splash of warm rain that will muffle their noise and restore to them their colour. Or the runnels that line the streets, down whose uneven surface one can almost already see the first creeping streams of water. Or, most of all, the sky, which seems, from the sheer futility of its contractions, from the experience of so many stillbirths, now to literally be birthing the new season; the sky, which any day will darken with finality, and not brighten again till it has restored the world to moisture and to pigment and to textured light. So it is that this season of rain – which, for being the agent of renewal and fertility, is bound etymologically to the Sanskrit word for a male bull – is never so remote as when it is nearest at hand.

Summer is the season he arrived in, returning his father to the country he had left forever; and it is the season, after a year of paralysis, of coming to terms with death, as it were, that he departs in. It is the kind of symmetry that might hint at futility, but it does not feel that way. The city contained the sleeping configurations of the past – his past – which, as long as his father was alive had not, for some reason, needed to be faced. But Toby's death had left Skanda suddenly exposed, as if the way was now clear for his own end. And what had been enough before came to feel like too little. The life that had been hardly more than an extension of his father's grief came to feel like too little. His father, when he was alive, had, no matter how nominally, embodied the past. But, with that body gone, it was as if he, Skanda, needed the child to come up in him from the depths of a buried past to merge with the adult, like a reflection rising to meet its object. It did not have to happen in any forced or deliberate way – it did not have to be a hard and tangible thing – but he had needed the past in some way to wash over him. He had needed it to be near, as much as he had once needed to escape it. 'Men need history,' Naipaul tells us, 'it helps them to have an idea of who they are. But history, like sanctity, can reside in the heart; it is enough that there is something there.'

They pass Khan Market, the closed shutters of BahriSons. Everywhere, all around him, from Fatehkot Apartments to his flat to the house on Curzon Road to the houses of his parents' friends, he sees coiled about him the Snake of Residue – śeṣa nāga or An-anta, the infinite.

They speed along the empty streets on their way to the new road. Kartik, in orange matching shorts and T-shirt, sleeps between them. Now not the defender of his house, now no longer sick with worry at having to keep his mother safe from intruders, he is calm, almost without anxiety. It will not be easy to know him, let alone to be part of his life – but Skanda feels, for some reason, that he, even more than Gauri, has been sent him: that he is part of his recovery. He is part of those little ways in which life allows us to set right what was wrong in our own life, to make whole what was incomplete. And when, that afternoon, a few weeks before, Skanda had glimpsed his rage and his terror, he had felt himself face to face with something so deeply comprehensible to him that he had hardly needed to put it into words. It had reminded him of the things that still lay buried in him beneath the thick overlay of his protections.

It showed me life and man as the mystery, the true religion of men, the grief and the glory.

But it was hard to keep life vital, hard not to let a system of life, a formula, a key, stand between one and one's life. He had done that, he knew, and, strangely – or, not so strangely – it was death that taught him to live again.

The new road lies like a fenced-up slab over the land, halving the distance to Agra. Even by Indian standards, it is full of dissonance and absurdity. An empty expressway, with grey and orange patrol jeeps racing up and down it, helplines, signs that say, 'Over-speeding will invite persecution [*sic*]'. The Indian scene is pushed back beyond the lines of barbed wire, and the figure of a lone farmer in white against the fields, or a small pink temple with its red flag fluttering in the hot breeze, come almost to seem like the scenery that scrolls behind a stationary vehicle on a film set. Its distortions of time and space, the homogenizing power of the frame, are incredible; they seem to remake the landscape, and, under pressure from this reworking, the U.P. of his childhood comes to seem inert, a landscape robbed of its power to stir memory. Will it go all the way to Kalasuryaketu one day? What will that mean for him? What will it do – this levelling and uncaring gaze – to the landscape of his childhood? To the ravined and eggshell hills that anticipate the Tamasā?

For now it goes no further than Agra. And Gauri laughs out loud when, after the exit, India returns with double force.

'They may as well write, "Exit: India!"'

She is dressed in a white salwar kurta with a red tinselled dupatta. And she has the urn in her hands. She took it from him within minutes of their setting out. It is what he likes most about her: her quiet understanding of things, her easy solemnity. She is also a practitioner of the unsaid. He has given her so little this year; and she, like someone terrified of expectation, has asked even less of him.

'How much time has this road saved us?' he asks Narindar, even as the car is engulfed in traffic, in chortling engines, in bicycle bells, in clouds of brown smoke.

'About two hours,' Narindar says. 'We should be there by 4 p.m.'

Lunch in Gwalior. Kartik asleep after a hunger-induced tantrum. The irresistible *Tempest*-like lull of afternoon, the whirr of the engine, the cool of the air-conditioner: *svap* in Sanskrit is to sleep, to dream, like the Anglo-Saxon *swefan*, the Latin *sopor*, soporific . . . When they wake, the sun is high and they are winding their way through that country of withered hills, their furrows deep as shadows, that enclose the Tamasā.

And then it is all coming fast at him. The town of memory, recently revisited, so now neither old nor new, standing at an odd angle to the past and present. Narindar's home town; and he drives through it with that aggression with which we want to remind the people we have left behind that we are both theirs and no longer theirs.

'Shiv Niwas?' he says, as the crossroads approach. 'Or Tripathi's?'

'Drop me off at Tripathi's.'

Gauri looks questioningly at Skanda, then understands. And, quietly, after a few minutes, she puts the ashes on the seat between them.

The car stops at the crossroads. Past the frilled arch of a large whitewashed gate, the road curls up to Shiv Niwas. Tripathi's house is to the right, at the base of the hill. At the centre of the crossroads, on the balding crest of a tiled roundabout, is the statue of a warrior queen, painted copper. Her shadow falls short over the little clearing in the town, on the periphery of which is the usual assemblage of chemists and auto-mechanics – the fossilized tread of a tractor's tyre in the dried mud – a few stray dogs sharing what little shade there is.

'I thought it might be raining,' Gauri says with sudden dismay, looking about at the dusty almost shadeless town on the banks of this sluggish – and yet unseen – river. Kartik, waking up slowly, twists in her arms. He wants to know who the statue is of. 'Ketubai,' Narindar tells him with reverence, and glancing into the rear-view mirror, adds, 'their ancestor.'

'You won't come up for a bit?' Gauri says, with something like desperation in her voice.

'No. Let me go and see Tripathi first.'

He doesn't know why it must be done this way, except that it was the way it had played out in his mind. And somehow the order seems important.

'Narindar will settle you in upstairs. And I'll be there shortly, in time for drinks on the terrace. It's been a long time since there were drinks on the terrace of Shiv Niwas.'

She smiles – and grave again – hands him the urn.

'OK. See you in a bit.'

He waits till the car sets off up the hill – imagines their first view of the river – then, the urn in his hands, he walks in the direction of Tripathi's house.

A beige and red curtain hangs like a nightgown from a springy wire in the doorway. The room, at once shaded and ablaze with tube light, is full of books in tall plywood cabinets with oblong glass windows. Mahesh, Tripathi's grandson, a slim restless young man in dark jeans and a football jersey, plays on his phone, its eerie green light reflected in his face. Tripathi, past the curtain, in the further room, is still asleep.

He would like to be woken up, Skanda knows, but Mahesh has presented it to him as a fait accompli – 'My grandfather still sleeping' – and Skanda does not force the matter. He can sense his restlessness. He watches him, sullen and silent, slumped in a red plastic chair, in this room, with its cemented floor and the treasures of his grandfather's erudition. Nothing of anything, it seems will remain in Mahesh. He is scoured clean of the past. And, predictably, almost on cue, when after some stalled attempts at conversation, he sees Skanda studying his grandfather's books, he says, 'Sanskrit, very old language. Mother of all languages.'

Skanda has his back to him when he hears the words and he is powerless to resist the dismay they produce in him. He has always known, implicitly, at least – he has seen it in Maniraja – that when culture dies, its slogans grow louder, its clichés become like articles of faith. But Mahesh . . . Tripathi's grandson! Who would have thought it? Something about his restlessness, when seen next to the drying up of the cultural stream, a process repeating throughout the country, gives him a sense of foreboding: of decay without end.

'Your grandfather hasn't taught you any Sanskrit?' Skanda says, still with his back to him.

'Why?' he says defensively. 'He teach me. I know Sanskrit.'

He is lying. When Skanda turns around to meet his gaze, he sees his face hot with shame. He may be restless, but he is not yet a liar. And the lie told, with his grandfather practically in earshot, embarrasses him. Not just the lie, but perhaps the cause of it, too. There is such a temptation – when faced with loss of this kind – to fall into lies. To let boastfulness and false pride fill the vacancy left in you. Left, by a process beyond your control, a process that is general and historical, but which, nonetheless, makes you feel responsible for your loss, makes you feel as if you – for your laxity and disregard – have been robbed of your cultural artefacts, singled out for extinction.

Their brief exchange wakes Tripathi, and when he discovers, while emerging from sleep, that Skanda has been kept waiting, he appears in a rage in the doorway, tearing away the sagging curtain.

'Damn fool. Good-for-nothing. Bloody goonda. You sit here, playing on your phone, *while* . . . Do you know who this is?! No tea? Not a glass of water? Oh, God. What am I to do with this boy? Damn fool. Idiot! Just get out! Get out!'

Mahesh shrinks from the abuse, but, almost immediately, like a man actively in search of injustice, something defiant enters his eyes.

Tripathi sees it and his anger grows. 'Get out, I say,' he yells hatefully. He looks like he's on the verge of hitting him.

'Tripathi saab, please, leave it . . .' Skanda inserts.

'No, Raja saab,' he says – he is the first to address him this way – 'he hates me, this boy, you don't know. He does everything in his power to humiliate me. He wants to heap scorn on all that is sacred in my life.'

'I'm going, I'm going,' Mahesh says, 'you don't have to tell me twice.'

And the roughness with which he says this next to Tripathi's antiquated, almost Victorian English, is so jarring that it draws out some women into the courtyard. A mother, a sister. This is obviously a familiar scene and they collect around Mahesh, shielding him from his grandfather's temper.

Tripathi sees them and says, 'Get this layabout away from me. And, for God's sake, offer Raja saab some tea, some water, something to eat. He's just driven down from Delhi.'

The women cover their heads and, at the sight of the gesture, Tripathi's temper cools. He strokes his bald head. His long dark face brightens a little.

'Come inside,' he says, cleaning his bifocals with the end of his kurta. His eyes, without the spectacles, are milky, and crescent measures of luminosity and sadness are visible on the edge of the deadening discs of cataract.

Inside, over tea and biscuits, in the room bathed in fluorescent light, Skanda says cautiously, 'How come you never taught him, Tripathi . . .?'

'Where would I teach him, Raja saab? I haven't even been able to teach him manners let alone Sanskrit.'

He sits back on his narrow bed and pulls up his cracked feet.

'But, you know, the one is not separate from the other. In fact, the one would have made the other possible—'

Tripathi cuts him short.

'What can I say? They would come back after school with their little satchels laden with books and homework. I didn't have the heart to press one more thing on them. And a thing that seemed so irrelevant to their lives. I wanted them to be free of that responsibility, as I had never been. Free of the obligation to our past, Raja saab. It was all over.'

He speaks out of the mood Mahesh has aroused in him. But now, as if aware of Skanda, as if aware of what he has come to do, he checks himself. And almost afraid to cause offence says softly, 'It is much better it all go. I mean: *go completely*. Then there is some small chance that they will feel its loss. And when they're ready – when they want their culture back – it'll be there, waiting for them in the West, like so much else. And they will come to it with fresh eyes, as your revered father once did, come to it with the pain of their loss, and it will mean something then, as it never meant anything before. But now, in this present environment, other things being equal,' he says, and chuckles, 'it is much better it go.'

'Pralaya?'

'Total pralaya,' he laughs. 'Total dissolution. Look,' he says, turning to face the wall he sits against, 'of all the images I keep from our culture, this is the one I cherish most.'

Skanda has not noticed it. It is garish and ugly, a busy hodgepodge of green and orange. But he sees now that it is of Vishnu. Vishnu after Dissolution, reposing on the Snake of Residue, which itself floats on the primal waters; and, from Vishnu's belly, has come the lotus calyx that contains Brahma.

'In my view,' Tripathi says, 'it is our incomparable contribution to the world of images. A perfect crystallization of our thought, of our ease with the cycle of creation and decay. The world is destroyed. Nothing remains but Shesha Naga – the snake of the world's residue! – floating on the waters, Vishnu reposing above. Time passes – aeons, maybe; the waters heat; and, from Vishnu's belly, comes the lotus, with its promise of regeneration. Its petals open to reveal Brahma and the world is reborn. No anxiety, no excitement. Neither for the end nor the beginning. Just peace and inevitability. The peace of the abyss, Raja saab: neutral, amoral, neither with negative nor positive charge. That is why it passeth all understanding. The other religions, they speak to us of Heaven and Hell, and we just smile. We think – Ha! – if only anyone cared so much as to bother sending you to Heaven or Hell!' He laughs, then sober again, he says, 'But that is the great mood of our culture, Raja saab, the *inimitable* mood, if I may say so. The mood of an indifferent and uncaring peace.'

Skanda smiles. He thinks of Mahesh, a moment before, of his restlessness, but he says nothing. He will never know this fabled peace of Tripathi's, this peace that passeth all understanding . . .

But they are not there that afternoon to dispute these things, and the shared awareness of this, of why they are together at all, seems to come to them at the same time.

Tripathi's eyes rest on the urn, and he says, somewhat nervously, 'Your father, Raja saab, was not a religious man.'

'I know, Tripathi.'

'Good. Because I wanted to tell you: I haven't prepared anything. This gesture of yours – which I approve of wholeheartedly, as would have your revered father – it has a natural poetry, a natural logic. And, in keeping with that, with the poetry of it, we will not bring in anything religious. Your father's interests, in any case, were always and ever literary. Kāvya was his religion, *The Birth of Kumara* his Bible, Kalidasa his prophet.'

'I know, Tripathi.'

The road to the river is of a pinkish-black stone. The houses are old-fashioned, their balconies slim and delicate. They overhang deep drains whose steep sides are coated in rich wet algae. In the distance, its surface flat and oily, is the river. And, along its earth bank, there are several long boats.

Suddenly, it is all very real. Not now a romantic or poetic thing, but logistical and real, real as the funeral had been. Perhaps it is the boats that make it that way. The boatman, a sinewy sparrow of a man, who has to be negotiated with; the tipping boat, as he gets in, and the rapid steadying movement of the little boatman along its cross plank. The urn of ashes, Tripathi's chapped palm in his, as he steps in after him. The poling out of the boat into the river, the endless drift. The cross-weave of the water disappearing into the placid and depleted expanse of the Tamasā. It gives him an awful feeling of futility that has always made a mockery of his experience with Experience. He peeks under the lid of the urn, and sees the blue knot of the polythene bag, the government form that says the ashes are human remains.

Then he feels Tripathi's gaze on him. He looks up and sees his long-toothed smile, his eyes bright with amusement.

'You're every bit your father's son,' he says. 'Always intellectualizing.'

'How do you mean?'

'You look so worried. What is it? What is the matter?'

'Tripathi, I feel so empty.'

'Raja saab, it's life – not a poem, not a work of literature – there is no tying together of knots at the end. We give it shape, but it has no shape; no plot, it is fluid as this river. Don't be cast down by its absurdities. I'm here, your father's old friend. He's here, too, in some form. And you're on a river whose name means darkness. But "whose waters are lucid as the mind of a good man". A river you've grown up around, a town which you have an ancient connection to. These are threads enough. You are where you ought to be; you're doing what is to be done, your kartavya. Feel easy about it.'

They have come halfway into the river. The darkening mass of the Shiv Niwas is visible. The great escarpment of stone steps. The outline of a temple's summit, its pointed flag fluttering. The faint sound of bells. The evening light begins to fade, but the western horizon still bears a line of red – a rakta | lekham – 'as with a bloodied sword,' the poet writes, 'left behind on the field of battle'.

He opens the blue polythene bag and sees the ashes – ashes once in the shape of a man, the ashes of Love's demise – with shards of bone. He stands in the boat, causing it to rock, and the boatman to go scuttling, crab-like, from side to side. Then, loosening the polythene knot, and holding open the mouth of the bag, he lets its contents fall out with a crude thump into the river, some taken up by the flow of water, some carried away by the hot breeze. He lets the bag go too, drifting over the river's surface, a lung filling slowly with liquid. Then, the government form and the urn, too, swallowed up by the river, with a pleasing gurgle and a great capping stone of a bubble.

It is done.

On the way back to the shore, Tripathi, the leathery mask of his face disappearing into the gloom, says, 'You feel fine, Raja saab?'

'I feel relieved, Tripathi. Is that a bad thing to say? When I think of the idea of the man my father was, I feel a great sadness. Enough even to bring me to tears. But when I think of the death of the physical man, of his body, I feel relief. I'm glad he's gone, Tripathi. I feel cut free.'

Tripathi lets the words vanish into the darkness, with that generosity we extend to the last words of a doomed man, regardless of what they are. Then, after some time, he says, 'This is how the great poems end, no? In a description of sunset, of nightfall, of moonrise. This is the end of the Birth, too. And I've always thought it the strongest argument against those who challenge the integrity of the eight cantos. It may be *The Birth of Kumara*, but it is a poem about the love of Shiva and Parvati. And, in the end, it is their union, akin to that of word and meaning, that is all. Isn't it? "A hundred or more seasons passing as one night, and the thirst yet unsated . . . a submarine fire in the depths." But come, let me take you back to the Shiv Niwas. Your guests must be waiting.'

There are drinks on the terrace of the Shiv Niwas. And Narindar, as if out of a private act of remembrance, an ode to Sharada and Laban, has made a special effort. He is full of a sense of occasion and takes care with the details. He has brought out the wrought-iron fanooses in whose cut-glass cavity he has lit cheap smoky candles, their shadowy patterns shrinking and swelling against the whitewash of a pillar; mosquito coils smoke from under the potted plants and peg tables; a battery-operated torch lies on its side on the white cloth of the bar, under a cloud of insects.

Gauri, in a white kurti and shorts, is drinking a gin and tonic. Kartik, in what seems like a strategic alliance, the special need boys like him have for male approval, has befriended Narindar, and follows him about in each of his chores from kitchen to house.

'You must bathe,' Tripathi says, as he sees Skanda off, 'I'll pass by later to say goodnight.'

Gauri's mood, in this hour before Kartik's bedtime, is invariably an extension of her son's. And she is calm. She knows how raw his nerves can be, and her face glows with the visible relief of seeing that the new place has not chaffed against them. He still has his hectic energy, but it is the last frazzled little burst before sleep.

'Should I put him to bed and see you outside?'

'Sure. I'm going to have a bath.'

'Here,' she says, and hands him a drink.

'Oh! It's not that kind of bath. Just an old-fashioned balti bath; hot water, if we're lucky.'

'Still.'

He takes the drink.

'Has he eaten his dinner?'

'Yes,' she says unthinkingly, and then something long and meaning and grateful enters her eyes. He knows that gratitude: it is the limitless thanks we feel when our concerns become those of another.

'See you back in a minute.'

•

They reconvene after what could not be more than fifteen minutes – and yet, there is something quieter and stiller and darker about the night. The tiredness of the journey has merged with the magical refreshment of a drink, a bath, the new and cleaner air. The almost inaudible presence of the river, which, as with the involuntary effect of architecture upon us, deepens the night, lends it gravitas, endows their words with weight. She says nothing of the rite, but, like a writer writing around her theme, says, 'You never talk of the intervening time, of the time in between.'

'In between what?'

'In between . . . Well, I mean how old was your father in 1992, when he left India?'

'Oh! I see. He was born in 1940, so fifty-two.'

'And so when he . . . ?'

'Seventy-four, on 1 November.'

'Right! So, a long time then. Did you see him much in those years, I mean, in the time between his leaving India and . . . ?'

'Yes. A lot, in fact. I went to college in England soon after, so, I saw him a lot, yes. And then we would meet on family holidays, too. The India-by-the-back-door-holidays, Rudrani used to call them.'

'Why?'

'Oh, because they were always in places that were part of the spread of ancient Indic culture – Angkor, Pollonaruwa, Borabadur – but were not in India, the modern country. He needed those places very badly in the end. To be near India, but not in India.'

'The immigrant syndrome, no?'

'Yes, I suppose, except Baba . . . He was like an emigrant from the past into the present. And he took it all so personally.'

'What?'

'The changes, you know. The rise of what he saw as "the Hindu element". His reasons for leaving India became the defining feature of his life. And it skewed his perspective. He was pretty unbalanced in the end, a crank almost. It was difficult to be around him. Even Rudrani found it hard. Because . . .'

His voice trails off.

'Because . . . ?'

Gauri does not see – she has her back to him – but Tripathi has appeared on the balcony. He stands at a distance, not wishing to disturb the conversation. His hand rests lightly on the rough rounded lip of the ramparts.

'Just wanted to see if everything was OK,' he says, when he sees he has their attention.

'All OK, Tripathi saab,' Skanda says, and gets up to greet him.

'The boy' – he still calls Narindar that – 'has made all the necessary preparations?'

'Yes, yes, all fine,' Skanda says. 'Tripathi saab, this is Gauri, my friend from Delhi. Gauri, this is Tripathi saab, a very dear and old friend of my father's. One of the few unbroken threads in our lives, no?'

'Tripathi saab!' Gauri says brightly, rising to meet him.

The old man bows his head slightly in greeting and places one hand on his breast.

Gauri, out of that concern city people express in rural places for the vagaries of weather, says, 'How long before the rains, Tripathi saab?'

'Oh, any minute now, madam,' he replies, 'tonight perhaps even. It's very still.'

Skanda veers off in the direction of the bar. The relief from the completion of the rite is sinking in. His father is dead a year; his remains are now part of the air of Kalasuryaketu, part of the water of the Tamasā. Skanda feels suddenly bold. And, half from genuine curiosity, half from the recklessness of his mood, he says, 'Tripathi, why don't you shed some light on this? Gauri was just asking me why it was difficult to be around Baba in the end?'

He turns around and sees Tripathi standing almost at attention. His hands folded, his face closed. He is afraid he has offended him. But Tripathi is simply waiting for his full attention. Then considering his reply, he says, addressing Gauri directly, 'The reason I would give is simple. Raja saab's revered father was impatient of life. He was a man with mumūrṣā. And there are few things, I'm sure you will agree, that make us more uneasy than someone eager for death?'

'Mumūrṣā?' Gauri says with wonder, and looks to Skanda, who, after a pause, says, 'It is the desiderative of our root for death – *mṛ*. Which is shared by the Latin *mors*, the German *Mord*, in English, murder.'

'But it didn't make you uneasy, Tripathi saab? This desire of his for death.'

'No, madam,' Tripathi says; and then, as if he has said too much, makes to leave.

'But why?' she presses him.

'I had better be going, madam. I don't want to disturb your evening with philosophical speculations.'

'No, please,' she says, oblivious of this little bit of theatre. 'Why?'

Tripathi smiles his sage and knowing smile and, taking a few steps back, giving a little bow, he says, 'I saw it as part of his great capacity for love. Now, really, I must say good night. Raja saab, I'm sure, will explain more . . .'

With this, he goes.

When they are alone again, Gauri looks to Skanda.

'What did he mean?' she says. 'Why did he say your father's wish to die was an extension of his capacity for Love?'

'Oh, it's rubbish, Gauri. It is something from theory, and so abstract and meaningless that it's not worth discussing. Really!'

But she can see that under his irritation his eyes have grown moist with emotion. Something in what Tripathi said has moved him deeply.

'Still . . .' she urges him softly.

The night is dense; it has an immense and oppressive weight. Skanda turns to face the river, in expectation, almost, of the moment when its surface will be pricked with rain. And, gazing out over the parapet, he says, with difficulty, as if the pressure of the night has allied itself with that of Gauri's question, 'It's from the kāmaśāstra. According to the ancient Indian theory of Erotics . . .' he says, and breaks off, his voice lost in the night air.

'Go on,' she says, after a long wait, 'According to the ancient Indian theory of Erotics . . . ?'

The returning words seem almost to startle him. He looks at her confusedly before emitting the little breath of a sigh.

'According to the kāmaśāstra,' he says, turning away again to face the unqualified darkness, liquid and still, 'Death is the tenth and last stage of love.'

A NOTE ABOUT THE AUTHOR

Aatish Taseer was born in 1980. He is the author of the memoir *Stranger to History: A Son's Journey Through Islamic Lands* and two novels: *The Temple-Goers*, which was short-listed for the Costa First Novel Award, and the highly acclaimed *Noon*. His work has been translated into more than a dozen languages. He lives in New Delhi and New York.